Blue Ridge Commons

environmental
history
and the
american
south

Blue Ridge Commons

Environmental Activism
and Forest History
in Western North Carolina

Kathryn Newfont

The University of Georgia Press

Athens & London

© 2012 by the University of Georgia Press
Athens, Georgia 30602
www.ugapress.org
All rights reserved
Set in Adobe Caslon Pro by Graphic Composition, Inc.

Printed digitally in the United States of America

Library of Congress Cataloging-in-Publication Data

Newfont, Kathryn.
   Blue Ridge commons : environmental activism and forest history
in western North Carolina / Kathryn Newfont.
      p. cm. — (Environmental history and the American South)
   Includes bibliographical references and index.
   ISBN-13: 978-0-8203-4124-8 (cloth : alk. paper)
   ISBN-10: 0-8203-4124-X (cloth : alk. paper)
   ISBN-13: 978-0-8203-4125-5 (pbk. : alk. paper)
   ISBN-10: 0-8203-4125-8 (pbk. : alk. paper)
      1. Forest conservation—North Carolina. 2. Forest conservation—Blue Ridge
Mountains Region. 3. Natural resources, Communal—North Carolina.
4. Natural resources, Communal—Blue Ridge Mountains Region.
5. Environmentalism—North Carolina. 6. Environmentalism—Blue Ridge
Mountains Region. 7. North Carolina—Environmental conditions.
8. Blue Ridge Mountains Region—Environmental conditions.
9. North Carolina—Politics and government.
10. Blue Ridge Mountains Region—Politics and government. I. Title.
   SD413.N65N49 2012
   333.75′16097568—dc23   2011027439

British Library Cataloging-in-Publication Data available

Cartography by David Wasserboehr

For

Carol
My fern-gathering mother

Stuart
My owl-spotting father

The Newfont kids
My rock-hopping, salamander-catching, ant-observing,
cave-exploring, sweet birch–chewing, kayak-paddling,
snake-handling, blueberry-picking, stick-whacking,
turtle-marveling, cucumber root–digging,
booney-stomping children

Esther
Who set my feet on the path

Jacquelyn
Who taught me to walk it

Dann
My brilliant husband
Always a beacon on the trail

And the forests that sustain us all

Europe has its cathedrals, and western North Carolina
has its native forests.
Esther Clouse Cunningham

I think the National Forests are our national treasures.
Bob Padgett

They regarded this country as their country, their common.
Gifford Pinchot

I find it safe to count on plenty of trouble.
Harold G. Wood

CONTENTS

FOREWORD

Environmental historians have been surprisingly slow to give their full attention to American environmentalism as a *social movement.* During its early years, the field was perhaps too close to the movement, the latter having helped to birth the former, but over the last two decades a surprising critical distance has replaced that closeness. This critical distance is rooted in the common assumption that postwar environmentalism has been less a broad social movement than a values revolution among the comfortable classes who see in the natural world a series of amenities—clean air and water, space for outdoor recreation, and scenic beauty. This conclusion that mainstream environmentalists have constructed their notions of normative nature as affluent urban and suburban consumers has led scholars to write critically about American environmentalism as a privileged political ideology. There is much truth in this characterization, but it is also one that has entrapped environmentalism within tight demographic confines. A growing literature on the environmental justice movement has challenged this narrow definition of what constitutes environmental activism to a degree, but it also has sustained the portrait of the environmental "mainstream" as exclusive and narrow in its interests.

To the extent that rural working people have entered this narrative about environmental activism, they have done so as opponents of environmentalism. In *Blue Ridge Commons,* her superb study of rural western Carolinians and their efforts to protect their region's forests, Kathy Newfont turns this story on its head. Newfont has found in western North Carolina a brand of activism she aptly calls "commons environmentalism"—an activism aimed at protecting a local forest commons for rural working people. And this "commons environmentalism" emerged, Newfont argues, at the same moment as the "wilderness environmentalism" that we have come to associate with the mainstream movement. Indeed, Newfont insists that we see commons environmentalism as the equal of wilderness environmentalism—as two stars in a larger constellation of postwar environmental concern.

To see commons users as environmental activists is to insist on the persistence and modernity of commons land use regimes. Environmental historians have come to assume that the commons and the land uses associated with it drifted to the margins and then largely disappeared more than a century ago, partly as a result of a general "transition to capitalism" across the long nineteenth century and partly as a result of federal conservation efforts to manage those lands that remained beyond the pale of that capitalist transition. In this telling, the traditional local resource commons, which often functioned on privately owned land, lost out to a nationalized commons as federal landownership grew and urban and suburban recreationalists increasingly dominated the management of public lands. Nothing better embodies this narrative than the ignominious history of national parks in the Blue Ridge, and particularly the removals of mountain residents during the creation of both the Great Smoky Mountains and Shenandoah National Parks. The creations of these two parks, which conveniently bracket the Blue Ridge geographically, provide poignant examples of how federal conservation erased human occupation in the name of wilderness preservation. But in Newfont's telling, the Blue Ridge commons outside of these national parks not only survived the coming of federal conservation to the region; to a surprising degree the commons thrived because of it, though in a new form. This is a story we are not used to hearing.

As Newfont shows in the first part of *Blue Ridge Commons*, the commons that western North Carolinians came to value and mobilized to protect in the postwar years was in fact a national forest commons created as a result of the Weeks Act of 1911, which provided the statutory mechanism for federal purchase of forestlands in the eastern United States. Indeed, one of the signal contributions of *Blue Ridge Commons* is its subtle and thorough rendering of the coming of the Forest Service and its land management to the mountains of the Southeast. While western North Carolinians treated the arrival of the Forest Service with due skepticism and sometimes even engaged in traditional forms of "commons defense" such as arson when their privileges seemed threatened, they also saw the Forest Service as preferable to the timber industry that had decimated Blue Ridge forests in the late nineteenth and early twentieth centuries. Indeed, many locals hoped that Forest Service stewardship would be restorative, and they worked hard to maintain their traditional commons practices as the Forest Service assumed managerial control over large portions of the region. Locals were not dispossessed of their traditional commons rights and privileges when the Forest Service arrived; instead, locals inscribed those rights into Forest Service management in creative ways, working with federal foresters to protect the local commons. In their guarded support for the coming of federal conservation to western North Carolina, commons users planted the seeds of the commons environmentalism that would germinate after World War II.

In the second half of *Blue Ridge Commons*, Newfont shifts her narrative to a remarkable series of environmental protest mobilizations in western North Carolina beginning in the 1960s. First, and perhaps not surprisingly, she shows that many western North Carolina activists resisted wilderness designations for lands located in nearby national forests in the wake of the passage of the Wilderness Act of 1964. Many of the region's residents suspected that wilderness designations would damage local extractive industries where they found employment, and they worried (not entirely accurately) that wilderness would limit their access to hunt, fish, and gather on national forestlands. As a number of other environmental historians have done, Newfont shows that the wilderness ideal was most resonant among those urban and suburban middle-class consumers traditionally assumed to be at the forefront of the environmental movement and that rural people who still relied on the resources of these forests for their living were more likely to resist wilderness designation. Had Newfont stopped there, she would have produced a useful contribution to a larger body of scholarship on how rural working-class people resisted wilderness environmentalism.

Luckily, she did not stop there. Instead, she painted a vastly more complicated portrait. First, in the Southern Nantahala area, just a stone's throw from where locals had opposed wilderness designation, Newfont found commons users who actually rallied support for and achieved wilderness designation. They did so by insisting that wilderness designation would in fact protect their commons privileges. Indeed, Newfont suggests that the most notable early wilderness success in the region could not have been achieved without the support of commons users. Then, in the years following the battle over wilderness designation for portions of the Nantahala and Pisgah National Forests, Newfont noticed, locals rose up repeatedly to oppose other forms of development on national forestlands. First, they opposed schemes to open large portions of these national forests to oil and gas development. Then, even more dramatically, they mobilized to oppose clearcutting, a timber-harvesting technique that had a devastating impact on the region's forest ecology. While these movements were not identical in their constituencies, they shared a core group of what Newfont shrewdly calls "swing voters." But how to explain their swings between what seemed like a decidedly antienvironmental position in their wilderness opposition and decidedly proenvironmental positions when it came to oil and gas drilling and clearcutting? Were these activists suffering from "environmental schizophrenia," to use Newfont's evocative phrase? No, they were not. Rather, these swing voters were consistent "commons environmentalists" who shared a deep attachment to the forests of western North Carolina as a natural and cultural heritage. They opposed these development efforts and worked both sides of the street on wilderness designation because they valued most of all the persistence of the commons.

As we celebrate the centennial of the Weeks Act, Kathy Newfont has given us a new and surprising history of the national forests that the act created—a history that not only revises our sense of the coming of national forests to the rural periphery but also expands our sense of what modern environmentalism is. *Blue Ridge Commons*, then, is a regional study with profound national implications. Newfont's original and far-reaching thesis is destined to send a new generation of social and environmental historians into the archives of other rural resource hinterlands to test her hypothesis and to build a fuller, richer portrait of postwar environmental mobilization.

Paul S. Sutter

ACKNOWLEDGMENTS

Though not literally visible, the generous support of an enormous circle of people and institutions is inscribed on every page of this book. I could never have brought this piece to your hands without that support. My list of debts is longer than I can fully enumerate here, so these paragraphs represent only a partial accounting. I trust they will give you a sense of the broader sustaining web that has made this work possible.

I must begin with Jacquelyn Dowd Hall, queen of my scholarly world. Jacquelyn's mentorship has been one of my life's great gifts. Without her shining example and infinitely wise and patient guidance, I would not be an historian at all. Her unflagging confidence in me and in this project carried me forward on countless occasions, from early interviews through published book. More than anyone else, Jacquelyn taught me the skills I have put into practice here. In a very real sense, this work is hers as well as mine.

Other key mentors at UNC–Chapel Hill included Peter Filene and David Whisnant. Both slogged through dissertation drafts meticulously, offered many insightful comments, and reliably raised important questions. Peter is also the most important writing teacher I have ever had. I am grateful to him for this book's very existence as well as any felicitous passages it may contain. David, in his inimitable and generous way, taught me to think about the Appalachian region. If I have managed to offer useful analysis here, it will be largely thanks to his skills as supportive gadfly.

My work also benefited from insights and guidance offered by a wide range of UNC and Duke University faculty during my time in graduate school, including Pete Andrews, Judith Bennett, Bill Chafe, Ray Gavins, Nancy Hewitt, Dottie Holland, Alison Isenberg, John Kasson, Suzanne Lebsock, and Della Pollock. I am particularly grateful to Pete Andrews for key encouragement of my interest in environment, to Judith Bennett for keen and forthright assessment of my writing and thinking, to Nancy Hewitt for complicating my understandings of places and peoples, and to Della Pollock for helping me find my own embodied voice.

I was as fortunate in my graduate colleagues at UNC and Duke as I was in my mentors. The magnificent Nettes—Stacy Braukman, Kirsten Delegard,

Natalie Fousekis, and Ginny Noble—offered laughter, collegiality, and brilliance in heaping measures. I also enjoyed these gifts from my wonderful housemates, Eve Duffy and Elizabeth Horst, who kept my mind and body nourished and never complained about my cartoonish clutter. Natalie, Ginny, Eve, Stacy, and Christa McGill also hosted me in their homes repeatedly, with stunning generosity, more times than I can begin to count— so many that I often had a key, and my own special room, and a thorough familiarity with the kitchen. I also sharpened my mind over meals and in gab sessions with Gavin Campbell, Sandra Hayslette, John Hepp, Jennifer Ritterhouse, Molly Rozum, and Kathy and Dave Walbert. Among all these friends, and much to my delight, an astonishing number proved to be outstanding chefs as well as first-rate academics. I savored their delicious dishes, although I worried a bit about whether excellence in cookery and in history *necessarily* went hand in hand.

Some of these friends were also colleagues in the superb Southern Oral History Program, where I had the good fortune to train and work. Through SOHP I met other wonderful people as well, including Rob Amberg, David Cecelski, Melynn Glusman, Pamela Grundy, Lu Ann Jones, Spencie Love, Beth Millwood, Joe Mosnier, Kelly Navies, and Alicia Rouverol. I am indebted to each of them for support, encouragement, and insight, offered in different ways and at different times throughout the years of this work.

I am also deeply grateful to all the people I interviewed for this project. Without their gifts of time, memories, and insights this book would not have been possible. Special thanks go to Esther Cunningham, whose initial interview launched me on this project. With unfailing grace and good humor, Esther agreed to further interviews, corresponded with me, and accommodated my many requests for additional information. Monroe Gilmour also proved remarkably generous. He lavished me with important sources from his personal files and regularly provided encouragement and information. Mary Kelly and Pat Cook also stood out, graciously accommodating what must have seemed to them interminable questioning.

I owe a great debt to past and current staff members of the Western North Carolina Alliance, especially Bob Gale, Norma Ivey, Julie Mayfield, and Brownie Newman. They steered me toward important people and documents, entrusted me with archival materials, and graciously tolerated my many intrusions into their work space. I also benefited from volunteer Linda Kane's careful work organizing WNCA materials. And I thank my friend Cynthia Camilleri for her willingness to serve as emergency WNCA office help.

Historians could not do their work without support from librarians and archivists, and I am grateful to the many fine professionals who assisted me. I found them at the National Archives, the Asheville-Buncombe Public Library system, the *Asheville Citizen-Times* office, National Forests in North Carolina headquarters, UNC's North Carolina Collection, the Forest History Society, the North Carolina State Archives, the Harriet Beecher Stowe Center, and the Macon County Historical Society. I also found high-quality support in Special Collections at the University of North Carolina at Asheville, Appalachian State University, and Western Carolina University. Cheryl Oakes, at the Forest History Society, deserves special mention for excellence so consistent it seems routine.

My colleagues at Mars Hill College's Liston B. Ramsey Center for Regional Studies have also proved invaluable. Peggy Harmon helped me to useful materials I might otherwise have overlooked. Richard Dillingham, whose encyclopedic knowledge of regional history continues to amaze me, was one of my earliest Mars Hill supporters and pointed me toward valuable sources. I am grateful to Cassie Robinson Pflegler for unearthing numerous archival treasures and nudging me sagely at key moments. I owe a great debt to Karen Paar for repeatedly helping me past key roadblocks and for readily offering both considerable research, writing, technical, and archival expertise and unstinting moral support.

Mars Hill College's Renfro Library, too, made substantial contributions to this project. Staffers there generously allowed me to extend and re-extend due dates and graciously accommodated my nearly endless stream of interlibrary loan requests. They helped me track down obscure pieces and offered gentle reminders when return deadlines loomed. I am particularly grateful to Bev Robertson and Penelope Lindsay for their patient and staunch library support.

I have also been fortunate to have the support of wonderful faculty colleagues and friends at Mars Hill. My splendid fellow professors in the History Department—Lucia Carter, John Gripentrog, Jim Lenburg, and Phyllis Smith—proved exemplary, in this as in so many things. They covered courses while I was away, offered useful tips and generous encouragement, and generally reminded me how lucky I am to inhabit third-floor Cornwell.

I am quite grateful to Matt Baldwin, Carol Boggess, Greg Clemons, Lora Coomer, Peggy Fender, Kathy Meacham, George Peery, Jason Pierce, Joanna Pierce, Paul Smith, Beth Vogler, and Ashby Walker, each of whom supported this project and its author in important ways on various occasions. And I sincerely thank Noel Kinnamon for repeatedly serving as my on-campus writing role model, counselor, cheerleader, and mentor. I am also indebted to my colleagues and friends Scott Pearson and Alan Smith for regularly sharing their immense knowledge of Appalachian forest ecology with me. I thank Alan, too, with deep gratitude, for patiently tolerating countless soliloquies on the rewards and challenges—especially challenges—of this work.

In addition, this project has benefited from the support of Mars Hill College administrators. I thank Dan Lunsford, Nina Pollard, John Wells, and Lyn White for encouraging this endeavor and making it possible for me to move forward with it. Lyn introduced me to the National Endowment for the Humanities, without whose support this book would still be in pieces on my desk. Dan, Nina, and John made arrangements that enabled me to win funding and take the leave time I needed to finish researching and writing the manuscript.

A long parade of students at Mars Hill College has also encouraged this project. They asked for updates, reserved advance autographed copies, modeled persistence and hard work, embraced revision, pushed me to think deeply about mountain forests and cultures, wrestled with environmental issues in history and the present day, shared stories and observations from their own lives, made me laugh, and reinforced my enthusiasm for pigs as historical actors. I thank you all.

I am grateful as well to participants in Mars Hill College's 2005 and 2006 NEH Landmarks of American History workshops for community college faculty, "Working the Woods." These fine educators not only reminded me why I do what I do but also encouraged me to continue the book project—even after they read part of the manuscript.

I have also enjoyed generous collegial support far beyond the halls of Mars Hill. Senior Appalachian history scholars Ron Eller, John Inscoe, and Gordon McKinney each offered important encouragement at critical times. Appalachian environmental and park historians Margaret Brown, Don Davis, Dan Pierce, Tim Silver, and Anne Mitchell Whisnant proved excellent role models and generous colleagues. Beyond the Appalachians, eminent environmental historians Richard Judd and Char Miller offered timely support and encouragement. Seasoned woods researcher John Alger gave me sage guidance to investigations in national forest records, including this memorable and all too apt line: "First, go to your doctor and get a prescription for Valium."

This project has benefited tremendously from the consistently excellent work of the team at University of Georgia Press. I am fortunate to have had that team standing shoulder to shoulder with me throughout the publication process. Paul Sutter, in particular, has been an exceptional partner in this book project, a patient and insightful ally for years. The finished product is far better than it could have been without his keen input and stalwart support. Derek Krissoff has also proved a wise, patient, and pleasant guide, as has John Joerschke. Both have always responded with grace and good humor to assorted challenges I have thrown at them. I am grateful to Mary M. Hill, whose careful copyedits improved clarity and consistency throughout. I also thank two anonymous reviewers engaged by the press; their thoughtful feedback has markedly improved the book.

Financial support for this work has come from a variety of sources. This project was born through Southern Oral History Program's Women's Leadership and Grassroots Activism initiative and continued through its Listening for a Change project. An Archie K. Davis Graduate Fellowship from SOHP supported key early-stage research.

In addition, the Graduate School at UNC and the Center for the Study of the American South provided timely grants. The graduate school awarded an Off-Campus Dissertation Fellowship and the center a Graduate Summer Research Grant. In my final year at UNC, the graduate school also provided critical financial support through the Peace R. Sullivan Dissertation Fellowship and awarded me membership in the Royster Society of Fellows. It is difficult to overstate the importance of those honors to the success of this work.

I am also very grateful to Mars Hill College and to the Appalachian College Association for essential postdoctoral research support. The Appalachian College Association provided a summer fellowship that enabled my work in the National Archives. Mars Hill College granted a four-course release that allowed me to continue the national forest research and to master the intricacies of early Pisgah and Nantahala history. The college also enabled me to accept fellowship leave, and support from its Faculty Enrichment and Renewal fund permitted conference presentations that sharpened my analyses.

I owe an immense debt of gratitude to the National Endowment for the Humanities for crucial support of this project's final stages. A Research Fellowship from the NEH enabled me to spend a full year writing and revising, readying the piece for peer review. I simply cannot express how important that support was. Without it, this book would not yet exist.

Finally, there is a wide circle of family and friends without whom I could never have completed this project. Lynn Appelbaum, Cynthia and Vince Camilleri, Robin Devlin, Carol and Stuart Fountain, Donna Hollinshead and the Thursday yogis, Lu Ann Jones, Woodeane MacDonald,

Leah McGrath, Loy and Connie Newby, Karen Paar, Alicia Rouverol, Alan Smith, Jay and Michelle Wilkins, and the entire Newfont family listened to endless hours of research and book-project news. Cynthia Camilleri, Heidi Hodges, Lynn Isgrig, Vinessa Landolt, and Keith Mastin cared for my children while I worked on various pieces. Blythe, Hannah, Adah, and Walker Ardyson hosted me in their home while I researched in Forest History Society archives. Patty, Darek, Ben, and Sam Newby housed, fed, and transported me during my stints at the National Archives and kept me properly hugged. My wonderful parents and parents-in-law, Carol and Stuart Fountain and Loy and Connie Newby, looked after the children and the house on many occasions and graciously put up with holiday absences. My brothers and sisters-in-law and nieces and nephews were always encouraging, as was my beloved grandmother.

My deepest gratitude goes to the other Newfonts. I thank my children for their patience, encouragement, and inspiring artwork. My dear ones, you could have complained when I disappeared into the archives or the study, but instead you cheered me on. You lighted this project, just as you have always lighted our home and our lives. I thank my husband, Dann, who for years allowed this project to take over his life and home as well as mine. His extraordinary generosity and luminous faith in me give this work its foundation. There are no words sufficient to thank you, Dann, for the incalculable gifts you have always lavished on me.

MAPS

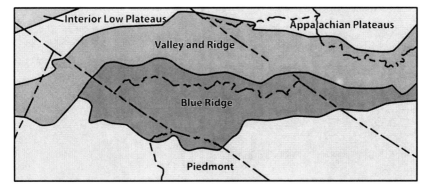

The southern Blue Ridge geological province stretches from north Georgia and northwestern South Carolina into western North Carolina and eastern Tennessee, and it continues north into southwestern Virginia. North Carolina's mountainous western counties lie in this province, and North Carolina encompasses more of the southern Blue Ridge than any other state. U.S. Geological Survey map.

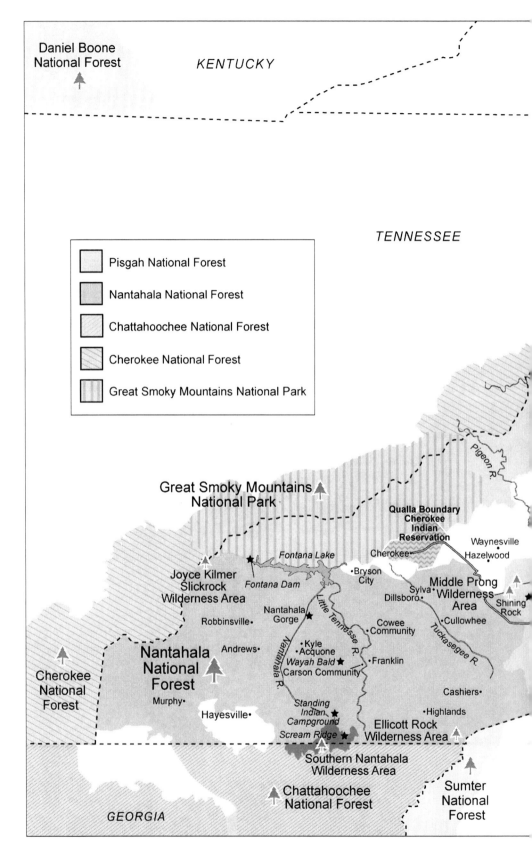

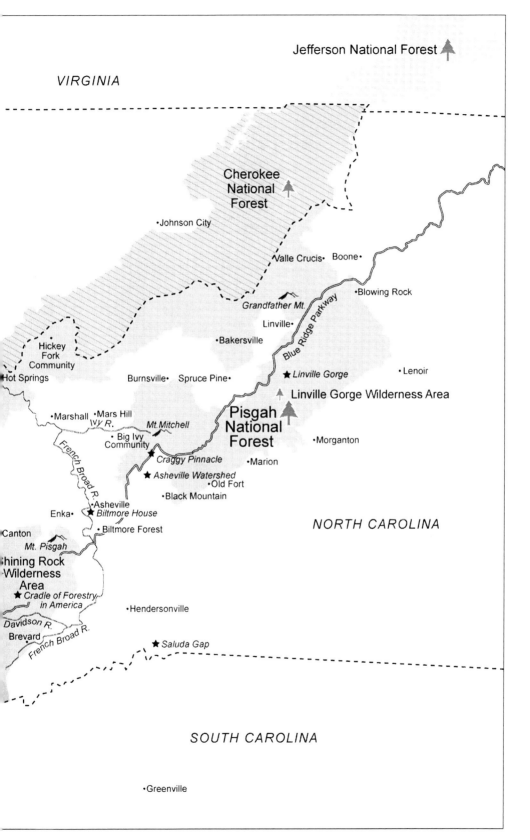

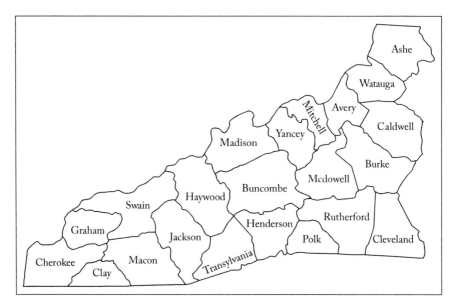

Western North Carolina counties.

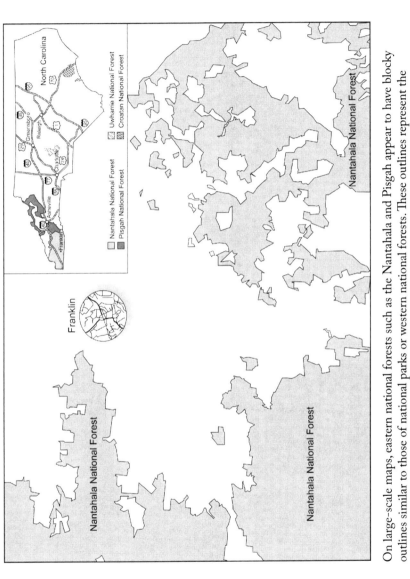

On large–scale maps, eastern national forests such as the Nantahala and Pisgah appear to have blocky outlines similar to those of national parks or western national forests. These outlines represent the "proclamation boundaries" of eastern forests, or the areas within which they have authority to acquire land. Their actual landholdings are far more irregular, reflecting their history of acquisition only from willing sellers. Close-up maps—such as this one of the Nantahala National Forest near Franklin—reveal a patchwork of ragged, snaking forest parcels scattered across the landscape. U.S. Forest Service map.

Blue Ridge Commons

Margaret Morley captured this beautiful image of a woman in the woods near Bryson City, North Carolina, around 1910. We have very little information about the woman, but she has quite likely harvested the commons forest. The sack she carries might contain nuts, roots, game, herbs, bark, fish, or other products native to the rich woods of the southern Blue Ridge. Courtesy of Harriet Beecher Stowe Center.

Of Forests and Commons

IN A BLACK-AND-WHITE PHOTOGRAPH taken around 1900, an elderly woman stands on a mountain path, surrounded and dwarfed by towering trees. In her right hand she carries a plain cloth sack—a "poke" in local parlance. The poke's contents round its sides, giving it volume and heft. She holds it in front of her long dark skirt, her left hand touching its fabric edge. A ruffled sunbonnet frames her face, and from beneath it, smiling slightly, she gazes directly at the camera lens.

Unanswered questions swirl around this woman in the Blue Ridge woods. Who was she? Where was she headed? Where had she been? What was she doing there in the forest?

We know more about the photographer who captured this beautiful image. Margaret Warner Morley, an educator, author, and biologist, regularly visited and eventually moved to Tryon, North Carolina. After a childhood in Brooklyn and studies in New York, Chicago, and Massachusetts, she spent much of her adulthood traveling the southern mountains, observing and photographing. In 1904 she gave a photo album including this image to her friend and host in Tryon, the noted playwright William Hooker Gillette. Morley's well-received 1913 book, *The Carolina Mountains*, includes another photo of the same woman, this time crossing a log footbridge over a mountain stream.[1]

Morley recorded very little information about these photos or their subjects. We wonder how she found the woman, why she chose to photograph her, how the two organized the photo shoot, and what the mountain woman thought of the experience. Did the woman in the woods ever see this image?

One tantalizing question is this: What did the woman's sack contain? There are many potential answers, most of them centered on the wooded commons.[2] Whoever she was, this Blue Ridge woman lived in one of the world's richest forest regions. She might have harvested any number of things from her neighborhood woods. In early spring she could have gathered wild vegetables such as "branch lettuce," "poke," and the flavorful, onion-like local delicacy called "ramps." Leaves in the surrounding forest look too well developed for that season, however, so probably the bag contained something else. Perhaps it was fall and the woman had been nutting, her sack bulging with chestnuts or hickories. Or she might have dug roots—perhaps ginseng for the Chinese market or sassafras for home use. Maybe she had gathered medicinals—black cohosh, wild goldenseal, bloodroot, among many possibilities. She might have taken mushrooms, bark, or leaves. Perhaps she picked galax, destined eventually for distant urban floral markets. She may have trapped fish or snared small mammals. She might have gathered seasonal wild fruits—fall buckberries, summer blueberries, late summer grapes.

Although the bag's precise contents must remain a mystery, the woman likely carried a harvest from the forest commons. If so, she would be one of countless Appalachian thousands to have done so. These southern mountain commons users, in turn, swell the ranks of untold millions who have harvested the globe's many commons. Morley's woman in the woods is just one in a vast army of these commons workers, their long lines stretching deep into the recesses of history and marching forward into the present day. Her story is only one of many commons stories that remain to be told.

Though commons systems have played an enormous role in human and environmental history around the world and over many centuries, until recently they have been poorly understood outside practitioner groups and a small circle of scholars. They have often been nearly invisible beyond their user sets. When noticed at all by nonusers, they have typically been misunderstood, oversimplified, and dismissed as archaic or impractical.[3]

In fact, commons systems when clearly viewed often prove complex, even sophisticated, as well as flexible and resilient. Some have lasted for centuries. Their power reaches into the present, and their history bears useful lessons.

In the last few decades, a rich literature has documented the commons and illuminated much of their variety and vitality. Scholars have identified types and categories of commons, compared systems of commons governance, traced threats to the commons, and described patterns of response to those threats. This literature offers insights with resonance for the southern Appalachians.

The woman in Margaret Morley's photograph walked a path in the heart of one of the world's great forests. Only the planet's tropical forests can surpass the biological diversity of North America's rich southern Appalachian woods. For centuries these woods have sustained the human communities living in and around them, and they continue to do so today. Within the great Appalachian forest, the Blue Ridge woods of North Carolina stand out. In the biological cache this region represents, Blue Ridge forests may be the crown jewels.

Even if it were the region's only qualification, this enormous biological richness would justify close historical study. But the western North Carolina mountains yield much more. Compelling political, economic, and cultural histories surround the forests. Close scrutiny of these histories reveals stories with implications stretching far beyond the Blue Ridge.

Exploring Blue Ridge history has reshaped my understanding of the conceptual underpinnings of U.S. environmentalism. It has led me to place the concept of "commons" alongside the concept of "wilderness" as central to American thought about nature. "Commons environmentalism" is the name I have given to the determined forest defense efforts of mostly rural, often working-class people in the southern Appalachians, people who were typically not friends to wilderness.

In its full expression, commons environmentalism proved every bit as powerful as wilderness environmentalism—arguably, even more so. In western North Carolina, it appeared in a series of late twentieth-century pitched battles over management of the sprawling Nantahala and Pisgah National Forests. Just as elsewhere, these postwar battles pitted industrialists against environmentalists. In Blue Ridge North Carolina, however, commons users (those same typically rural and often working-class Appalachians) served as "swing voters" in these battles. The side that most effectively hitched commons culture to its wagon won. Moreover, commons environmentalists sometimes championed forest protection proposals so sweepingly ambitious that mainstream environmental groups proved unwilling to support them.

The contours of these heated contests cannot be understood outside the region's long history of forest use. As the Morley photograph illustrates, Blue Ridge forests served as harvest grounds for generations of inhabitants. These people hunted and fished wildlife and dug, tapped, cut, and gathered plant resources. Whole economies relied on the woods, among them the eighteenth-century deerskin trade, the nineteenth-century livestock business, and the twentieth-century leather-tanning industry.

Beginning in the late eighteenth century and continuing into the twentieth, private owners held nearly all Blue Ridge lands. But that did not prevent local people from using the forests as de facto commons. Local custom treated privately owned but "unimproved" woods as semipublic, fair game for hunting, fishing, gathering, and the like. Until at least the late nineteenth century, local law agreed.

In the early twentieth century, the U.S. government recognized both the national importance of southern Appalachian forests and the massive timber-industry devastation then wrecking them. To protect what it saw as a critical set of U.S. resources, the federal government began purchasing southern highland forests on a grand scale. It established an extensive series of national forests under United States Forest Service (USFS) management, including western North Carolina's Pisgah and Nantahala. By the end of World War II, the USFS had become the largest landholder in the region, a status it enjoys to the present day.

This establishment of national forests in the southern Appalachians proved a sea change in the region's forest history. With federal purchase, formerly de facto commons woods now became de jure commons, lands actually owned by the public through the vehicle of government. Commons users also gained some input into management of these lands, as the USFS answered at least indirectly to the nation's citizenry. The national forest system also served as a brake on the wholesale forest destruction that often continued—even into the present day—on private lands in the southern mountains.

Though she probably never used the word, the woman in Margaret Morley's photograph can lead us into an American commons. This book explores the concept of the commons and its enduring power in Blue Ridge history: economic, cultural, political, and environmental. Though the region is unusually rich in natural treasures, this story is not unique. There are many other commons users waiting to take us into many other harvest grounds. This book tells only one of many possible American commons tales.

Following our guide, let us step into the woods.

Southern Blue Ridge Forests

Earth's richest temperate forests drape the southern folds of North America's Appalachian mountain chain. These woods, dazzling in their biological diversity, host tens of thousands of plant, animal, insect, and microbe species, many rare and some unique. Like the planet's other great biodiversity sinks—its oceans and tropical forests—the Appalachian slopes continue to reward science with new and surprising discoveries.[4]

The complicated geology that gave rise to the mountains enabled them to provide habitat for this dazzling array of flora and fauna. At least two collisions between North America and the European and African continental plates contributed to the Appalachians' complex stone foundations. Immense geological uplifts, overturning rock formations, erosion, and deposition sculpted the rich contours of the southern highlands. The result of this chaotic history was a topography in which older rocks overlay younger rocks and unusual geological combinations occurred at various elevations and faced every compass direction. In addition, wildly different subclimates—from near rain forest to near desert conditions—patchworked the hills.[5]

Within this rich southern Appalachian landscape, the southern Blue Ridge geological province stands out as a crown jewel, perhaps the richest realm of all. A single Blue Ridge cove may rival all of Europe in the number of tree species it sustains. The forest's wealth extends to other arenas as well. Scientists estimate that some one hundred thousand total species may inhabit the Great Smoky Mountains National Park, which encompasses about eight hundred square miles in Blue Ridge North Carolina and Tennessee. As of 2009, biologists had recorded more than 17,000 species in the park, including over 1,600 vascular plants, 350 ferns and mosses, 240 birds, 100 crustaceans, 75 fishes, 65 mammals, 40 amphibians, and 40 reptiles. Less glamorous categories yielded even more staggering numbers: 2,700 fungi, 2,400 beetles, 1,800 moths and butterflies, 1,000 algae, 900 flies, 580 lichens, and 500 spiders. Work in the park between 1998 and 2009 documented over 6,500 species previously unknown to inhabit it and yielded over 900 species entirely new to science. In Blue Ridge western North Carolina, biologists have identified 35 types of botanical communities, some extremely rare. This area also provides the richest salamander habitat on earth—over 50 species make homes there, alongside 14 different species of frogs and toads. One hundred types of snails roam the woods, and 23 types of bivalve mollusks survive in North Carolina's mountain streams.[6]

Acre for acre, no other temperate region on earth can surpass the southern Blue Ridge in biological wealth. In recognition of its enormous riches, the United Nations has included parts of the Blue Ridge in the international biosphere reserve system and has named the Great Smoky Mountains National Park a World Heritage Site. In 1968 the park numbered among the very first designated biosphere reserve units, and today the Blue Ridge hosts four of six official units in the Southern Appalachian Biosphere Reserve.[7]

Though state lines fragment the Blue Ridge province, its heart lies in western North Carolina. Political boundaries often fail to mirror geological distinctions, and this is particularly true in the Appalachian mountains. The southern Blue Ridge spreads over portions of Georgia, South Carolina, North Carolina, Tennessee, and Virginia. North Carolina encompasses more of the province than any other state, however, including important features such as the Black Mountain Range, home of Mount Mitchell, the highest peak in eastern North America. Three of the four Blue Ridge international biosphere reserve units lie entirely in western North Carolina; the fourth straddles the North Carolina–Tennessee line.[8]

Thus, western North Carolina represents a kind of ecological heartland. The biological hub of the rich southern Appalachian region, North Carolina's mountain forests act as a green treasure trove for the nation, for the continent, and even for the globe. The U.S. Congress affirmed this reality in 2003 when it designated the state's highlands as the Blue Ridge National Heritage Area, citing the region's wealth in both nature and culture.[9]

Nantahala and Pisgah National Forest Commons

The USFS holds over a million acres in this ecological jewel of a region, far more than any other landowner. It entered the region after the 1911 Weeks Act gave the federal government authority to purchase eastern lands, and by 1940 it had become the largest landholder in the southern Blue Ridge province. The agency's Nantahala and Pisgah National Forests encompass huge swathes of the North Carolina mountains, surrounding some communities and reaching tendrils into many more. Small wonder, then, that USFS land management decisions have had profound effects both on Blue Ridge flora and fauna and on the people of western North Carolina.[10]

Margaret Morley's woman in the woods walked her mountain path just as the enormous sea change of federal ownership was about to sweep the Blue Ridge. With the arrival of the national forests in the southern Appalachians after 1911, the region became host to a vast de jure forest commons, one that supported hunting, fishing, gathering, and, for a few decades, grazing. This commons, unlike the de facto commons it replaced, enjoyed recognition through formal law. The cultural and economic importance of this federal commons grew in the twentieth century, especially as development claimed an increasing share of private land after World War II.

The Nantahala and Pisgah National Forests meet the two key criteria of common-property management systems. First, significant resources are communally held. The trees, streams, wildlife, and flora in the forests are widely recognized as valuable resources. They are publicly owned, which is one form of common ownership.[11] Different elements of the forest are held by different government entities—North Carolina state government owns the opossums, for instance, while the federal government owns the lichens—but all national forest resources are in the public domain.

Second, these publicly owned resources are deliberately managed. The USFS has broad authority over resources in the Pisgah and Nantahala National Forests, and it actively manages these resources. It decides, for instance, where, how, and when to cut trees.

The agency also makes many national forest resources widely accessible.

For a fairly small fee, hunters and anglers can purchase rights to take wildlife on hundreds of thousands of forest acres and in thousands of mountain streams. Modest fees also purchase permits to gather various marketable plant species, such as ginseng, galax, mosses, and Fraser fir cones and seedlings. The USFS also sells thousands of moderately priced firewood permits each year. In the late twentieth century, the agency could not say with precision how many people used its woods, but certainly many thousands harvested Nantahala and Pisgah resources every year.[12]

The North Carolina Wildlife Resources Commission (NCWRC) is also an active forest resource manager. The state commission has authority over all wildlife in North Carolina, including the animals on federal lands. Where the Forest Service manages Nantahala and Pisgah flora, the commission manages fauna. Commission regulations specify where and when anglers can fish for trout, for instance, what equipment they can use, how many trophies they can take home from each day's outing, and how big these fish can be. Through its system of permits, the commission also determines who can legally harvest trout, and through its stocking program, it governs which streams will have which kinds of fish.

These two agencies are central commons managers, but the bureaucracy governing national forestlands is still more complicated. The Bureau of Land Management, which is under the Department of the Interior rather than Agriculture, controls mineral resources on all federal public lands, including the national forests. Thus, when a petroleum exploration rush came to the Nantahala and Pisgah in the early 1980s, a third agency stepped into the commons-administration spotlight. The Bureau of Land Management is not typically involved in day-to-day commons management throughout the forest as the Forest Service and Wildlife Commission are, but it does play a central role in any question of mineral-resource development, and it is closely involved with managing any active mineral sectors of the forest.

This, then, is the western North Carolina national forest commons. In the 1970s and 1980s it comprised roughly one million acres of mountain forestland, countless streams, and parts of several rivers. Innumerable wild animals, trees, and other plants lived within its borders. Untold mineral deposits lay beneath its surface. All of these resources were publicly owned, and one state and two federal government agencies shared responsibility for managing them. In the late twentieth century, this was a hunting, fishing, and gathering commons, though it had previously—and fairly recently, in places—been a grazing commons as well.[13]

Mountain residents worried about enclosure threats to these commons forests. Enclosure concerns surfaced in every major regional USFS management debate from the 1930s onward. When the 1976 National Forest Management Act gave real power to public input, these concerns came roaring to the surface.[14] They drew force from the long history of commons forest use in the southern Appalachians and from the commons model of forest thought it supported.[15]

Local residents' Nantahala and Pisgah advocacy has proved spirited, persistent, and often quite effective. Commons traditions, which give many residents a sense of woods ownership, have fueled it, as has the knowledge that, as taxpaying American citizens, they actually have co-owned USFS lands. Like a powerful motor running continuously and revving occasionally, debates about forest policy hummed throughout western North Carolina's late twentieth-century history, from time to time erupting into dramatic and even dangerous confrontations.

Toward the end of the twentieth century, three striking clashes centered on questions of wilderness designation, petroleum development, and clearcut timber harvesting on the Nantahala and Pisgah. In the late 1970s, the entire southern Appalachian region seemed to hover on the verge of violent explosion during the Roadless Area Review and Evaluation (RARE II) process initiated by President Jimmy Carter's administration. An effort to expand the federal wilderness system created under the 1964 Wilderness Act, RARE II met with fierce local resistance and enjoyed only minimal success in the North Carolina mountains. RARE II advocates, including national environmental groups such as the Wilderness Society, came out of the process largely defeated and keenly disappointed.

Yet just a few years later, before the wilderness-battle dust had even settled, North Carolina's rural mountain residents raised loud and determined voices again, this time to oppose petroleum exploration and clearcut timber harvesting in the national forests. They fought industrial development with a vigor and tenacity that took Forest Service officials completely by surprise. In this second round of campaigns, some longtime residents' goals were actually *more* far-reaching than national environmental groups such as the Sierra Club were willing to support.

At first glance, this history might seem to indicate that mountain people suffered a kind of environmental schizophrenia. They fought against forest protection, then for protection, as if they could not make up their minds. A closer look, however, reveals logic beneath this apparent paradox. The key lies in the intersections between regional forest history and culture and regional forest politics. In order to understand late twentieth-century environmental politics in the southern mountains, then, one must turn to the region's environmental history.[16]

The Idea of the Commons

The idea of wilderness failed to resonate with many longtime mountain residents. It typically seemed to them elitist, economically unsound, and historically dishonest. They had "Trouble with Wilderness" along the lines William Cronon traced in his pathbreaking article.[17] But their rejection of wilderness environmentalism did not necessarily mean they were hostile to all types of forest conservation. As a few perceptive activists in the region realized, some of the same cultural ground that had yielded opposition to wilderness could also produce support for other kinds of forest protection. Longtime mountain residents both rejected wilderness environmentalism and built a regional forest protection movement on their own powerful model. They practiced what I call "commons environmentalism."

The concept of the commons has existed in various forms across many human cultures over millennia. The word "commons" whisks many of us immediately to past centuries and distant lands. Especially in the United States, where private property holds center stage, we rarely think in terms of commons systems. Yet these systems are very much alive and affect all our lives, as frequent references to the "global commons" among contemporary environmentalists attest.

Moreover, although it has long been nearly invisible, the commons has deep roots in the United States. It is as American as apple pie.[18] Though the U.S. commitment to private property has been far better publicized and understood, the commons has been no less fundamental to American history and culture. It is not possible in the space of this book to fully trace the contours of American commons systems past and present. Suffice it to say that the Appalachian woods featured in this volume are but one of many such systems across the United States through its history.

But what is the commons? Briefly, any resource that is widely accessible, used by many people, and communally owned may be considered a commons. Commons resources are not privately owned by any single person or group, though within a commons some specific resources may be reserved for certain claimants. Commons systems are regulated and managed either through formal laws and rules or through informal traditions and social sanctions. Illegal or unsanctioned harvest of commons resources is considered poaching, theft, or invasion, and these infractions are punished. Commons systems are dynamic. They are nearly always contested, and they are subject to change over time. One enemy to commons systems takes the form of "enclosure" moves, or attempts at privatization.[19]

In the southern Appalachians, a commons model of forest thought had roots in a nineteenth-century economy dependent on small-scale woods extraction. It lived on, however, in traditions important to twentieth-century rural culture—hunting, fishing, berrying, herb gathering, and the like. Local residents often valued mountain forests as working and peopled commons harvest grounds, not as unspoiled wilderness.[20] They saw any policy that threatened to remove large tracts from commons use as enclosure, though they did not use that term. Whatever form it took—wilderness designation or industrial development—perceived forest enclosure met with determined resistance.

Insights from the Appalachians

Exploring western North Carolina's commons history yields many benefits. First, the Nantahala and Pisgah National Forests encompass a lion's share of the southern Blue Ridge province's rich woods. The history and politics surrounding these forests have had, and will continue to have, real ramifications for this global treasure. As world species loss and global climate change heighten concerns about deforestation—which contributes to both—the planet's remaining forest wealth becomes ever more precious. Investigating the history of how this wealth has been managed and where and how that management has succeeded and failed takes on new urgency.[21]

Second, western North Carolina's forest contests represent one of the twentieth century's most consequential social movements at work on the ground in one of North America's richest environments. In other words, this history illuminates what happened when the rubber hit the road—when environmental movement rubber, that is, hit southern Blue Ridge road. Since neither the postwar environmental movement nor the southern Appalachian region has yet received its full historical due, it is worth lingering over this point.

The American environmental movement was one of the most important developments to shape U.S. history in the postwar period. Like other giants of the time—the civil rights movement and the Cold War, for instance—its long reach extended not only into law and politics but also into economics, philosophy, and culture. Environmentalist thinkers troubled key American concepts such as "property" and "progress"; they questioned basic categories such as "nature" and "human." In politics, the movement etched its mark into national, state, and local legislation; into legal briefs and court decisions; and into electoral contests at every level. It also carved into the very landscape of the nation, leaving its signature in the forests, plains, deserts, and wetlands; in the air, soil, and water; and even among the animals, plants, and insects. Americans everywhere continue to feel its influence in countless ways. Diplomats negotiating international treaties walk in its shadow, and so do everyday Americans confronting empty soda bottles. Like other giants of the postwar period, the environmental movement and its legacy are still unfolding, still shaping politics and culture in the twenty-first century.

In spite of this enormous influence, however, we still know relatively little about the history of American environmentalism. Compared to the voluminous literature on the Cold War or the civil rights movement, for instance, the literature on the environmental movement in the United States is still remarkably thin. Excellent pioneering work provided initial scaffolding, tracing the movement's origins and limning its broad outlines. More recently, fine case studies have illuminated particular instances of competing claims and conflict over specific sets of natural resources. These nuanced explorations have enriched our understanding of the movement as a whole, and this book aims to join their number. Nonetheless, the history of this crucial movement has barely reached adolescence.[22]

Despite decades of excellent work from scholars of the Appalachians, the same can be said for southern mountain history. Incredibly, students of the southern highlands still have to work hard to convince national audiences that the region is not a parochial backwater—that it actually has been and continues to be a part of the United States and that it, like other, more respected regions, may have something to teach the nation. Appalachian people still groan under the weight of a century and a half's worth of negative stereotyping. Too often their fellow citizens seem incapable of seeing the region through anything other than the denigrating and antiquated "ignorant hillbilly" lenses developed by visitors after the Civil War. Distorted even then, these lenses today have become essentially opaque, obscuring far more than they reveal. The resulting cultural blindness endangers both would-be seers and the would-be seen.

This blindness has tangible and potent negative results for people and for the environment. The most horrific recent example comes in the form of mountaintop removal, a method of coal mining that brings to the Appalachians environmental devastation on a nearly incomprehensible scale. Entire peaks are decapitated, and the resulting "debris" is dumped in streams and valleys. Waste from the process often outweighs coal produced by a factor of twenty or even thirty. It is impossible to undo the ecological annihilation this process wreaks on some of the continent's richest forests. Social and cultural devastations to neighboring communities mirror the environmental havoc. Whole neighborhoods disappear or are reduced to desperation.[23]

Despite these realities, local residents have fought mountaintop removal fiercely and relentlessly, battling tooth and nail, with dignity and savvy, and often at great personal risk. Yet this courageous resistance and the ruination that inspires it have barely registered in the national consciousness. It is difficult to imagine a parallel scenario occurring in another U.S. mountain region—the Adirondacks, the Colorado Rockies, the Sierra Nevada. The outrage would be seen as national and would not be tolerated; the resistance would be difficult to ignore. Only because too many other Americans think of southern highland residents as "backward," segregated in "a world apart," has this set of natural and human demolitions achieved multiple-decade longevity.[24]

Infuriating, damaging, and inaccurate as negative stereotypes of Appalachian people are, in the broadest sense they are not surprising. Lowland peoples in other parts of the world also paint their highland neighbors with a negative brush, deriding them as violent, drunken, dirty, diseased, and incestuous.[25] Metropolitans stigmatize rural peoples. And those unfamiliar with the commons—with its systems, practices, and knowledge—frequently denigrate commons users.[26] Small wonder, then, that southern Appalachian residents, who fit all these categories, have borne such a heavy negative burden.

In reality, the southern Appalachian region is far richer and more complex than most Americans realize. Like other parts of the United States, it has its cities, towns, and countrysides, its urban, suburban, and rural neighborhoods. Like other regions, it hosts—and has long hosted—substantial racial and ethnic diversity. Wealthy, middling, and poor people call it home. Longtime residents work alongside recent immigrants. Factories, universities, farms, hospitals, resorts, mines, and restaurants dot the region. Inhabitants identify with a variety of religious traditions and with none at all. Every conceivable type of music visits Appalachian airwaves and residents' earpieces.

The region has never been cut off from the wider world, and clearly not in the last five hundred years. It has long had cultural, economic, political, and other ties to places far beyond its boundaries. Economic exchange illustrates the larger pattern. Global trade networks have included the Blue Ridge since at least the seventeenth century, and the region's residents participated in continental trade networks centuries before that. In the eighteenth century, staggering numbers of Blue Ridge deerskins crossed the Atlantic in the lucrative peltries trade. The nineteenth century saw Appalachian ginseng travel to Asian markets and mountain livestock undergird the international cotton trade. In the twentieth century, the region became a national center of the crucial leather-tanning industry, and South American hides arrived by the trainload to be processed using tannic acid extracted from native trees. Also in the twentieth century, New Yorkers bought Blue Ridge chestnuts on their city streets, and Ohioans made fortunes in mountain medicinals. The list goes on: railroads transformed the region in the nineteenth century, interstate highways crossed it in the twentieth, the Internet ushered in the twenty-first.

As this history demonstrates, the Appalachian region is by no means a separate land and has not been one. Instead, it is and has long been one of many sections that together make up the United States of America. Genuine knowledge about southern highland history, cultures, and ecologies tends to reveal kinships—rather than stark contrasts—with other regions. I have had colleagues from New England, the Chesapeake, the Great Lakes, and the Louisiana bayous, for instance, point out regional parallels. In discussions of Appalachian forest history, scholars from Texas, Minnesota, Ohio, Washington, Florida, Montana, New Mexico, New York, and California have told me they see analogous patterns in their states.[27] In turn, my own understanding of the southern Appalachians has been informed by resonant insights from the Adirondacks, the Grand Canyon, the Illinois River, Glacier National Park, rural New England, Chicago, and the Chesapeake Bay.[28] Work on national forests in Oregon, New Mexico, Minnesota, Maine, Montana, Idaho, South Dakota, California, Alabama, and Alaska has provided useful parallels.[29] Beyond North America, scholarship treating Cameroon, Kenya, India, Norway, Poland, Japan, Switzerland, and the Amazon rainforests has brought insights.[30]

For these reasons I believe this book illuminates a story that is not unique or isolated. Rather, it provides a close-up examination of one corner in an extremely broad and complex tapestry. I am convinced that commons culture and practice were not at all unique to the southern mountains and that other instances of commons environmentalism in American history exist but are currently invisible because we lack the tools to recognize their pattern.

Illuminating the commons, making its contours visible and its outline recognizable, is a key goal of this book. Our histories of the United States—especially but not only our environmental histories—will be incomplete as long as they leave out past commons. Our understandings of the American environmental movement, so central to postwar U.S. history, will also be incomplete without commons environmentalism.

The commons is powerful, but it cannot be useful if we cannot see it clearly. The wellsprings of commons environmentalism run deep, but they cannot be tapped if we do not know they are there. Without a visible commons, commons environmentalism cannot be available as a strategy.

Like the planet's glaciers, forests globally are shrinking, in retreat. We need to utilize every possible tool and strategy if we are to reverse this deadly process. Western North Carolina's forest history can help draw attention to a set of tools that has too often been overlooked, at least in the United States. It can provide a useable past for those working today to protect Earth's great forests, in the Appalachians and elsewhere.

The toxic habit of treating forest landscapes as disposable mirrors the unjust custom of dismissing Appalachian people. Both ignore compelling evidence, and both are dangerous. As Gurney Norman astutely observed, "The mountain people are leaders and teachers of civic virtue for the nation, not scabs upon the body politic as the negative hillbilly stereotype would have it."[31] This study offers one example of that leadership and teaching. It is the story of a widely maligned people building a powerful forest protection movement from the sturdy materials of their commons history and culture. Like the Blue Ridge forest itself, this story contains lessons for us all.

ONE

"The Custom of Our Country"

The Appalachian Forest Commons

ONE SUNDAY IN EARLY 2010, during a record-setting winter of seemingly continuous snowstorms and perpetual school closings, columnist Dale Neal met two empty-sacked galax hunters coming down a path in Pisgah National Forest. The newspaperman had taken advantage of a rare weekend break in the freezing temperatures to hike with his dog along Daniel Ridge Trail. A record-setting economic recession, even more dramatic than the winter, also gripped the country. The two galax hunters braved Pisgah's snowy woods in hopes of earning money during these hard times. They sought the glossy leaves of galax, a ground-hugging native evergreen. For a few pennies apiece, they could sell the attractive leaves to dealers servicing the nation's florist industry.

Their efforts on this day proved fruitless, however. As Neal observed, "Galax was out there, but it was anybody's guess where under eight inches of snow." He worried about the two men, who wore only thin protection against the cold. They had walked for miles, the snow had soaked their jeans, and one was coughing noticeably. The reporter identified them as Hispanic and noted their broken English. He wondered what "deeper anxieties" had driven the men to the woods, imagining how they must be struggling to provide food, warmth, and clothing for their families. For him, these galax pickers and their empty bags stood alongside Walker Evans's Depression era sharecroppers as iconic images of poverty and suffering during economic crisis.[1]

The two men may have been breaking the law, as Neal recognized. They might have been in the United States without required documentation. They might have been seeking to harvest galax without a national forest permit. Neal noted these possibilities but focused on the "desperation" that must have driven the men to endure physical hardship and exposure in the icy woods for what at best would have been saleable harvest worth only a few dollars. The most they could have hoped to earn, he wrote, was $1.85 per twenty-five galax leaves. Despite this small payoff, the North Carolina Horticultural Research Station reported an increase in galax harvesting during the recession, usually by people who were "underpaid or unemployed."[2]

This contemporary encounter illustrates a series of long-standing patterns in the history of the Appalachian commons forest. It underscores commons harvest's economic importance and links products of the southern mountain woods to distant markets. It highlights the critical role of commons harvest in subsistence strategies, particularly of the poor. And it points to the often tricky relationship between commons harvest and formal law.

For more than three centuries, these patterns have marked the southern Appalachians.[3] Dale Neal's account of galax pickers in the snow illustrates a recent chapter in a very long story. Commons harvest, like the forest itself, has changed over time. Some key products, such as deerskins and free-range hogs, have risen to central roles and then fallen away. Other products, such as ginseng, have remained more steadily in demand. The cast of forest characters has also changed. Hispanic galax hunters, for example, are among the most recent entrants. But the basic outlines of an economy tied to forests have persisted.

Defining "Commons"

At the most basic level, the word "commons" can be employed to describe any significant set of resources that is communally owned, used, or managed. "Significant" often, but not always, means economically substantial. It can also mean socially or culturally valuable. True commons are managed, either formally or informally. Rules prescribe who may access the resources, when, how, where, and how often. The word "commons" can refer not only to the resources themselves but also to the governance systems that regulate their use.[4]

Because they are managed, commons are not "open-access." In other words, not just anyone can use a commons resource whenever and however she might like. Rules restrict access, and violations are punished.[5]

Commons stand in contrast to private ownership, where one person or entity holds near-complete, near-exclusive rights to a set of resources. In the commons, many claimants assert such rights. Some claims can coexist, but others compete. When competing claims are mutually exclusive or reciprocally detrimental, they must be settled. Settlements can be reached through formal or informal commons governance and through negotiation, adjudication, or force.

While private property can be treated as commodity, commons thinkers reject straightforward commodity definitions of communal resources. They typically see these definitions as overly simplistic and ultimately misguided. More ominously, these thinkers charge that commodification can ignore fundamental realities and wreak catastrophic destruction on key resources and all those who depend on them. Thus, they refuse formulations equating commons resources with commodities, and they often do so regardless of law.[6]

Like private property regimes, however, commons systems are governed. Rules may be determined by a specific governing body and formally documented, or they may be informally produced by a community of users and enforced by social sanction. Like governance, policing may be either formal or informal. Whatever the means, commons systems are monitored, and rule infractions are penalized.

Commons are often both inclusive and exclusive. They define certain resource users in and others out. Governance systems typically uphold the rights of in-group users whose claims are seen as legitimate while simultaneously denying the claims of other "invalid" would-be users. These excluded prospective users are usually seen as encroaching outsiders.

Commons are marked by ongoing conflict, and contests over them can be tense, even violent. Conflict can occur among in-group users, who may struggle to expand their commons claims at each other's expense. Conflict occurs as they attempt to encroach on one another and to defend themselves from encroachment. Conflict can also occur between users as a collective, on the one hand, and would-be users who have been excluded or who have recently arrived, on the other. Both types of conflict—intra-user and user-outsider—may occur simultaneously.

Commons systems change over time—sometimes gradually, sometimes suddenly. Change can be driven by shifts in the resource base, in the user community, or in relevant technology. Environmental variations of all kinds can affect the resource base, for instance, and these can be naturally occurring or human created. Climate fluctuation, weather events, species introductions, pollutants, and the like can transform ecologies or even bring about resource collapse. Select users may gain access and power over resources at the expense of other established users, or all users may lose access and power to new claimants who do not abide by previously established rules. New technologies can bring sweeping change, as can warfare or state intervention.

Commons systems are often local, but they may function on larger scales. They may or may not be congruent with the state. They may coincide with, overlap with, or exist outside of formal governmental structures at the local, state, national, or international level. In contemporary systems, it is nearly impossible for commons to be independent of established governments, but this has not always been the case.

Enclosure, or privatization, is a perpetual enemy to commons systems. Commons users typically meet enclosure threats with determined resistance, using every tool at their disposal. Usually, those spearheading enclosure attempts are elites—fewer in number but armed with greater economic and political power than the existing commons user group. These elites may or may not have local ties and power bases. Either way, they almost always have connections to distant and powerful economic and political networks. To defend traditionally communal resources against such formidable would-be privatizers, commons users—who usually come from poor and middling classes—often resort to subterfuge and secret attack. They typically target the agents and apparatus of enclosure. Sometimes, as a desperation move, they may assail the resource itself. They rely on one another to conceal information about these defense efforts, including the identities and whereabouts of perpetrators, especially if their actions have broken the law.

Commons systems can exist with or without the support of formal law, though lack of legal standing leaves them especially vulnerable to enclosure. A de facto commons functions without legal backing, while a de jure commons has the force of law. De facto commons can exist, for instance, on land that is privately held, especially if the owner is largely absentee. Since commons practice in such a case would not carry legal recognition, governance could not be enforced through law. Nonetheless, such a commons might enjoy widespread cultural sanction, have governance through informal means, and thrive for many generations. It could crumble suddenly, however, if the private owner decided to use the land for purposes inimical to commons. Commons users would have little recourse in such a case.[7]

De jure commons are actually owned communally and recognized as legitimate under the law. They are more likely than de facto commons to have formal structures of regulation and governance. Their legal standing braces these commons systems to better resist enclosure threats, though it does not render them invulnerable. Like de facto commons, de jure commons may enjoy broad cultural support and prosper for generations. Particular groups may own these commons, or they may be state property. Defenders of de jure commons are more likely than de facto users to work within legal frameworks and in cooperation with agents of government. De facto commons practitioners have little incentive to do so, while for de jure users, these avenues can provide powerful antienclosure weapons and allies.

State or public ownership and governance can create or promote commons systems, and this form of commons has played an increasingly important role in the last century and a half. State ownership is not necessary to commons practice, however, and by itself does not automatically yield commons systems. In some cases state management may undermine commons practice, while in others state ownership may support or enable such practice. State and commons properties are not always easily differentiated, and a thorough discussion of the range of relationships between state and commons is beyond the scope of this book. Suffice it to say that state or public ownership may be but is not necessarily congruent with commons management and practice.

Historical specificity is crucial to understanding commons systems. These systems exist in particular times and places, they are used by particular individuals, and they are governed by particular customs or specific bodies. Internal and external circumstances affecting these systems change, and the systems respond either by making definite adaptations to accommodate these changes or by succumbing in the face of them. In all of this, specificity is vital.[8]

Across time and space, commons systems have been remarkably diverse, both in the resources they have managed and in the schemes they have employed to manage them. Within the general definition of commons, nearly infinite variety is possible.[9]

Natural-Resource Commons

The Blue Ridge forest commons, centerpiece of this story, is one example of a *natural-resource commons*, a harvest ground for plant and animal resources. This type of commons includes not only elements of the natural world, such as deadwood, birds, nuts, and fish, but also the human activities involved in harvesting these elements, such as gathering, hunting, and fishing. Natural-resource commons are the most concrete and best-documented types—in a sense, the classic commons. They are varied and complex, involving not only forests but also fisheries, grasslands, fresh waters, and the like. Examples abound, from across the planet and throughout the centuries.[10]

Historically, natural-resource commons have taken four forms: fishing, gathering, grazing, and hunting. Two or more of these forms have often overlapped. All these forms played central roles in Blue Ridge forest history and culture, and all contributed to the emergence of commons environmentalism.

Fishing commons have developed around a wide range of waters—fresh, salt, and brackish; flowing and still; vast as oceans and tiny as tide pools; enduring as the Mississippi and fleeting as its floodwaters. Even a short list of such commons would include oceans, bays, marshes, estuaries, lakes, rivers, swamps, creeks, and a variety of other wetlands. Historically, fishing commons have been regulated both informally and formally, with a trajectory toward increasing state regulation over time.

The Appalachians' abundant watercourses supported fishing commons for centuries and continue to do so today. Early peoples harvested a variety of native fish with their hands and used baskets, spears, traps, and poisons. These methods persisted into the twentieth century, joined by cane poles, trotlines, commercial rods and reels, and even dynamite. Introduced species, damming, chemical pollutants, soil erosion, and a variety of other factors changed ecologies in the region's waterways, but the fishing commons persisted wherever fish lived. Well into the twentieth century its governance was largely local and informal. In western North Carolina, formal governance began after World War II, when the newly formed North Carolina Wildlife Resources Commission (NCWRC) took on fishing regulation. Fishing continued under the new state system, with some practitioners—especially sportsmen and better-off residents who did not need fish for subsistence—purchasing licenses and abiding by season and bag limits. Others, particularly those who relied on fishing for food, continued traditional practices regardless of the law.[11]

Hunting commons have found support in forests, grasslands, swamps, tundras, and whaled seas. Also known as "wildlife commons," these systems treat wild animals as the property of those able to take them successfully. Early Blue Ridge hunters used stone weapons, such as spears and atlatls, and their descendants developed powerful bows and deadly arrows. Europeans introduced new technologies of hunting and war, such as guns, bullets, and steel knives. These became increasingly sophisticated, eventually yielding high-power rifles and rapid-fire machine guns. Contemporary hunters have a range of technologies at their disposal, including these weapons as well as automobiles, helicopters, and airplanes, radio communication systems, satellite tracking devices, and Global Positioning System locators.

In the Native American wildlife commons, game animals belonged only to themselves until taken by a hunter, at which point they became his property. Particular groups claimed certain game lands and defended them from outside would-be users. Disputes could be settled by negotiation, trade, ballgame competition, or warfare. Ritual observance and prayer surrounded hunting, and widely shared cultural taboos served to brake overharvest.[12] Formal state attempts at hunting regulation began in the early eighteenth century, when colonial governments issued orders respecting deer and predators. These achieved only partial success, and hunting in the mountains continued largely without effective state regulation into the twentieth century. After World War II, when the NCWRC was established, regulation became more systematic. Commission efforts to govern and police the hunting commons are not entirely successful even today, though they do enjoy broad cooperation, and some violators are caught and punished.[13]

Gathering commons typically center on botanical resources, including fuel, wild plant foods, craft and building materials, and medicinals. They may also include some animal and insect products, particularly dung and honey. Grasslands, wetlands, and especially forests have hosted such commons. Under gathering commons systems, plant materials, fungi, insect creations, and animal leavings belong to those who find and harvest them. These commons have typically been regulated informally, but here too there is a trend toward increased state regulation over time.

In the Blue Ridge, gathering commons governance remained largely local and informal until after 1916, when the United States Forest Service (USFS) began gaining control over huge swathes of woods. The USFS focused its initial efforts almost exclusively on timber species and watershed protection, and at first the gathering commons barely registered on its administrative radar. Only later did it begin to recognize the importance of nontimber plant species on its lands and to regulate their harvest accordingly. Even today, though the agency issues plant-gathering permits and occasionally nabs plant poachers, the USFS has only a scant outline of the value of "nontimber forest products" on its lands. In the Appalachians, the gathering commons remains the least well organized, least well documented, least thoroughly regulated, and least policed of the present-day natural-resource forest commons.[14]

A *grazing* or *livestock commons* thrived in the Blue Ridge for more than two centuries, beginning in the early days of European settlement. Native Appalachian peoples did not practice livestock husbandry and at first resisted its introduction. Both Europe and Africa supported herding cultures at the time of contact with the Americas, and Europeans introduced grazing animals practically the moment they set foot on North American shores. Hernando de Soto, for instance, included not only humans but hogs and horses in the 1539 expeditionary force that eventually made its way to the Blue Ridge. By the early 1700s, Cherokee people had adopted hogs as a food source, and toward the end of the century, some Cherokee women had taken up cattle husbandry. Open-range herding became a subsistence centerpiece for almost all mountain families in the nineteenth century, and by the antebellum period, livestock export had emerged as critical to the region's market economy. Toward the end of the century, "stock laws" or "fence laws" began to close the open range, but it persisted in some parts of western North Carolina until World War II.[15]

A combination of local custom and formal regulation governed the Appalachian grazing range through most of its history. Early colonial rules supported Cherokee rights to shoot grazing animals that wandered beyond English territory, for instance. By the nineteenth century, a system of county "range masters" had developed, and mountain families identified their hogs and cattle by branding. They registered brands with a local official who also adjudicated livestock disputes. With state support, western North Carolina counties began closing the livestock range in the last decades of the nineteenth century, and by World War II open-range grazing legally continued only on national forestlands. These too soon closed, largely in favor of the wildlife or hunting commons and mostly at the behest of sportsmen organized through the NCWRC.[16]

Natural-Resource Commons History: A Brief Overview

By the time American and European peoples came in contact, struggles over access to the commons in England already had a history centuries deep and had left a paper trail going back at least as far as Magna Carta. A full exploration of this sweeping history is beyond the scope of this book, but a brief summary is useful to understanding the Blue Ridge.

A second keystone treaty, the Charter of the Forest, was issued with Magna Carta in 1215. The Forest Charter gave formal recognition to long-standing customary use rights, such as the right to gather firewood and building material and the right to graze animals on commonly held land. This twin charter has not enjoyed Magna Carta's renown, but together the two documents became the founding Charters of English Liberties and the basis for English common law.[17]

English commoners mounted staunch defenses of common rights before and long after King John signed the Great Charters. Despite their efforts and the Forest Charter, use rights to commons eroded, and land privatization by nobility continued. English law increasingly supported wealthy enclosers rather than poor commoners in class struggles over game and fish. By the 1500s, commons enclosures had reached crisis proportions in many parts of the British Isles, and this process undercut countless citizens' ability to obtain even basic subsistence. Punishments for commons lawbreaking grew increasingly severe, eventually including imprisonment, torture, and death. Nonetheless, an "underground law"—accepted by much of the British population—stood in counterpoint.[18]

No matter what parliamentary law said, the thinking went, the laws of nature and of God determined that things in a state of nature rightly belonged to everyone. Wildlife, according to this view, could not be privately held. No one's property while alive, native animals became the hunter's property once killed. Poaching in privately held woods thus became both a pragmatic response to rural hunger and a morally grounded activity. Police and middling country gentry often seemed to sympathize with poor poachers, as the former frequently overlooked violations and the latter sometimes organized their own poaching expeditions. The idea of common property rights came to resonate with meaning for class struggle and to take on a revolutionary dimension.[19]

British and other European colonists brought these ideas with them to the Americas, and New World law and culture grew to reflect them. Many immigrants to North America were essentially refugees from enclosure, migrating precisely because, having been stripped of customary use rights, they had lost the capacity to sustain themselves in their home communities. Small wonder, then, that these migrants determined to protect similar use rights in their new setting. Hostility to Old World enclosure patterns informed New World colonists' efforts to make game and fish widely accessible by rule of the commons. Colonial charters and early legal cases reflected these efforts. An understanding of the American Revolution as a return to basic rights further buttressed commons law and culture in the new nation. Thus, like the idea of wilderness, the idea of the commons is deeply rooted in American soil.[20]

Scholars still have an incomplete understanding of early Native American commons traditions, but colonists' observations of Native practice could only have strengthened allegiance to commons. Nearly all American Indian economies relied on commons-style harvest. Wild game and fish made up a significant portion of indigenous peoples' diets, and animal parts were used in tools, dress, housing, medicine, and ceremony. Plant gathering also sustained Native communities and provided food, medicine, fiber, dye, and fuel as well as building, clothing, craft, and tool materials. Communal landownership typified American Indian societies, and so too did communal land maintenance.

Though few colonists adopted Native cultures wholesale, many elements of these cultures did appear in colonial thought and practice. As one visitor to southwestern Virginia in the 1740s observed, "White people are found here, who live like savages." Since the ethnocentric word "savages" referred to American Indian groups, this comment suggests how much the Appalachian region's early settlers had adopted Native ways of living.[21] White residents of southwestern Virginia could not "live like savages" without studying their neighbors' strategies, techniques, and practices. The visitor noted that his hosts slept on bearskins, wore deerskins, and ate wild meat; clearly, they had learned to hunt native animal species, cure hides, fashion buckskins, and prepare game dishes. "Hunting is their chief occupation," the visitor noted. They would also have learned about indigenous plant species—which to eat, which to avoid, when and how to harvest, how to prepare and store. On the eastern flank of the Blue Ridge, for instance, Moravian settlers learned to value the medicinal properties of seneca, or snakeroot. With help from their Native neighbors, they dug large quantities for shipment to English and French markets.[22]

There is even evidence that settlers may have adopted Native commons-maintenance techniques, such as the large-scale use of fire to improve hunting grounds. Many early commentators noted Cherokees' and other Native peoples' seasonal woods-burning practices, which cleared the forest of underbrush and reduced competition for nut-bearing trees. Settlers also relied on seasonal fire as a tool to clear pastures and improve hunting.[23]

And fishing, trapping, and gathering technologies developed by Cherokee people and their ancestors also showed up in settler households, as did the foods these technologies helped deliver. No matter what Margaret Morley's woman in the woods carried in her bag, then, we can be nearly certain that many Appalachian generations before her—settlers, Cherokees, and Woodland peoples—had harvested the same thing.[24]

Early Appalachian Commons Economies

In the southern Appalachian region, forest harvest has supplied household and neighborhood needs and has provided products for exchange, often through networks linked to distant markets. It has played both these roles for more than five centuries, beginning with mountain prehistory.

Pre-Columbian Appalachians certainly relied on forest products even after they adopted agriculture. There is even evidence suggesting that, during the Mississippian period (1000–1540 C.E.), their consumption of wild foods made mountain peoples healthier than their lowland counterparts. Highland Mississippians gathered and consumed nuts in huge quantities, including chestnuts, butternuts, walnuts, hazelnuts, beechnuts, and chinquapins. They also dined extensively on native fruits, among them persimmons, mulberries, pawpaws, cherries, plums, huckleberries, strawberries, blackberries, and grapes.[25]

Some evidence suggests that prehistoric highlanders may have traded forest products to distant markets. Certainly, beginning around 300 B.C.E., Appalachian peoples participated in trade networks linking them to southern coasts, to Florida, to the lower Mississippi, and eventually to the Great Lakes area. It is difficult to know precisely what changed hands besides rocks, minerals, shells, ceramics, and other durable materials that have weathered the centuries. The mountain region produced many less-durable forest goods that probably found buyers in other areas, including wild plant medicines and animal pelts.[26]

After Mississippian collapse, Cherokee people continued to rely on a field and forest economy. Like their forebears, they hunted, fished, and trapped native wildlife, and they gathered wild plant foods, medicines, building materials, and the like. They also participated in far-flung trade networks with other Native peoples and eventually with Europeans. During the seventeenth and eighteenth centuries, European traders—first Spanish and later French and English—valued exchange with the peoples of the southern mountains, and many of the goods they sought came from highland forests. By the 1680s trade outposts near the mountains conducted a brisk business exchanging European goods for deerskins, medicinal plants, chestnuts, handmade baskets, and woven cane mats.[27] All these trade goods either came directly from the woods or utilized products that did. Forest hunting and gathering yielded the first three: deerskins, medicinal plants, and chestnuts. The two manufactured items, baskets and mats, also drew on native forests. Cherokee women made stunning baskets and sturdy, attractive mats from rivercane, a semidomesticated native plant, and from split forest woods, such as white oak. The women dyed these raw materials with tints obtained from forest plants, including bloodroot, black walnut, and butternut.[28] Beginning in the 1750s, Cherokee root-diggers began harvesting ginseng for the insatiable Chinese market.[29]

The early trade in these goods became big international business. By 1740, for instance, the fledgling English trading post in Augusta, Georgia, hosted some six hundred men who made a living through exchange with mountain peoples.[30] Since Augusta provided only one of several outlets for Appalachian products, and since the trade lasted for decades, the southern mountain export-import business must have supported English colonials by the thousands. In the Proprietary era, some 10 percent of South Carolina's white male population claimed "Indian trader" as its occupation, and

Charlestown trading house agents earned almost twice as much as plantation overseers. John Lawson observed that self-employed traders in North Carolina "throve as fast as any men." Though forest-based Appalachian exchange did not exclusively support this vibrant segment of the colonial economy, it made enormous contributions.[31]

The Transatlantic Deerskin Trade

The deerskin trade, in particular, evolved into a massive transatlantic operation. By 1700, Appalachian deerhide had caught the attention of English traders seeking to profit from the voracious European peltry market. Native peoples produced beautifully soft and supple leathers from white-tailed deer hides, and these leathers' pleasing textures and warm buff colors consistently drew European admiration. Leather served many critical purposes in European societies, as artisans used it to make everything from equine harness to clothing and bookbindings. Even before devastating cattle epidemics squeezed European animal-skin supplies, English explorers tapped the economic potential of Carolina deerskins. When bovine disease swept Europe beginning in 1710, demand for American deerskins skyrocketed. As a result, the southern Appalachian region, rich in white-tailed deer, became ever more tightly entwined in the international peltry market, and the region's forested hunting commons emerged as a player on the global economic stage.[32]

Occasional colonial records hint at the enormous scale and value of the eighteenth-century mountain deerskin trade. In the middle decades of the eighteenth century, for instance, merchants in Augusta, Georgia, bought some two thousand packhorse loads of animal skins each year, many of them from Cherokee country.[33] In 1735 deerskin traders lugging Cherokee peltries to colonial outposts employed some eight hundred horses as pack animals.[34] These animals would have carried dozens of hides apiece; a conservative estimate puts their annual haul at around fifty thousand skins. A proficient hunter could annually harvest some fifty deer, and in 1751 at least two thousand Cherokee hunters supplied the deerskin trade. Here too a conservative estimate puts their yearly take in the range of fifty thousand.[35]

Competition for the valuable deerhides became so fierce that one exasperated South Carolina trader, writing in 1751, charged that Cherokee hunters returning to home villages could barely "dress their skins" before a trader's emissary showed up to collect the take. Though he certainly exaggerated, his vivid imagery—one envisions colonial traders hovering anxiously outside successful Cherokee hunters' homes—underscores the white-tailed deer market's compelling power.[36]

Deerskin leather became so valuable that it served as a form of currency. A 1717 trade agreement between a South Carolina official and a Native leader set prices for common goods: a gun could be purchased for thirty-five skins; a yard of stroud cloth for eight; an ax or broad hoe for five; a hatchet or narrow hoe for three; thirty bullets, a pair of scissors, a knife, or twelve flints for one. Native peoples also carried out exchanges among themselves in pounds of leather.[37]

It is impossible to know with precision the scale of the Appalachian deerskin trade, but certainly it was substantial. Colonial documents abound with hints. Some ten thousand deerskins reportedly left Virginia each year between 1699 and 1715, while approximately four times that number shipped annually from Charleston.[38] Between 1739 and 1751, more than five million pounds of deerskins departed Charleston, probably representing roughly 2.5 million hides. In 1748 the South Carolina port exported some 160,000 deerskins. Another 2.5 million pounds of deerskins—the hides of roughly one million deer—left Savannah between 1755 and 1772. The Appalachian region provided only a portion of these total numbers, as the trade encompassed the entire Southeast.[39]

Yet the Appalachian contribution was certainly significant and probably enormous. Very conservative estimates have the Cherokee harvesting over half a million deer during the height of the trade, between 1739 and 1761, and less conservative estimates put the number much higher, at 1.25 million. It seems likely that Cherokee hunters dispatched at least a million deer between 1739 and 1772 and perhaps far more. Creeks and Shawnees also hunted in the mountains, and their peltries typically left the continent through other venues: New Orleans, Saint Augustine, and the Ohio Valley Company. Over the whole course of the vast deerskin trade, there can be little question that deer harvests in the mountains reached well into seven figures.[40]

Warfare between 1760 and 1780 devastated Cherokee society and reshaped the deerskin trade. Under the scorched-earth policies of English and U.S. military leaders, entire villages were destroyed as well as countless acres of crops and orchards. Cherokee people responded to these crises with an inward turn. They stepped up intratribal leather exchange and scaled down their participation in the transatlantic trade. The international deerskin trade continued, but white "long hunters" supplied an increasing share of its hides.[41]

Formal Regulation in the Colonial Grazing and Hunting Commons

Throughout the eighteenth century, the Appalachian forest continued to serve as a hunting and gathering commons, and during this period it became a grazing commons as well, an open range for livestock. By the early 1700s, Cherokee communities in the southern highlands had taken up hog raising. They penned the animals during the growing season and then turned them loose to forage in the woods after the crops were in. The Cherokees were less quick to adopt cattle husbandry, and in the early eighteenth century, they clashed with frontier herdsmen over cattle. Cherokee hunters treated free-ranging cattle as game animals. Like deer and other wildlife, these roaming animals posed danger to the Cherokees' unfenced cornfields and provided a source of food and raw materials. From the Cherokees' point of view, it made sense to shoot these cattle. English herders, on the other hand, resented losing valuable animals to Cherokee marksmen.[42]

In 1730 British authorities wrote an "article of friendship and commerce" aimed at easing these tensions. In it the British monarch gave the Cherokees "the privilege of living where they please" and proposed that English newcomers avoid settling near established Cherokee towns, "for fear that [Cherokee] young people sho'd kill the Cattle and young Lambs & so quarrel with the English and Hurt them."[43] This article may represent the earliest colonial attempt at formal commons regulation in the southern mountains. It placed the burden of accommodation on herdsmen rather than farmers, urging cattle raisers to keep livestock away from Cherokee settlements and recognizing that herdsmen ran heavy loss risks if they failed to do so.

By the late eighteenth century, the tide had turned in the herdsmen's favor. Partly in response to military destruction of their fields and orchards in the 1760s and 1770s, Cherokees turned increasingly to cattle herding and to the crop fencing it required. English newcomers to the region also found it necessary to protect their crops from all manner of woods inhabitants, including hogs and cattle. They built and maintained sturdy fences designed to ward off the cropland depredations of semiwild livestock as well as deer and other wild forest animals. Nearly all mountain families raised hogs as well as crops, and pork became the central meat for Appalachians of all descriptions during the colonial period. Nearly all culture groups also hunted, adding buffalo, deer, elk, bear, turkey, rabbit, squirrel, raccoon, opossum, grouse, duck, goose, quail, and swan to their corn-and-pork-based bill of fare.[44]

Hunting in the Appalachian forest commons went formally unregulated only until the mid-eighteenth century. Responding to the complaints of highland livestock owners, North Carolina began offering cash bounties for panther, wolf, and wildcat scalps in 1748. The colony thus encouraged large-scale destruction of these commons-dwelling predators. In 1764 alone a single county, Rowan, paid bounties for forty-one wolves, thirteen wildcats, and five panthers. By the 1830s states throughout the southern mountains offered around $3.00 a scalp for these animals, and western North Carolina bounty hunters earned $2.50 for a wolf scalp of any size. Some hunters responded to this rule by following mother wolves to their dens, killing the pups, and letting the mothers go free to provide another year's litter of scalps.[45] The bounty system illustrates how users of the grazing commons successfully demanded state intervention to improve commons conditions. The practice of cashing in wolf litters while in effect reinvesting adult females demonstrates how savvy users of the hunting commons maximized profits from the state wolf-scalp market initiated by commons herdsmen.

Early state intervention in the forest commons also took the form of wildlife hunting regulations. Colonial market hunting decimated buffalo, elk, and deer herds in North Carolina and throughout the Appalachians. Market hunters killed big game in every season, often taking only the valuable hides and leaving the meat to rot. Especially in the case of deer, this destruction drew the attention of legislative bodies, which passed laws designed to curtail the slaughter. Beginning in 1745, North and South Carolina passed a series of laws against what they considered hunting abuses, aiming "to prevent killing Deer at unseasonable Time," for instance. Later legislation in both colonies restricted night shooting, proscribed doe and fawn hunting, and prohibited killing deer only for skins. Assemblies also attempted to regulate deer-hunting seasons, restricting some spring and some fall hunting.[46]

These attempts at commons regulation fell short of their goals, however, and did little to protect deer populations in settled areas. Where the bounty system provided cash incentives to kill, early attempts at hunting regulation came with few concrete incentives to refrain from killing. And deerskins continued to be so valuable that they were often used as currency. In fact, in 1768 the province of North Carolina itself began accepting deerskins in lieu of cash tax payments, in effect encouraging with its tax policies the very behaviors it sought to discourage with its wildlife regulations. The state made night deer hunting a misdemeanor in 1784 and restricted it further in 1810. But enforcement was lax, consequences were relatively minor, and deerskins were very valuable, so these regulations had little effect on hunting practice.[47]

Nineteenth-Century Commons Economies

For most of the nineteenth century, a pattern of crop and livestock raising supplemented with small-scale forest extraction typified the rural mountain economy. Beginning in the early part of the century, a landscape of farmed valleys and wooded slopes reflecting this corn-woodland agricultural system developed. Most mountain farmers helped sculpt this landscape by concentrating agriculture in their lowland acreage and keeping large tracts of their land on the slopes wooded. A few determined homesteaders settled on the ridges, but most higher-elevation lands remained forested, and effectively commons, through the last decades of the century.[48] As late as 1900, most Blue Ridge farmers kept at least 60 percent of their land wooded, and many maintained forest on 90 percent. Farm families turned to these "woodlot" tracts for a host of crucial forest products: firewood and building wood for fences, homes, barns, tools, and sheds; nuts, mushrooms, honey, fish, game animals, grapes, berries, and other fruit for food; herbs, barks, and roots for medicine; rich foraging grounds for livestock.[49]

As in other field-and-forest regions, local custom treated "improved" farmlands and "unimproved" woodlands differently, with cleared and planted lands squarely in the private property column but wooded lands inhabiting a gray area between public and private—fair game for local hunting and fishing expeditions, not fair game for timber harvesting. Even if privately owned, as nearly all were from the late colonial period until the early twentieth century, woods were considered semipublic—effectively, commons. A pattern of large-scale absentee ownership emerged early in the region's European American settlement history and strengthened this de facto commons custom by leaving whole sections of the forest largely unsupervised for decades.[50]

As in the eighteenth century, a variety of harvests took place in the nineteenth-century commons forest, but grazing now replaced hunting as preeminent. Big game populations continued to dwindle, and hog and cattle populations continued to rise. Only the Civil War, which took a toll on human and animal populations alike, interrupted this pattern, and then only temporarily.[51] Forest plant gatherers also continued to carry on their largely unregulated work, and wild plant materials provided a quiet but steady stream in the region's economic flow.[52]

French botanist André Michaux, who visited the North Carolina mountains in 1802, recorded his observations about the region's trade patterns in a list indicating the wooded commons' centrality. In Morganton, Michaux noted, mountain residents could purchase goods imported from England via Charleston, South Carolina. They "give in exchange," he wrote, "a part of their produce which consists chiefly of dried hams, butter, tallow, bear and stag skins, and ginseng, which they bring from the mountains."[53] Nearly all these goods came directly or indirectly from the forest. Hams traced to the wooded grazing commons, where hogs ranged freely. The wildlife commons provided bear and stag skins. Tallow came from bears or hogs, and thus it too was a commons product. The gathering commons yielded ginseng. Only butter stood as a possible exception, and it too would have been at least partially a commons product, as cattle often ranged the woods alongside hogs.

Agricultural products joined forest and livestock products as the century progressed and more land came under the plow, but the wooded commons never lost importance. Writing from Brevard in the 1860s, Leander Gash listed trade goods including "hams, venison, hides, and feathers, chestnuts, chestnut bark, apples, cabbages, wild honey and mountain herbs." In this list, feathers, apples, and cabbages represented nonforest farm products, while the other seven entries relied on the wooded commons.[54]

Both lists, with hams at top, hint at the growing centrality of the live-stock commons. By including venison and deerskins, both also suggest the ongoing importance of the wildlife commons. And through their ginseng and mountain herb entries, both lists indicate continuing use of the gathering commons.

Ginseng proved quite valuable due to voracious demand from Chinese markets, where it was considered potent medicine. In Yancey County in the 1830s, three factories prepared enormous quantities of wild ginseng for international shipping. In 1837 these outfits handled 86,000 pounds of green roots, bound for Philadelphia and then for China. Buncombe County merchants sold an estimated 181,000 pounds of ginseng in 1850. Since freshly dug ginseng roots typically weigh only a few ounces, these operations must have handled them by the millions. Root diggers by the tens of thousands earned income supplying ginseng on this scale. Buncombe County in 1850 averaged more than ten pounds of ginseng collected per man, woman, and child living in its boundaries. Though residents of neighboring counties doubtless contributed to the Buncombe total, this average suggests the enormous scale on which ginseng digging took place. A. T. Davidson remembered "great companies of mountaineers . . . with packed horses and oxen" making their way to ginseng facilities in Yancey County. Delivery time became "a great rendezvous for the people," he recalled.[55]

For some, ginseng even provided a primary source of income, as it did for Betsy Calloway of Watauga County. A young unwed mother in the

1820s and 1830s, Calloway had few opportunities to obtain a living, so she turned to the "only cash article" in the area. She earned a reputation as a "master sanger" and sold her roots as far away as Abingdon, Virginia, and Blountville, Tennessee. She supported seven children with ginseng earnings and with the proceeds from reportedly excellent maple sugar and syrup she made each year. Other women used similar commons-based strategies and earned community recognition for their strength and resourcefulness.[56]

Betsy Calloway's example underscores the Blue Ridge forest commons' importance for the poor and for women and children. This is a typical pattern in commons systems, which often provide basic subsistence. As far back as the 1215 Charter of the Forest, English thought had considered the right to commons-based subsistence fundamental. This idea enjoyed currency in western North Carolina, as an 1892 letter to the *Watauga Democrat* makes clear. John Winebarger, weighing in against a proposal to close the open grazing range, wrote that poor people "have the same right to turn their stock on our lands as they have to dig roots, gather herbs, and skin our timber: which has always been the custom of our country." Winebarger's letter suggested a bedrock right to commons harvest and a durable "custom of our country" sustaining this right.[57]

Nineteenth-Century Grazing Commons

During the antebellum period, the grazing commons emerged as a central pillar of the Blue Ridge economy. As early as 1752, an explorer described the Carolina mountains as "incomparable" for stock raising. Before the turn of the nineteenth century, settlers flooded the highlands, drawn by fine air and water and "especially the pasturage," observed André Michaux. By 1800 western North Carolina hogs and cattle routinely made their way to markets in Charleston, Savannah, Norfolk, and Philadelphia. A few decades later, livestock dominated local agricultural production, and famed University of North Carolina geologist Elisha Mitchell exaggerated only somewhat when he described the region as a "country of herdsmen and shepherds."[58]

The open-range forest grew in economic importance, until by the antebellum era it dominated trade throughout western North Carolina. Nearly every mountain farm raised livestock for home consumption and sold surplus hogs, cattle, and sheep for transport to distant markets. Some mountain drovers earned a living by raising animals expressly for these markets. And the occasional savvy businessman, such as Buncombe County's James McConnell Smith, amassed a fortune by gaining control of a critical site along the livestock trade routes.[59] Animal flesh became the mountain South's most important antebellum export, linking it especially to the international cotton economy. After the War of 1812, southern planters increasingly devoted every available acre to cotton and imported basic food supplies, including meat from the highlands. Mountain livestock prices fluctuated with the cotton market, as southern planters typically offered about half as much for a pound of pork as they collected for a pound of cotton.[60]

Supplying meat to the cotton belt became enormous business. Frederick Jackson Turner estimated that over a million dollars' worth of livestock passed through North Carolina's Saluda Gap in 1824 alone en route to southern markets. During 1828 the Buncombe Turnpike was completed, making human and animal travel over the Blue Ridge easier and more affordable. The turnpike cemented Asheville's position as a hub of the region's livestock industry. By the late 1830s, over 140,000 animals annually tromped through the Buncombe County cowtown on their way south to market centers. A similar number—rising as high as 160,000—made the trek each year for the rest of the antebellum era. Sales of mountain livestock commanded an estimated $2 to $3 million a year.[61]

Supplying feed to these southbound animals proved profitable to mountain farmers and to innkeepers living near major livestock arteries. A series of stands along the stock roads offered food and overnight rest to drovers and their herds. These stands might host 5,000 animals in a single night and as many as 110,000 in a season. Feeding all this stock required enormous stores of corn, and area farmers profited from the ready market. Stand owners also earned a comfortable living and often became prosperous leaders of their communities.[62]

The highlands' vast forested grazing commons made all these lucrative enterprises possible. Through much of the year, mountain farmers and drovers fed their livestock on the abundant offerings that native forests reliably provided. As western North Carolina chronicler John Preston Arthur noted, "The mast rarely failed." In the fall, herdsmen turned cows and hogs out to forage for chestnuts, hickory nuts, acorns, and the like, often leaving them all winter. Occasionally, swine-keepers made sheltered beds for their animals during extreme weather, but for the most part the hogs fended for themselves. "For many it was literally a case of 'root, hog, or die,'" Arthur wrote.[63]

This system, which relied heavily on forest offerings, worked so well that it elicited approving comments from wealthy travelers such as famed landscape architect Frederick Law Olmsted. Olmsted observed that the chestnut mast in the Blue Ridge was "remarkably fine" and yielded hogs "of superior taste" that looked better than he had seen "anywhere else in the South."

To be sure, elsewhere in his writings, Olmsted commented disapprovingly about mountain cattle husbandry. "In the severest weather [cattle] are fed only occasionally," he wrote, "even by the better class of farmers." Olmsted did not understand that upland forests provided rich mast for cattle just as for pigs and that supplementary feeding became necessary only under unusually harsh conditions.[64]

Nineteenth-century North Carolina law gave counties the authority to regulate local livestock practice, and mountain counties elected to keep the grazing range open through nearly the entire century. Beginning in the early 1800s, some eastern counties passed "stock laws" or "fence laws" requiring that animals rather than crops be fenced. The highlands, however, continued as open-range territory with only rare exceptions. Voting districts within counties could withdraw from the mountains' open range by passing stock laws of their own, but few did so. To enforce such laws, a district had to fence its entire perimeter, and hardly any voters were willing to go to this trouble and expense.[65]

Instead, most western districts opted to participate in a lightly regulated open-range system overseen by county "range masters." Informal branding codes for recording livestock ownership had emerged early in the history of the forest range, and range masters systematized these codes. County regulations usually required herd owners to register their marks with the range master and to go to him when disputes over free-ranging livestock arose. By the mid-nineteenth century, most western North Carolina counties had adopted such a system.[66]

The open-range system meant that one could earn a living in the mountains without holding legal title to land. Since colonial times, western North Carolina had followed typical Appalachian land-distribution patterns, in which large holdings were concentrated in a few hands and much of the population was without property. Open-range law and open-season custom mitigated to some extent the polarizing effects of this pattern. Together with the hunting and gathering commons, the open range enabled western North Carolina's majority population of smallholders and landless tenants to wrest a living from the mountains. Without land of their own, highland residents could still survive and even prosper by raising what one historian called "four-legged crops."[67]

Weighing in against 1892 proposals to close the range in parts of Watauga County, Leander L. Greene explained how landless farmers could use the open range to pursue their dreams of landownership. "The poor fellow as soon as he lands in Watauga if he uses industry and economy soon begins to own stock and then for a few years he converts his stock into a nice little happy home for his family," Greene wrote. He detailed how this process worked. "The renter can easily make enough during the summer to keep his stock over winter and then range all of his stock free for about seven months in the year. The growth and increase cost him nothing," he concluded.[68]

The lucrative livestock trade collapsed alongside the rest of the southern economy as a result of the Civil War, but the open-range grazing commons continued into the last decades of the nineteenth century. Even then, it closed only gradually, and in a few places in western North Carolina, open-range grazing remained in effect through the 1940s.

The Grazing Commons Closes

A series of challenges to the open-range system mounted as the nineteenth century drew to a close. Towns sprouted in the mountains, many of them tied to the growing tourist industry. Town residents and tourism promoters often advocated new stock laws that would replace the open range with fenced pens and pastures. Writing in a western North Carolina newspaper in 1892, D. B. Dougherty explained, "In the thickly settled parts of the country the people are favorable to the stock law, but in the more sparsely settled sections there is opposition to the law."[69]

Debates over the fate of the range made for heated politics. In 1886 Buncombe County's Democratic open-rangers openly revolted against their pro–stock law leadership. Led by local politico Richmond Pearson, the renegade Democrats successfully joined with Republicans in an anti–stock law coalition. In Watauga County in 1892, the *Watauga Democrat*, Boone's pro–stock law newspaper, printed anti–stock law reassurances on behalf of Democratic General Assembly candidate Edward Lovill. "Already we hear of a lie being circulated that Capt. Lovill is going to put the county under the fence law," wrote the *Democrat*; "this is a miserable falsehood intended to injure him in the election." Earlier that year, the newspaper had conceded that "the stock law is not booming much these days."[70]

By the turn of the century, that situation had changed. Blowing Rock, a Watauga County tourist town, voted in the stock law in 1900. The following year the North Carolina legislature closed the range in Watauga, Caldwell, and Mitchell Counties. The state legislation contained local option clauses, but boundary responsibilities shifted to open-range supporters. Any free-range districts must now shoulder the burden of fencing their perimeters in order to prevent animals from wandering into nearby closed-range townships.[71]

Debates about the stock law, in western North Carolina as elsewhere in the South, pitted elites, townspeople, and advocates of a new industrial order against the poor, country dwellers, and defenders of the traditional agricultural economy. Issues of class loomed large in these debates. As the *Watauga Democrat* noted after the 1901 success of the law it had long advocated, the new private-range system was "a blessing for the upper, but a curse to the unfortunate lower class of our people." Nine years before, when the Watauga County towns of Valle Crucis and Blowing Rock had considered withdrawing from the open range, letter writers had explained just how they expected the stock law to prove a curse to the county's poorer residents.[72]

Prosperous farmer and Republican politician Leander L. Greene opposed the stock law, citing class concerns especially. In a letter to the editor, Greene remembered "a number of good citizens of Watauga County who came here a few years ago from counties south of the Blue Ridge without any capital, save a little stock. They rented land to cultivate, ranged a little stock, had the benefits of free mast for their hogs, and now they own homes of their own." Greene explained that this progression had been possible because "the free advantages offered poor people in our Co. so far excell advantages in counties south of us, where the stock law is in force." In the Blue Ridge, an impoverished but industrious man could realistically aspire to be a landowner in only a few years. "This is Watauga without a stock law," wrote Greene. "Truly it is a paradise for the poor man, and a delightful abode for all who live within her borders." Contrast this sunny portrait with "a picture of this county under the curse of the stock law," Greene urged. Starving hogs and dead sheep would replace healthy livestock, and hard-working poor families would wind up exhausted and desperate paupers rather than sturdy homeowners. "Free range and free mast is half the battle," Greene concluded. "Deprive our people of that and in a few years you look upon this lovely land, the boasted paradise of the poor man, converted by the stock law into a wilderness of distress and poverty."[73]

This classic enclosure battle not only highlighted archetypal elite-versus-commoner class issues but also triggered a series of ageless commons defense tactics. John Winebarger barely veiled a prediction or threat of retaliatory arson if the stock law were passed. If Watauga townships voted it in, he wrote, "and another burdensome tax is levied on us to build a fence, it would not be two years, in my opinion, before it would be destroyed by fire. As we all know, there are more or less forest fires burning every spring and fall." Whether or not Winebarger knew it, he was reaching for an ancient weapon of commons defense. Faced with enclosure threats from the upper classes, lower-class commoners had for many centuries invoked and wielded fire.[74]

The state legislature's regional approach to the stock law circumvented opponents such as Winebarger by insuring that they would have to do more than destroy fences to reopen the range. Free-range proponents cast about for other ways to fight the new system. The *Watauga Democrat* reported "a regular uprising of the people in all parts of the county" shortly after the law was passed and noted that residents were circulating at least four petitions asking county commissioners to fence Watauga out of the newly closed range. In a letter to the paper, John Hodges called the 1901 stock law "corrupt legislation against the will of the people" and urged his neighbors to ignore it. "We fear no stock law," Hodges thundered, and "we will put more stock on the range this year than we ever have." For Hodges, the question was one of basic liberties; "a law of nature" superseded the stock law. "We are fully determined to maintain and protect our liberties, our rights, and our freedom at all hazards against any invasion whatever," he wrote, joining a long line of American commons defenders who used the national lexicon of rights, freedoms, and liberties.[75]

Neither the petition drives nor Hodges's charges of unconstitutionality succeeded in reestablishing the open range, and large landholders quickly profited from the new system. A few months after the law passed, the going rate for Watauga cow pasture was around two dollars per head. Hog production in the county dropped from a high of 12,405 in 1880 to 9,990 in 1900 and 5,868 in 1910. Still, some Watauga herdsmen apparently continued to resist the closed range by ignoring the stock law, just as John Hodges had urged. Several months after the state legislation passed, the *Democrat* complained that "some citizens of this county are openly violating the stock law and setting at defiance the same by turning their stock upon the common range." Free-range livestock owners risked small fines and impoundment of their animals, but some local herders seem to have continued running these risks. Though Watauga's de jure commons grazing range closed in 1901, a semiunderground de facto open range persisted decades later.[76]

Other mountain counties eventually followed where Watauga led, and by 1920 much of the western North Carolina range had closed. In the southwestern corner of the state, however, it persisted until the 1940s, at least on national forestlands. Taylor Crockett remembered the range remaining open until the Forest Service and the North Carolina Wildlife Resources Commission began creating wildlife refuges in the mid-1940s. "That took a lot of activity out of the woods," Crockett explained to interviewers. According to Crockett, it was a hunting-commons project that sounded the final death knell of western North Carolina's 250-year-old grazing commons.[77]

The open range lingered in memory decades after it ceased to exist in the forests, and livestock memory was alive and well in late twentieth-century southwestern North Carolina. In 1978 lifelong Franklin resident Carrie Stewart told student interviewers that she remembered rounding up the family's cows every Sunday during her turn-of-the-century girlhood. "At that time they didn't have this fence law," Stewart explained, "and you could turn your cows out and they could go anywhere they wanted to. So after Sunday school we'd go out and hunt up our cows and bring them in." Stewart was part of Franklin's small African American community, and her testimony suggests the historical importance of the open range for black as well as white mountain residents and for women as well as men.[78]

Through this memory and experience, the long arm of the open range reached into late twentieth-century forest politics. Franklin-area forest activists Taylor Crockett and Jim Cunningham, for instance, remembered running hogs on the Nantahala National Forest during their 1920s youth. Both were avid hunters, but both also cut their woodsmen's teeth in open-range hog roundups.[79]

Chestnut Blight: "A National Calamity"

As the people of western North Carolina debated the merits of the stock law, a deadly scourge swept toward their commons forests. A fungus, most likely imported on Asian chestnut stock from China and Japan, began killing American chestnuts through much of the eastern seaboard. Eventually, it would all but eliminate the estimated 3.5 to 4 billion mature chestnuts that grew in eastern North America.[80]

The American chestnut was a dominant species in the Appalachian forest, an ecosystem cornerstone. It contributed one of every four trees through much of its two-hundred-million-acre range, and in some places one of every two. The majestic trees soared into forest canopies as far north as Maine, as far south as Alabama, and as far west as Ohio, Kentucky, and Mississippi. In early summer their creamy blossoms dotted the southern mountains "like big, potted flowers." In fall the trees dropped immense numbers of nuts, tucked in spiny burrs, onto the forest floor.[81]

The American chestnut provided a primary source of hard mast for any number of wild animals, including game species such as black bear, deer, squirrel, and wild turkey. Old-timers who remembered the preblight woods told tales of bears so chestnut-fat they could barely run. Chestnuts also provided important fodder for free-range livestock, especially hogs. Untold thousands of wild and semidomesticated animals relied on the high-protein and reliably plentiful fall nuts to fatten for Appalachian winters. Humans too gathered the nuts to use as table food and livestock feed and to sell or barter. Thus, the chestnut served as a cornerstone supplier for the hunting, grazing, and gathering commons.

Mountain people also prized chestnut wood for its beauty and its weather-resistant qualities and sought it out for barns and furniture, musical instruments and coffins, and especially fence posts and rails. Appalachian people used chestnut bark as well for dye and tanning leather. Western North Carolina's sizeable turn-of-the-century leather-tanning industry consumed enormous quantities of chestnut bark and kept countless men busy gathering it.[82]

In 1904 a forester with the New York Zoological Park—the "Bronx Zoo"—noticed cankers on American chestnuts there. Though he worked to remove diseased wood, his efforts proved futile. Within the year some 98 percent of Bronx chestnuts showed signs of the infection, and trees soon died by the score. By 1908 the lethal blight had spread and was killing trees from Massachusetts to Maryland. In 1912 North Carolina foresters began scouting the state's mountains for signs of the fungus's inevitable arrival—"a foregone conclusion," state forester John Simcox Holmes wrote. By 1916, despite a large-scale resistance effort in Pennsylvania, the fungus had begun felling Virginia's chestnuts. It headed south at an estimated twenty-four miles a year, its light asexual spores carried by wind, and its adhesive sexual spores clinging to migrating birds and other travelers. Foresters estimated the disease would eventually take more than a quarter of the North Carolina highlands' standing timber. Between 1917 and 1920 infected trees began appearing in the Black Mountains near Mount Mitchell. By 1925 one of every ten chestnut trees in higher-elevation Yancey County showed signs of the disease, as did one of every five in lower-elevation Buncombe. In the 1920s and 1930s trees across the region succumbed, and by 1950 the mature American chestnut had all but ceased to exist.[83]

The ecological, economic, and cultural importance of the chestnut loss is impossible to calculate fully and all but impossible even to fathom. North Carolina forester Holmes called the tree's loss "not only a State but a National calamity." One historian likened the passing of the chestnut to "a whole world dying," and certainly it is difficult to exaggerate the profound sense of loss that many mountain residents shared. In western North Carolina, chestnuts wound through the fabric of daily life. Macon County hunter Taylor Crockett remembered waking up as a child to the sound of chestnuts falling on the roof of his home. They made a sound like shotgun blasts, he told interviewers. Countless people remembered gathering chestnuts by the bushel, hauling them to town, and eating them all winter. When the blight came, local people coined a term for the sound of giant chestnut skeletons crashing in the woods—"clear day thunder."[84]

The chestnut's disappearance greatly impoverished the Appalachian hunting, grazing, and gathering commons. Sportsmen "gloomily predicted drastic reductions" in deer, turkey, bear, and small game animal populations. Subsistence hunting became more difficult, as species from squirrel to quail felt the effects of lost plenty. Free-range hogs fared worse than they had when the oil-rich nuts lay in piles on the forest floor. Cattle had to do without the enormous trees' shade and storm shelter. Farmers' turkey flocks had to find other forage.[85]

Before the blight, human chestnut gatherers had plied the woods in numbers so large as to command foresters' notice. A 1902 Appalachian forest study conducted by the U.S. Department of Agriculture noted "the collection of nuts" as "an important industry." Forester John Simcox Holmes worried that western counties' great crowds of chestnut gatherers substantially increased the risk of forest fire in the fall woods.[86] The chestnut gatherers ate and stored nuts themselves and sold their surplus to local merchants. Roasted, the tasty nuts proved a delicacy on the streets of mountain towns and eastern cities. Supplying these markets enabled local people to earn much-needed cash income. Western North Carolina farmers hauled wagonloads of nuts to Asheville, where they sold them on the street or supplied local restaurants and hotels serving the tourist trade. Blue Ridge chestnuts also made their way to major cities such as Baltimore, Philadelphia, and New York.[87]

Evidence suggests that, true to commons patterns, the chestnut trade especially served poor families and women and children. One mountain resident likened the nuts to "the manna that God sent to feed the Israelites." Wrote another, "It was the chestnuts that kept the family going." A third, speaking of his impoverished childhood, remembered chestnut season as "a time of year when we had food." The Virginia Department of Agriculture noted that "income from the commercial nut crop goes largely to the women and children in the mountainous sections." A mountain woman seemed to concur when she described a chestnut grove as "a better provider than a man." And "easier to have around, too," she added mordantly. Numerous adults recalled gathering the nuts as children, some for basic subsistence and others for important cash income. A Georgia observer remembered whole families coming out of the coves to trade chestnuts for winter supplies. One historian found evidence that the poorest residents of south-western Virginia used chestnuts to settle store debts. Chestnut harvesting continued on a reduced scale at least through the 1930s, but by killing the chestnut trees, the blight ended this vital seasonal business.[88]

Though the nut market ended as a result of the blight, in other ways the chestnut kept on giving. Wood and bark gathering continued, for instance, as tannin remained even after the tree died. American chestnut wood and bark held especially high concentrations of tannin, which enabled the tree's famed resistance to decay. In the late nineteenth and early twentieth centuries, the Blue Ridge region emerged as an international center for the leather-tanning industry, largely thanks to the proximity of critical forest resources. At that time, industrial-scale leather tanning required enormous amounts of tannin in the form of "extract wood" or "tanbark" or of heavy liquid "extract" from that bark and wood. Both forms proved expensive to ship—the bark and wood because of its volume and the liquid because of its weight. Industry leaders found it cheaper to ship hides to the tannin source rather than the other way around. Thus, train cars full of rawhides from as far away as South America made their way to Old Fort, North Carolina, where one leather tannery operated.[89]

In 1912 North Carolina forest agents reported that Champion Fibre Company in Canton, the region's largest chestnut consumer, took in roughly three hundred cords of wood per day. The wood came from as far as 150 miles away, much of it by rail. Though it was the biggest, Champion was only one of nine major tannin producers in western North Carolina. In 1914, just across the border in Virginia, another nine plants operated.[90] It took a huge workforce to keep the tanneries in acid bark and wood. A few people made a living primarily in tanbark—a Swain County man, for instance, listed "tanbark peeler" as his full-time work. A great many more participated in the industry seasonally and part time, and some families paid off farms by selling tanbark. The work was so pervasive that advocates for a federal forest reserve in the southern Appalachians listed bark gatherers alongside lumbermen as among those who would benefit from a continuous future wood supply.[91]

Tanbark gathering was a gray-area activity, at once part of the commons and yet closely related to timber harvesting, which was governed by different rules. The question of who had the right to peel tanbark on certain lands did arise. For instance, disputes arose between Cherokee people, who regularly sold bark to a tannery in Andrews, North Carolina, and their neighbors, who sometimes reportedly trespassed on Cherokee lands and sometimes accused Cherokees of trespassing on theirs.[92]

This portion of the chestnut market continued to operate, though in gradually declining amounts, after the blight hit. One western North Carolina man recalled paying off his farm with gathered tanbark in the late 1930s. In Macon County in 1936, chestnut salvage ranked as the principal forest-related occupation.[93] In the early 1940s, Billy Long delivered six truckloads a day, the equivalent of one traincar load, of "dead chestnut" to Dillard, Georgia.[94] Champion operated its extract plant until 1951, and a crew of full-time "bull gang" acid wood haulers worked in Canton until that unit closed.

In a few cases, ingenious mountain residents found ways to use chestnut even later. Worms drilled tiny holes in the fallen logs, and "wormy chestnut" became a sought-after wood. As late as the 1970s, Lloyd Fish of Madison County supplemented his income with chestnut stumps. He hauled these out of the woods, then hand-split them into shingles and decorative boards.[95]

Enclosing the Commons: Industrial Timber Harvests

While the menacing chestnut blight galloped south, industrial timber harvesting liquidated vast swathes of the Appalachian forest. The devastating harvests of the late nineteenth and early twentieth centuries dramatically changed Blue Ridge commons woods and set in motion processes that eventually created the Pisgah and Nantahala National Forests. The southern mountain timber boom deforested the region on an enormous, nearly unimaginable scale. It permanently changed the highland landscape by removing most of its irreplaceable centuries-old trees and subjecting what remained to a vicious cycle of fire and flood. The combined impact of timber removal, on the one hand, and the relentless circle of burning and erosion in its aftermath, on the other, also greatly impoverished the region's soils. Together these processes rendered whole sections of the mountain region nearly unrecognizable, some almost lunar in appearance.

Industrial timber harvests effectively enclosed and nearly destroyed much of the mountain forest commons. Yet they also inspired a movement that eventually recovered and even strengthened that commons. The scale of the destruction alarmed many mountain residents, and some sought ways to limit its impact. The successful post–Civil War creation of federal forest reserves and national parks in the West inspired a few to suggest this alternative. They began organizing campaigns to establish similar tracts in the East. These campaigns ultimately led to the creation of the Pisgah and Nantahala National Forests as well as seven other national forests and two national parks in the southern Appalachians. By 1930 the USFS held two million acres in the southern mountains, and this number eventually grew to over six million.

The southern Appalachian timber boom continued a national story of massive timber harvesting that began along the eastern seaboard, logged out coastal forests and the forests of New England, then moved to the Great Lakes area. Wherever it went, this large-scale timber harvesting left destruction in its wake. It removed enormous swathes of forest and left behind tattered landscapes plagued by fire and erosion. The large-scale harvests effectively demolished what had often been de facto commons forests. Few forms of enclosure could be more absolute than mowing down and hauling off millions of privatized trees.[96]

Insatiable demand for wood spurred these destructive harvests. Critical sectors of the early industrial economy—energy, communication, packaging, construction, and land and sea transportation among them—relied on the ready availability of wood and wood products. After New England's rich forests fell to the ax, large timber operators turned their attention to the Great Lakes region. By the close of the Civil War, industrialization was in full swing, and demand for wood grew to staggering new heights. Great Lakes timber was soon logged out, and the voracious timber industry began to look about for fresh sources. Southern mountain forests had largely escaped the early harvests due to access difficulties and prohibitive transportation costs. But now, in the last decades of the nineteenth century, the Appalachian forests stood as the richest remaining in the East. New industrial technologies, particularly railroads, made them more accessible than previously and less costly to harvest and transport.

Railroad building required enormous amounts of capital, and few southern Appalachian residents had access to assets on the necessary scale. Most industrial timber operations in the region, therefore, relied on outside investment sources. People of the southern mountains had participated in national and global economies for at least two centuries, and forest resources had always been central to their participation. Large-scale landholding by distant and absentee owners had likewise long been a fact of the region's history. Nevertheless, industrial timber harvesting ushered in a new era. It changed landownership patterns on a grand scale, damaged or destroyed large sections of the forest commons, tied the southern mountain region more tightly to the global economy, and made it more susceptible to the vagaries of that economy.[97]

Timber harvesting in the southern Appalachians took place in two rough phases. Between 1880 and 1900, the harvests were smaller in scale, less capital intensive, and less destructive than they became after the turn of the century. Animal labor and water power played key roles in transporting logs to market during this early period, while railroads gained ascendancy in the 1900s.

Forests harvested in the earlier period were selectively cut, or "high-graded," meaning operators took the best trees and left everything else. During this stage, timber ventures were relatively low-capital affairs, typically scattered through the forest. Loggers used horses and oxen to transport logs long distances to mills, and only the best logs brought prices justifying this expense. Enormous trees—giants centuries old and often measuring six or more feet in diameter and as much as twenty-five feet in circumference— fell during this period. The most valuable species went first—ash, cherry, oak, walnut, and "yellow" or "tulip" poplar. These first large cutting operations showed little consideration for other woods resources, future harvests, or the health of the forest. They left the woods damaged and cutover. Even so, after these operations the landscape remained recognizable as forest. Though tattered, a remnant canopy endured, and small game and understory plants could survive.[98]

Still, even in this early period, outside capital and large-scale operations made their presence felt. Big companies with international financial backing bought huge tracts of mountain land and acquired timber rights to even more acreage. Their operations left lasting scars, and profits went outside the region, as did most of the lumber itself.[99] In Newport, Tennessee, in the early 1880s, for example, the Scottish Carolina Timber and Land Company bought ten square miles of land. Funding came from Glasgow, Scotland, and Cape Town, South Africa. The company built a sawmill in Newport and brought a French Canadian workforce into the area. To supply the Newport mill, it purchased 120,000 acres in North Carolina's Haywood and Madison Counties. By 1888 a Maine lumberman had set up a bandmill in Jackson County, along the Tuckaseigee River, and the Linville Land, Manufacturing, and Mining Company had begun cutting timber in Avery County.[100]

The pace of development quickened in the 1890s. Knoxville's Unaka Timber Company, Michigan's Crosby Lumber Company, New York's Foreign Hardwood Log Company, Illinois's Dickson-Mason Lumber Company, and New York's Tuckaseigee Timber Company bought western North Carolina acreage heavily. Crosby purchased 47,000 acres, Dickson-Mason acquired 34,000, and the two New York firms obtained at least 75,000 each. Around the turn of the century, at least sixteen big timber outfits owned hundreds of thousands of acres in western North Carolina, and sawmills in Lenoir, Pinola, and Nantahala each produced more than fifty thousand board feet daily.[101] The largest of these firms, the William M. Ritter Lumber Company of Ohio, held nearly two hundred thousand acres in the state's mountains. Ritter also had substantial holdings in West Virginia, Kentucky, Virginia, and eastern Tennessee. By 1913 it had obtained more than two billion board feet of Appalachian hardwood timber. Ritter became the world's largest hardwood flooring producer, and its owner earned fame as "the dean of the Hardwood Lumbermen of America." As Ritter flooring, Appalachian woods graced elegant hotels in North America and private palaces in Europe.[102]

In 1900 the southern Appalachian region contributed nearly a third of the nation's hardwood timber cut, and production continued to grow until the 1909 peak, when nearly four billion board feet—almost 40 percent of the national hardwood figure—poured from the southern mountains. These numbers declined as the timber boom liquidated more and more of the region's forest stock. Some 2.4 billion board feet came from the region in 1919, and 2 billion in 1929.[103]

Nor were hardwoods the region's only important forest product, as leather-tanning operations also moved into western North Carolina. Toxaway Tanning Company, Brevard Tanning Company, and other tannin producers established operations in the late 1800s. By 1900 large tanneries operated in Morganton, Brevard, Lenoir, Asheville, Marion, Hazelwood, Waynesville, Andrews, and Murphy, and dozens of small operations also dotted the region. These tanneries kept thousands of mountain residents busy supplying the immense stores of high-tannin bark and "extract wood" they demanded.[104]

In a move that would affect the region dramatically for over a century, Ohio's Champion Fibre Company opened a pulp mill in Canton, North Carolina, in 1905. The company used the Blue Ridge operation as supplier for a lucrative Ohio paper mill owned by Champion Coated Paper. Owner Peter G. Thompson purchased some three hundred thousand acres in western North Carolina. By 1911 Thompson had also organized Champion Lumber Company and had purchased another one hundred thousand acres. When World War I began, Champion employed some seven thousand people in its various operations, including one thousand at the Canton plant.[105]

Local landholders usually faced serious disadvantages as they dealt with these large and well-capitalized companies. Timber operators nearly always had the upper hand in wealth, education, familiarity with the law, and knowledge of international markets, and their elite connections and large bankrolls also furnished political clout. Industry agents astutely leveraged all these advantages as they made land deals. This imbalance of power left many mountain residents embittered in the wake of land and timber-rights transfers. Many felt that they had been tricked, cheated, swindled—even robbed outright. Resentments often lingered long after the sawyers came and the trees fell. Later landholders, including the USFS, inherited this offended landscape.[106]

Through much of the nineteenth century, economic transactions in the southern mountains typically took place among people who knew each other and had long-term business and social relationships. A system of neighborly mutual exchange lay at the base of the local economy. In this system, personal loyalties overlapped with business loyalties, and where and with whom one "traded" was part of the fabric of one's family and community life. Even business deals linking the region to international markets often followed this pattern. Such a system made sense when all participants expected to have long-standing ties. In that situation, cultivating a reputation for loyalty, trustworthiness, and fair dealing could be a shrewd business tactic.[107]

Timber companies typically operated from a different and much less personal business model. They did not expect to have long-standing business relationships with people in the southern mountains. In fact, as one operator freely admitted, maximizing profit was their central aim: the goal was to "cut and get out." Thus, the companies had little incentive to recognize or honor the interests of local people. As federal field investigators observed in a report President Theodore Roosevelt sent to Congress in 1902: "The home and permanent interests of the lumberman are generally in another state or region, and his interests in these mountains begins and ends with the hope of profit."[108]

This state of affairs led to a series of transactions heavily skewed toward timber company interests. Local landholders often had little idea of the value of their lands or the trees on them and typically sold acreage or timber rights for paltry sums. Huge centuries-old tulip poplars, white and red oaks, and black cherry trees often changed hands for twenty-five to seventy-five cents a tree. In one revealing example, a pair of speculating agents based in New York endeavored to obtain timber rights to 33,000 acres belonging to western North Carolina's Cherokee Indian band. The agents first offered $30,000 for the rights, then apparently more than doubled the offer to $66,000. The fact of Cherokee ownership eventually led to involvement by the federal commissioner of Indian affairs and the secretary of the interior. Government officials estimated the value of the timber in question at

$1,195,000, nearly twenty times the highest offered price and roughly forty times the initial offer. The Interior Department killed the deal on grounds that the proffered sum was pitifully inadequate. Most landowners, of course, lacked the information-gathering capacity of the federal government, and many similarly lopsided deals doubtless went through. Moreover, company agents sometimes misled landowners about the terms of the contracts they signed. In those cases, mountain residents had little recourse when they realized, too late, the agents' dishonesty. Timbermen also used their far superior access to legal expertise, taking advantage of widespread title uncertainties to claim lands longtime residents considered their own.[109]

The timber boom affected the Blue Ridge human landscape nearly as dramatically as its physical landscape. It displaced many mountain families and left most of those who stayed with less acreage, spurred outmigration, and slowed population growth or halted it altogether. Between 1880 and 1900, for instance, western North Carolina's Macon and Graham Counties had grown at a faster rate than the state average, but between 1900 and 1910, they expanded hardly at all, while much of the state continued to grow robustly. In the same period, farm acreage dropped about 20 percent in southwestern North Carolina, southeastern Tennessee, and north Georgia.[110] Lumber companies prompted these developments by buying many small farms and assembling them into huge timber tracts. Former owners typically moved out. In 1912, for example, the USFS examined 21,000 acres in far southwestern North Carolina. Owned by the Macon Lumber Company, these lands—which once hosted agricultural communities—now supported an "only settler . . . the keeper employed by the Company."

At the same time, hundreds of logging camps and sawmill towns grew up as part of the timber boom. The camps were always temporary, but some of the towns became permanent. In North Carolina, Bryson City, Fontana, and Ravensford began as mill towns. Towns also grew around other woods industries. Carl Schenck described the Champion Fibre Company operations and the town of Canton—which Champion built to support its pulp plant—as "the most gigantic enterprise which western North Carolina had ever seen." Enka later developed around a Dutch-owned rayon factory, and a Mead Corporation cardboard factory joined the tannery in Sylva. The region's population diversified as local men and crews imported from Pennsylvania, New York, Michigan, and overseas combined to bring in the timber.

Local landowning families' desire to preserve productive woodlots served as a brake on the timber boom's environmental destruction. Farmers sold timber from their wooded acreage, but these small sales were usually less damaging than the wholesale approach the lumber companies employed on larger tracts. Farmers' land proved more likely to remain at least partially forested. As late as 1940, it was common for the region's farmers to keep 40 percent of their acreage wooded, and commons-style harvest went forward on this woodlot acreage.[111]

After 1900, as more capital-intensive timber harvest methods gained ascendancy, environmental damage became more acute. Railroads snaked into the hills, bringing portable sawmills with them. By bringing the purchase point closer to the harvest point, the railroads slashed transportation costs and made it profitable to cut smaller trees. Operators began clearcutting, or taking every tree regardless of size or species. They left only piles of slash behind—discarded branches and tree tops. Dried, these heaps became an invitation to fire. Locomotive sparks or lightning strikes ignited huge conflagrations that burned uncontrollably. The fires scorched deeply into the earth, destroying root structures, worms, and microorganisms. Rains coming after the fires washed away the parched and loosened soil, leaving the ground scarred and gullied. Unlike earlier harvests, this phase of logging and its aftermath left desolate landscapes where the forests had been. Only ghosts and shattered fragments of the woods remained. In western North Carolina, the slopes of Mount Mitchell became one such wasteland. Acre upon treeless acre stretched across the mountain, a barren landscape of charred stumps (see figure 4).[112]

Even at its peak, however, the timber boom left large areas nearly untouched. Southwestern North Carolina was one such area, and in the 1920s large parts of what became the Nantahala National Forest had never been cut. Even when these rugged sections were logged in the 1930s, they did not suffer the devastation the Mount Mitchell area experienced in the 1920s. Catastrophe in places like Mount Mitchell, however, rather than rough continuities in places like Nantahala, set in motion processes that eventually created de jure commons where de facto commons had been. In response to flooding and other devastation in the wake of the industrial timber harvests, the federal government began purchasing forest acreage in the southern mountains. The Weeks Act of 1911 gave the young United States Forest Service authority to acquire lands in the east for watershed protection and opened a new era in Blue Ridge commons history.

TWO

Response to Devastation
Organizing Forests in the Southern Appalachians

IF THEY COULD WREST their attention from the world's first Ferris wheel, a fifteen-hundred-pound Venus de Milo statue in chocolate, a seventy-foot illuminated lightbulb tower, and other showy attractions, visitors to the 1893 World's Fair in Chicago could take in a more muted exhibit: a display of practical forestry in western North Carolina. Gifford Pinchot, a young forester working on George W. Vanderbilt's extravagant Biltmore Estate near Asheville, had prepared the display. Pinchot had been at Biltmore just over a year, and he ran an early American experiment in scientific forestry there, using methods he had recently learned in Europe. Vanderbilt and Pinchot hoped the exhibit might garner attention from at least some of the estimated 25 million visitors who attended the heralded Columbian Exposition in Chicago's beautifully prepared White City.[1]

To accompany the World's Fair exhibit, Pinchot prepared a small booklet, *Biltmore Forest*, describing what he called "the attempt to treat Biltmore Forest systematically." The leaflet's opening pages included a map of the property, and in the text Pinchot outlined the condition of the forest, the work that had been done, and the project's costs and revenues. When he arrived at the estate, he wrote, "The condition of a large part of the forest was deplorable in the extreme." While not the near-lunar landscape that would eventually confront foresters in other places, Biltmore Forest had suffered grave damage. Heavily cutover, widely grazed by free-range cattle, and often burned, the woods were in tatters. Pinchot banished cattle and fire. He also prescribed and began carrying out "a series of improvement cuttings." He did not cut where doing so would be dangerous to soil retention, and he did not cut where the work would cost more than the value of the wood it produced. In other places he replanted. And in places he simply decided no active management at all should take place—that "the forest must be allowed absolute rest."[2]

In the booklet, Pinchot explained how he also made a concerted effort to study and describe Biltmore Forest. He divided the seven-thousand-acre tract into numbered sections, each containing around 5.7 acres. He made detailed notations about each section on a series of six hundred index cards. He recorded each parcel's elevation, slope direction, percent incline, soil type, and forest floor condition. He estimated the amount and types of timber and noted which species and age classes predominated. Finally, on each card the young forester recorded his management recommendations.[3]

Toward the end of the pamphlet, Pinchot offered some conclusions about the Biltmore experiment's value. "Of the silvicultural character of American trees," the fledgling forester wrote, "we are [largely] ignorant." The Biltmore effort could be "expected to yield much information of general value," helping to address that knowledge vacuum. "But above all," he continued, "it will be useful in defining and helping to solve the problems with which American forestry must deal."[4]

Gifford Pinchot later became the first chief forester of the U.S. Forest Service. He played a monumental role in all things related to national forests and in the broader conservation movement. Few figures loom larger in the history of American conservation. The work he did preparing the Biltmore Forest World's Fair pamphlet paled in comparison to jobs he would later undertake at the highest levels. Yet in many ways, it also foreshadowed a number of the issues and challenges he and other forest conservationists would face in the coming decades.[5]

Systematizing native forests was not easily done. Obstacles lurked at every turn. Pinchot and his successor at Biltmore, Carl Schenck, learned this almost immediately. They used every tool at their disposal—maps, axes, fences, wardens, logging crews, and much more—to order the forests. Their considerable brainpower and dauntless work ethic contributed substantially to the endeavor, as did Vanderbilt's plentiful financial backing. Yet they never fully succeeded, as both foresters readily conceded.[6]

The systems Pinchot and Schenck tried to use at Biltmore focused almost entirely on commercial timber species. They considered the dizzying variety of other species in the Appalachian forests as quite secondary and as a downright nuisance when competing with commercially valuable trees. In his World's Fair pamphlet, for instance, Pinchot provided a short list of commercial timber species and a longer general list of tree species and made no mention at all of any other forest species. Forest management priorities other than timber—watershed protection, wildlife habitat, and the like—barely registered with Pinchot and Schenck. The systems they developed, then, considered only a small portion of the native forest. Yet systematizing even this much proved enormously challenging.[7]

To understand responses to the devastating timber harvests in the southern Appalachians, we turn first to Pinchot and the Forest Service he sculpted. We then explore the series of events that led to the establishment of national forests in western North Carolina.

Pinchot's Forest Service

Gifford Pinchot established himself as the most visible figure in the history of the early Forest Service. Its central founding father, he set the course for the fledgling Forest Service's long-term trajectory. He also established the Department of Agriculture, rather than the Department of the Interior, as the administrative home of federal forestry. And with the help of his long-time friend and close political ally President Theodore Roosevelt, Pinchot engineered an enormous land transfer. The 1905 Transfer Act moved jurisdiction over the nation's forest reserves, which had been with Interior, to the Department of Agriculture.

The question of whether national forests should be controlled by Interior or Agriculture drew lively debate early in the history of federal forest management. Since 1881 the Department of Agriculture had housed a Division of Forestry. Intended largely as a farmers' consulting agency, it had fairly light responsibilities, a minimal budget, and no lands to manage. The first forest reserves, created after the 1891 General Land Law Revision Act authorized them, were administered by the General Land Office within the Interior Department. The 1897 Organic Act offered initial forest reserve management guidelines, aimed at the secretary of the interior.[8]

Bernard Fernow, who had served as chief of Agriculture's Division of Forestry, left the position in 1898, and Gifford Pinchot succeeded him. From his new academic position, Fernow called for greater Agriculture Department involvement in national forest management. Pinchot, Agriculture's new forestry chief, had previously worked as a "confidential forest agent" with Interior. A brilliant political tactician, Pinchot began laying the groundwork for an increased role for Agriculture while continuing his ties to Interior. By 1901 Interior was patrolling the reserves, but Agriculture was examining them and making forest management decisions. On reserve matters, Pinchot reported directly to the secretary of the interior, bypassing his supervisor in Agriculture.[9]

Interior's General Land Office was mostly in the business of transferring public lands to private ownership. But private lumbering had ravaged landscapes, caused destructive fires and floods, and wasted dismaying amounts of timber. The Land Office also had a sordid history of corruption and ineptitude. Interior's Geological Survey had a better track record and shared some responsibility for the reserves. Still, Pinchot saw the effort to shift forest reserves from Land Office control to Agriculture as a proactive conservationist move. Extractive industries initially opposed it.

Theodore Roosevelt's succession to the presidency after William McKinley's September 1901 assassination brought new energy to the transfer effort. McKinley had expressed support for the transfer idea but had warned about significant political barriers. Roosevelt proposed the transfer within months of taking office. His first attempt failed, but his resounding 1904 election victory offered another opportunity. Pinchot mounted a remarkable publicity campaign and spearheaded a tireless lobbying effort to forward transfer legislation. In 1905 the Transfer Act placed the forest reserves under the jurisdiction of Agriculture's Bureau of Forestry, which Pinchot headed. Within two years, Pinchot had renamed the reserves "national forests" and his Bureau of Forestry the "Forest Service."[10]

A trained forester himself, Pinchot believed a corps of professional experts should manage the nation's forest reserves. He set about turning the Forest Service into such a corps. In 1905 Pinchot summarized the basic management principles he applied to the forest reserves. He laid out these ideas in a letter delivered the day President Theodore Roosevelt signed the Transfer Act. The letter officially came to Pinchot himself from agriculture secretary James Wilson, but Wilson simply signed the document. Pinchot had authored it, and it framed his guiding principles. Together with the Organic Act of 1897—which outlined reserve goals as producing a continuous supply of timber and protecting watersheds and charged reserve managers with guarding the forests against fires and other "depredations"—these principles guided national forest management for over seven decades.[11]

Pinchot's forest philosophy emphasized use, as his italics in Wilson's letter make clear. "All the resources of the reserves are for *use*," Pinchot-for-Wilson wrote, "and this use must be brought about in a thoroughly prompt and businesslike manner, under such restrictions only as will insure the permanence of these resources." Pinchot's vision for proper use meant that "all land is to be devoted to its most productive use for the permanent good of the whole people, and not for the temporary benefit of individuals or companies." He was no friend to large commercial interests, which he saw as ignoring the public welfare in pursuit of private gain, but neither was he an enthusiast for preservation, which he deplored as "nonuse."

Pinchot and leading preservationist John Muir, who had previously been friends and allies, famously opposed one another over the Hetch Hetchy dam project in California's Yosemite National Park. Pinchot supported the project as a rational use of the Hetch Hetchy Valley that would provide needed water resources to San Francisco. Muir opposed it on grounds that the project represented a wanton and shortsighted assault on the breathtaking Hetch Hetchy Valley—in his view, a splendor of creation that should be preserved by the Park Service for future generations rather than irreparably flooded by this one. Eventually, Muir and the preservationists lost the Hetch Hetchy battle, the O'Shaughnessy Dam was built, and a bitter split between preservationists and utilitarian conservationists ensued.[12]

Gifford Pinchot's utilitarian version of conservation required active forest management to ensure good timber productivity and continuous high yield. As his biographer, Char Miller, noted, Pinchot saw "the axe as double-edged, a tool that could both destroy and revitalize." The forester deplored the tool's destructive use, but he aimed to deploy it for regenerative purposes. He saw his Forest Service as a sort of management and engineering team at work in a kind of giant forest factory producing goods and services useful to human beings.[13]

Pinchot hoped to establish an autonomous agency whose forest reserve management decisions would be based on its technocratic expertise and its disinterested commitment to the public good. The Forest Service could not maintain the sort of political autonomy he initially envisioned. It quickly came under interest-group pressures and lost aspects of its early independence. Pinchot himself experienced the receiving end of hardball politics when President Howard Taft—Roosevelt's successor—fired him in early 1910.[14]

Even after this defeat, Pinchot continued to influence national forest affairs, and significant parts of his vision endured. During Pinchot's tenure as chief and for more than six decades afterward the USFS did enjoy relative autonomy, though like all government institutions it was more or less continuously embroiled in political power struggles. The Forest Service continued to emphasize technocratic expertise, and professionals trained in "scientific forestry" continued to dominate its ranks. In theory, multiple uses with an eye on the long term continued to be its watchword, though in practice commodity production—and especially timber harvesting—took precedence over all other uses.[15]

Pinchot's legacy remained with the Forest Service deep into the twentieth century and helped shape forest politics even after the 1976 National Forest Management Act enabled significant public participation. Pinchot resisted activist public input into his agency, and he built an organization that continued to do so long after his departure. He firmly believed that forest management decisions should be made by technocratic experts rather than through democratic participation, and he established in the USFS an enduring culture built on that belief. In one sense, the American public had never been far from the Forest Service, especially in the East, where national forestlands entwined with private holdings. There the national forests had neighbors by the hundred thousands and soon hosted users by the millions. In another sense, however, Pinchot and his successors kept the American citizenry at arm's length and continued to do so long after the public and a broad range of scientists clamored for a larger role.[16]

Pinchot's Forest Service eventually became the largest landholder in the western North Carolina region where he first worked as a professional forester. A variety of factors, including his stint at Biltmore, contributed to this development.

Pinchot Comes to Biltmore

In 1889, at the same time timber industrialists turned increased attention toward the southern mountains, so too did George Vanderbilt, scion of one of the world's wealthiest families. He began buying lands in western North Carolina for what would eventually become the 125,000-acre estate of palatial Biltmore House. Most of the acreage he purchased was cutover and damaged farm and woodland. Vanderbilt hired North America's foremost landscape architect, Frederick Law Olmsted, to help him transform these ragged grounds into the aristocratic retreat he envisioned. Olmsted advised Vanderbilt to make Biltmore Estate the first U.S. site to be managed under the system of "practical," or "scientific," forestry then practiced in Europe. Young Gifford Pinchot, son of a longtime Olmsted friend, had recently returned to the United States after studying forestry in France and Switzerland. Olmsted suggested that Vanderbilt hire the young man to manage Biltmore woods. Vanderbilt followed Olmsted's advice, and Pinchot accepted the position.[17]

Like his employer, Gifford Pinchot moved in patrician and international circles. Thanks to his wealthy and well-connected family, he was accustomed to hobnobbing with elites on both sides of the Atlantic. William Tecumseh Sherman, for instance, the famous Civil War general and leading Republican, was a dear family friend and a frequent visitor at the family's several homes. Gifford spent three years of his boyhood living in Europe and eventually followed other men in his mother's family to Yale University.

During his senior year, wanting advice about a possible career in forestry, he went straight to the top. He sought out the nation's leading forest lights: former U.S. Commissioner of Agriculture George B. Loring; U.S. Chief of the Forestry Division Bernard Fernow; and botanist Charles Sprague Sargent, head of Harvard's Arnold Arboretum, publisher of the elite magazine *Garden and Forest*, and author of one of the nation's most important forest inventories.[18]

Pinchot's pursuit of a forestry career eventually led him back across the Atlantic and into the orbit of Dietrich Brandis, perhaps the most widely respected European forester of the day. A German by birth, Brandis had trained in German scientific forestry, considered cutting-edge in the nineteenth and early twentieth centuries. He had made his career with the British Empire and had charge of managing the rich tropical forests of British India. Pinchot thus learned to think of forestry in international terms. He admired German forestry but thought it inadequate to American contexts. He especially valued Brandis's experience in India and saw parallels to his own situation in the United States.

Pinchot, who had loved the outdoors since boyhood and was an avid hunter and fisherman, deplored the ravages of industrial timber harvests across the United States. He thought of himself as a missionary for "practical forestry," which he saw as the responsible alternative to unchecked lumbering. As a practical forester, he aimed to manage timber species in such a way as to insure a continuing crop. Like lumbermen, he would cut trees but always with an eye to future harvests, never with the "cut and get out" approach that had decimated so much of the continent's green canopy.

Pinchot brought a missionary's zeal to his work, a keenness expressed at Biltmore and evident throughout his long and influential career. The young man persuaded Vanderbilt to put his western North Carolina woods under a scientific forestry management system. He touted the system as both pioneering American experiment and sound financial investment.

The "Biltmore Experiment"

Vanderbilt's celebrity and deep pockets, combined with Pinchot's ambitions for himself and the woods he managed and supported by both men's social networks, made the "Biltmore experiment" in scientific forestry a national phenomenon. Luminaries such as John Muir, Bernard Fernow, and Charles Sprague Sargent visited Biltmore. Together with Pinchot himself, these men were among the most important leaders of the nation's growing conservation movement. Biltmore Forest showcased itself to an international audience, as we have seen, at the 1893 World's Fair. When Pinchot parted ways with Vanderbilt, he recommended German forester Carl Alwin Schenck as his successor. Schenck organized Biltmore Forest School, the first school of professional forestry in the United States, and this groundbreaking institution added further to Biltmore's national reputation as a forestry pioneer. Some of Schenck's students made their way to important positions in private forestry, academic forestry, and the USFS. They strengthened ties Pinchot had already forged between Biltmore, the USFS, and professional forestry.[19]

When the Weeks Act passed in 1911, the USFS already had Vanderbilt's property in mind as a highly desirable purchase. Over time, the agency bought most of the estate's 125,000 acres, which became the core of Pisgah National Forest. Under the USFS, Pisgah eventually grew to include over five hundred thousand acres.[20]

Gifford Pinchot spent three years at Biltmore reforesting damaged areas, inventorying Vanderbilt's holdings, managing the estate arboretum, carrying out small logging operations, and supervising the estate's acquisition of tens of thousands of acres. The Vanderbilts called the roughly seven thousand acres nearest their mansion Biltmore Forest. The rest, sprawling holdings that stretched to Mount Pisgah, became Pisgah Forest.[21]

In many ways, the Biltmore and Pisgah Forest experience in western North Carolina presaged that of the USFS throughout the southern Appalachians. Foresters at Biltmore were among the first in the United States to attempt to manage native forests using scientific forestry methods. They were also among the first to attempt to restore forests to health after timber harvests had devastated them. And they found themselves, as USFS personnel later would, navigating the complicated terrain of local forest-use tradition.[22]

Forest managers at Biltmore confronted challenges the USFS would later encounter, among them trespass, fire protection, and the problem of "inholdings." First Pinchot and then Schenck wrestled with these problems.

Biltmore and the Commons

As both Pinchot and Schenck noted, though Vanderbilt eventually acquired enormous swathes of Appalachian woodland, local people did not view it as strictly private property. In his autobiography, Pinchot perceptively noted, "They regarded this country as their country, their common." Schenck agreed and went even further. "The real owner of Pisgah Forest was not George W. Vanderbilt," he wrote, "but these mountaineers, who were using his property for farming, pasturing, and hunting at their own pleasure."[23]

The two foresters disagreed about how best to approach this situation. Schenck determined to protect Vanderbilt's property by every means at his disposal, while Pinchot expended considerably less energy on the issue. Schenck criticized Pinchot for failing to curb local uses, charging that Pinchot "apparently took these inroads on the rights of the proprietor for granted." For his part, Pinchot believed Schenck underestimated the importance of neighborly relations in successful forestry. He credited Brandis with teaching "a great truth which most German foresters had never grasped—that in the long run Forestry cannot succeed unless the people who live in and near the forest are for it and not against it."[24]

Pinchot also believed Schenck was too high-handed toward Pisgah's neighbors. He vividly remembered a scene from his travels in Germany when an elderly peasant "stood silent, head bent, cap in both hands" at the approach of a professional forester, who "stalked by without the slightest sign that he knew the peasant was on earth." Pinchot believed Schenck expected similar behavior from his Blue Ridge neighbors and that local people found the German forester's attitude galling. "He thought of them as peasants," Pinchot wrote. "They thought of themselves as independent American citizens—and of course, they were right."[25]

In addition, Pinchot expressed sympathy for mountain people, who typically "lived very far from high" and "needed everything usable" in the forest, "pasture, fish, and game—to supplement the very meager living they were able to scratch from the soil." He recognized that cattle and hogs had free range "by immemorial custom and by law." He noted that local people "knew nothing of game preserves, and but little of property rights." And although he lamented the condition of the forest he found, he described the small farmers who had formerly owned it as having been "obliged" by poverty "to use without reserve all the resources" at their disposal.[26]

Schenck, however, objected staunchly to what he called "the usurpation of the natives." "To my own European feeling," he wrote, "they were equal to theft and robbery." He believed the rights of private property trumped any potential concern with local need or neighborhood relations. He thought it his duty, regardless of consequences, to do everything in his power to protect Vanderbilt's holdings from the commons uses to which Pisgah's neighbors were accustomed. Schenck poured enormous energies into this project, though he found his efforts repeatedly stymied.[27]

Schenck's autobiography contains evidence of an ongoing forest contest between the German forester and his commons-minded neighbors. Several

incidents reveal both the lengths to which Schenck was willing to go to enforce Vanderbilt's property rights and the determined resistance with which
local people met his efforts. In addition to his own authority, the forester
used fences and private wardens in his quest to wrest control of the forest
away from Vanderbilt's neighbors, and he called on local law enforcement
for assistance. In their turn, the neighbors used fence cutting, arson, and
arms as tools of resistance, and they too seem to have sought aid from local
lawmen—apparently with more success than Schenck.

One set of dramatic conflicts revolved around fencing. Schenck esteemed fences as a way to keep out uninvited neighbors and their livestock.
He noted with approval "a strong wire fence, six feet high" encircling much
of the original Biltmore Forest. He believed it was "unique at the time in
western North Carolina," and he saw it as most useful for keeping "intruders, including fire fiends," out of the private forest.[28] Neighbors objected to
such fences, however, and apparently looked for opportune moments to take
them down. When he returned to Pisgah Forest in July 1900 after two months
in Germany, for instance, Schenck learned to his dismay that eight miles of
boundary-marking and cattle-excluding barbed-wire fence "had been cut
to pieces" while he was away. Moreover, "gigantic fires had celebrated my
absence," he reported. Among other things, these fires had destroyed five
houses in the Vanderbilt woods, houses Schenck used as headquarters for
his rangers.[29]

The attacks on Schenck's fences and cabins in the summer of 1900 were
clearly deliberate, and they have all the marks of a textbook case of commons defense. Fence cutting and arson are among commons users' ancient
weapons against attempted privatization. In this case, Pisgah neighbors
purposely wielded them against the infrastructure of Schenck's enclosure.
He intended the fences to keep out free-range livestock, and he intended
the cabins to house guardians of the private forest. As both the forester and
the local people understood, without these structures it was all but impossible for Schenck to control access to his employer's holdings.

Residents also doubtless recognized that Schenck represented Biltmore's most determined opponent of their commons traditions. They did
indeed "celebrate" his absence. Biltmore's neighbors apparently agreed with
Schenck that they were "the real owners" of Pisgah Forest, and they intended to keep it that way. Thus, the moment he turned his back, they did
everything in their power to undo the work he had thus far accomplished
toward enclosure of their de facto commons. By making war on his enclosure arsenal, they insured greater forest access for themselves on his return.

If the local sheriff arrested suspected arsonists and fence cutters in 1900,

Schenck did not record the fact. More likely nothing happened, as so often proved the case when Schenck turned to the neighborhood and to local law enforcement for support. The forester remembered his frustrating experience battling moonshiners active on the Pisgah Forest, for instance. "It was in vain that I offered a premium for the discovery of any moonshine still," he lamented. When Schenck or his rangers stumbled on a still, it "was removed before I could get the sheriff to seize it." Most locals, including the sheriff, lived in fear of moonshiners, Schenck believed, and he attributed to this fear their reluctance to cooperate with his own efforts to remove active stills from Vanderbilt property. It is also probable that many neighbors, perhaps including the sheriff, felt more sympathy toward local moonshiners' efforts to earn a living than toward the foreign forester's efforts to police his largely absentee multimillionaire employer's woods.[30]

On another occasion, Schenck found himself in danger when he confronted a fisherman plying the Davidson River as it ran through Vanderbilt lands. The man had left a buggy along the public road, a road Schenck wished he could close, along with all others through Vanderbilt property, precisely because it "allowed free access to the moonshiners, the cattle drivers, the hunters, and the prospective squatters." Schenck traced the buggy owner to the river and asked him to stop fishing. The fisherman responded with an oath and a refusal to budge. Schenck announced that he would take the man's buggy to Brevard in quest of the sheriff and proceeded to do so. In response, the fisherman pursued Schenck and drew a gun, challenging the forester to draw his own weapon. Schenck had earlier decided not to carry a gun, noting, "I was no match for a mountaineer." He believed he was safer "going unarmed and making it known that I was unarmed." He dismounted the buggy at gunpoint and edged away.[31]

The forester eventually did report this incident to Brevard's sheriff but got no response. Again Schenck attributed the lack of action to fear, but it is possible to imagine other reasons the sheriff might have been reluctant to press charges. A law officer might legitimately disagree with Schenck's belief that he had caught the fisherman trespassing and poaching. According to local custom, the man had done nothing wrong. He had used a public road to access the public Davidson River. Rivers, like "unimproved" forests, were considered legitimate commons. The buggy Schenck had taken, on the other hand, was clearly private property. Schenck's seizing it could be considered outright thievery.

Add to that the class dimensions of this encounter, and it is clear that local sympathy would have leaned heavily toward the neighborhood commons fisherman rather than the imported private forester in an American aristocrat's employ. The fisherman would have been seen as quietly minding his own business and the forester as arrogantly troublemaking, meddling high-handedly where he had no business. Small wonder, then, if the sheriff, a member of the local community whose job security and quality of life relied on neighborhood support, chose simply to ignore Schenck's complaint.[32]

Schenck confronted one final issue that the Forest Service would later inherit, the question of "inholdings." This term referred to land within the broader forest still held by other owners. To Schenck's consternation, "in the southernmost part of Pisgah Forest the size and the number of the interior holdings were so great that Vanderbilt's property in the aggregate was smaller than that of the holders." Some three hundred farms in the Pink Beds area interspersed Vanderbilt lands. Schenck believed these interior holdings represented an insurmountable barrier to true forestry, and he prioritized their acquisition. But Vanderbilt was never able to purchase most of them, and the USFS inherited the patchwork landscape years later.[33]

Federal Forest Reserves

By 1900, just as industrial timber harvests in the southern Appalachians increased and Pisgah neighbors torched Carl Schenck's fences and ranger houses, a system of national forests had developed in the United States. Concerns about protecting western forests and waters spurred the creation of this system, which began as a series of forest reserves in the western states. Through an 1891 amendment to the General Land Law Revision Act, Congress gave the president authority to designate large stretches of wooded federal lands as forest reserves. At that time, the federal government had enormous landholdings in the western states. The 1891 Creative Act essentially enabled U.S. presidents to "reserve," or continue federal ownership of, some of these lands rather than move them into the private domain.

Between 1891 and 1893, President William Henry Harrison used the Creative Act to designate fifteen forest reserves totaling thirteen million acres, and President Grover Cleveland later added five million acres to the system. The Creative Act offered little direction or infrastructure for managing the reserves once created, however. Congress addressed this issue in the 1897 Organic Act, which provided the first legislative framework for managing federal forest reserves. Lively debates about who should be responsible for reserve management continued for years, ending finally in 1905, when legislation designated the Department of Agriculture's Division of Forestry—

later the U.S. Forest Service—as the reserves' administrative home.[34] By that time, the federal forest reserve system had grown to 63 million acres, all in the West. It would expand again to 151 million western acres by 1907, when it became the National Forest System.[35]

Although the federal forest reserve system initially involved only western lands, calls quickly came for expanding it into the East, and especially into the southern mountains. Even before Congress created the forest reserve system in 1891, at least one public proposal for a federal public lands initiative in the southern Appalachians had occurred. Like most early proposals, this one had in mind a national park in the style of Yellowstone rather than a timber-producing reserve.

Created in 1872, Yellowstone was the first national park in the United States. It inspired calls for other such parks, including one from Boston physician Henry O. Marcy for a national park in the southern mountains. Marcy proposed his Appalachian park in an 1885 presentation to the American Academy of Medicine in New York City. He emphasized that such a park could secure the region's health benefits and extend these benefits to more Americans. In 1892 leading botanist Charles Sprague Sargent published a call for a southern Appalachian park in his well-respected and widely circulated magazine, *Garden and Forest*. Sargent, too, seems to have had a Yellowstone-style model in mind. He saw the proposed park as a means of preserving the area's rich botanical communities and providing recreational opportunities to citizens in the East. Gifford Pinchot remembered Joseph A. Holmes, North Carolina's state geologist, mentioning a similar idea to him on a Biltmore Estate visit at around the same time. Sargent's well-publicized proposal apparently sparked a brief flurry of activity. In 1893 the North Carolina legislature passed a resolution supporting the park proposal. That same year the North Carolina Press Association also did and drew up a memorial petitioning Congress to create such a park. North Carolina representative John S. Henderson introduced the petition to Congress in 1894, but the proposal never got out of committee. Still, by the turn of the twentieth century, an organized movement to establish an Appalachian National Park had emerged. Under its aegis, forest reserve supporters—including Pinchot—soon built momentum toward expanding the forest reserve system into the East.[36]

The Appalachian National Park Association

In 1899, on a fishing trip near the western North Carolina town of Sapphire, Dr. Chase P. Ambler told an angling buddy that he would like to see a national park in the southern mountains. Ambler had recently moved to Asheville from Ohio, and his friend Judge William R. Day had come to visit from that state. The two fishermen discussed the idea as they plied the June waters. A few days later, Day gave Ambler some notes sketching a plan for making the envisioned park become a reality. The judge proposed lobbying for the park through an Asheville-based group to be organized with assistance from the local Board of Trade.[37]

When the fishing trip ended and Ambler returned to Asheville, he went right to work implementing Day's plan. He enlisted support from A. H. McQuilkin, a magazine publisher who owned a print shop in Asheville. He also partnered with George H. Smathers to try to bring a proposal to Congress. Smathers, an attorney, represented timber and railroad companies in the area. He and others likely helped press the effort away from a preservationist park and toward a timber-producing reserve. In any case, Ambler and Smathers worked to recruit U.S. senator Jeter C. Pritchard, an influential Republican from North Carolina. Ambler and his team then drew up a petition explaining why the park was necessary. In it they discussed the lack of any such park in the South; the fact that visitors by the thousands sought out western North Carolina's scenery, climate, and forests; the area's easy accessibility to much of the East, from New York to the Deep South; and the ready availability of affordable land. They lingered over the devastating effects of lumbering and tanneries on forests, with a particular emphasis on loss of game and fish.[38]

In September the *Asheville Citizen* came out in support of the proposed park, and Senator Pritchard came aboard. In October the Asheville Board of Trade organized a Parks and Forestry Committee and named McQuilkin chairman and Ambler secretary. The new committee sought newspaper publicity in North Carolina and neighboring states. It also distributed petitions through the public schools, quite widely in North Carolina, and with less success in Tennessee, South Carolina, Alabama, and Georgia.[39]

Now the Board of Trade, in an effort to gather broader support, began thinking about an association with multistate representation. Organizers invited southern states, cities, and civic organizations to send delegates to an inaugural meeting. They planned to set up a formal group to press Congress for a park in the Blue Ridge or Great Smokies. When the invitation went out, it proposed "organizing an association for the promotion of a Southern National Park and Forest Reserve."[40]

In response to the Board of Trade invitation, a well-heeled group gathered at Asheville's fashionable Battery Park Hotel in November 1899.

Southern urban professionals—newspapermen, attorneys, scientists, physicians, merchants, politicians, and the like—made up its ranks. Out of the group's discussions emerged the Appalachian National Park Association, complete with officers and bylaws. The organization planned to call on Congress to "secure the establishment of a park in the mountains of western North Carolina." When the last of their formal meetings ended, members of the new association headed to the Biltmore Estate for a driving tour.[41]

Originally, the group envisioned a park on the Yellowstone model rather than a timber reserve. As Chase Ambler explored rural Buncombe County on weekend hunting and fishing trips, he grew increasingly alarmed at the appalling devastation he saw after timber harvests—fires, flooding, and dramatic wildlife habitat destruction. It would be "negligence of the grossest kind," Ambler declared at the initial meeting, "if a portion of this grand and picturesque place be not preserved in its natural condition." The *Asheville Citizen* ran a front-page cartoon in support of the association—a graphic image of denuded mountains.[42]

Within two years, however, the organization had amended its goals and begun pushing for a timber-producing forest reserve rather than a preservationist park. This shift likely came about as a combined result of lobbying efforts from timber-friendly group members such as Smathers and of Washington politics involving Division of Forestry chief Gifford Pinchot, Senator Jeter Pritchard, and Senator Marion Butler, also of North Carolina. In any case, the association eventually found favor with big lumber companies and professional foresters. Small timber operators did not rally to it, however, and it did not enjoy broad support from local people outside Asheville.[43]

Once established, the Appalachian National Park Association moved quickly. In January 1900 the new organization partnered with New England's Appalachian Mountain Club to propose a plan to Congress. The plan called on the federal government to create "a great forest reserve" in the East through purchase of eastern woodlands. A flurry of bills—scores of them, in fact—with similar aims came before Congress in the ensuing decade, some specifically targeting the southern Appalachians and others aimed more generally at the East.[44]

The Park Association found a powerful ally in Senator Pritchard, who offered continued support. "The acknowledged leader of the Republican Party of the South," Pritchard worked closely with Republican President William McKinley and later with his successor, fellow Republican Theodore Roosevelt. Pritchard was also a mountain native. He grew up in eastern Tennessee and moved to western North Carolina as a teenager. He lived initially in Mitchell County and launched his political career from Marshall, the seat of North Carolina's mountainous Madison County.[45]

Via Pritchard's sponsorship, backed by Appalachian National Park Association lobbying and by tactical consultation with Gifford Pinchot, in 1900 Congress appropriated $5,000 for the southern Appalachian project. It charged the secretary of agriculture "to investigate the forest conditions in the Southern Appalachian Mountain region of western North Carolina and adjacent States." The legislation's focus on North Carolina not only reflected Pritchard's influence, the Park Association's advocacy, and Pinchot's ties to the region but also set precedent for the important role the Tar Heel State's mountains would play in federal forest policy.[46]

Federal Investigations of Southern Appalachian Forests

Armed with the congressional appropriation of $5,000, in 1900 federal investigators set about making field examinations into southern mountain forest conditions. The Department of Agriculture's Division of Forestry led the effort, with support from the Department of the Interior's Geological Survey. Secretary of Agriculture James Wilson and Gifford Pinchot visited the region and spent some ten days personally studying its conditions. From the top of North Carolina's Mount Mitchell, the highest peak in eastern North America, Wilson and his team viewed vast unbroken swathes of forest, but elsewhere they saw devastation from timber harvest and the fire, flood, and erosion that often followed in its wake. Together the surveyors examined some 9.6 million acres, and their work exposed an alarming state of affairs.[47]

In January 1901 President William McKinley, who supported the Appalachian forest reserve initiative, sent a disquieting preliminary report to Congress. In his segment of the report, Secretary of Agriculture Wilson linked "extensive destruction of our forests" with "increase in the irregularity of the flow of water in important streams." In May and August 1901 terrific floods ravaged the southern Appalachians, fortifying his point and quickening interest in the question of southern forests. North Carolina's Jackson, Mitchell, and McDowell Counties suffered traumatic losses. In the tiny Mitchell County community of Bakersville, Cane Creek's swollen waters destroyed seven houses. Before the end of 1901, Wilson submitted the finished report to President Roosevelt, who in turn delivered it promptly to Congress.[48]

The report dramatically captured disturbing conditions in the mountain South, including ruinous fires, disastrous flooding, and widespread soil leaching and erosion. Destructive lumbering practices and poor farming patterns yielded these devastating results, the document concluded. "Logging operations have generally shown an inexcusable slovenliness," researchers wrote. The authors accompanied their vivid descriptions of these problems with striking photographs illustrating the damage. Over a century later, these graphic images still carry power.[49]

President Roosevelt announced that the report "unmistakably" demonstrated a need for forest reserves in the region. He had called for such reserves already in his First Annual Message to Congress in 1901, sections of which Gifford Pinchot had penned. He now endorsed the plan anew, arguing that it would strengthen the southern economy and enhance flood control. The 1902 report he submitted to Congress recommended the nation aim for five million acres of forest reserve in the southern Appalachians.[50]

Gifford Pinchot's close involvement with the survey project further cemented the shift from the Appalachian National Park Association's initial call for a park (where timber would not be harvested) to President Roosevelt's call for reserves (where it would). Pinchot was a dedicated forest reserve evangelist with little interest in preservationist parks, and he worked closely with Roosevelt throughout the time both were in Washington. His stamp is clear on the 1902 report.[51]

The Appalachian National Park Association continued its advocacy and undertook a mass mailing campaign to build support for the forest reserve proposal. The National Hardwood Lumber Association and the National Lumber Manufacturers Association passed supporting resolutions in 1902. These groups, which represented mostly large operators, had opposed the initial park idea. They embraced reserves, however, seeing federal purchase as a potential venue for divesting themselves of cutover lands and lessening their tax duties while still retaining enormous tracts in the regional timber base. In 1903, in a move signaling how completely the original park effort had shifted focus, the Appalachian National Park Association changed its name, replacing "Park" with "Forest Reserve."[52]

The Southern Appalachian Forest Reserve Movement

The move to establish an Appalachian forest reserve as well as a reserve in New England's White Mountains continued throughout the first decade of the twentieth century, culminating finally in the Weeks Act of 1911. The proposal kept gathering support and eventually garnered over seventy endorsing resolutions sent to Congress. These came from a variety of organizations, including chambers of commerce, garden clubs, universities, and various conservation groups.[53]

Within this expanding base of proponents, the 1905 endorsement of the American Forestry Association (AFA) proved key. That group was stronger and enjoyed broader membership than either the Appalachian National Forest Reserve Association or its New England partner, the Society for the Protection of New Hampshire Forests. The AFA had lobbied effectively for passage of the 1891 National Forest Reserve Act, which had created the federal forest system. In 1899, shortly after the Appalachian National Park Association held its organizational meeting, the AFA had passed a resolution expressing "gratification at the prospect" of a park and forest reservation in "the southern Alleghanies." The AFA now strengthened coordination between the two regional groups and gave the effort a national base of support. Eventually, the Appalachian group actually disbanded, turning over leadership to the larger organization.[54]

Despite its growing body of support, significant impediments faced the eastern forest reserve movement. As President Roosevelt wrote to a friend in 1906, "There are grave practical difficulties in the way" of the "great South Appalachian preserve" he and other proponents envisioned. Congress saw nearly fifty Appalachian or eastern forest reserve bills introduced during the period between 1900 and 1910. One after another, they all went down to defeat.[55]

Speaker of the House Joseph Cannon strongly opposed the eastern forest reserve proposals and proved himself a formidable foe. "Not one cent for scenery," the Illinois Republican famously proclaimed. One contemporary observer suggested Cannon might be more powerful than the president. In any case, Cannon's astute political maneuvering generated numerous obstacles for forest reserve proponents, who found themselves facing a protracted battle of wills. Pinchot believed "a little rioting" was in order, but in the end sheer doggedness carried the day.[56]

Eastern reserves proved far more complicated to accomplish than their western counterparts. In the West, reserves could be carved out of existing federal holdings. But the federal government no longer owned land in the East; private owners held all eastern lands, and long had. Unless large-scale private land donors could be found, the only way to establish an eastern forest reserve was to purchase lands from current owners. Questions loomed about the federal government's authority and ability to make such a move.

One set of questions revolved around the issue of states' rights. By 1901, however, this issue had essentially disappeared, as North Carolina and five other southern states passed legislation endorsing the federal government's right to purchase lands within their borders and relinquishing the right to tax those lands. The broader issue of political support in the South did not disappear, however, as many southern politicians fiercely opposed the proposals. One historian described the reserve idea as "akin to heresy" in at least four southern states, including North Carolina.[57]

A second and particularly knotty question concerned the federal government's right to purchase lands at all. The first eastern reserve proposal intended to condemn lands using the power of eminent domain. The House Judiciary Committee declared that bill unconstitutional. It saw the proposed condemnations and even land purchases in general as outside the bounds of the federal government's constitutional authority. An editorial writer for the AFA's journal, *Forestry and Irrigation*, scoffed at that ruling. Nevertheless, the question of constitutionality had enormous repercussions for the debate.[58]

Reserve proponents changed tactics and began emphasizing the role of forests in protecting watersheds. They argued that since the federal government had the power to regulate commerce, it could protect the navigable waterways that served as commercial transportation routes. Nearly all the East's navigable rivers had headwaters in the Appalachian chain. Forests helped prevent flooding, reserve supporters contended, and therefore had beneficial effects on navigation. Thus, the federal government could purchase headwater forests. Proponents amended eastern reserve proposals to target only forests situated at the headwaters of navigable rivers.[59]

A lively debate ensued about the relationship between forests and flood prevention, with reserve proponents linking deforestation to flooding and others questioning this link. The debate was not new; the Appalachian National Park Association had entered fully into it in 1902, for example. Association members carted two six-foot-high miniature mountains to Congress, where they offered members of the House Agriculture Committee a demonstration of the relationship between forests and floods. One mountain had replica "forests" on it, in the form of sponge, moss, and evergreen twigs. The other, bare and gullied, represented the results of deforestation. An association member mounted a stepladder and simulated highland rain by pouring water from a sprinkling can onto the two models. The water ran off the bare model "with a gush," the association reported, and caused "devastating floods" in the model lowlands. Water falling on the "forested" mountain, on the other hand, "was held in the humus and given up slowly in the form of springs, thus regulating the water supply in the lowlands," the association concluded.[60]

Years later, in his testimony before congressional committees, Gifford

Pinchot offered a similar, though less elaborate, demonstration. He poured water over a photograph—held at a slant—of a deforested area and pointed out how quickly the water ran off. He then poured water over an ink blotter held at a similar angle and underscored how little of the water ran off the edge, the paper having absorbed most. He told legislators the two papers were analogous to denuded areas and healthy forests.[61]

Not everyone accepted these kinds of analogies, and Pinchot found an especially effective adversary in the Army Corps of Engineers' Hiram M. Crittendon. Crittendon questioned the relationship between forests and flooding in a lengthy paper he presented to the American Society of Civil Engineers in 1908. Among other things, Crittendon noted that well-forested Yellowstone National Park had seen acute flooding. This kind of evidence, he argued, disproved the assertion that forests always prevented floods. The Weather Bureau and a past president of the Mississippi River Commission concurred.[62]

A series of events seemed to reinforce reserve proponents' arguments, however, and to undercut their opposition. In 1907 disastrous flooding along the Monongahela and Ohio Rivers wreaked widespread and costly havoc. Swollen waters swept people and livestock to their deaths and left homes destroyed and agricultural land devastated. The Monongahela torrent caused some $100 million in damages, and the city of Pittsburgh suffered an additional $8 million. Headwater areas of both flooding rivers had been heavily cutover. Observers drew links between this upstream logging deforestation and the ruinous downstream floods.[63]

Three years later, cataclysmic fires swept through Montana, Idaho, and other parts of the Northwest. Writing about the proposed eastern forest reserves, one historian noted that "western opposition in the Senate . . . had gone up in the smoke of [the] holocaust in Idaho." Together the fires and floods convinced many people that decades of industrial logging were having pernicious effects and that government action was warranted.[64]

Crittenden and others continued to question links between forests and flood prevention, but the U.S. Geological Survey supported Forest Service claims that a link did exist, and the House Committee on Agriculture overwhelmingly embraced that view. By 1910 even the House Judiciary Committee conceded that the federal government could purchase headwater forestlands to protect navigation. The committee reiterated, however, that forest preservation alone did not justify federal purchase.[65]

Congressman John Weeks of Massachusetts, who had supported the idea of eastern federal forest reserves since 1906, repeatedly sponsored eastern reserve legislation. Versions of his bill had passed the House before, and again one did in June 1910. Against the backdrop of nightmarish western fires, Senate opposition—which had kept similar bills from passing earlier—lost strength. That chamber added a provision establishing a commission of the U.S. Geological Survey to confirm that all acreage purchased under the bill helped protect navigation, then passed the bill in February 1911. Less than a month later, on March 1, President William Howard Taft signed the bill, and the Weeks Act became law.[66]

The Weeks Act

The 1911 Weeks Act proved to be a watershed piece of legislation. It began a process that ultimately resulted in federal purchase of over 24 million acres in the East for national forests. In 2009 the Forest Service held authority over eastern lands with a total area greater than that of Vermont, New Hampshire, New Jersey, Connecticut, Delaware, and Rhode Island combined. The Weeks Act also served as a spearhead initiative for land purchases by other federal agencies, including the National Park Service, the Tennessee Valley Authority, and the U.S. Fish and Wildlife Service. Together these other agencies also eventually acquired millions of eastern acres. Thus, the federal government, which held essentially no eastern land before the Weeks Act, has since become one of the East's—and especially the southern Appalachians'—most important landholders.

The act authorized the federal government to purchase "such forested, cut-over, or denuded lands within the watersheds of navigable streams as . . . may be necessary to the regulation of the flow of navigable streams." It approved $11 million to finance these purchases and established the National Forest Reservation Commission to oversee them. The seven-member commission included three cabinet secretaries (agriculture, interior, and war), two senators, and two representatives. The Speaker of the House would appoint the representatives and the president of the Senate the senators.[67]

The Weeks Act directed the secretary of agriculture to recommend lands for federal purchase. It gave the National Forest Reservation Commission authority to consider and approve recommended tracts and to establish prices for those tracts. It spread the budget of $11 million over fiscal years 1910 to 1915. Congress intended these funds both as a pool of purchase monies and as financing to cover examination and survey costs. Once the commission had approved a land parcel and fixed a price for it, the secretary of agriculture had authority to purchase the parcel at that price on behalf of the United States. Before sales could be finalized, the U.S. Geological Survey must determine that the tracts would "promote or protect" navigation and the attorney general must agree that the United States could claim "safe title."[68]

The Weeks Act allowed the secretary of agriculture to divide acquired lands into specific national forests for purposes of administration. It stipulated that purchased lands "be permanently reserved, held, and administered as national forest lands." Only small tracts of agricultural land could be excepted from this rule and sold as homesteads at the secretary of agriculture's discretion. The act did allow purchase of lands where timber or mineral rights were reserved but stipulated that agreements must be reached about how those resources would be removed. Finally, the act required that 5 percent of any national forest receipts in a given year be paid to the states within which the forests lay "for the benefit of public schools and public roads" in host counties.[69]

Though the Weeks Act never mentioned specific regions, it was implicitly aimed at the southern Appalachians and the White Mountains. Eastern forest reserve lobbying efforts had long focused on these areas, and many of the East's navigable waterways had headwaters in them. The Forest Service had studied these sections for a decade and already had approximate purchase targets in mind. Thus, when the act passed, the Forest Service turned its attention immediately to these sections.[70]

THREE

Plenty of Trouble

Creating Federal Forests in the Blue Ridge

R. CLIFFORD HALL, a forest examiner with the Forest Service, had a strange encounter while working in the Nantahala area a few months after the Weeks Act passed. It was July 1911, and Hall had been in the North Carolina highlands about a month, part of a vanguard team working to procure lands for the federal government. He spent most days in the woods, "in camp," at times having packed in with animals. Occasionally, he made trips to nearby towns to procure supplies, send and receive mail, and run any other necessary errands. On one such trip to Andrews, "an old man who gave his name as Tom Holland" sought Hall out. The man offered "a very confused line of talk about matters of which I have no knowledge," Hall reported to his supervisor in Washington, D.C. As best Hall understood it, Tom Holland wished to inform the USFS that he and a neighbor, J. C. Huskins, had served as chainmen on a lumber company survey of a five-thousand-acre tract in the Nantahala area and that rumors of their deaths had been exaggerated.[1]

Two entities claimed the tract in question: the federal government and the Hiawassee Lumber Company. The government had acquired the parcel years before the Weeks Act through U.S. Treasury Department confiscation. Now that the Forest Service was acquiring eastern lands, Treasury planned to transfer the tract, which lay within the Nantahala national forest purchase unit, to Agriculture. The Hiawassee Lumber Company contested Treasury's federal claim, citing a competing paper title. The dispute went to court. It was tied up in early-stage litigation at the time Holland spoke with Hall. According to Hall, Tom Holland seemed to think the two former chainmen's "testimony might be of value to the government." For that reason, Holland suggested, "the other side represented them as dead." Examiner Hall expressed doubt whether "this information is of any real importance" but passed it to D.C. nonetheless.[2]

This exchange offers a glimpse into the complicated world of national forest acquisition in the southern Appalachians. First, it illustrates the legal morass the Forest Service entered when it began work in the region. Tangles of competing claims had long been a problem, and things had become even more complicated with the arrival of industrial timber outfits. This particular case went all the way to the Supreme Court, which ruled in the government's favor in 1915, reversing an earlier court of appeals decision. Court battles were exceptional, especially on that level, but legal chaos was not.[3]

Second, the conversation highlights both the dishonest shenanigans in which some timber companies engaged and also how the Forest Service had to navigate in the context of this chicanery. Assuming Tom Holland's story was accurate, Hiawassee Lumber Company deliberately suppressed evidence in a court of law. The Forest Service expressed confidence the government would prevail in court without Holland's proffered testimony, and nothing further apparently came of the exchange. But the kinds of legal thuggery Holland described were all too common among companies working in the region.[4]

Third, Hall's letter hints at the cultural divide looming between himself and Holland—and, by extension, between Forest Service employees and the local people they moved among, often quite temporarily. Forest examiners and other skilled Weeks Act crew leaders were, like Hall, typically young, well educated, and rooted in places far from the southern Appalachians. "Chainman," on the other hand, was considered an unskilled position, one usually filled by local labor. Chainmen had responsibility only to hold one end of a survey chain in place while other team members took measurements and recorded information from the other end. The position did not even require basic literacy. Older men like Holland could fill it as well as younger men as long as they were good in the woods.

Elsewhere, Hall indicated just how differently he viewed these two worker categories. A few weeks after he talked with Holland, Hall told the D.C. office he planned "to try the experiment of sending only one man on a strip to do both mapping and estimating, with a native to watch the rear end of the chain." The "man" would be a trained Forest Service employee, probably from elsewhere, who would do the crucial technical work. The "native" need only assist by holding the chain. So thoroughly did he discount the proposed local chainman's value that Hall thought of the two-man crew he described as fundamentally a one-man operation.[5]

Hall's description of Holland's communication—"a very confused line of talk"—further underscores this divide. Hall recognized that Holland's conversation largely treated matters Hall himself knew nothing about. But he nevertheless dismissed the exchange as almost certainly unimportant. He seems to have passed the information along only on the off chance that he was wrong. One can only guess at what Holland might have said beyond what Hall recorded. It seems clear, however, that the older man offered information he thought could be valuable to the Forest Service. He probably included particulars about the history of Hiawassee Lumber Company's involvement with the disputed tract, and he may have tried to explain why his experience as chainman could prove false the company's current claims.

In a sense, Tom Holland and Clifford Hall were scouts, advance guards in what would become a long chain of interactions between mountain residents and the USFS. Hall and his fellow land examiners represented the beginnings of a tidal wave of change coming to communities like Holland's Andrews. The coming of the Forest Service into the southern Appalachians marked a watershed not only in the forests' history but also in the history—political, economic, and cultural—of the entire region.

The Weeks Act served as an opening wedge for substantial federal presence in the southern mountains, a federal presence that would grow so large as to make the region more comparable, at least in this particular, to the West than to other parts of the East. The Forest Service proved to be the vanguard agency in a series of federal initiatives that would eventually have an enormous role in the region, permanently transforming it. The series would grow to include the National Park Service, the Tennessee Valley Authority, the Bureau of Land Management, the U.S. Fish and Wildlife Service, and the Appalachian Regional Commission.

The establishment of national forests in the southern Appalachians also marked a turning point in the history of the mountain commons. With this development, the long-standing de facto forest commons became a de jure commons owned by the federal government and regulated by federal and state agencies. This new publicly owned commons proved challenging both to create and to manage. Like most commons systems, it was hotly contested terrain. And it was not without its victims. Yet the creation of national forests, difficult and contested as it was, also ushered in a new era of vitality for the wooded mountain commons. It enabled continuity in commons experience and traditions even as it brought change in forest management and regulation. And although it did not bring an end to enclosure threats, it did eventually enable local people to combat these threats in ways that would have been nearly impossible if the forests had been privately owned.

The process of creating national forests in the southern mountains was long and complicated. It began decades before the Weeks Act of 1911 and the official designation of the Pisgah National Forest in 1916, and it continued for decades after. It involved a diverse array of mountain people—farmers, businessmen, scientists, politicians; rich, poor, and middling; young and old; rural and urban; landowner and tenant; native and newcomer. Some welcomed the national forests' arrival and expansion; others resisted their creation and growth.

Under the Forest Service, privately owned land that had long been used as if it were commons forest became publicly owned land—actual commons forest. High ridges and midslopes typically went to the Forest Service, while richer bottomlands and lower slopes remained in private hands. Thus, the pattern of Forest Service ownership replicated in de jure form long-established de facto commons patterns: lowlands were private grounds; highlands were public woods.[6]

The Forest Service's combination of benign neglect, zealous fire suppression, erosion control, and limited reforestation also enabled cutover mountain forests to recover some of their former richness. And the agency's multiple-use mandate dovetailed nicely with traditional commons practice. Thus, the industrial onslaught on the southern mountain forests indirectly enabled the continuation and even the revitalization of the wooded highland commons.[7]

The Weeks Act in Western North Carolina

When President Howard Taft signed the Weeks Act into law on March 1, 1911, it was as if he had sounded a starting gun in Washington, D.C., and the southern Appalachians. Within a week the National Forest Reservation Commission had been appointed, had held its first meeting, and had chosen Secretary of War Henry L. Stimson as its presiding officer. During the decade before the Weeks Act became law, the Forest Service had anticipated its advent and had worked to prepare purchase unit boundary proposals. Now it rushed to put finishing touches on these proposals and deliver them to the commission.[8]

The term "purchase unit" initially referred to a body of land at the headwaters of a navigable river, at least one hundred thousand acres in size, and deemed suitable for federal purchase under the act. Once the commission had approved purchase unit boundaries, the Forest Service would have authority to advertise for and pursue specific tracts within them. When sufficient lands in an area had been obtained, the agency would designate the lands a national forest. The Forest Service did not have to acquire all lands within the purchase unit before creating national forests. In fact, it proved nearly impossible to acquire more than a fraction of the land within a given purchase unit boundary in the East. In the last quarter of the twentieth century, after decades of purchasing, most national forests in the southern Appalachians included only a third to half the authorized purchase unit area, though in a few places the percentage edged as high as two-thirds.[9]

But all this lay in the future. After the Weeks Act passed, the immediate task was to designate purchase units. Forest Service chief Henry Graves—Gifford Pinchot's hand-picked successor—quickly delegated thirty-five men to the task of finalizing purchase unit proposals. In early March the agency scrambled to finish surveying and mapping suggested purchase units, and it quickly delivered these proposals to the newly appointed commission. Before month's end that body had approved thirteen purchase units, seven of them in the southern Appalachians. Of these, five included lands in western North Carolina—Mount Mitchell, Nantahala, Pisgah, Smoky Mountains, and Yadkin. In 1912 the commission established four more purchase units in the southern mountains, and three of these—Boone, Georgia, and Unaka—included North Carolina lands.[10]

Most purchase units were actually much larger than the stipulated minimum of 100,000 acres. Nearly all in the southern mountains topped 200,000 acres, with only the Yadkin as an exception—and even that included more than 194,000. The Mount Mitchell unit encompassed nearly 215,000 acres, and the Boone some 240,000. The Pisgah unit incorporated over 358,000 acres, while the Unaka and Georgia units stood around 475,000 each. Nantahala and Smoky Mountains topped the list, as Nantahala came in just under 600,000 acres and Smoky Mountains just over.[11]

Western North Carolina, which had long been at the epicenter of the eastern national forest movement, thus emerged as a keystone in the eastern federal forest system. Almost half of the original seventeen eastern purchase units created in 1911 and 1912 included North Carolina lands, as did eight of the eleven southern Appalachian boundaries. Of the eight purchase units that included North Carolina acreage, four lay entirely within the state: Mount Mitchell, Pisgah, Yadkin, and Boone. Together these accounted for just over one million targeted acres. The two largest units, Smoky Mountains and Nantahala, straddled the North Carolina–Tennessee line. North Carolina also claimed shares of the two next largest—the Georgia, which it shared with that state, and the Unaka, which it shared with Tennessee. At least a third of the total purchase unit acreage in the southern Appalachians—and probably some 1.7 million of a total 4 million acres—lay in North Carolina. Thus, the state hosted a substantially greater subset of proposed eastern forests than any other.[12]

Western North Carolina's Pisgah and Nantahala were also among the earliest of the eastern national forests. The National Forest Reservation Commission's first purchase was a North Carolina tract in McDowell County, near Marion. This 8,100-acre tract, previously owned by the Burke McDowell Lumber Company, changed hands in December 1911 and eventually became part of the Pisgah National Forest. The Forest Service purchased the real nucleus of the Pisgah—some 87,000 acres—from the Biltmore Estate. The agency began purchase negotiations in 1913, but George Vanderbilt died before the parties reached agreement. His widow, Edith Vanderbilt, continued the process and finalized the sale in 1914. She requested the "Pisgah" name be kept. The Pisgah became the first official Appalachian national forest in 1916.[13]

In 1918 Virginia's Natural Bridge and Shenandoah National Forests joined the Pisgah, and in 1920 five more federal forests received official recognition in the region. These included the Boone, Nantahala, and Unaka, which lay partially or entirely in North Carolina; the Monongahela in West Virginia; and the Cherokee in Tennessee. Boundaries and names changed substantially in the early days. In North Carolina only the Pisgah and Nantahala retained their original names, as the Cherokee also did in Tennessee. North Carolina's Boone National Forest existed for only a few months and was subsumed into the Pisgah in 1921. The multistate Unaka lasted a bit longer but was divided among the Pisgah, Cherokee, and Virginia's Jefferson National Forest in 1923 and 1936. The Nantahala originally included lands in Tennessee, but as multistate forests proved especially difficult to administer, these holdings eventually were sheared away to be incorporated into the Cherokee. Similarly, parts of the Cherokee lay in North Carolina. In 2009 some three hundred acres still did.[14]

The original purchase unit boundaries met a range of fates. The Yadkin unit, for example, was essentially stillborn. It never saw much activity and yielded no purchases. Though it remained on the books in 2009, it was effectively moribund and had been for the better part of a century.[15]

The Smoky Mountain unit also went belly-up, but for different reasons. The Forest Service demonstrated some initial enthusiasm about this purchase unit, the largest in the East. By 1912 agency crews had begun work in the area, examining and surveying tracts offered by—among others—the Little River Lumber Company, one of the district's largest landholders. Several smallholders had received National Forest Reservation Commission approval for their offers by the following year. More groundwork went forward, and some eight thousand Little River Lumber acres had also received purchase approval by 1915. But no sales were ever finalized. Despite the significant early investment, land title research in the unit uncovered a legal landscape so impossibly thorny that by 1923 the USFS had essentially abandoned its efforts. It was not at all clear the Little River Company actually held title to its many claims, and the company eventually revoked its offer to sell. Seeing no way forward, the National Forest Reservation Commission dissolved the purchase unit. Partly as a result of the Forest Service's inability to gain a Smokies foothold, in the 1920s a renewed national park movement focused its efforts in that area.[16]

Work on the Mount Mitchell unit ran into similar, though less pronounced, difficulties. Again, legal questions loomed, and this time the agency also encountered resolute local resistance. But the Forest Service did acquire lands in the unit, and these eventually became part of the Pisgah National Forest. Lumber companies maintained control over much of the section, however, and beginning in 1912 they clearcut its lush spruce-fir growth so completely as to render parts of the mountain virtually lunar. The Forest Service was powerless to stop this destruction. Local tourism interests and state officials grew increasingly alarmed at the rapidly deteriorating conditions on North Carolina's most famous peak. An article entitled "Destroying Mount Mitchell" appeared in the February 1915 issue of the national journal *American Forestry* and helped prod state government into action. In 1915 the North Carolina state legislature passed a bill authorizing funding for a park at the site. By 1916 the government had purchased Mitchell's summit and designated it as North Carolina's first state park.[17]

Thus, the original eight North Carolina purchase units established in 1911 and 1912 yielded wildly different results. Yadkin never got started, and Smoky Mountains imploded after an energetic beginning. Despite a rocky start, Mount Mitchell generated some acreage, which eventually became part of the Pisgah National Forest. Successful acquisition of the sweeping Vanderbilt lands guaranteed a future for Pisgah. Though lower profile than the Vanderbilt sale, a number of large timber-company purchases in the Nantahala unit put a solid foundation under the Nantahala National Forest. Boone and Unaka flourished enough to become independent national forests but enjoyed this status only briefly. The entire Boone soon merged into the Pisgah, as did the North Carolina portion of the Unaka. It is not clear precisely what happened to North Carolina portions of the Georgia unit, which straddled the North Carolina–Georgia line. Tracts in Georgia eventually became part of the Chattahoochee National Forest, and any tracts purchased on the North Carolina side would ultimately have become part of the Nantahala National Forest.[18]

The period between 1911 and 1916 saw the heaviest acquisition activity in the southern Appalachians, though eastern purchases continued at a reduced but fairly steady rate through 1931. Sprawling tracts in the present-day Pisgah, Nantahala, Chattahoochee, Cherokee, and Jefferson National Forests came into federal ownership during that very early period. By 1914 the Forest Service had purchased some 850,000 acres in the southern Appalachians, an area larger than the state of Rhode Island. By 1920 the agency owned 250,000 acres in western North Carolina. Acquisitions continued at a slower pace until a second flurry of purchases took place under Franklin Delano Roosevelt's Depression era presidential administration. Before that second round began, however, the federal government had acquired over four million acres under the Weeks Act. Some of these lands were in New England's White Mountains, where the original goal had been to acquire between five hundred thousand and one million acres. Far more lay in the southern Appalachians, where the federal government initially aimed to purchase five million acres.[19]

Though many families offered small tracts of three hundred acres or less, most early purchases came from large landholders offering at least two thousand. Roughly 80 percent of the Pisgah National Forest came from twenty-nine sellers, for instance, and some 60 percent of the Nantahala came from twenty-two. Most of these lands came from timber companies and some from land speculation outfits and private estates.[20]

USFS Land Acquisition: The Process

Once the National Forest Reservation Commission authorized eastern purchase unit boundaries, the USFS quickly set about acquiring lands within those boundaries. During its first wave of large-scale eastern land acquisition—which took place between 1911, when the Weeks Act became law, and 1918, when the United States entered World War I—the federal government obtained roughly 1.25 million forest acres in the Appalachian South, an area the size of Delaware.[21] The process was long, complicated, expensive, and fraught with difficulty at nearly every turn. In Washington, Forest Service administrators pushed for speed, efficiency, and cost minimization. They felt a sense of urgency and wanted to acquire lands as quickly as possible before congressional money and interest ran out. Crews working on the ground found it difficult to complete the work as speedily and cheaply as their supervisors hoped. Chaotic title records, overlapping claims, precipitous terrain, ruthless weather, unreliable communication, limited transportation, and occasionally hostile neighbors proved formidable obstacles to smooth acquisition. At any point the process could stall or wash out entirely, no matter how much time, energy, and expense had been invested.

On its surface the acquisition process was fairly straightforward. Through advertisements in local newspapers, the Forest Service announced its interest in purchasing lands within the approved boundaries. Landowners then contacted the agency with offers to sell. The Forest Service conducted preliminary examinations of each proffered parcel for its physical condition and legal standing. If it found the unit suitable and the title clear, the Forest Service took out an option to purchase and conducted more detailed and formal examinations. The formal examinations included close scrutiny of legal titles, a timber cruise, and a survey. Detailed tract descriptions based on this work went to the National Forest Reservation Commission, along with a yea or nay purchase recommendation and a suggested price.

The commission considered each tract and either approved or denied purchase. For approved parcels, it set prices. Landowners could accept or decline the official government offer. They could also hold out for higher payments. If that happened, the USFS resubmitted paperwork on the tract to the commission, along with a price recommendation. If it recommended a price higher than the original offer, the agency explained its rationale. Similarly, if it advocated sticking to the original price, it justified that position. Again the commission ruled on the parcel in question. Extended price negotiations could repeat the process many times, as happened in the case of the Vanderbilt lands.

Once an offer had been accepted and a contract signed, the machinery of final payment and title transfer began. It moved at a glacial pace. The Forest Service conducted formal surveys of the parcels and worked to resolve any outstanding legal questions. The agency lacked manpower adequate to the task of processing the huge number of tracts it purchased, and a backlog built up, both of title research and of survey work. Even once these tasks had been completed, further delays lurked. In some cases there was a wait for funds to become available. The final exchange occurred months (in the best cases) or even several years after the commission's ultimate decision.[22]

Difficulties plagued every step of this process, from the initial tract and title examination straight through to the final payment and title transfer. The Forest Service considered streamlining the process by condemning lands outright—by exercising the government's power of eminent domain, as later occurred with Park Service lands in the Smokies, Shenandoah, and Blue Ridge Parkway. This option proved especially attractive when price negotiations dragged on, making an already cumbersome and expensive process even more difficult and costly. The agency opted not to pursue this path, however, and continued to purchase lands from willing sellers at negotiated prices. It used only "friendly condemnation," a tool for clearing land titles in otherwise impossibly tangled cases.[23]

Mapping the Land

In order to purchase and manage lands in the southern mountains, the federal government must first gain an intellectual foothold in the region—it must rationalize and make coherent the intricate, dizzyingly complex highland landscape. Maps proved crucial to this effort. Mapmaking occurred in practically every phase of the process and served as a central pillar in the government's acquisition efforts (see figure 6).[24]

Ultimately, the Forest Service needed detailed survey maps distinguishing precise boundaries of properties it acquired. Landholders could almost never provide such maps. Drawings therefore had to be painstakingly created, usually by examination and survey crews working long hours on the ground.

The U.S. Geological Survey had compiled topographical maps of the region, but otherwise the Forest Service found itself working in an information vacuum. Local governments typically could not even supply the agency with maps showing a county's basic outlines. Immediately after the Weeks Act passed, the Washington office wrote to every western North Carolina county requesting a map. It hoped to purchase maps indicating the county borders, major townships, and as much as possible the boundaries of particular landholdings in the county. In reply after reply local officials regretted their inability to fulfill these requests.

As A. L. Hardin, Transylvania County surveyor, informed the Forest Service, "There has never been any County Map." County officials used the Geological Survey maps, he explained. J. C. Drake, surveyor for Henderson County, had much the same message. "There is no map . . . that I know of," he wrote, "that will give you the information that you want." Jackson County's T. R. Zachary echoed this view and concluded that "it would be hard to get the information you seem to want."[25]

This lack of basic information proved a formidable barrier. Time and time again, before the Forest Service could turn attention to a particular acquisition proposal, it had to put money and manpower toward establishing essential starting points.

The most dramatic example came in the Nantahala area, where the Forest Service surveyed the nearly thirty-mile Macon-Swain county line for the first time. The boundary between the two counties had been established in 1871, but no formal survey had ever been done. As USFS crews worked on tracts in the Nantahala purchase unit, they found they needed to know precisely where this county line lay. By 1914 the agency had concluded that there was no way, short of assigning one of its own teams to the project, to determine the boundary's exact location.[26]

Swain and Macon officials offered to contribute monies toward a formal survey, but there was no mechanism in place for the USFS to accept payment from outside sources. Even if there had been, the counties' proffered $70 would have covered only a tiny fraction of the total cost, which the Forest Service calculated at more than $900. A full USFS survey crew spent most of the summer of 1914 on the county line project. It was the most difficult, expensive, and time-consuming endeavor that crew undertook that season.[27]

Percy Ferebee accounted for the high cost of the survey and the long timeline it required in a report to supervisors in Washington. "The country through which the Macon-Swain County Line runs is so rough," he explained, "that offsetting is impracticable and you run three times a total distance of 29.55 miles to get a true line without offsetting." In other words, his crew trekked some ninety working miles in its effort to properly map the boundary, and this in country so steep and rugged as to make ordinary survey methods impossible.[28]

Ferebee was not the first to find the costs of mapping western North Carolina forests dismayingly high. George Vanderbilt commissioned a topographic map of Biltmore Forest's 7,250 acres, "the best map I had ever seen," Carl Schenck observed. It gave contour intervals every five feet. The forest management map Gifford Pinchot included at the beginning of his 1893 World's Fair pamphlet was based on that more detailed chart. The fine Biltmore Forest map cost Vanderbilt the staggering sum of $30,000. When Schenck requested a similar map for the roughly one hundred thousand acres under his care, even Vanderbilt balked at the expense. Assuming parallel costs, the price tag would have run beyond $400,000. Schenck remembered the incident as one of only two times his employer rebuffed him. But the German forester considered a good topographic map essential; without it, he wrote, "my task in Pisgah Forest could not be accomplished." Vanderbilt had a sketch map of the entire property, and he told Schenck that drawing must suffice. When the Forest Service bought Pisgah, they found the Vanderbilt crew still had only vague—"sketch map"—ideas about the forest's boundaries.[29]

Gradually, through countless hours spent researching titles, seeking out old landmarks, surveying boundaries, and sometimes just improvising, the

Forest Service filled out myriad blank spaces and developed detailed maps of the properties it purchased. In some places old boundary trees simply could not be located, and then the USFS asked neighboring property owners to sign agreements establishing new corners.[30] In the most dramatic instances, court decisions or legislation ultimately finalized official boundaries. But in most cases, painstaking work in courthouses and on the ground eventually yielded results, and the Appalachian forest gradually bloomed with stakes marked "U.S." Reams and reams of gathered documents in the National Archives and state national forest offices testify to the enormously laborious process behind USFS land acquisition and behind the daunting task of establishing an intellectual foothold on the Appalachian landscape.

Measuring the Timber

Establishing formal boundaries marked only one step in the process of rationalizing the Appalachian forests. For foresters, a second crucial step involved calculating timber values. Here too the southern Appalachian forests proved challenging.

Foresters considered only a handful of species when estimating a tract's timber value. They mentally transformed living trees of these species into a relatively short list of timber forest products. They usually ignored or decried other species, and "nontimber forest products" such as ginseng, moss, galax, mushrooms, and animal hides did not enter into their calculations. Nor did other goods and services, such as clean water and aesthetic values. Yet despite the comparative simplicity of their methods, Appalachian tracts proved very difficult to evaluate.[31]

Foresters used "volume tables" to calculate trees' timber value. These volume tables, which were specific to each species, enabled men on the ground to estimate a tree's monetary worth based on its overall height and its diameter at breast height, or DBH. Volume tables could help a forester estimate how many board feet of lumber a tree would yield, or how many cords of firewood, or how many fence posts.

In July 1911 R. Clifford Hall wrote from a camp in the Nantahala unit, outlining "several questions" that "have arisen in connection with working up the estimates." "We are dividing this tract into estimate units on a watershed basis," he explained, "and will figure out the average acre for each type [of forest product] on each estimate unit. I believe that this method will give the most satisfactory results for this region." To record his calculations he requested "100 of the smaller sized computing sheets . . . ruled for tabulation." But before he could complete the work he needed guidance from D.C. First, nothing in the best available handbook of volume tables treated trees under fourteen inches DBH. But Hall had instructions to include all trees ten inches DBH or larger. How should he work up estimates for the smaller trees? Hall also found himself "lacking suitable tables" for a host of species, including black birch, basswood, hickory, locust, black gum, and pitch pine. How should he handle these species? And was there a table available for estimating locust fence-post yield?[32]

The Washington office sent Hall some additional volume tables but suggested he approximate in many cases. Hall's supervisor proposed a method for calculating smaller trees' board-foot yield, which, while not especially accurate, would yield numbers "conservative and sufficiently reliable." The D.C. office found tables for hickory and pitch pine but said that for black birch, basswood, locust, and black gum "there are no reliable figures." Hall would just have to do the best he could. Similarly, for locust posts the office suggested Hall work out his own conversion estimates. "It is probable that the system of estimating that you are now using," the supervisor continued, "will be adopted throughout the work." In other words, Hall was breaking trail for other estimators working in the region, and whatever he invented would likely become the standard.[33]

By 1914 the Forest Service had developed fill-in-the-blank tables for examiners to use. The forms asked men in the field to note ten species of trees and to record the "stand per acre" and the "stumpage value per unit" for each. Using these numbers, field crews were to calculate the sawtimber "stumpage value per acre" of each species for a given tract. The table also included entry blanks for eight other forest products: extract wood, hemlock and oak bark, hemlock and poplar pulp, white oak railroad ties, and poles and posts. Examiners were to calculate the average value per acre of sawtimber, add the average value per acre of other products, and add this total to the average value per acre of the land itself. The resulting sum yielded the USFS "total value per acre of tract." At least one crew leader found these forms mystifying and returned a package of them to D.C., believing they must have been sent by mistake.[34]

Logistical Challenges

As it gathered necessary information, the Forest Service confronted formidable logistical challenges on the ground in rugged western North Carolina. Transportation proved difficult, communication erratic, and weather onerous. Even the most basic tasks—getting crews of six to eight men to examination and survey sites, housing and feeding them adequately once there, and enabling them to report on their work and to receive orders from D.C.—proved fraught with difficulty. Again and again the agency lost time, money, and labor to undelivered communications, arduous travel, delayed supply shipments, and debilitating weather.

A cable telegram R. Clifford Hall sent to D.C. headquarters on his first venture into western North Carolina in 1911 hinted at the difficulties ahead. "Must enter track with Pack animals," Hall wired.[35] Another telegram, from the Washington office to the field, proved undeliverable. "Party 6 miles in country," Western Union reported. "No telephone. We had to mail a copy." In 1912 Harold G. Wood wrote a message to his supervisors underscoring the difficulties he faced. "More than half of this month's work necessitated a walk of from 2 to 4 miles to and from camp," he noted. "Country very rough."[36] Hall had done Weeks Act work in Georgia but found North Carolina's mountains even more challenging. "The small size of most of the tracts offered and the roughness of the country limits the extent of the section that can be covered from a single camp to an area much smaller than was possible in Georgia," he wrote to the D.C. office.[37]

Crew chiefs struggled to fit the difficult realities of Weeks Act fieldwork into standard reporting forms. In a work report for October 1911, O. D. Ingall broke down into six categories the 233 total man-days an eleven-man team had spent on Nantahala examinations. His list included days spent conducting strip surveys, days spent on base and boundary work, days spent on office work, and the like. Ingall also placed eleven man-days in a revealing category he labeled "Lost, rain, failure to locate land, etc."[38] This category seems not to have gone over well with Ingall's D.C. bosses; it disappeared in the November report, never to be seen again. Eventually, Washington provided a bad weather category, but there was no formal mechanism for crew chiefs to report time lost attempting to locate boundaries or wandering rudderless in the woods.[39]

Wet weather could make examination work difficult or impossible and bring misery to life in the camps. "A very wet month," wrote Harold G. Wood from the Nantahala area in July 1912, "the crew being wet for over twenty consecutive days, with the exception of intervening Sunday. Camp equipment and bedding wet during this time."[40] The following year James Denman's crew worked through another wet July in the same purchase boundary. "Weather: Rainy," wrote Denman. "Remarks: High cost per mile due to rainy weather, excessive heavy laurel growth encountered & remote location of camp relative to base of supplies."[41]

Winter weather posed another set of challenges. "I feel that the work is going very well despite the short days, inaccessibility, and cold weather,"

Ingall reported in early November 1911. "The party has had no accidents or ill health and the men are all hard workers & do excellent work considering their comparative inexperience."[42] Two weeks later he sounded a note of concern. His crew had no heat source other than an open fire, as the camp stoves he ordered had not yet arrived. Ingall blamed "the procrastination & prevarication of the native teamsters" for the delay. He hoped the equipment would soon appear; he knew it had left Andrews five days earlier. "The conditions are such that it is well nigh impossible to see ahead more than a few days at a time," he wrote. "I shall be better able to give an opinion on how long the weather will let us work by the end of the week. Last night was the coldest so far. At eight o'clock this morning the thermometer registered 14 degrees."[43] By December, even with stoves, Ingall was ready to close up shop. His crew had soldiered on so far. "The local surveyors however say that January & February are usually very bad months here," he warned. "The snow and ice on the rocky north slopes makes the going both dangerous and slow. The roads also from now on get steadily worse & moving and getting in supplies are growing increasingly difficult. I think perhaps it would be better to call off the work here as soon as it can be wound up and move out of here."[44]

As Ingall's reference to getting in supplies indicated, housing and feeding woods crews could be quite challenging. At one point in 1911, perhaps as a response to the difficulty of transporting supplies to backwoods camps, the Forest Service toyed with the idea of requiring some examination parties to live "on the country." Someone in D.C. apparently thought the men could accomplish the work while providing themselves with a steady diet of wild game and fresh berries. Hall quite vigorously opposed this idea. He lobbied for a continuation of the current system, which he thought already challenging enough. "Conditions are such," he reported, "that the men suffer from lack of sleep and digestible food, and besides being unable to do their best work, soon become greatly dissatisfied."[45] His phrase "lack of digestible food" leaves one wondering exactly what the USFS fed its crews. Maybe the men would have been better off fending for themselves after all; with any luck, they might have bagged a wild turkey and served it with roasted chestnuts.

Harold G. Wood's 1912 crew seems to have fared better, at least in the matter of rations. "As to my cook," Wood wrote, "I would be totally at sea should I lose him for he cannot be equaled in this country and it is mainly through him and his efforts that such good harmony has existed in my crew this season."[46] This team especially needed creature comforts, as former chief M. Stuart Davis apparently robbed the men by absconding with their USFS paychecks. It took a long time to straighten out the resulting financial mess, and the crew went unpaid for months. Also, this group suffered near-continuous rain and sodden bedding in the month of July. Yet Wood claimed "good harmony." Cook Canada Fouts must indeed have been a wonder.[47]

Even when examination sites were accessible enough to be worked from town bases, arranging accommodations could prove challenging. In 1914 Hall pleaded for haste in his crew's new assignment. "It would be well to have the instructions for the disposition of the men reach me by Feb 10 without fail," he wrote from the Mount Mitchell area on February 6. "Our 'land lady' refuses to keep the woods crew after that date; in fact, has been keeping us under protest since the first of the month owing to the early breakfast required by the woods crew. The regular boarding house is full, and it would be very difficult to find accommodations for a few days or a week."[48]

On other occasions, proprietors proved more accommodating. Assigned to set straight the M. Stuart Davis embezzlement debacle, Ingall asked permission to pay two Franklin businesspeople whose fees Davis had also taken. "The lady who runs the hotel says she does not know the amount of the bill as she left it to Davis to calculate and merely signed receipts on his promise to settle up later," he wrote from Kyle. Davis had turned in the USFS paperwork, including receipts, and then skipped town once the money arrived. "Of course I have only the word of these people," Ingall wrote, "but they are both people of very good reputation and I personally am willing to take their word in the matter. At any rate I shall pay these bills myself very shortly as the people around here very naturally hold me responsible in a way and I have already guaranteed them payment of these bills."[49]

In general, relations between USFS crews and local businesspeople seem to have been cordial, as Ingall's post-Davis correspondence suggests. Concerns about local business rarely made their way to Washington. Ingall's "prevaricating teamsters" and Hall's landlady "under protest" seem to have been exceptions. The Weeks Act crew leaders made hundreds of transactions with local merchants, proprietors, and teamsters, and in general these seem to have flowed smoothly, never registering in Washington beyond routine paperwork.

Another of Ingall's reports in the wake of the Davis embezzlement scandal hints at the scale of routine Weeks Act business. Urging the Washington office to fast-track payments to the people Davis had robbed, Ingall wrote, "We owe one of these small country merchants $150. They cannot get credit with their wholesalers for any great amount nor any length of time."[50] The sum Ingall mentioned probably represented about two months' supplies for Davis's woods crew. Assuming this to be a fairly representative number and remembering that Davis also robbed the local hotel proprietor, it becomes clear the USFS examination effort represented a significant boost to local economies.

USFS Land Acquisition: Examination and Survey Challenges

As the Forest Service went about the work of examination, challenges originated both on the ground and in the courthouse. In the initial phase of the acquisition process, government agents conducted physical examinations of proffered tracts and also investigated owners' legal claims to title for those tracts. Establishing clear titles proved particularly taxing, but neither process was without its difficulties.

During physical examinations, government crews visited sites and walked over them, gathering information to include in descriptive reports for the USFS. Teams conducted preliminary technical surveys of a property, recorded its use history, described its current conditions, and estimated its timber value. If the acquisition process moved forward, versions of their reports eventually went to the National Forest Reservation Commission.

Physical examinations proved difficult for several reasons. First, owners sometimes had only vague notions of where boundary lines lay or of how much acreage they actually owned. In some cases their claims were outright false. These problems became even more apparent at the stage of formal surveying, but they reared their heads already in early examinations. Even when owners offered particulars, it was sometimes difficult to locate tracts, as knowledgeable guides were not always available and landmark descriptions could be idiosyncratic. Also, the parcels in question often included rugged terrain that was extremely demanding to navigate. Finally, rough weather often slowed the work or even prevented it altogether, especially as winter came on.[51]

These difficulties became clear almost as soon as government crews arrived in western North Carolina. Forest Service personnel confronted them repeatedly in 1911. Ingall reported on one elusive tract in the Nantahala area: "I tried to locate the land according to [the landholder's] directions and lost thereby four one man days." He advocated that the agency drop these lands from its agenda, as they proved impossible "to examine in an economical way."[52] About a different tract in the same vicinity, Ingall informed his supervisors that "the boundaries are in such shape that we can only hope to get a very approximate estimate."[53] USFS lumberman Daniel W. Adams reported on a tract in the Mount Mitchell area: "I had some trouble locating their lands but later, I was informed that they were located on Chestnut Wood Mountain and that 'Newberry's Fork' referred to in the description is a portion of Curtis Creek." Adams also noted a case in which timber company officials "decline to furnish [a] guide to show these lands." He believed his time would be best spent elsewhere. "However," he concluded in a letter to Washington, "if you desire, I will endeavor to locate their lands."[54]

Similar difficulties arose when formal survey teams moved in. In 1914 James Denman led a crew surveying the Vanderbilt lands for the Pisgah unit. He found that "no one either in Vanderbilt employ or otherwise seems to know much about the location of their lands on the ground."[55] Given Vanderbilt's enormous resources and the property's history of professional management, Pisgah Forest tracts should have been among the best mastered in the region. Nevertheless, even here USFS personnel found themselves facing an enormous basic challenge: to determine where exactly the proprietor's holdings lay.

R. F. Hemingway, writing from the Nantahala unit in 1915, echoed these frustrations. He and his team had worked diligently on preparing an ownership map for the unit, he said, but had run into "numerous obstacles." These had come "in the shape of incomplete and inaccurate descriptions, no descriptions at all, the hesitancy with which owners produced their descriptions, surface measurement," a lack of map support from Washington, a heavy administrative workload, and a run of terrible weather. They would do the best they could, but in this case, as in so many, they would not make the deadline Washington had set.[56]

A humorous story circulating in the early USFS acquisition period underscored the herculean character of the tasks field crews confronted. "I am told," wrote William L. Hall in 1914, of a land grant that "began at a white cow on a mountain side. Needless to say, the white cow cannot now be located." Though this purported grant was probably apocryphal, invented to poke fun at an infuriating situation, the joke highlighted a very real problem. "At a mud hole in the road" was an official description Gifford Pinchot remembered for one boundary corner of a farm George Vanderbilt purchased. A USFS researcher in Macon County came across one grant that officially "started in a brook." Landmarks like these proved only slightly less elusive than the fabled white cow.[57]

USFS Land Acquisition: Title Claims Challenges

Besides conducting physical examinations, the government also researched title claims for proffered tracts. This proved to be a particularly thorny stage in the land acquisition process. Researchers for the government found, as had timber agents before them, a near-nightmarish legal mess. It is all but impossible to overstate the degree of chaos they confronted. "The title situation is about as bad," wrote William L. Hall in a cogent summary, "as a generation of men could have made it had they started out for the purpose of entangling the titles."[58] Claims overlapped, record keeping was spotty, boundaries were vague. Sometimes no written title record existed for a given tract, and sometimes multiple competing records existed. Sharp timber agents had leveraged this legal confusion to their companies' advantage, often with little regard for ethical niceties or the interests of long-term residents and claimants. "Shrewd men went through these mountains buying standing timber and paying for it with a song, if with that," wrote one historian of the region. In some cases the companies had essentially stolen the land.[59]

Government examinations occasionally turned up this chicanery; in a few cases timber company claims turned out to have no legal standing whatsoever. Daniel W. Adams reported that one company's claimed offer of 2,560 acres had proved, upon only cursory legal examination, to include at most a scant 560 acres. Adams expected even that reduced number not to hold. "I doubt very seriously the validity of their claims," he wrote to the Washington office.[60] Companies such as this one had further convoluted an already problematic state of legal affairs. Coming into the region on their heels, Forest Service agents confronted an even more challenging legal landscape than that the companies had themselves encountered.

In one especially complex Nantahala case, dozens of competing claims proved impossible to untangle over the course of decades. In 1868 the Treasury Department had confiscated lands formerly belonging to E. B. Olmstead in the aftermath of his embezzling from the Post Office. Treasury deeded the parcels to Agriculture in 1912. When the Forest Service arrived to examine the lands in 1913, chaos ensued. Scores of local people claimed portions of the property and "were not generally aware of the Government's claim to ownership." Some claims were sorted out successfully, but many persisted. In the end federal legislation—the 1934 Weaver Act—proved necessary to cut through this Gordian knot, satisfy all twenty-two remaining claimants, and establish clear title for the government.[61]

As the Olmstead case underscores, federal agents demonstrated much greater concern than timber agents to establish the legitimacy of title claims and to settle with claimants on terms to which these claimants agreed. They made serious efforts to unravel complicated and conflicting claims and to sort through title records as fully as possible. Several sources of motivation lay behind these efforts.

Unlike typical timber companies, the USFS planned to have a long-term presence in the region. Perceptive officials understood that today's sellers were tomorrow's neighbors, and they wished to begin on good terms with these neighbors as often as possible.

Also, the USFS, as a federal agency, had goals different from those of a for-profit corporation. It was more concerned with process legitimacy. By law, it could not acquire lands if clear title could not be established. It therefore could not engage in the questionable acquisition practices some timber companies had used. Also, making money was not its raison d'être. In fact, the agency had been conceived as a response to the excesses of for-profit timbering, mining, and other resource extraction industries. Thus, although it wished to acquire lands as cheaply as possible, it could not and did not seek out opportunities to defraud landowners.

A final and related source of motivation flowed from the Forest Service's reliance on Congress for funding. This dependence made the USFS sensitive to political pressure. It did not wish to have senators and representatives flooded with mail from irate constituents railing against abuses.

This is not to say that the agency's land acquisition track record was perfect or that no landholder had legitimate reason for grievance against it. Far from it—for would-be sellers, especially smallholders, aggravation dogged every step of the process, and payment delays caused real hardship. The USFS recognized the payment lag issue, and beginning in 1913 field agents repeatedly advocated that it be addressed. Despite their efforts, problems persisted. The Forest Service blamed government attorneys for failing to streamline the process. In 1940 a USFS report summed up the agency's frustration. "Much ill will results from preposterous delays in making final payment because of highly technical legal demands from legal authorities," researchers affirmed. The Forest Service had "fought for years for a more rational handling" of payment issues, but "little real progress has been made until just recently." Whatever the reason, it is certainly true that payment delays plagued the USFS acquisition process throughout its peak stages and that many landowners suffered—sometimes acutely—as a result.[62]

Nevertheless, it is also entirely clear that the USFS amassed a far more admirable record in the southern Appalachians than the timber and coal companies it often supplanted. Its methods were also less high-handed toward local landowners than those later used to obtain National Park Service and TVA lands in the region.[63]

1930s Purchases

The Great Depression had dramatic effects on the southern Appalachian region and ushered in a second period of large-scale USFS land acquisition. The 1924 Clarke-McNary Act helped set the stage for this development by expanding the rationale for federal forest purchases. The Weeks Act had allowed only purchases that would protect headwaters of navigable streams. Clarke-McNary enlarged "headwaters" to "watersheds," thus considerably increasing the area eligible for purchase. The 1924 act also added "production of timber" as a purchase justification, a change swelling the agency's purchasing authority virtually without bounds.[64]

The southern Appalachian region felt the force of the nationwide economic collapse acutely. Industry declined precipitately. Timber production had peaked in 1909, and it now fell dramatically. In Georgia, for example, one thousand sawmill operations closed between 1929 and 1932. Coal production had already been stagnant in the 1920s, and it too decreased steeply after 1929. By 1933 the industry's workforce had dropped to a quarter-century low. The textile industry also suffered, throwing thousands out of work.[65]

At the same time, a kind of perfect storm collapsed agriculture in the region. That sector too had shown signs of crisis during the 1920s in the Appalachians as throughout the country. Now, in the 1930s, unemployed industrial workers reversed the region's long out-migration trend and headed to mountain homeplaces in hopes of scratching out a living. But area soils could no longer sustain the slash-and-burn techniques that had characterized mountain agriculture for generations. Nor could old systems of neighborly exchange and caring suffice to meet huge basic needs.[66]

To make matters worse, the chestnut blight hit at precisely the same time. The deadly fungus removed the giant trees that had long provided reliable food sources for humans, wildlife, and livestock. Mountain communities also lost an important cash crop as disease collapsed the profitable chestnut trade.[67]

This multipronged crisis showed up in dramatic fashion as land prices plummeted and tax delinquency rates soared across the region. Land valued at five dollars per acre in 1925 in upland Georgia lost 40 percent of its value, falling to three dollars by 1934, with no buyers even at that price. In

North Carolina's eastern Blue Ridge—the area around the headwaters of the Yadkin–Pee Dee River system—over 50 percent of farmlands and some 33 percent of forestlands had fallen into tax delinquency at the height of the crisis. A few counties in that vicinity saw delinquency rates rise as high as 90 percent.[68]

President Franklin Delano Roosevelt saw the national forests as critical elements in his New Deal recovery plans. Within a month of his inauguration in March 1933, Roosevelt had convinced Congress to pass the Emergency Conservation Work Act, which aimed to put young unemployed men to work in a series of nationwide conservation efforts. A few weeks later, the first Civilian Conservation Corps (CCC) camp had opened in the George Washington National Forest in highland Virginia. By July the CCC housed three hundred thousand men in camps around the nation.[69] In the program's beginning, the Forest Service employed all CCC recruits. Other agencies eventually became involved, but at least half the "CCC boys" worked on the national forests throughout the program's nine-year duration.[70]

Before the end of his famous first "100 days" in office, Franklin Roosevelt issued an executive order designating $20 million for eastern national forestland purchases. Like the Weeks Act before it, this order served as a kind of starting gun for a flurry of acquisition activity in the southern mountains. Almost immediately a new host of surveyors, timber cruisers, title examiners, land agents, secretaries, assistants, and the like appeared in the region, and a new round of office securing, equipment procuring, housing, and feeding began.[71]

Emergency Conservation Work leaders pointed out that it would be less cumbersome and less expensive for the federal government to buy lands in the East as employment sites for young CCC recruits than it would be to shoulder the logistical burdens and financial costs of shipping eastern men to western job sites. Throngs of young jobless men inhabited eastern cities, and prices for Appalachian land had hit rock bottom. With these facts in mind, Emergency Conservation Work, which ran the CCC, allocated $10 million from its budget for eastern forestland purchases in 1934.[72]

New Deal architects also considered eastern forestland purchases to serve another key goal, that of easing rural suffering. Through a host of initiatives, the New Deal took aim at agricultural reform and alleviating rural poverty. One Roosevelt administration strategy involved removing farm families from "submarginal" lands that could not support them with the idea that they might then relocate to better situations.[73] The 1933 National Industrial Recovery Act and the 1935 Emergency Relief Act expanded the federal government's land-purchasing authority, permitting it to buy lands that had been cutover and eroded. In the Appalachian region, the federal government could thus purchase unproductive lands outright and return them to forest under USFS jurisdiction. During the New Deal era, it did this on a grand scale.

Together the Nantahala and Pisgah encompassed a little under four hundred thousand acres in 1930 after nearly two decades of purchasing. Ten years later, in 1940, they had more than doubled their holdings—to a total just under eight hundred thousand acres. This pattern held across the southern Appalachians; USFS holdings in the region increased from roughly two million acres in 1930 to some five million in 1940. By 1940 the agency's southern mountain holdings surpassed the combined area of Connecticut and Delaware.[74]

Many newly acquired lands had very low price tags; some badly damaged tracts cost only two dollars an acre. A few parcels commanded much higher prices, most notably, the rare uncut Gennett Lumber Company holding that eventually became Joyce Kilmer Memorial Forest.[75]

Where USFS purchases after the Weeks Act had focused especially on large holdings, New Deal buying generally featured smaller tracts. In 1935 and 1936 the agency made hundreds of land purchases, many involving parcels fewer than two hundred acres and some of farms with fewer than ten. At one point the Forest Service thought it might acquire significant new Nantahala and Pisgah lands through the Agricultural Adjustment Administration's Land Policy Section in North Carolina. Regional forester Joseph C. Kircher submitted a list of 3,774 farms he recommended as possible additions to the two national forests, and a number of targeted farmers optioned their land. Funding for the AAA program dried up before the two agencies could hammer out a detailed agreement, however, and no purchases occurred through that channel. Through its own agency program, the USFS did acquire some of the parcels later.[76]

In 1935 a budget of $15 million enabled this purchasing, but funding levels dropped quickly after that. Between 1936 and 1941, an annual average $3 million financed USFS land purchases throughout the nation. After World War II began, even this number dropped precipitately.[77]

One aim of Forest Service purchasing in the New Deal period had been to inject cash into local economies. Land payments, the thinking went, would be felt not only by sellers themselves but also by others in their communities. But as in earlier periods, delays plagued the purchase process. As a result, despite the quick New Deal start USFS acquisition had in 1933, the effects of its purchasing were not felt until 1935 and 1936.[78]

Far more than the Weeks Act lands had, the New Deal lands brought with them a great many tenant families. Often these tenants were very poor people with nowhere else to go. This development put the Forest Service in a new and uncomfortable position as large-scale landlord. Officials worried about the ramshackle condition of many newly acquired tenant homes, for example. "Should we provide something besides bare board walls?" asked personnel, describing the answers to such questions as "above the head of the average forester."[79]

Finally, New Deal era lands were often in much worse shape than the Weeks Act era purchases had been. They were nearly all cutover, and some were badly eroded. As the 1930s wore on, the condition of offered properties generally grew worse. The USFS set its CCC crews to work repairing the damage, replanting trees, and controlling erosion. Decades later, Forest Service personnel who began work with the agency during this period vividly remembered and took great pride in these enormous restoration efforts.

End of the Acquisition Eras

Though USFS purchasing continued after the outbreak of World War II and goes on even into the present day, the agency acquired most of its Appalachian holdings before 1941. Roughly 80 percent of today's Nantahala and Pisgah National Forests, for instance, came into federal ownership before the war. In 1940 the Forest Service held 454,560 acres in the Pisgah and 325,930 in the Nantahala. These numbers edged up in the coming decades, but except for a brief recreation-driven flurry during the 1960s, the purchasing frenzy that marked the Weeks Act and New Deal eras did not return. Mountain lands grew in value during the postwar period also, especially in popular tourist areas.[80]

With its major purchases between 1914 and 1918 the Forest Service established an enormous presence in western North Carolina. By the dawn of World War II it had become the largest single landholder in the state's mountain region. By 1970 the Nantahala and Pisgah National Forests encompassed around nine hundred thousand mountain acres—at least one-tenth of the land in nearly every mountain county and over half the land in some. When the millennium turned, the Forest Service held over one million acres in western North Carolina. Together its Pisgah and Nantahala holdings encompass an area larger than the state of Rhode Island, including Narragansett Bay.

By the end of the 1930s Forest Service holdings also accounted for a substantial percentage of wooded land in the mountains, and this percentage increased as development claimed ever more private woods. The USFS mandate to manage its holdings for "multiple uses"—including small-scale as well as large-scale forest extraction—made these tracts de jure as well as de facto commons. In 1982 Macon County's *Franklin Press* noted a pattern that was true throughout the region: "The largest portion of non-posted, available-to-the-public land falls under Forest Service jurisdiction." In other words, the national forests had become the wooded commons.[81]

This publicly owned commons set western North Carolina apart from some other areas of the Appalachians. In West Virginia, for example, coal companies held most large forested tracts. Local residents treated these lands as de facto commons. Since they were privately rather than publicly held lands, however, commons users had little recourse when corporate owners bulldozed the woods. The fact of government ownership poised western North Carolina commons users to better defend their forests.[82]

During its first several decades in the southern Appalachians, the USFS served an important role as forest caretaker and restorer. Through a rigorous campaign of fire suppression, coupled with erosion control measures, reforestation efforts, and simple benign neglect, the agency helped enable one of the great conservation success stories in U.S. history. Though the ancient forests could not be replaced, lush second-growth forest eventually reclothed many damaged Appalachian slopes under USFS management.

At the same time, the agency oversaw harvest of nearly all the old-growth Appalachian forest it had purchased. Some 30 percent of the woods the USFS acquired in the years after the Weeks Act had never been cut. Almost none of that ancient forest remains today. The agency's focus on timber, together with its commitment to scientific management, led it to see old-growth forest as "overmature" or "decadent," in need of improving by harvest. As a result, the preservationist impulse that inspired Chase Ambler and others to work on behalf of federal landholding in the region went largely unfulfilled.[83]

The Forest Service's decision to buy only from willing sellers had two important long-term consequences. It produced less local animosity than the condemnation methods used to establish the Great Smoky Mountains National Park, the Shenandoah National Park, the Blue Ridge Parkway, various TVA and other government dam projects, and eventually the Mount Rogers National Recreation Area. Hostilities stemming from Shenandoah and Smokies land condemnations, for example, continued to produce headaches for the National Park Service throughout the twentieth century. Since the Forest Service had not forced mountain families to leave their homes, it did not have this set of problems. Relations between the Forest Service and local residents were not always cordial, but they were at least not marked by the displacement-driven indignation that continuously plagued the Park Service. This was true until the 1960s, when the Forest Service condemned lands in Virginia's Mount Rogers vicinity for a national recreation area.[84]

The piecemeal character of Nantahala and Pisgah holdings also stemmed from the USFS decision to purchase only from willing sellers. Where the Park Service simply drew a boundary and condemned everything within it, the Forest Service acquired lands more haphazardly. The agency's designated purchase unit boundaries were large and blocky, similar in shape to national parks. On maps of the United States the eastern national forests usually look much like the western forests (which were carved, blocklike, out of existing federal holdings) or the parks.[85]

Upon closer inspection, however—at the county level, for instance—important differences become clear. Within the forest's "proclamation boundaries" only the lands the Forest Service successfully purchased actually became national forest. Behind the blocky outline lies a series of ragged, snaking forests scattered across the landscape. George Vanderbilt's Pisgah property, for example, had private holdings patchworked through it, much to Carl Schenck's annoyance. When the Forest Service bought Pisgah, it inherited this mosaic. This pattern held throughout the East. Even the largest national forest blocks contained "inholdings" of private property entirely surrounded by publicly owned forest. The forests also included small "islands" completely surrounded by private lands. Long fingers of private property reached into the public forests, and national forest tendrils extended into private lands. Thus, any eastern national "forest" was not so much a single forest as a collection of assorted forests woven across the fabric of the landscape (see map, p. xxiii).[86]

The sheer extent of North Carolina's national forests gave weight to their presence in the region, and these convoluted boundaries insured a certain intimacy. In effect, as early as 1920 and continuing into the present day, the North Carolina national forests were "in everybody's backyard"—or at least quite literally in thousands of rural mountain backyards.[87]

FIGURE I. Like this young woman, photographed near Banner Elk in 1939, generations of western North Carolina residents have supplemented their earnings by harvesting galax in the forest commons. The floral industry has long valued galax, a native Blue Ridge plant, for its attractive leaves, which are round and glossy. Harvested leaves might end up in faraway cities such as New York or Philadelphia. Galax picking and other forms of commons harvest continue into the present day, especially on national forestlands, where gathering permits may be purchased for a small fee. Courtesy of North Carolina State Archives.

HOG DROVERS.

FIGURE 2. Western North Carolina's native forests have long played a central role in the region's economy. In the mid-nineteenth century, livestock—particularly hogs but also cattle, sheep, and turkeys—foraged in the open-range woods and became a leading Blue Ridge export. Great droves of animals, such as the hogs shown in this 1857 illustration for *Harper's New Monthly Magazine*, marched to urban markets. Hundreds of thousands of animals made the trek each fall. Sale of free-range stock brought income to countless mountain families, and many other residents earned a living by providing ancillary services such as overnight accommodations and feed for traveling animals.

FIGURE 3. The old-growth Blue Ridge forest included trees far larger than those typically found in today's second- and third-growth woods. These giants, photographed around 1910 in the Santeetlah Creek area of Graham County, North Carolina, dwarf the timbermen standing among them. The two trees in front are American chestnut, while poplar dominates the background. Both were valuable timber species. Industrial timber harvests in the first decades of the twentieth century took nearly all such towering giants. Courtesy of the Forest History Society.

FIGURE 4. The barren slopes of Mount Mitchell, photographed here in June 1923, demonstrate the devastating effects industrial timber harvests often had on Blue Ridge forests. Many operators took a "cut and get out" approach, showing little concern for the future health of the forest. A relentless cycle of fire and erosion often followed large-scale timber operations, leaving soils scorched and barren. As a result of these ravages, near-lunar landscapes of charred stumps appeared where vast forests had previously spread. Congress passed the 1911 Weeks Act and established a series of national forests in the East in response to this wholesale forest destruction. National Archives photograph.

FIGURE 5. After the Weeks Act of 1911 gave the federal government authority to purchase forestlands in the East, survey crews like this one fanned across the Appalachians. Well-educated young men from outside the mountains usually headed the crews. Local men, typically less well-educated, routinely served in lower-paid crew positions. In 1912, Jonathan Keith Esser, a Pennsylvanian who had studied forestry at the Biltmore School, worked with a crew surveying mountain tracts in North Carolina, Tennessee, and Virginia. He documented his experiences in a series of photographs. Esser's caption for this photo underscores the distance he, like other Forest Service men from outside the region, saw between himself and local people. From right to left Esser identified these crew members as himself, "Sam Detwiler, 2 native helpers, Lippincott." The local workers go unnamed. Courtesy of the Forest History Society.

FIGURE 6. Detailed mapmaking lay at the heart of Forest Service acquisition work, but mapping North Carolina's rugged mountain terrain proved extraordinarily difficult. Agency crews often found even basic starting points difficult to locate. Here, in a photo taken by Jonathan Keith Esser in 1912, a team consults with a local informant. Here too, Esser's caption illustrates the cultural divide he and other Forest Service crew members saw between themselves and the local people with whom they worked. In this case Esser emphasized local dialect: "A mountaineer 'pintin' out some of the 'kentry' from a map. The nonchalant gent against the tree is our 'chef.'" Courtesy of the Forest History Society.

FIGURE 7. After the Weeks Act, Forest Service field crews surveying tracts in the southern Appalachians worked from temporary woods camps such as this one, photographed by Jonathan Keith Esser in 1912. This "office tent" seems to have doubled as a sleeping quarters. Esser's caption pointed out his crewmates' "patent sailor hammock bed." Courtesy of the Forest History Society.

FIGURE 8. USFS crews surveying the southern Appalachians lived in the woods for months at a time. Few records of their responses to this life survive in the archives, but this beautiful photo from the spring of 1912 contains some hints. Jonathan Keith Esser framed the shot to capture the forest as well as the tent and his absorbed crewmate. His caption, "Shaw's composition of oak bottoms and 2nd story of dogwood in full bloom," suggests both his forestry training and his aesthetic appreciation of the blossoming woods. Courtesy of the Forest History Society.

FIGURE 9. After the 1976 National Forest Management Act required the Forest Service to solicit public input into forest decision making, Nantahala and Pisgah officials repeatedly faced packed halls like this one. At meetings about wilderness designation, petroleum leasing, and long-term management plans, concerned citizens such as these poured out their forest concerns. Widespread and passionate participation in such meetings throughout the Blue Ridge underscored the importance of federal forestlands to local residents. Courtesy of the Western North Carolina Alliance.

FIGURE 10. Noted outdoorsman Taylor Crockett, pictured here with one of the Plott hounds he bred as bear-hunting dogs, led an effort to win wilderness designation for the proposed Southern Nantahala Wilderness Area during the RARE II process. Crockett and many of his supporters made commons-friendly arguments on behalf of wilderness designation, emphasizing the Southern Nantahala's quality as a hunting and fishing ground and its ready accessibility to local people. They maintained that plans to clearcut in the area represented an enclosure threat, and they cast wilderness designation as an effective tool of commons defense. Their efforts paid off, and the Southern Nantahala became the only entirely new wilderness area created in western North Carolina as a result of the RARE II process. Courtesy of North Carolina Wildlife Resources Commission.

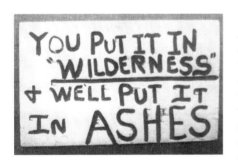

FIGURE 11. The southern Appalachian region proved a hotbed of antiwilderness activism during the RARE II process of the late 1970s. Wilderness opponents used commons-friendly arguments to draw mountain residents to their cause, casting themselves as agents of commons defense and wilderness designation as a form of commons enclosure. These arguments successfully tapped deep wells of commons attachment, as this forthright hand-lettered sign illustrates. The sign appeared in Georgia's Chattahoochee National Forest, which bordered North Carolina's Nantahala. In a classic commons defense move, messages such as this threatened "enclosed" wilderness with retaliatory arson. U.S. Forest Service photograph. Courtesy of Chattahoochee National Forest.

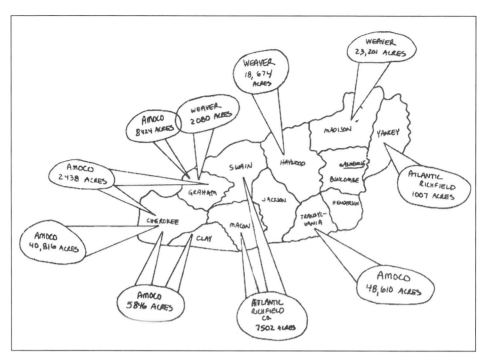

FIGURE 12. In the early 1980s, petroleum companies leased hundreds of thousands of acres in western North Carolina, including nearly all the Pisgah and Nantahala National Forests. This situation alarmed many forest users, who worried that oil and gas development would destroy the woods for other uses. Esther Cunningham and David Liden organized the Western North Carolina Alliance in response to the lease issue. An early WNCA newsletter carried this illustration showing how much acreage three leading companies had leased in each county. Courtesy of the Western North Carolina Alliance.

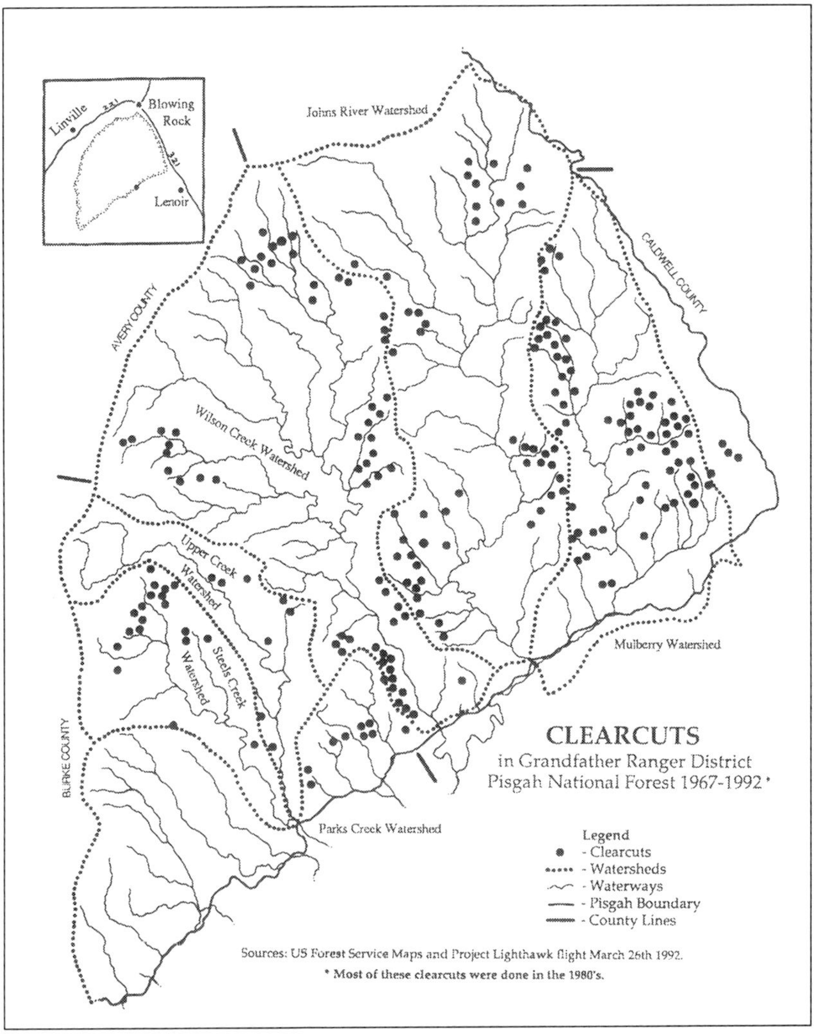
Linville
221
Blowing Rock
221
Lenoir
Johns River Watershed
CALDWELL COUNTY
AVERY COUNTY
Wilson Creek Watershed
Upper Creek Watershed
Steels Creek Watershed
Mulberry Watershed
BURKE COUNTY
Parks Creek Watershed
CLEARCUTS
in Grandfather Ranger District
Pisgah National Forest 1967-1992 *
Legend
- Clearcuts
- Watersheds
- Waterways
- Pisgah Boundary
- County Lines
Sources: US Forest Service Maps and Project Lighthawk flight March 26th 1992.
* Most of these clearcuts were done in the 1980's.

FIGURE 13. In the decades after World War II, the Forest Service stepped up timber harvesting throughout the national forests and turned increasingly to clearcutting as a harvest method. By the late 1960s, clearcutting had reappeared in eastern national forestlands, including the Pisgah and Nantahala. The young Western North Carolina Alliance opposed wholesale clearcutting, just as it had petroleum development, on grounds that it destroyed the public forests for other uses. This drawing of clearcutting sites in the Pisgah's Grandfather District appeared in a WNCA newsletter and captured the scale of Forest Service clearcutting. The clearcuts depicted here took place between 1967 and 1992; the map's creators pointed out that most of the cuts occurred in the 1980s. Courtesy of the Western North Carolina Alliance.

FIGURE 14. Mary Kelly, shown here standing in a clearcut, served as Western North Carolina Alliance coordinator during the critical years before and after the organization's 1989 Cut the Clearcutting! campaign. Clearcutting, a timber harvest technique that took every tree, drew fire from a wide range of Blue Ridge residents. They objected not only to its abysmal aesthetic but also—and more importantly for many—to its long-lasting destructive effects on native forests. Clearcutting effectively removed woods many western North Carolinians prized as commons harvest grounds, and affected forests took decades to recover. Through the Cut the Clearcutting! campaign, WNCA activists gave residents an organized opportunity to express their often passionate opposition to the practice. Courtesy of the Western North Carolina Alliance.

FIGURE 15. Walton Smith (holding center stick) spent his career with the Forest Service but became a vocal critic of the agency during his retirement. In Smith's view, large-scale clearcutting amounted to bad forestry. He advocated selective harvest techniques instead, which left behind a forest canopy more compatible with other uses, including commons-style hunting, fishing, and gathering. Smith often held forestry training sessions such as this one and taught scores of Western North Carolina Alliance volunteers to assess trees' timber value. He put his amateur citizen foresters to work doing professional-quality timber surveys, and he used the data they collected to mount sophisticated technical challenges to Forest Service harvest plans. Courtesy of the Western North Carolina Alliance.

FIGURE 16. In the mid-1980s, a group of leading Western North Carolina Alliance activists gathered at the Carson Community building in Macon County to celebrate victory on a timber sale appeal. The festivities included a birthday cake for David Liden's young son. From left to right: Rob Kelly, Esther Cunningham, Lindsey Liden, Walton Smith, Gill Heywood, Dee Smith, Dick Heywood, Bob Padgett, David Liden. Courtesy of the Western North Carolina Alliance.

FIGURE 17. A petition drive served as centerpiece for the Western North Carolina Alliance's 1989 Cut the Clearcutting! campaign. In this photo, campaign organizer Monroe Gilmour stands beside the giant petition during an anticlearcutting rally in Asheville. The document included more than 15,500 signatures when the WNCA delivered it to National Forests in North Carolina headquarters. The effort eventually gathered over 20,000 signatures expressing opposition to large-scale clearcutting in the Nantahala and Pisgah forests. Courtesy of the Western North Carolina Alliance.

FIGURE 18. Marching behind a "Cut the Clearcutting" banner, forest activists carry a giant anticlearcutting petition through the streets of Asheville, North Carolina. Fully unfurled, the petition stretched over four city blocks. The activists delivered the huge document to National Forests in North Carolina offices as part of the Western North Carolina Alliance's Cut the Clearcutting! Day, April 15, 1989. Courtesy of the Western North Carolina Alliance.

FIGURE 19. This cartoon by David Barbour appeared in the Western North Carolina Alliance newsletter, *Accent,* in the spring of 1994. The drawing depicts native Blue Ridge wildlife—a raccoon, bear, deer, and songbird—celebrating the demise of clearcutting as a timber harvest method. The cartoon appeared after the Forest Service released its revised fifty-year management plan for the Nantahala and Pisgah National Forests. The original plan, released in 1984, had drawn passionate criticism for its wholesale embrace of clearcutting. The revised plan took a very different approach, dramatically reducing timber harvest levels and nearly eliminating clearcutting as a harvest method. WNCA activists, many of whom had fought clearcutting for years, shared the jubilance expressed in Barbour's cartoon. Courtesy of David Barbour, Carolina Cartoons.

FOUR

De Jure Commons

National Forests and
Blue Ridge Neighbors

O. D. INGALL WORRIED ABOUT David Guffy. He admired the mountain man's quick mind, exemplary work ethic, and thorough trustworthiness. The forest assistant knew how hard Guffy had worked with one of the Nantahala examination parties, how he had given "excellent satisfaction" from the moment the work began. He knew Macon Timber Company managers had also trusted Guffy—had even requested that he move onto one of the abandoned farms their business had purchased and serve as caretaker. Guffy had done so, had built himself a house, and had cleared and planted six acres. He had lived on the site for several years and had thought he was settling in for the long term. Now the land was changing hands, and Ingall feared for Guffy's future if the USFS turned him out.

Guffy would have made a fine forest ranger, Ingall believed. He was "a very clever fellow," but the fact that he could neither read nor write disqualified him. If he lost the farm he had built, Ingall frankly did not know what Guffy would do. For all his hard work, he was "without any capital." Besides, Ingall well knew that "cheap farms are very scarce in this vicinity of late." If Guffy did need to leave, he had best start thinking of alternatives as soon as possible. The forest assistant could think of only one solution to the dilemma. He would write to Washington, D.C., on Guffy's behalf, asking that the man be allowed to stay in his home, cultivate his small patch, maintain his rail fences, and cut his annual supply of firewood in the neighboring forest. In return, Guffy could serve the agency as a fire guard and occasional laborer. "Since he has been in charge the fires have decreased to a minimum," Ingall wrote, playing his ace.[1]

Ingall's politic letter met with a favorable reception in Washington. William L. Hall wrote that the crew chief could "assure Mr. David Guffy that the Government will not interfere with him this season or require any payment for the land which he is occupying. However," the assistant forester continued, "if he wishes to continue to cultivate the land on which he is now living he should make direct application to that effect." Again Hall offered reassurance. "I see no reason why he should not be given a special use permit to occupy this land as it is more valuable for agriculture than for forestry. Moreover, the point that you make about his being able to protect the land from fire is a good one." Ingall had won Guffy a reprieve.[2]

The correspondence between Ingall and Hall offers a glimpse into the economic and social context the Forest Service entered when it began purchasing lands in western North Carolina. Tenant farming was common, and landless farmers such as Guffy had few options if they were turned off the land they worked. Most tenants on lands the Forest Service acquired did not have an Ingall to advocate for them. Some applied for and received special-use permits like the one Hall suggested for Guffy, but others left the area. Population growth in heavily USFS counties usually slowed or stopped altogether in the decades after Weeks Act purchases began, in striking contrast to counties with no Forest Service presence. Out-migration had often begun or accelerated when big companies such as Macon Timber moved into an area, and it typically continued where the Forest Service took over.[3]

At the same time, the Forest Service offered employment opportunities to some mountain residents who did stay. As Ingall understood, the agency especially valued local help in its efforts to fight fire. David Guffy and many others stood to benefit by cooperating in USFS fire prevention. Not only might Guffy hold on to his home, but men like him could land official positions as firefighters and forest guards, earning income while spreading the Forest Service gospel of fire prevention. Around 1915 forest guards in Georgia earned fifty dollars a month. By 1940 the Forest Service even provided some designated fire wardens with home telephones to expedite reporting. As a result, farmers working closely with the agency might boast the first telephones in their neighborhoods.[4]

Other employment opportunities also came through the Forest Service. Local men found work building trails and fire towers. The agency spent a considerable sum—almost $100,000—on fire prevention work in the Smoky Mountains purchase unit before its demise, for instance. Much of the funding went to local workers, who erected a fire tower on Rich Mountain—now in the Pisgah National Forest—and constructed a network of supporting trails. Later, as the apparatus of national forest administration developed and the agency established district ranger offices, local men obtained jobs as laborers and technical assistants, and local women sometimes landed clerical positions.[5]

Ingall's suggestion that David Guffy would make a valuable forest ranger also fits larger patterns. The USFS sought out promising local men for positions in the agency. Across the line in north Georgia, W. Arthur Woody started with the Forest Service just as David Guffy had, as a laborer on a 1912 examination crew. By 1918 Woody had become a district ranger, a position he kept for the rest of his career—some twenty-seven years. Had Guffy been better educated, he might have followed a similar path.[6]

Finally, the question of special-use permits that William Hall raised played an enormous role in Forest Service history. Its effects continue into the present day. Some landless tenants such as David Guffy had permits to remain on the land either for free or by paying a relatively small fee. Some elderly landholders sold tracts to the agency but reserved lifetime occupancy and use rights. Other mountain residents had special-use permits to cut firewood, fenceposts, tanbark, or dogwood—the last in demand by the textile industry. Occasionally, special-use permits allowed holders to build summer homes, resort hotels, or industrial operations. Special-use permits could strengthen relations between the Forest Service and local people, as seemed likely in David Guffy's case. On the other hand, the agency concluded in 1940, most likely "all of this special use business is so much taken for granted by local people that it has little influence" on their attitudes toward the USFS, "except when they are refused some desired privilege. Such disapprovals," the report concluded, "result in more or less hostility and resentment."[7]

The Forest Service's arrival marked a turning point in David Guffy's world and in the worlds of countless other Appalachians. Like him, innumerable mountain residents would find their lives permanently changed as the federal agency became a major landholder. Developments in the aftermath of the Weeks Act transformed the region, ushering in a new era of increased federal presence and a pattern of local-federal interaction on a scale so large it would have been unimaginable even a decade earlier. Few developments have been equally important to the region's history.

Mixed Local Responses to the Early Forest Service Presence

Despite its tremendous importance, historians have thus far found little surviving record of local people's responses to early federal landholding in the region. Occasionally, the regional press announced large USFS purchases, and USFS documents recorded some interactions with local people, but the record of mountain residents' reactions is nonetheless sparse.[8]

Newspapers carried scant coverage. Historian Ronald Eller reported "little local reaction to the creation of the National Forest Reserves" recorded in the *Asheville Citizen* between 1910 and 1920. He concluded that "most local residents reacted indifferently to the [Weeks Act] legislation."[9]

At least one early ranger account supports this interpretation. "For several years the people . . . did not seem to know what to think of the government owning this land," wrote Roscoe C. Nicholson, a district ranger in north Georgia's Rabun County, just over the North Carolina line. Uncertainty is not precisely indifference, but it is a close cousin.[10]

Examiners working in the region offered conflicting reports, recording both skepticism and embrace. D. W. Adams, a timber cruiser working in western North Carolina, reported from Acquone in September 1911: "The people generally, particularly on the Mt. Mitchell unit, have been decidedly skeptical as to the purchase of lands by the government." Just a few months later, in February 1912, forest examiner Verne Rhoades wrote of the Unaka area: "The people in general regard most favorably the movement on the part of the government to purchase these mountain lands."[11]

There are many possible explanations for these disparate accounts, but they must remain speculative. It is possible the two areas had different timbering histories. Certainly, the Mitchell area had hosted particularly heated timber disputes. But Adams seemed to suggest that he had run into similar, if less pronounced, "decided skepticism" in other areas as well. It is also possible that local people reacted to Adams with more hostility than to Rhoades. As a Forest Service timber cruiser, Adams may have seemed to local eyes essentially indistinguishable from a private lumberman; he did precisely the same work. In his forest examiner role, Rhoades may have seemed less threatening. It is also possible that Rhoades simply had a defter local touch, a greater ability to relate to local people. He had graduated from western North Carolina's Biltmore School of Forestry, so he had a history in the area. And he later became the first supervisor of the Pisgah National Forest, so the agency must have had confidence in his ability to work in the region.[12]

USFS historians point to the number of tracts local residents readily offered for sale as evidence of positive agency reception. Just four months after the Weeks Act passed, some 1,264,000 acres had been offered for sale, most by large landowners but many by smallholders. Timber companies often welcomed government purchase, both as a means to get rid of cutover or unprofitable lands and as a strategy for reducing their tax responsibilities. Speculative land purchases could turn a profit via sale to the government as well. Many small landholders also jumped at government purchase opportunities, and for some of the same reasons. Sale to the USFS could yield significant profits, lessen one's tax duties, and provide a way to dispose of unwanted, exhausted, or unprofitable farms.[13]

In the early days, local landholders strategically used land agents to drive up prices. This strategy evidently worked. Assistant forester William Hall reported in September 1911 that agents made it "difficult for the government to buy at a reasonable price." Soon after, the USFS made it a policy not to work with such agents and to deal only with landowners directly. Forest Service officials also noted that, in the high-stakes land acquisition game, agents sometimes pressured or tried to bribe examiners to prioritize, advocate for, or ease the progress of tracts in which they had an interest. Washington officials warned field personnel to be constantly on guard against these tactics and announced what amounted to a zero-tolerance policy for participation in unscrupulous schemes.[14]

While some mountain landowners evidently welcomed the opportunity to sell lands to the government, other residents reportedly worried about the ramifications of government ownership. According to Georgia ranger Roscoe C. Nicholson, "Some of them did not like the idea of taking the land out from under taxation. Some thought they would be forced to sell their land and move out." In succeeding decades, both these concerns proved astute.[15]

Taxation Concerns Prove Well-Founded

"The question of taxation bothers many . . . people," wrote forest examiner Verne Rhoades, reporting on the Unaka purchase unit in 1912, "especially the smaller owners, who think they will have to meet higher taxes when land purchased by the government is removed from the total acreage of assessable property." Unaka-area landowners could hardly have been more prescient. Over the following decades, events played out precisely as they feared in their neighborhood and in every county where the Forest Service purchased significant acreage.[16]

The issue of lost tax base was very real. Federal lands enjoyed exemption from local and state taxation. As federal landholding in the southern Appalachians grew, this situation presented increasing challenges for local governments. Even the agency itself recognized the difficulty. The Weeks Act originally allotted 5 percent of all revenues generated from federal forestlands—meaning timber sales—to the counties hosting those lands. The National Forest Reservation Commission considered the taxation issue beginning in 1911 and recommended an increase to 25 percent in 1913. That policy stayed in effect for over half a century, despite repeated complaints from Appalachian counties.[17]

In a 1919 *Journal of Forestry* article touting the benefits of the national forests to the southern Appalachian region, Forest Service spokesman William L. Hall offered an assessment of the tax issue. He noted that "at first there is a loss to the counties in taxes." But he expected the loss to prove temporary, to be "overcome as soon as business sets up on the Forests in a moderate degree." The issue proved more intractable than Hall anticipated, however.[18]

In 1936 the Society of American Foresters, which opposed continuing federal forest acquisition, raised the issue of lost tax revenue. In the throes of economic depression, mountain counties found themselves particularly hard-pressed to provide basic services. The 25 percent provision provided monies only when the agency received timber revenues. Since much of the land under Forest Service supervision in the southern Appalachians had been cutover or farmed, it could not be harvested. At the time the Forest Service was in the midst of its second large-scale round of acquisitions, and most of the land it purchased would not provide merchantable timber for decades. Thus, the 25 percent policy offered little relief to struggling mountain county governments.[19]

The Forest Service responded to these concerns by initiating a series of studies. The studies examined financial conditions in several host counties, including North Carolina's Macon County. In 1936 the federal government owned 43 percent of Macon's land base. Nearly all the rest was included in the Nantahala purchase unit and therefore was also eligible for federal ownership. The chestnut blight had devastated the area's forests, and they were not likely to yield high-quality timber for decades. Researchers found Macon records in extreme disarray, but they determined that the county suffered very high tax delinquency rates and was essentially broke, able to provide only meager services. Fortunately, the state had shouldered much of the financial responsibility for schools and roads. Despite its dire circumstances, the Forest Service study concluded that the county had gained more than it had lost by the agency's presence. Employment opportunities, free-use permits, road building and maintenance, use of USFS telephone lines, and recreation area development had more than compensated for the lost tax revenue, researchers concluded. Yet there could be no doubt that Macon's financial outlook was bleak indeed.[20]

Forest Service chief Henry Graves, who succeeded Gifford Pinchot, noted the taxation issue in correspondence addressing a 1937 forest-acquisition proposal from the Tennessee Valley Authority. TVA forester Edward C. M. Richards advocated a huge expansion of the Forest Service presence in the Tennessee Valley. He suggested the Forest Service buy up the area's struggling farms on a scale so grand as to quadruple its holdings, catapulting them from roughly 2.5 million acres to nearly 10 million. "There is one thing that is bothering me," wrote forester Graves in reference to this proposal, "and this applies to all undertakings involving large expansion of the public forests. This is the issue of taxation."[21]

Decades later, officials in Fannin County, Georgia, echoed this concern, noting "a steady undermining of our tax base" and pointing to USFS landownership as the cause. The John Hay Whitney Foundation also drew attention to the issue in a 1974 report linking large-scale USFS landholding in the southern mountains to persistent regional poverty. Report authors argued that "Appalachian people are bearing an unfair share of the cost of maintaining a National Forest system—and are getting very few of the benefits." They pointed especially to the tax issue, estimating lost revenues to local governments at $10 million annually. This lost revenue produced a dramatic cumulative effect, the report contended, and lay behind the common regional "irony of high taxes on the one hand, and low public services on the other." Restricted revenue due to large federal landholding undermined local governments' capacity to provide schools, roads, policing, health programs, and other necessary public services. National forests thus compromised "the ability of mountain counties to govern—and finance—themselves" and "helped in creating . . . poverty areas" in the Appalachians, the report concluded.[22]

The issue of lost tax base went unaddressed until 1976, when Congress passed the Payments in Lieu of Taxes Act. This measure required the USFS to make minimum annual payments of $0.75 per acre to counties hosting federal forestlands. It replaced the earlier system. By allotting local governments 25 percent of Forest Service timber receipts from sales within their boundaries, that system had tied county finances directly to USFS timber harvest. The system had left county governments with wildly fluctuating and hopelessly unpredictable finances. The new minimum-payment system improved the situation dramatically. It provided far more generous as well as far more reliable funding to county governments. Even in the heaviest timber harvest years of the late 1960s and early 1970s, local governments had netted only about $0.26 per acre, and when timber sales lagged, the numbers dropped deep into single digits. In 1972, for instance, the average payment per acre across the Appalachian region was only $0.135 and ranged from a low of $0.04 in Virginia to a high of $0.267 in Georgia. Thus, the leap to $0.75 represented an enormous improvement, though it was still only about half the rate of private property taxes per acre across the region.[23]

Displacement Fears Realized

Mountain residents' early concerns about forced sales proved as well-founded as their concerns about lost tax revenue. In fact, the National Forest Reservation Commission did consider using condemnation as a land acquisition tactic. Forced removals could have transpired as a result. The commission ultimately rejected the idea as likely to yield serious opposition and create USFS enemies. But within three decades several thousand mountain families were forced to endure devastating removals to make way for the Great Smoky Mountains National Park, the Shenandoah National Park, the Blue Ridge Parkway, the Tennessee Valley Authority dam system, and the Army Corps of Engineers uranium facility at Oak Ridge.[24] The trauma of these removals persisted for decades in local memory and colored regional attitudes toward all federal landholding agencies and indeed toward the U.S. government itself. Fallout from the Smoky Mountains removals, for instance, caused legal headaches and public relations problems for the National Park Service well into the twenty-first century.[25]

It is important to note that the Forest Service bore no direct responsibility for these later removals. Only because the Weeks Act, its bill of entrée, also served as a kind of legislative doorman for all federal landholding in the region could the agency be considered to have any role at all. Through most of its history the Forest Service acquired lands only from willing sellers, despite the many difficulties this policy caused.

The USFS developed a tool it called "friendly condemnation," but this device was categorically different from the straight condemnation procedures used on other agencies' behalf. It did not compel sale. Friendly condemnation aimed only to establish clear title in cases where would-be sellers' land records were muddled or nonexistent. In a typical case the landholder's claim went uncontested, but legal research failed to uncover a paper trail that clearly documented ownership. Usually, the agency and the landowner reached agreement on all points, including price, beforehand. Then the government, which could not purchase lands without clear title, used friendly condemnation to clear a legal path for the sale. The landholder could negotiate a price or refuse altogether to sell, options strict condemnation prohibited. In some instances, however, the agency proceeded with friendly condemnation before the landholder was satisfied with price. These cases doubtless provoked resentment.[26]

Especially in the 1930s, when the federal government undertook an array of Appalachian projects through an alphabet soup of agencies, local people may have had difficulty distinguishing Forest Service land acquisition policies from the more inflexible ones of other agencies. For instance, dam construction projects under the Tennessee Valley Authority could not go forward until the authority had acquired all affected parcels. TVA therefore could not tolerate the delays so typical in USFS land purchasing. It developed its own policy, called "no-trading." TVA officials examined each tract included in engineers' plans and made price recommendations to a committee of three. The committee then determined purchase prices. TVA notified landholders of its prices, and if a landholder did not acquiesce, the agency promptly began condemnation procedures. Thus, landholders had no choice about whether to sell or how much to demand.[27]

Methods used to acquire lands for the Great Smoky Mountains National Park, the Shenandoah National Park, and the Blue Ridge Parkway proved similarly uncompromising. Working in this context and alongside these other federal agencies, Forest Service acquisitions were necessarily affected. It seems likely the agency's decision to move forward with some friendly condemnations before landholders had agreed to a price may have been influenced by the larger atmosphere of inflexible federal purchasing. In any case, local people often resented Forest Service acquisitions in this era. In their view, the agency took advantage of widespread financial desperation to pick up lands at bargain-basement prices. This idea gained traction when the government bought many farms sold at sheriffs' auctions for tax delinquency. Though not literally forced to remove, as so many of their neighbors were, many Depression era national forest sellers nonetheless felt coerced. The agency had not directly forced their hands, but in a desolate economic landscape offering pitifully few options, it was as if it had.[28]

Moreover, some landholders felt swindled when Forest Service surveys determined they owned less acreage than they had claimed. Smaller tracts meant federal payments lower than landholders had anticipated. Surveys almost as often turned up greater acreage than owners had claimed, but this was no consolation to those for whom the verdict went the other way.[29]

Also exacerbating the sense of forced removal were many cases of squatters and tenants who had to move when the lands they occupied changed hands. These farmers did not own land, but many, like David Guffy, had homes they had built and lands they had cleared on property formally owned by others. Many worked land held by absentee owners. Squatters and tenants often felt they had some claim to the lands in which they had invested their labor. Particularly in the case of squatters, however, such claims held no legal standing. The Forest Service allowed some people to stay; indeed, it became a major landlord during the Depression era. It could not or would not accommodate others, however, and these people often left feeling sorely aggrieved. In some cases, the Forest Service razed buildings on its property to prevent reoccupation. "Sometimes tumble-down shanties and cabins are demolished," wrote William L. Hall, "because the site is unfavorable for a home." In these cases, clearly, local people did experience forced removal.[30]

In other less direct ways, early concerns about "moving out" also proved substantial. Hall wrote that "scores of abandoned cabins, school houses, and churches bear witness" to depopulation in the decades before the Weeks Act. "The entrance of the Government into the situation," he continued, "carries this movement forward to some extent." For those left in the region, he wrote, "life has in fact become harder than it was before their neighbors began to leave because it has been more difficult to keep up churches, schools and roads." He saw all this as evidence that the "heroic" experiment in mountain farm life had failed, and he posited the national forest presence as the key to a new and more prosperous system.[31] But by 1919 Hall and the Forest Service had recognized "decrease in population due to the acquisition of lands" for national forests as a pattern in mountain communities. Neighborhoods where the agency purchased many small farms saw markedly slowed population growth and even population loss in the decades following purchase.[32]

In the early 1970s, when the Forest Service condemned lands and forced residents to leave what became the Mount Rogers National Recreation Area, it joined the parade of outright federal removers. The agency noted that it condemned only twenty tracts with full-time residents, but a local organization countered that "everyone in the affected area has either lost land or had friends or relatives who did." The Citizens for Southwest Virginia group charged that people with "ancestral homes" in the area "were coerced into selling their land at a fraction of its worth." Its newsletter portrayed the USFS as "making sweeps through the area taking thousands of acres at a time while assuring residents 'that's all the land we're going to buy.'" Then, the group declared, "a few months later they will sweep through again enlarging their borders." In the end, the Forest Service condemned a total of around 7,100 acres for the recreation area. Like the Park Service before it, the Forest Service found itself facing a public-relations disaster in the aftermath of land condemnations. Resentments in the Mount Rogers area plagued forest managers for decades.[33]

Thus, early fears of forced sales and compulsory removal proved prophetic. The Weeks Act itself did not forthrightly strip mountain people of their homes against their wills. It did, however, serve as spearhead legislation for a gigantic federal public lands acquisition process that eventually did precisely that.

USFS Land Acquisition Brings Opportunities and Frustrations

The enormous land acquisition process brought employment opportunities to some mountain men. Full-time USFS employees in the southern Appalachians tended to be credentialed men from other regions, but local men often staffed temporary field crews. The field assistant, cook, and chainman positions they typically filled paid far less and carried fewer benefits than the higher-ranking forest assistant and examiner positions. Even these low-level positions proved very attractive to men in the area, however, as they compared favorably to the limited list of other economic opportunities available. Though the Forest Service laid off nearly all its local workforce when it closed the field season in December, mountain men were accustomed to temporary seasonal work—in logging camps and sawmills, for instance.

Local men on USFS examination crews expressed eagerness to stay on, despite the rigors of life in back country camps. Anticipating the oncoming end of the field season in November 1911, O. D. Ingall reported: "I have interviewed all the men & they all want to continue work as long as it holds out."[34] An earlier report from Ingall's supervisor, R. Clifford Hall, underscores the strength of this preference. Hall noted how area crews "suffer from lack of sleep and digestible food."[35] Ingall's crew had endured these conditions, yet they wished to continue the work. And their crew chief, pleased with their record, lobbied to keep them on. "I should hate to see the party break up," Ingall noted, "as the boys are all very congenial & used to working together."[36]

High wages probably account for much of this initial enthusiasm for Forest Service work. In 1911 forest assistants working in western North Carolina earned fifty dollars a month plus room and board. Supervisors such as Hall and Ingall earned at least double that amount, but the fifty-dollar salary was hard to match elsewhere in the mountains. USFS wages for local men actually went down after 1911. This decrease probably came about as agency officials coped with the high costs of acquisition work in western North Carolina, on the one hand, and realized the availability of low-cost local labor, on the other. In 1913 James Denman reported favorably on "the very efficient corps of assistants" he had attracted to his team "by raising wages from thirty to thirty-five dollars a month."[37] Standard wages for forest assistants thus seem to have dropped some 40 percent between the fall of 1911 and the spring of 1913. Correspondence from the field hints at one possible reason for this dramatic decline. Crew leader D. M. Gibson reported a plan to use day labor, "which I can get very easy at $1.50 per day or less," to fill in occasional gaps in his team. Around the same time, workers in the timber industry earned comparable wages for dangerous work in difficult conditions, often far from their homes.[38]

While mountain men often welcomed USFS work, local landowners frequently grew frustrated with the Forest Service, beginning at the examination stage. Delay emerged very quickly as a major source of dissatisfaction. The land acquisition process moved much more slowly than the agency had originally envisioned, and this was especially true for the smaller parcels typically offered by local landholders. When the USFS first began conducting land examinations in 1911, it tried to study all lands offered in a given area, regardless of size. As quickly became apparent, however, the acquisition process for any tract was difficult, expensive, and time-consuming. Officials soon realized that their initial undifferentiated approach was untenable. Before the end of 1911, for example, North Carolina ground crew supervisor O. D. Ingall wrote to Washington headquarters advocating a change in strategy. "We shall have to adopt the regular methods of timberland buyers and concentrate on the bigger tracts until we get 'control' of a certain district," he urged. After that, he continued, "we can pick the smaller areas at our convenience."[39]

As Ingall understood, in order to craft an operable unit in a given district, the government needed to attain critical mass in landownership. If it could not purchase large tracts in a particular area (sections with thousands or, even better, tens of thousands of acres), then it had little interest in adjoining smaller tracts (parcels with tens or hundreds of acres). Money and manpower for the complex acquisition process were quite limited, as Ingall knew all too well. "I have more than I can do," he wrote in the same letter, appealing for help even as he acknowledged that the agency was "short of men." With labor scarce and outsized tracts most critical, it made sense from a strategic perspective to prioritize the largest pieces and then, once these had been secured, to turn attention to the smaller parcels.[40]

As a result of this strategy, however, many small landholders—who were typically local people of modest means—waited months or even years for the government to initiate action in response to their offers. Meanwhile, they watched while USFS employees worked more hastily on neighboring tracts belonging to large timber companies. These corporations, as we have seen, usually had capital backing on a large scale and often answered to headquarters outside the region. Small wonder, then, if mountain residents concluded that the Forest Service put the interests of wealthy outsiders ahead of their own.

This perception probably drew increased force from the cultural similarities timbermen and foresters often shared and that divided both from most rural Appalachian people. Just as many timbermen had, Forest Service crew chiefs typically hailed from outside the region. Like the timber operators, they usually came from northern and midwestern states. They were college graduates. That fact alone set them apart, since a college education remained well out of reach for most Americans—including most Blue Ridge Americans—before World War I. Though the Forest Service advocated a different approach to timber harvesting than that practiced by most private operators, it was nonetheless avowedly in the timber business. Thus, its employees used the terminology of "board feet," "volume tables," "strip surveys," and "senior lappages" familiar to timbermen.

No such cozy commonalities united Forest Service employees and the rural mountain people who lived near national forestlands. On the contrary, a cultural divide yawned between them. This was true even when relations between the two were fairly cordial. Assistant forester William L. Hall, writing a 1919 promotional article touting the economic and social benefits of the southern Appalachian national forests in the *Journal of Forestry*, captured this divide. Hall's descriptions of mountain people drew on what even in that day were hoary negative stereotypes. "These are the genuine Appalachian mountaineers," he declared, "who, until a few years ago, had no outlet for their products and none for their energies except the manufacture of moonshine liquor and the maintenance of community feuds."[41] The USFS provided an uplifting presence in the region, Hall argued, a remedy for the poverty, lawlessness, and violence that decades of ugly stereotyping taught him to believe typical among Appalachian southerners.[42] Hall's piece cast the Forest Service as a kind of Progressive reformer organization in the mountain South, and that interpretation put the federal agency alongside a host of other contemporary reform efforts in the region. In all these endeavors, well-educated reformers from outside the region sought to improve mountain people, whom they cast as ignorant or even pathological.[43]

Though misleading stereotypes lay behind much of Hall's writing about the southern mountains, the poverty problem was real. O. D. Ingall's concerns about David Guffy underscore this point, and further evidence runs throughout the USFS documentary record. Men scrambled to work on government crews. Forest examiners worried that local people struggled to carry on if their land payments were delayed, that local shopkeepers suffered if their bills were not settled promptly, that woods crew families risked real privation if paychecks failed to arrive on schedule. Of the Davis party, victims of wrongdoing by a USFS crew leader, R. F. Hemingway wrote: "Several of these men have families to support and long delays, such as they have had to put up with, have caused them great inconvenience to say the least."[44]

Hemingway's pointed comment hints at the magnitude of suffering the Forest Service's perpetual acquisition holdups must have caused many mountain smallholders. Delays plagued every stage of the acquisition process. Initial examinations moved slowly, title searches inched along, formal surveys made slow progress, the commission review process crawled forward, and the wait for final payments seemed interminable. USFS ground crew leaders working in the region regularly advocated for more expedited attention to local concerns but apparently to little avail.

By the end of June 1911, Appalachian landowners had already offered to sell 1,264,022 acres. Only about an eighth—some 150,000 acres—had been examined. Ground crews lobbied for more manpower and cast about for more efficient ways to complete examinations. By August 1911, as more land offers rolled in, Daniel W. Adams urged the D.C. office to hire enough men for another examination party. "It is quite obvious," he wrote, "that there is more land listed on the Nantahala River shed than can be examined by Mr. Hall's party this season." Adams feared that if the work continued at its current pace, landholders "may become impatient and unfavorably impressed with our tardy action in regard to the examinations."[45]

Similar problems lingered in 1914. "When this land was listed we gave the owners the assurance that their land would be examined at once," wrote forest examiner Robert J. Noyes from the Mount Mitchell unit. "I think that this land should be examined as soon as possible in order to keep good faith with the owners."[46]

Responding to news that the National Forest Commission would not meet in September 1911 as initially planned but would convene instead in December, Adams worried about local repercussions. "I very much fear that this delay," he wrote from the Mount Mitchell unit, "will seriously handicap future operations in that locality."[47] Adams advocated a commission meeting in spite of lawmakers' recess, even if only part of the group could be assembled.

Regarding boundary and title searches, forest examiner Verne Rhoades offered a Pisgah example in 1915. "Today," he wrote, "there may not be a single grant laid down for the simple reason" that his team did not have the information they needed to begin the fieldwork. "The consequence is that the men must look up some of the old deeds in the courthouse to see if they can find anything to give them a key to the situation," Rhoades explained. "Multiply such an instance by similar others," he continued, and the Washington office would understand why he could not predict with any accuracy when he would complete work in a given district.[48]

Forest examiner L. L. Bishop expressed frustration with the glacial pace of title clearance, which involved both Forest Service personnel and the district attorney. "What I want to point out is just this," Bishop wrote to Washington. "The title work on this Area is not getting on." The Forest Service title examiner was doing the best he could with his tiny staff. "This, however, is not of interest to the people who sold their land two years ago and who have to wait at least four months yet for their money. Judging from the past it will be nearer 8 months than 4," Bishop fumed. "Something seems to be radically wrong." Moreover, he concluded, "the fact that no one is being paid for their land has and is standing very much in the way of our making further purchases on this Area."[49]

In 1913 Nantahala-area forest examiner Rowland F. Hemingway, who seems to have been regularly accosted by local landowners waiting for news on their holdings, wrote to D.C. for guidance. "I must candidly confess that I am up a tree as to what to say to them except to be patient and wait," he reported.[50] Bishop confronted the same issue in 1915. "I feel that anything that can reasonably be done to hasten payment should be done," he wrote from the Mount Mitchell unit, "that it is due the vendors that it be done. Some of these people are actually distressed because they have not received pay for their land."[51] Bishop might have had J. M. Bradley in mind, an elderly man who had awaited payment so long that his family members "were afraid that he would lose his mind over it."[52]

USFS and Timber Legacy: The Dillinghams of Big Ivy

While delays drove some landowners to distraction, others charged the Forest Service with wrongfully acquiring their land. When Ingall suggested that the government adopt timber companies' methods for gaining control of a district, he did not mean the agency should use questionable tactics. But Ingall's suggestion offers a useful reminder that all USFS acquisitions took place against the backdrop of industrial timber harvesting. The USFS inherited a landscape stamped with timbermen's marks, and this fact often hovered just below the surface of interactions between local people and the agency.

Resentments against real or perceived timber company abuses in a given region could haunt USFS acquisition efforts. This happened in the Big Ivy neighborhood, where Ed and E. F. Dillingham spearheaded stout extended-family resistance to USFS purchases. Big Ivy nestled at the base of the Black Mountain range in the Forest Service's Mount Mitchell purchase unit. The Forest Service hoped to acquire lands offered by Phillip Heintz on behalf of the Big Ivy Timber Company, but members of the Dillingham family considered some of these lands to be their own. Ed and E. F. Dillingham fought tooth and nail against Forest Service efforts to acquire the contested tracts.

The Dillinghams claimed full title to three tracts offered by Big Ivy Timber and a partial interest in two others. Some of these five contested parcels encompassed vast swathes. The Dillinghams claimed a one-twentieth interest in the "entire watershed of Big Butte creek," for instance. Others were more limited. One full title claim, for example, included seventy-five acres below Craggy Pinnacle. Ed Dillingham felt so strongly about the Pinnacle tract that he built a fence around it. USFS examiner of surveys Thomas A. Cox Jr. reported that he had given Dillingham "every assurance that his claim would be regarded and his rights cared for," but Dillingham remained defiant. He vowed that the government crew "would never finish the survey," Cox wrote. Moreover, Cox continued, Dillingham went "to every length to forceably [sic] stop the survey and have me arrested."[53]

Ed and E. F. Dillingham served as spokesmen for five sets of Big Ivy residents contesting Big Ivy Timber Company title claims. In the first case, J. A. Allen and T. A. Dillingham prepared written title claims and submitted them to the USFS through Ed Dillingham. These claimants "very respectfully" requested that certain tracts "be excepted from the boundary to be conveyed by Mr. Heintz as he has no right title or interest therein." They pointed to specific registered deeds to support their claims.[54] Residents also filed four other claims, each of them verbal rather than written. The Forest Service listed E. F. Dillingham as "representative" on the first two of these, which had been filed by groups—of Dillingham heirs, in one case. C. H. Dillingham filed the third verbal claim, and Harriet Dillingham et al. filed the fourth. In all but one of these four cases, claimants also offered supporting deeds.[55]

Examiner of surveys Thomas Cox regarded the Dillingham claims with skepticism. He considered two of the supporting deeds fraudulent and one void. Since a fourth claim cited no deed, he believed four of the five claims to be essentially invalid. The fifth claim, from Harriet Dillingham et al. for one-twentieth interest in the Big Butte watershed, offered a supporting registered deed that Cox did not dismiss outright.[56]

One deed—offered in support of the written J. A. Allen and T. A. Dillingham claims—Thomas Cox considered fraudulent because it had been registered in 1913, decades after its claimed 1889 date. The deed, he wrote, "appears to have been located 35 years ago at instigation of the Dillinghams, then after some trouble, set aside for a more favorable time to press same." A second deed supporting the Allen/Dillingham claim was undated but "said [by Ed Dillingham] to be an old deed and registered." A third deed, registered in 1903, also supported the claims. It cited lands held by Alfred Burton Dillingham and passed to J. Andrew Allen.

In spite of his belief that one of these key documents was fraudulent, Thomas Cox thought it possible the Dillinghams might prevail on the first claim. He sent a sketched map of the contested lands to Washington with the Dillingham/Allen claims labeled "1" and "1b." T. A. Dillingham "will contest for '1' and can hold '1b' if '1' is held," Cox informed his supervisors.[57]

Both these claims involved the Dillingham family inheritance. The first treated lands held by Ed Dillingham's great-grandfather Thomas Foster Dillingham, who died in 1881. The second involved lands Ed Dillingham claimed had been passed from his grandfather Albert Gay Dillingham to his father, Job Farris Dillingham.[58]

Ed Dillingham and E. F. Dillingham used every tool at their disposal to prevent the Forest Service from acquiring lands they believed the Big Ivy Timber Company had no right to offer. While Ed Dillingham built fences and threatened the USFS examiner with arrest, E. F. Dillingham convinced his son, who worked as an axman on the government crew, to walk off the job. He seems also to have influenced his neighbors not to take the younger Dillingham's place, as Cox reported he had great difficulty replacing the man. And, wrote Cox, "due to his influence," it became impossible "to get any local aid on the survey."[59]

After researching the tracts in question, the agency concluded that the family had falsified claims. The Dillinghams, for their part, based their claims on verbal agreements and family inheritance that had not been formalized at the courthouse or had been formalized belatedly, after the Big Ivy Timber titles were registered. Despite the government's contention that the legal record supported the company's claims, the Dillinghams seem to have felt that their own claims carried more legitimacy.

It is impossible to know what really happened in Big Ivy. It might be that Ed Dillingham and his supporters were opportunistic rogues who saw a chance to make money and falsified claims in hopes of doing so, as some government agents hinted. It is possible, as survey examiner Thomas Cox speculated, that the Dillinghams simply hoped to delay government acquisition as long as possible so as to continue their own de facto use of the contested forest.[60] Perhaps they knew their claims would not stand up in court but bought themselves time by filing anyway.

It is also possible that timber agents had backstabbed or taken advantage of the Dillinghams, as family members seemed to suggest. It is conceivable, even likely, that the transactions the Dillinghams described actually did take place and were considered binding under the old system of verbal agreement and neighborly exchange. The Big Ivy Company might have said one thing in a face-to-face meeting the Dillinghams considered binding and then done another in the all-important courthouse.

Importantly, residents of the Big Ivy neighborhood seem to have sided with the Dillinghams against the Forest Service and the Big Ivy Timber Company. No one from the community stepped forward to fill the place left when E. F. Dillingham's son left his job, in spite of the attractions that position must have had for local men. And the tone in Thomas Cox's correspondence is one of frustration that the whole neighborhood had turned against him.

It is possible that Ed Dillingham, who was from a prominent family with a long history in the region, had a reputation as someone it was best not to cross. It is also possible that local residents believed his claims were legitimate and cheered for him in his fight against timber company claims they saw as fraudulent and against government acquisition efforts based on those unfounded claims. Perhaps they supported Dillingham out of solidarity.

In any case, versions of this story replayed countless times in the southern mountains. Private caretakers such as Carl Schenck or government agents such as Thomas Cox ran up against local behavior they considered beyond the pale, then expressed frustration when they received little support from the neighborhood. Schenck could not get moonshine stills confiscated; Denman could not replace his axman. Evidently, many longtime mountain residents held ideas about justice and fair play that stood in contrast to those held by newcomer agents such as Schenck and Denman—and behaved accordingly.[61]

Whatever their goals may have been, and whatever history lay behind them, it is clear that Ed and E. F. Dillingham were willing to go to great lengths to accomplish their aims. Their resistance efforts proved formidable. With their fence building, arrest attempt, claims filing, axman walk-off, and campaign for neighborhood noncooperation, the Dillinghams created a substantial obstacle course for USFS agents working in Big Ivy. They erected legal and physical barriers to the work, caused a labor shortage (in a labor-rich land, no less), and blackened the Forest Service's image in the community. Though in the end the government denied Dillingham claims and honored those of Big Ivy Timber, the family's efforts were not without effect. They caused the Forest Service a great deal of aggravation, expense, and delay, and they left the agency with a public relations mess in the Big Ivy neighborhood and with few, if any, local allies.

Thus, timber company history dogged USFS efforts in Big Ivy, as it did in many communities across the southern mountains. In effect, simply by entering the neighborhood, the agency stepped into an already boiling landownership cauldron. Similar cauldrons, full of local anger and resentment, simmered all over the southern mountains. And who had sparked the fires and set the kettles to boil? Local people blamed timber companies.

By buying land from Big Ivy Timber, the USFS may have seemed to Ed Dillingham and his neighbors to have sided with the corporation against the local man. The Forest Service would have roundly denied any such accusation. Legal research convinced the agency that Big Ivy Timber Company's claims were legitimate and the Dillinghams' were not, so it could hardly have acted otherwise. The legal paper trail was bedrock for the Forest Service, no matter which way it pointed.

And in fact the legal paper trail could cut both ways. In some cases, it did not support a timber company's title claims, and in those cases, the agency refused to buy from the company. In one striking example, the Forest Service even dissolved the entire Smoky Mountains purchase unit after the Little River Lumber Company's large claims in that unit could not be verified to its satisfaction.[62]

Usually, however, timber companies' superior access to legal expertise insured victory in land disputes with local residents, as happened in Big Ivy. That case was far more typical; the Smoky Mountains case was an exception. And of course, life was far easier for Forest Service officials if they were dealing with fewer landowners. As they raced deadlines, coped with tight budgets, and faced a growing work backlog, it might have been tempting to decide in favor of lumber companies if any legal case could be made to do so. Even if that never happened, what the Forest Service saw as a combination of wise strategy and upright fair play may have looked to local eyes like a penchant for privileging large companies over smallholders. Not only did timber company lands come first in the acquisition queue, but also the Forest Service usually honored timber company claims in disputed cases.

Foresters and the Commons

Finally, Pisgah and Nantahala neighbors expressed a range of concerns centered on the forest commons. Commons use continued in the federal forests, but rules changed and priorities shifted. Blue Ridge residents worried about how USFS managers might reshape the commons forests and whether their accustomed harvests could continue.

Some of these concerns clustered around the issue of grazing. Supervisor Inman F. Eldredge, a graduate of the Biltmore School of Forestry, described a "hostile atmosphere" surrounding his early work. "The settlers ... were against you because the Forest Service hemmed them in," he remembered. "The stock men were against you because you were going to regulate them and make them pay for grazing, count their cattle and limit where they could go." Ranger Roscoe C. Nicholson echoed this assessment. "Perhaps most of them thought at first that if they were stopped from burning out the woods they would never have any more free range," he wrote.[63]

The issues Eldredge and Nicholson raised proved critical to the Forest Service's mountain neighbors. The custom of firing the woods pitted local husbandmen against determined Forest Service officials, and the question of grazing fees loomed large.

Because fires had done and continued to do enormous damage to forests in the southern Appalachians, the Forest Service placed heavy emphasis on fire prevention. "Against fires the Government takes an unswerving attitude of opposition," wrote William L. Hall. Though logging locomotives probably bore responsibility for many of the most destructive fires, the limited burning customary in the region could spiral out of control, with devastating results. In any case, the Forest Service's antifire priorities put the agency on a collision course with local people accustomed to semiannually firing the woods to improve pasturage, deter snakes, and destroy insect pests. As Eldredge remembered, "The people right down on the ground, the settlers, the people who lived in the woods ... were the greatest, ablest, and most energetic set of wood-burners that any foresters have had to contend with."[64]

William L. Hall reported a debate he had with a north Georgia man on the question of livestock and fire. The man asked whether the government would continue to allow local people to run stock on the forests it acquired. Hall replied in the affirmative. The man then inquired about whether he and his neighbors would be allowed to burn the woods. No, answered Hall. To the north Georgian's mind, if fire could not be used, then stock might just as well be prohibited. "The people could not live there if the woods were not burned," Hall remembered this man's arguing. Without regular fires, the Georgian feared that "the underbrush would grow thick, that snakes and 'varmints' would increase, and that the cows would get milksick." "No amount of argument was convincing to this man," Hall recalled.[65]

The Georgia man doubtless spoke for many. In any case, some of the southern mountains' "energetic set of woodburners" continued their long-standing customs. William L. Hall reported: "So used have the people become to the burning of the woods" that "in spring or autumn during a dry week one may go through the Appalachians, even through the centres such as Asheville and Knoxville, with the air so full of smoke as to obscure the mountains, yet there will be little comment."[66] Claude Darnell, recalling his Blue Ridge boyhood to Foxfire interviewers in 1975, told them: "I've seen these woods afire plumb around here—just a ring all the way around the mountains." "They used to burn them—not all the trees, just the underbrush," he explained to the students, "so the cattle could have somethin' to eat."[67]

Foresters used a range of tactics to deter this burning. At least two early north Georgia rangers employed bloodhounds to track offenders. One former USFS official remembered how effective that method proved in Rabun County. A local man "had been setting fires each year in the spring to get the country in shape for his stock," J. Herbert Stone remembered. The stockman stopped the year after the dogs' reputation got around, reportedly remarking, "I don't want any bloodhound tearing the seat out of my britches." As a result, Stone concluded, "the fire record for that particular drainage improved tremendously."[68]

On the other hand, "there are no better firefighters anywhere than these mountaineers," William L. Hall averred. "Even women will leave their work and go to help the Government fight fire." Where forest officers worked with area residents, appointed local fire wardens, and developed "community interest," their effort "quickly solves the fire problem."[69]

This dual pattern continued through the early decades of Forest Service ownership in the Appalachians. On the one hand, the agency developed cooperative antifire partnerships with many local people, and the success of this effort seems to have grown over time. On the other hand, Forest Service personnel took a hard line against fire, using every means at its disposal to prevent and fight fires and to penalize fire-starters—both local and visiting.[70]

One intriguing firefighting partnership involved moonshiners, the unsanctioned whiskey distillers who often set up their illegal operations on national forests. A USFS employee who began work on Virginia's Jefferson

National Forest in 1931 lauded moonshiners as among the agency's readiest firefighting teammates. "Moonshiners were our best friends," he remembered. Agency employees' laissez-faire attitude toward moonshining made possible this partnership. "We didn't bother them, and they didn't bother us," recalled one Jefferson ranger. In fact, rangers on the Jefferson claimed "they had never seen a single still" on Forest Service lands (though they had), and they did not cooperate with local or federal law-enforcement officers' antimoonshine inquiries. Rangers on the Monongahela and the Pisgah took a similar attitude. Pisgah personnel deliberately avoided still sites, and at least one Pisgah district ranger placed regular orders with a local moonshiner. In that case, the two masked their exchanges under the liquor producer's dogwood-cutting permit. This tolerant attitude toward moonshining itself partly reflected the agency's fire prevention priorities. Virginia national forest historian Will Sarvis reported that the Jefferson rangers "feared the number of incendiary fires would increase if they cooperated with the authorities."[71]

Efforts such as these gradually reduced all kinds of fire on the Appalachian national forests, including range fires, and stockmen continued to worry about grazing. The Forest Service listed range as a legitimate use in its 1940 publication, "National Forests in the Southern Appalachians." "Grazing, though not so important here as on many of the western national forests," the agency explained, "is another of the multiple uses of forest land."[72]

But local people often associated Forest Service purchase with the closing of the range. As early as 1916, the year Pisgah became a national forest, local concern over grazing prohibitions reached the desk of U.S. senator Lee S. Overman. The North Carolina Democrat wrote to chief forester Henry Graves inquiring about the ban. Graves replied that the land could not support cattle in addition to the large wildlife population it harbored. George Vanderbilt had managed Pisgah for game, and the Forest Service continued to do so, as directed by President Woodrow Wilson's National Game Preserve mandate. Since Pisgah was a federal game preserve, wild animals took priority.[73]

The Nantahala range stayed open for some twenty-five years, but some local people thought of it as having closed with the arrival of the USFS. "We stayed there 'til the government closed us out," Will Zoellner told north Georgia's Foxfire interviewers in 1977. "I had so much cattle, so many hogs, I couldn't put them on my land and keep 'em alive. I had to have that mast." Although the USFS permitted hog grazing, Zoellner told the students he could no longer afford to keep hogs when he had to pay the agency's fee.

"But then, ninety cents a head if you want to graze 'em on the open range. I couldn't pay ninety cents for six hundred head of hogs with the rogues and rascals stealin' half of 'em." And "the cattle, the government wouldn't let them go at all. They said that the cows would browse the timber down— wouldn't let it grow." Richard Norton told a similar story. "When the government took it over, they wasn't no tellin' how many thousand of cattle and hogs that was raised up in there," he explained to Foxfire interviewers in 1975. "We had seventy-five head up in there," Norton continued, "back when they made me take my hogs out of there." Zoellner, Norton, and other Foxfire interviewees remembered the plentiful meat they obtained through the free-range system. "Now I can't even buy a good mess of meat," Norton lamented, "and it costs me $11 to go deer huntin'."[74]

On the question of livestock, however, Forest Service personnel could also be good neighbors. R. M. "Mack" Dickerson told Foxfire interviewers about four cattle that disappeared into the Nantahala National Forest in early 1945. A Forest Service worker tending a deer-raising project found the cattle, rounded them up, penned them, kept them fed and watered, and alerted the owners of their whereabouts. Some thirty years later, Dickerson remembered with gratitude the "forest feller's" neighborly care.[75]

As Norton's and Dickerson's comments indicated, Forest Service purchases also meant dramatic, though gradual, changes in the hunting commons. Slowly that commons gained ascendancy throughout the Appalachian national forests, and the livestock commons dwindled, losing ground in the 1920s and 1930s and finally closing altogether after World War II. The two processes were related, as the Overman-Graves correspondence about Pisgah's grazing ban revealed. Eventually, concerns about wildlife put the last nails in Nantahala's free-range coffin, just as it had earlier in Pisgah.

The deer-raising project Mack Dickerson remembered was part of this process. As the agency gained administrative control over its lands, it initiated wildlife rehabilitation projects focused on popular game species such as deer and turkey, which had sustained heavy population losses in previous decades. A deer preserve had long operated on Vanderbilt lands, for instance, and USFS personnel continued that work. In fact, just a few weeks after establishing the Pisgah National Forest in 1916, President Woodrow Wilson also designated it Pisgah National Game Preserve. In the 1930s Pisgah personnel developed increasingly elaborate systems for raising young deer in fenced stations. They released the animals on the larger forest and eventually shipped them to other national and state forests throughout the East. Dickerson's Nantahala "forest feller" probably tended deer originally raised on the Pisgah.[76]

Pisgah officials guarded their deer from harm almost as zealously as they guarded their forests from fire. "Dogs on the preserve considered predator and shown no quarter," they wrote in one telling example. They backed these words with action: in 1924 wardens reported killing 102 dogs. Some of these would have been feral, but others must have belonged to local families. The policy doubtless angered many hunters who lost prized animals. By 1925 the dog-kill numbers had dropped to forty-six, and a USFS report attributed the difference to more hunters keeping their dogs at home. In 1928, though the "no quarter" policy remained in effect, Pisgah authorities reported "every effort made by the wardens to return valuable animals to their owners."[77]

Hunters eyed the Pisgah deer herd eagerly, but Pisgah officials took trespass hunting quite seriously. In 1929 USFS personnel on the preserve brought twenty-nine trespass cases to the courts and secured twenty convictions. The year before they had reported "losses from trespass almost negligible." But protecting the deer from trespass, they noted, was "an unremitting and increasingly arduous job."[78]

Hunters made deer protection more difficult by devising clever new strategies to gain access to the USFS deer herd. The deer lost legal protection if they wandered off preserve grounds, and hunters went to great lengths to make sure they did just that. Hunt clubs with land adjacent to the preserve lured the animals to their property. They sowed favorite white-tailed deer food crops (wheat, rye, clover, and corn), and they baited deer with salt licks. Dismayed by high losses in 1927, when an estimated seven hundred deer had been killed when they "drifted from the preserve," wardens took a page from the hunters' playbook. They sowed food crops and installed salt licks on the Pisgah and did cut their losses.

Eventually, Pisgah wardens became so successful at raising deer that the herd began threatening timber species reproduction. At that point—in the early 1930s—wardens initiated a series of controlled hunts to thin the population. These, of course, proved extremely popular with hunters. Sportsmen from around the country flocked to the Pisgah, as did hundreds of local hunters. Demand grew so great that USFS officials began holding lotteries to determine participation. Some local subsistence hunters, caught in the throes of the Depression and anxious for a chance to secure meat for their families, came out winners in the drawing, but others did not. Those turned away doubtless resented the fact that wealthy out-of-state sport hunters won many slots. Forest Service regulations also prohibited hunting on the preserve during most of the year, including most of the state's deer season. Local hunters who violated this prohibition risked arrest and prosecution.

They may have wondered why, if deer populations were too high, the Forest Service did not simply open the preserve to deer hunting in accordance with North Carolina state hunting regulations.

Eventually, Pisgah rangers did precisely that. As of the mid-1940s they followed a federal-state cooperative model that had developed in Virginia by 1938. Under this model Forest Service officials and North Carolina's state Wildlife Commission shared responsibility for wildlife management. They divided fees from state hunting licenses and used the money to fund cooperative stocking efforts, habitat development projects, and other joint fish-and-game initiatives. Through the program sportsmen purchased annual North Carolina state hunting and fishing licenses. For an additional fee, they could also purchase special "stamps" giving them rights to hunt and fish on USFS property. This permit system made wildlife taking widely available but also put a price on that taking. Hence Richard Norton's pointed comment: "It costs me $11 to go deer huntin'."[79]

Forest Service officials in western North Carolina spent considerably less time and effort on the gathering commons than they did on the grazing and hunting commons and left a sparse documentary record. They clearly disapproved of some gathering practices, especially the tradition of skinning trees to make berry buckets from the bark. On the whole, however, they seem largely to have ignored local gathering. Since for the most part gathering did not threaten timber, Forest Service personnel may have permitted it to continue essentially unregulated, at least until sometime after World War II.

In 1924 Pisgah Forest supervisor Verne Rhoades provided an extensive list of "special uses" available on the national forests. Gathering was conspicuous only by its absence. Rhoades included "apiaries, stone quarries, gravel pits, pastures, railroad and flume rights-of-way, municipal water supply, tobacco beds, tree nurseries, sanitaria, hotels, stores, garages, restaurants, school houses, and what not." Of these, only "apiaries" could possibly be considered a gathering commons use. The Forest Service sometimes allowed farmers to keep beehives on land they had sold to the government. The bees plied the forest, and the farmers harvested the insects' honey.[80]

In his 1914 article, "To Remake the Appalachians: A New Order in the Mountains that Is Founded on Forestry," William L. Hall used huckleberry pickers as negative exemplars, as demonstrating the kinds of behaviors that required "remaking" by forestry. Hall included a photograph of two men holding chestnut bark they had collected and from which they would make berry buckets, or "toots." Using plant fibers, crafters sewed bark panels together to make the gathering buckets. This bark-bucket technology had been in use for centuries in the southern mountains, first by Mississippian era ancestors of the Cherokees, who likely developed it. Hall considered the bark buckets "an unprofitable use of the forest," as he announced in the photo caption. He described bark gathering as "an immediate economy but ultimately an absurd extravagance because the girdling ruins the trees." For Hall, timber production trumped all other uses, including this long-standing gathering-commons practice.[81]

Other hints of continued vitality in the gathering commons occasionally appear. In 1942, for example, Blue Ridge Parkway landscape architect Stanley Abbott reported meeting "three very colorful mountain women" near Linville, North Carolina. The three "emerged from the woods on the roadside, each with a gunny sack filled with galax leaves." When Abbott asked the women where they had gathered the leaves, one of them reportedly replied, "We ain't picked none on the Scenic. We knowed you can't pick them near the road." Abbott did not pursue the matter further, but Pisgah National Forest lands surrounded the Parkway near Linville. And though Parkway regulations prohibited galax picking, Pisgah regulations did not. The women may well have filled their sacks on nearby national forestlands.[82]

Until World War II, the USFS emphasis on small timber sales in the Appalachians fit nicely with commons practice. William L. Hall envisioned transforming the region into "a forest community instead of an agricultural community," with opportunities "for people to work permanently in the timber business." In 1914 Hall predicted that "timber cutting will provide remunerative contracts for a number of small operators and provide labor for thirty or forty men" in communities near the national forests.[83] A few years later, Hall believed his vision showed signs of becoming a reality. "Small sales suit the Government," he stated, "and they suit the local people." Before the Forest Service purchased Appalachian lands "there was no opportunity for small timber operators," Hall wrote. But now local men could become timber buyers, "sometimes in a very small way." The Forest Service made "numerous sales . . . for less than $100." As a result, Hall wrote, "improved standards of living are coming in."[84]

On the eve of World War II, Forest Service policy still favored small sales. In the Appalachians, sales of less than $500 made up roughly 90 percent of agency timber transactions in the early 1940s.[85] The agency also allowed permits to cut dogwood and tanbark, the former in demand for textile mill shuttles, the latter for the leather-tanning industry. And the early Forest Service offered free-use permits allowing local people to cut trees for firewood and fencing and for lumber for homes, schools, and churches—all free of charge. Using free-use permits, area residents could also remove building stone from national forestlands. The agency emphasized that these permits aimed to help local families secure their basic needs and were not intended to benefit for-profit enterprises.[86]

After World War II these patterns shifted, and the USFS began to embrace policies that put it on a collision course with commons users as with much of the American public. High postwar demands for wood and increasingly cordial relations with the timber industry helped ratchet up harvest levels on the national forests and sapped the agency's earlier commitment to small Appalachian sales, free-use permits, and other commons-friendly policies. At the same time, postwar development on private lands claimed ever more Blue Ridge forest, and a tourism boom spurred skyrocketing demand for outdoor recreation. As more stakeholders made more demands on a shrinking forest pool, commons users felt the squeeze. The federal forests became more precious, and commoners feared their enclosure at the hands of recreationists and industrialists.[87]

By the 1970s a perfect forest storm was brewing, both at the national level and in the Appalachians. A concerned Congress had wrested control of some national forestlands away from the Forest Service. Gifford Pinchot's agency had grown increasingly committed to a timber harvest method he called "tree butchery." Gifford Bryce Pinchot, in a move he saw as upholding his late father's legacy, had supported an Appalachian turkey hunters' lawsuit against the USFS. The landmark suit had worked its way through federal courts and had shut down the agency's timber harvest program nationwide.[88]

These developments paved the way for the National Forest Management Act of 1976, which shifted national forest ground by requiring public input into USFS decision making.[89] Because the Pisgah and Nantahala forests had long supported commons practice, in the Blue Ridge public input often took the form of passionate commons defense.

FIVE

Contested Forests

Commons, Clearcutting, and Wilderness

ON AUGUST 3, 1978, Ralph Sanders issued a stirring call to arms. In a letter to the *Franklin (N.C.) Press,* Sanders drew readers' attention to "a matter of grave importance" he was "prepared to fight . . . in every way possible." Sanders had recently learned of an intolerably discriminatory state law that would soon go into effect, and he was organizing in response. Over one hundred people had joined his cause already. They had formed an association and elected him president. Sanders and his allies were now working to get the organization officially chartered "so we will be better prepared to defend our rights." Sanders asked for more help, with a clarion call to turn "this great State of ours" around and "take this fight to the Capitol if necessary."[1]

The offending law was a North Carolina Wildlife Resources Commission regulation that allowed Macon County sportsmen to hunt with dogs only on Tuesday and Friday nights, and the fledgling organization Sanders headed was the Macon County Coon Hunting Club. To those unfamiliar with the Blue Ridge forest commons, the sense of passion and high stakes in Sanders's letter might seem out of all proportion to its subject. But local hunters heard the call and met it with an equally passionate response. They rushed to join the cause, and soon the coon club had enrolled nearly two hundred dues-paying members. It quickly turned back the offensive only-on-Tuesdays-and-Fridays proposal, and it established itself as a political organization to be reckoned with in Macon County.[2]

The coon hunters found the proposed restriction discriminatory because it did not apply to all counties and because it did not cover hunting with foxhounds. Residents of neighboring Clay and Cherokee Counties could continue to hunt their hounds any night of the season, so Macon hunters felt geographically singled out. Foxhunting clubs also won themselves an exemption, and this galled raccoon hunters, particularly since foxhunters tended to be wealthy outsiders, while coon hunters tended to be less-wealthy longtime local residents.[3]

The new rule represented only a small change in the enormous code governing North Carolina hunting and fishing, but for the Macon hunters, far more was at stake than the occasional Wednesday night trophy. As an *Asheville Citizen-Times* journalist later reported, they saw the proposed regulation as nothing less than "a threat to their sport." To them it seemed that the very survival of coon hunting was on the line and with it something bigger.[4]

Coon hunters saw themselves as defending not only a sport but also a set of memories and cultural practices that tied them to their families, to each other, and to their forests and that set them apart from others. The last lines of Ralph Sanders's letter gestured toward this larger project. "I speak," he wrote, "for every Father and son . . . who have walked into the woods on a cool brisk night with their hound dogs."[5]

For Sanders, coon hunting was not just an amusement but a tradition dense with cultural meaning. It included the companionship between a father and son, the working partnership between a hunter and his dogs, and the experience of cool, brisk nights spent in the woods. Blue Ridge bear hunter and forest activist Hoyte Dillingham echoed Sanders when he described hunting to writer Chris Bolgiano as "part of the heritage we grew up with." When Bolgiano asked if he meant that it was a sort of bonding experience, Dillingham said yes. "It's a bonding between you, the forest, the dogs, and the people." The coon hunters saw themselves as working on behalf of everyone who shared this powerful experience.[6]

Like Sanders and Dillingham, many twentieth-century mountain residents with deep roots in the region inherited a constellation of ideas, stories, and artifacts centered on the wooded commons. The commons model of forest thought had its origins in earlier economies dependent on small-scale forest extraction, but it lived on in traditions important to twentieth-century rural mountain culture—hunting, fishing, herb gathering, and the like. By this time commons harvesting had lost its central place in the regional economy, though it still retained some economic clout. Its cultural importance, however, continued undiminished.

As Sanders's and Dillingham's descriptions indicated, commons culture painted the woods as familiar, peopled, and richly historical. It stood in stark opposition to the wilderness model of forest thought, which posited forests as wild and ahistorical, by definition human-free, "an area where earth and its community of life are untrammeled by man, where man himself is a visitor who does not remain," read the 1964 Wilderness Act.[7] In the Blue Ridge, commons culture found expression in place-names; in forest tales, recollections, histories, and observations; in the material culture of recipes, guns, dogs, and trophy displays; in the organizational culture of hunting and fishing clubs; and in concerns over forest rules, regulations, and enforcement. This broadly shared commons culture connected forest users with their communities' past and future, valued hard-earned forest skills and experiential knowledge, and gave local residents a sense of forest ownership.

After the 1976 National Forest Management Act granted federal forest neighbors unprecedented power to influence USFS decision making, Blue Ridge commons users rushed to wield it. As contests over the future of the Nantahala and Pisgah forests heated up in the 1970s and 1980s, astute organizers worked to mobilize commons culture in the political arena. In debates over wilderness designation, petroleum exploration, and clearcut timber harvesting on the national forests, many voices issued calls to commons arms. And just as happened with the coon hunters, these passionate calls inspired passionate responses.

National Forest Use

Throughout the twentieth century, commons-style harvest continued in the Blue Ridge national forests. Like the Macon coon hunters, many people relied on the woods for recreational harvest. Others supplemented their livings with forest products such as galax, firewood, berries, fish, game, herbs, and roots. It is impossible to know harvest levels with any precision, but it is clear these products were significant to many households.

The Forest Service offered low-cost plant permits to moss, herb, and pine needle gatherers and to some shrub diggers. It sold Fraser fir cones to aspiring Christmas tree growers for around four dollars a bushel. By the 1970s Christmas trees were quickly overtaking tobacco as the region's leading agricultural product, and nearly all the industry's seed materials came from national forestlands. The North Carolina Department of Agriculture estimated that five hundred people earned income through ginseng digging in 1978. Most of the ginseng, too, would have come from national forestlands.[8]

Firewood was probably the most ubiquitous national forest product to make its way to Blue Ridge homes. The *Franklin Press* reported in 1981 that most Macon County households either heated exclusively with wood or supplemented with it. The national forests provided an important source of this fuel. In 1982 a Macon County family could purchase two pickup truckloads of firewood—enough to take a household through weeks of winter—from the USFS for ten dollars. In the winter of 1977–78 the Pisgah District of the Pisgah National Forest—one of eight ranger districts in western North Carolina—issued more than 4,150 such permits.[9]

A good supply of firewood could make a material difference to a family's well-being, as a 1978 *Franklin Press* article illustrated. The *Press* profiled the Carvers, a local family struggling to make ends meet after a debilitating illness struck husband Kenneth. He still cut heater wood, and wife Myrtice Carver gardened and canned to provide the family's winter food supply. The *Press* praised both Carvers for their industriousness, running photographs of Kenneth beside his firewood pile and Myrtice beside her pantry shelves, which included one hundred quarts of blackberries. The article did not specify the Carvers' wood and berry sources, but both products may well have come from neighboring Nantahala lands.[10]

Federal Lands History in Western North Carolina

While local people continued to harvest Blue Ridge forests, outside the region these forests' popularity as recreation sites grew. The southern Appalachians had long been among the nation's favorite eastern playgrounds, and in the 1930s large federal sums went into enhancing this status. In western North Carolina, the Blue Ridge Parkway and the Great Smoky Mountains National Park stood as two primary examples. The federal Tennessee Valley Authority also built dams in the region, partly to generate hydroelectric power and partly to provide lake-based recreation. Each of these projects required local sacrifice on behalf of national goals.[11]

Proponents argued for the Great Smoky Mountains National Park and the Blue Ridge Parkway initiatives in terms of the enjoyment they could provide to people within easy traveling distance. The parks would essentially function as national recreation areas. Some local boosters enthusiastically promoted the projects, but they tended to be elites from urban communities such as Asheville and Knoxville, which stood to reap large tourism-industry benefits from federal park initiatives while shouldering few of the costs.[12]

Park and Parkway boosters downplayed the negative effects those projects had on local people, but these effects were real and in some cases devastating. Whole communities were forcibly removed and their histories erased to make way for the Great Smoky Mountains National Park, for instance. People in these communities traditionally relied on agriculture for a living, but few found affordable farms to replace the ones they lost. The park thus took from them not only home and community but also livelihood—and this in the teeth of the Great Depression.[13]

The Blue Ridge Parkway exacted a similar toll. It too forced families to relocate during the economic crisis, and it left farms along its course diminished and fragmented. Moreover, in a region unmistakably hobbled by the lack of a basic transportation infrastructure, the federal government prioritized a *scenic* highway. The motorway's ban on commercial and farm vehicles underscored how little it was intended to serve local needs.[14]

Rural residents typically came away feeling railroaded and resentful if they lost land or suffered displacement due to park development. It seemed to them that they had been asked to make enormous sacrifices so that wealthy outsiders could enjoy federally funded pleasure grounds. Though only a small portion of the mountain population directly suffered the worst park and parkway effects, rural people across the region came away believing that outside elites and the federal government would willingly surrender mountain homes, jobs, and communities on behalf of "playgrounds" for the well-off.[15]

Western North Carolina's late-1970s wilderness controversies took place against this historical backdrop, and they cannot be understood outside it. Regional federal lands history hummed constantly beneath debates about wilderness designation and sometimes came roaring to the surface. Demonstrators in Franklin protested "We Have Given All We Can to Parks," for instance, specifically referencing this history and its regional toll.[16]

In 1978 memories of the painful Depression era displacements were still quite fresh. An ongoing struggle between the Park Service and families evicted from the Hazel Creek drainage, for instance, regularly made local papers. The families had lost homes and land to the Tennessee Valley Authority, which later transferred its holdings to the Park Service. When TVA completed the Fontana Dam in 1945, it became all but impossible for onetime residents even to visit their old homesites—Fontana Lake flooded the roadbed. Access to Hazel Creek's twenty-six family cemeteries became a particularly galling issue. The Park Service had promised the families a North Shore Road around the lake, but it ran into environmental and financial troubles that eventually doomed the project. Some Hazel Creek families saw this failure to provide the road as an intolerable case of insult added to injury.[17]

In 1978 Hazel Creek families, Great Smoky Mountains National Park officials, and area politicians worked on the thirty-three-year-old problem of cemetery access quite publicly. Park Superintendent Boyd Evison addressed the issue in local papers. Congressman Lamar Gudger announced his determination to find a permanent solution and expressed sympathy for the former Hazel Creek residents, many of whom still lived in Swain County.[18]

New sets of problems arising from western North Carolina's status as a national playground also made headlines in area papers. In Macon County, for instance, residents of the Nantahala community along Highway 19 vented frustration with campers and canoeists visiting the Nantahala Gorge. Visitors parked willy-nilly, sometimes even in the road, and they blocked traffic as they carried canoes to the river. Campers used every available inch of land and left trash and toilet paper littering the ground. With no public restrooms in the area, neighbors worried about potential health hazards. Some residents also feared for local women's safety. Community spokesman John Wagner told Macon County commissioners that the entire situation was "just a mess, a big aggravating mess." Wagner delivered a grievance petition signed by six hundred neighbors. The community had complained to the landholder, Nantahala Power and Light, but "the only progress we've seen is more and more people." "I'm not against them using the river," Wagner explained, but the community did object to becoming "a campers' village," under siege by insolent litterbug canoeists.[19]

Local people, then, found it difficult to ignore the costs associated with western North Carolina's status as a national playground. Wilderness opponents in the 1970s debates frequently referenced these costs. Wilderness advocates, however, often seemed unaware of the high historical and contemporary toll. When wilderness proponents based their arguments on the needs of "eastern population center" residents, they inadvertently marched in what local residents might legitimately see as a long enclosure and displacement parade. National-style wilderness advocates could appear not to have Macon County residents' needs in mind, just as Smoky Mountains Park boosters had not had Cattaloochee residents' needs in mind and Fontana Dam planners had not had Hazel Creek residents' needs in mind.

The Great Smoky Mountains National Park

The Great Smoky Mountains National Park loomed as the central structure in the federal lands backdrop against which western North Carolina's wilderness debates took place. Though not itself affected by the Forest Service survey, the park remained a vital presence during the controversy. Wilderness supporters seldom mentioned it, but wilderness detractors frequently did. The federal park served as a sort of shorthand reference to the tensions between national and local land-use priorities and to the insider versus outsider cultural politics that typified discussions of the wilderness issue.

Local people typically viewed the park as a place for outsiders to enjoy. They themselves more often made use of the national forests. As Mark

Taylor, writing for *Wildlife in North Carolina*, explained, the park "caters to a different crowd than the National Forest." By 1977 the Great Smoky Mountains National Park had already become the federal park system's most heavily used unit. It promised to become even more popular as "ever-growing crowds of urbanites seeking relief from the crowded cities and suburbs of the eastern seaboard" flocked to it, Taylor wrote. Yet local people seldom visited the park. They preferred lands administered by the Forest Service, explained Taylor, "because they can cut firewood on the forest, some make a living logging it, and they can hunt on it." Where the park served as a playground for outsiders, the forests provided harvest grounds for local residents.[20]

For *Wildlife* readers, as for many local people, the difference in NPS and USFS hunting policy was emblematic. "On Forest Service land, hunting and fishing is encouraged," Taylor wrote for the magazine. "The hunter is an unwelcome guest on Park land, however." This dramatic distinction, between "encouraged" hunters and "unwelcome" hunters, reflected the clientele gulf many longtime mountain residents saw yawning between park and forests. The warmly welcoming forests were "ours," the coolly uninviting park was "theirs."[21]

Western North Carolina grassroots forest activist Mary Kelly offered an insight into the links between hunters and mountain communities as a whole. "When you're tapped into the hunters you know you're striking a chord in the whole rural community," she explained. It was as if the hunters were a string on a musical instrument, producing sound that reverberated far beyond the instrument itself. In the same way, the ban on Great Smokies hunting sounded a cultural knell deep into mountain communities. Distinctions between national park and national forest lands might seem small to outside visitors, but cultural differences bulked large in local thinking.[22]

Like many hunters, *Wildlife in North Carolina*'s Mark Taylor chafed against the Smokies' prohibition. "Without a doubt, many of the people visiting the park would object if hunting were allowed within its boundaries," he wrote. "Yet one wonders why a hunter couldn't be allowed in some parts of the park for a little while each year." Park Superintendent Boyd Evison explained the Park Service rationale. "We feel that hunting isn't compatible with our philosophy of managing the park," he said, "and that it would conflict with other uses and upset many of the visitors." Park visitors' potential objections were a central reason for the hunting ban in both Evison's and Taylor's accounts.[23]

A divide thus loomed between park visitors who did not like hunting and neighborhood woods users for whom hunting represented a primary source of forest enjoyment. This divide proved a stumbling block in the path of good relations between the park and local communities. As Taylor explained, the Park Service's preservationist philosophy "has riled many local people." They felt they had been shut out of the forests, their priorities trumped by those of wealthy outsiders. The park, in local minds, had been enclosed.[24]

Where the Great Smoky Mountains National Park often seemed to local people essentially a private preserve set apart from the rest of the region, the national forests seemed a public commons entwined into it. These different perceptions reflected the two sets of federal lands' different histories as well as their managing agencies' different structures and philosophies. Where the park had been established by fiat and its inhabitants forced to leave, the forests had been gradually acquired from willing sellers. Consequently, local people expressed less ill will toward the USFS. Also, a single large block of land formed the park—officials decided where boundaries should be and then removed everyone who had lived within them. The forests, on the other hand, scattered through the region in multiple jagged pieces, braiding through many communities. They were physically woven into the larger landscape.[25]

Moreover, the Forest Service had for decades deliberately cultivated good relationships with local people. It sited district ranger offices in rural communities, so USFS employees had frequent contact with forest neighbors. From its inception the agency employed local women as secretaries and local men as technicians, rangers, and firefighters, often bringing much-needed income to neighboring families. The Forest Service sometimes offered perquisites to cooperative neighbors, such as providing in-home phones to farmers serving as fire wardens. It worked closely with hunting and fishing groups on wildlife management projects, and it offered free and inexpensive firewood permits as well as permits for a host of other forest products, including ginseng, galax, Fraser fir cones, and native mosses. And its emphasis on small timber sales favored the family-sized operations that typified Appalachian industry into the 1950s and 1960s. Tensions certainly existed between the USFS and local communities, but close ties also did.[26]

These contrasting views—of the park as an exclusive preserve for outsiders and the forests as an accessible commons for locals—surfaced early in the wilderness debates and continued to be important as it unfolded. Opponents likened proposed wilderness areas to the Great Smoky Mountains National Park. They saw the Forest Service study as an attempt to remove lands from the forest commons and reserve them, parklike, for the use of wealthy visitors.

Clearcutting

In the decades after World War II, as second-growth forests in the southern Appalachians matured and the nation's demand for wood products skyrocketed, the Forest Service shifted out of the caretaker and restorer role it had previously held and began to emphasize timber harvesting.[27]

Before the 1960s, the Forest Service relied on all-aged management as the chief forest supervision method in the southern Appalachians. All-aged management involved selective cutting, which required foresters to walk through the woods "cruising timber," or assessing trees for their timber potential. Cruisers marked mature trees for harvest, and only these designated trees were cut. Professional foresters preferred this method during the first half of the twentieth century. Carl Schenck, for instance, had practiced and taught it at Biltmore. He took pride in the fact that he had personally marked every tree to be cut on the property during his tenure. The system was called all-aged management or uneven-aged management because after a selection timber harvest, trees of various ages remained. Since selection cuts took only some trees, the method also left behind a forest canopy.[28]

After World War II, foresters turned increasingly away from this method and toward even-aged management. By the mid-1960s, even-aged management had taken center stage as a forest supervision system, and clearcutting had become the dominant method of timber harvesting on U.S. national forests. With clearcutting, every tree on a given tract was cut regardless of age, size, species, or timber quality. No timber cruising was necessary. Forest managers simply marked the perimeter of a sale area, and timber buyers cut everything within the perimeter. The trees that eventually grew in a clearcut site would be all the same age.[29]

In 1914 William Hall had written that "clear cutting as a rule will not be desirable in the Appalachians." He advocated selection cutting, with "a large proportion of the stand always remaining." By 1969, however, clearcutting accounted for about 50 percent of timber harvested in the southern Appalachians, and this percentage grew over the following two decades. Proponents argued that shade-intolerant Appalachian hardwoods regenerated better after clearcutting than they did after selection harvests. The method was also simpler and more economical than selection cutting. And the region's pulp and paper mills enhanced clearcutting's attractions by providing a ready market for trees too young or of the wrong species to make valuable sawtimber.[30]

To the lay observer, the visible aftermath was the most obvious difference between clearcutting and selective harvest techniques. When carefully done, selective harvesting could be all but invisible to the untrained eye. An *Asheville Citizen* reporter looking out over a western North Carolina timber plantation under all-aged management, for instance, noted that he could not discern where trees had recently been cut, though he had seen logs come to the sawmill that very day.[31]

Even the greenest of forest novices could never have missed a clearcut, however. Clearcuts left behind desolate-looking landscapes, muddy piles of brush, slash, and debris gashed by huge logging-road scars. They shocked the senses. Critics cast about for words to describe their visual havoc. Clearcutting sites were lunar, barren, hideous, denuded, devastated. They looked like the aftermath of an explosion or the end of the world.[32]

Even clearcutting advocates readily conceded the method's abysmal aesthetic. "A fresh clearcut is not an attractive place," wrote forester Charles E. McGee in a 1970 *Journal of Forestry* article. McGee supported clearcutting as sound silvicultural practice, but he recognized that clearcuts were visually appalling. After a clearcut "the land has an aura of total devastation," he continued, "an appearance of total ruin." Clearcutting aftermath "will shock even the most casual passerby." Foresters should remember that "a forest visitor's first contact with a clearcut operation is apt to be a traumatic and lasting experience." If they wished to continue using even-aged management techniques in the southern Appalachians, McGee wrote, silviculturists should take steps to limit clearcutting's negative visual impacts. The practice would only gain public acceptance if forest professionals mounted an ambitious educational campaign and did everything in their power to minimize its "spoiled environment" aftermath.[33]

Foresters like McGee may not have realized that clearcutting's ugliness was not the only—nor, for many opponents, even the primary—reason to oppose the practice. For many southern Appalachian critics, the central issue was not ugly aftermath but incompatibility with other forest uses. By taking whole stands of the forest, clearcutting essentially destroyed their usefulness as hunting, gathering, and camping grounds as well as scenic sites. As one forester noted, local people typically were "used to seeing a tree cut" and did not object to timber harvesting. However, whereas selection timber harvest methods left behind a usable forest commons, large-scale clearcutting did not. The method transformed a multiple-use forest stand into a single-use timbering site, in effect "enclosing" the commons forest. Wholesale clearcutting effectively removed the public woods and gave over their resources to the exclusive use of a single entity—in this case, a timber company.[34]

Thus, in their impact on the forest commons, clearcutting and other even-aged management practices proved categorically different from selective harvest techniques. Local people often deplored clearcutting's visual havoc, but many of their objections were more utilitarian than aesthetic. These commons-based objections eventually embroiled the Forest Service in one of its greatest controversies.[35]

The Monongahela Case

By the time Charles McGee published his article on clearcutting aesthetics in the southern Appalachians, heated clearcutting objections were already pouring out of the region, especially out of West Virginia's Monongahela National Forest neighborhood. The Monongahela was a Forest Service success story. The area straddling West Virginia's Alleghany Front had been so badly burned and cutover around the turn of the twentieth century that it became known as the Great Burn and the Great Brush Patch. Under Forest Service stewardship the district had gradually recovered, and by the 1960s much of it boasted valuable commercial forest, including large stands of mature hardwoods. By the late 1960s the Monongahela National Forest drew roughly one million visitor-days of use and provided a central attraction for West Virginia's one-billion-dollar tourist industry. Until 1964 the forest was under all-aged management. In that year Forest Service officials moved the "Mon," as it was affectionately called, to an even-aged system.[36]

In no time at all, Monongahela's managers found themselves in the middle of a public-relations nightmare. Eventually that nightmare grew to national importance. But if Charles McGee penned his "Clearcutting and Aesthetics" article in response to rumblings from the Mon, he misjudged those rumblings. Clearcutting opponents did object to the visual assault the harvest technique produced. Their criticisms, however, went far beyond aesthetics. Prettifying clearcuts would not blunt the critiques of many even-aged management opponents, including those spearheading the anticlearcutting movement in Monongahela.

In many ways, the critical Monongahela battle foreshadowed western North Carolina's anticlearcutting campaigns years later. For both sets of clearcutting opponents, aesthetic issues were significant but not basic. More important was the way clearcutting destroyed the forest for other uses. The destruction of hunting and gathering forest commons provoked anticlearcutting ire in West Virginia as it did in western North Carolina. Once roused to action, commons-inspired clearcutting foes joined forces with those interested in protecting mountain viewsheds. But the prime mover in West Virginia as in the North Carolina highlands was the removal of commons forest, not the visual affronts of clearcutting.

This commons-based concern about clearcutting was apparent from the beginning of West Virginia opposition to the new even-aged management system officials began to employ on the Mon. Local clearcutting opposition first found voice when a group of irate squirrel and turkey hunters, upset because some of their favorite hunting grounds had been clearcut, complained to the Forest Service. Rebuffed by foresters, the hunters took their case to the West Virginia legislature. Joining forces with tourist-industry business owners concerned about scenic quality, the hunters persuaded the legislature to pass a 1964 resolution calling for scrutiny of timber harvest practices on the Monongahela. The Forest Service's even-aged plan had been in place for less than a year, and already it was embroiled in controversy so hot as to inflame the state legislative branch.[37]

Monongahela managers moved forward in spite of the opposition. The West Virginia legislature passed another resolution in 1967, but clearcutting continued apace. Monongahela foresters performed a 550-acre clearcutting experiment on a tract near Richwood, West Virginia. This clearcut destroyed a well-connected local politician's favorite turkey-hunting grounds and scarred the view from a Richwood golf club. The Forest Service did itself no favors by clearcutting in the wealthy golf club's viewshed, but it made its most resolute enemies by destroying prime hunting grounds. The Richwood cut set in motion a series of events that eventually brought a nationwide halt to Forest Service clearcutting.[38]

In 1969 West Virginia hunters took their complaints to the top USFS echelons and paid a visit to the Washington, D.C., office of Forest Service chief Edward Cliff. Cliff wrote in his memoirs that the Monongahela group was "very upset because there was some timber harvesting [clearcutting] in the area that they had been using for years for turkey hunting. They felt that the cutting that was being done was not compatible with hunting. They demanded that this be stopped." Cliff's memories of this meeting are revealing. He did not mention the Mon delegation's expressing any aesthetic concerns about West Virginia clearcuts. Visual issues were conspicuous only by their absence. The West Virginia hunters had come to Chief Cliff's Washington office on a mission to defend their commons forests.[39]

Chief Cliff did not realize he was meeting the vanguard of what would prove to be a formidable commons-defense force. In fact, he dismissed the 1969 West Virginia clearcutting objections as "a very self-centered protest from a very small segment of the population who wanted the national forest to be managed just for their own personal pleasure." The Forest Service chief underestimated both the enormous popularity of commons-style national forest use in the Monongahela and the mammoth proportions of clearcutting opposition in West Virginia. The angry turkey hunters were not simply vociferous self-interested outliers. Instead, they represented the dangerous tip of a huge anticlearcutting iceberg on a direct collision course with Forest Service policy. Chief Cliff would come to regret this large miscalculation.[40]

In 1970 the turkey hunters and other clearcutting opponents ushered through the West Virginia legislature yet another resolution calling into question the Forest Service's Monongahela management practices. Finally, the Forest Service initiated its own review of timber harvesting on the Mon and found a range of problems. Managers had inadequately assessed wildlife range and habitat requirements and had failed to plan for wildlife needs. They had not properly enforced logging and road construction guidelines, and erosion and reduced water quality had resulted. Nor had managers paid adequate attention to scenic quality. Large and poorly planned clearcuts had caused "unnecessary visual blight."[41]

Yet still the clearcutting continued. Critics again took their complaints to Washington, D.C.—this time to Congress. By now angry westerners had joined the Monongahela hunters in their outpouring of clearcutting hostility. Responding to these various constituents, Congress held a series of long and volatile 1971 hearings on public forest management. As a result of these hearings, the Forest Service made some small policy changes. It vowed to use the clearcutting technique less frequently and on smaller tracts. Most of the changes addressed visual problems. The agency reduced the size of clearcuts and emphasized adequate clearcut "landscape design." The West Virginia turkey hunters' central concern, commons hunting-ground destruction, went unaddressed. Nor did Congress follow up the hearings with legislation. Clearcutting opponents, wary of agency assurances, increasingly turned to the courts for relief. Monongahela turkey hunters brought the most important of a series of conservationist lawsuits against the Forest Service.[42]

Richwood, West Virginia's well-connected politician–turkey hunter knew members of the sportsmen's organization the Izaak Walton League. He and fellow turkey enthusiasts worked with the league to bring an anticlearcutting lawsuit focused on Monongahela practice. Many local residents supported the lawsuit. Older West Virginians remembered when the Mon had been the Great Burn and the Great Brush Patch, and they did not like the jarring reminders of those bad old days that Forest Service officials had recently been serving up. Other conservation groups joined the Izaak Walton League suit as well. The West Virginia Highlands Conservancy wanted to preserve the state's viewsheds and attendant tourism. Two national groups, the Sierra Club and the Natural Resources Defense Council, also signed on. At this point, the Monongahela lawsuit participants represented a range of forest concerns. It is important to remember, however, that the turkey hunters initiated the suit as part of their resolute defense of commons hunting grounds. Other groups brought important ideas and resources to the bandwagon, but the commons harvesters had started it rolling.[43]

The turkey hunters, the Izaak Walton League, and their supporters based their case on the 1897 Organic Act, which one historian described as "an almost forgotten dinosaur of a law." This was a surprise move, since reams of legislation affecting the national forests had passed through Congress in the seven decades since 1897, and a great many important new public lands laws had been enacted in the dozen or so years before West Virginians filed their 1973 lawsuit. Yet none of this legislation had overturned the 1897 Organic Act. It still stood, amended but not annulled. And clearcutting opponents found in the act language that even-aged techniques seemed clearly to violate.[44]

The Organic Act stipulated that federal foresters could harvest only dead, mature, and large-growth trees and that these must be individually marked and removed. Clearcutting took all trees, not just mature and dead trees. In fact, all even-aged management techniques prescribed cutting for whole stands rather than particular trees. Thus, these forestry methods violated the specific terms of the 1897 Organic Act, the Monongahela team argued. The Organic Act proved an apt tool of commons defense. Commons users by definition believed in forest harvest. They saw timber harvesting as legitimate, but only if it did not damage the forest for other uses. Organic Act requirements dovetailed nicely with this view by allowing timber harvesting but limiting its extent. If Organic Act terms were enforced, the Forest Service could cut timber, but it would have to do so more slowly and less wholesale. This, of course, was precisely what Monongahela plaintiffs wanted. Though industry spokespeople later accused lawsuit conservationists of setting out to ban timber harvesting, the charge was ungrounded. Clearcutting opponents hoped to limit the amount and type of harvesting in the national forest but not to ban it outright.[45]

Because the Organic Act's language was so clear, conservationists expected to win their lawsuit. Because clearcutting had gone on for at least a third of the time the law had been on the books, the Forest Service expected to win. Monongahela lawyers filed their suit, *West Virginia Division of the Izaak Walton League v. Butz*, on May 14, 1973. West Virginia's federal district court acted on it with relative speed. On November 6 the court ruled for the turkey hunters against the Forest Service, agreeing that national forest clearcutting was illegal, a violation of Organic Act terms. The national implications of this decision were enormous. Glen O. Robinson, a knowledgeable contemporary observer, wrote: "If upheld on appeal and if accepted by other federal circuits, this ruling would have an almost incalculable impact on timber management in the national forests." It would bring a halt to clearcutting and all other forms of even-aged management that the Forest Service routinely used. The USFS appealed the West Virginia court's ruling, but on August 21, 1975, the United States Court of Appeals for the Fourth Circuit upheld the Monongahela decision, agreeing that turkey hunters were right and the Forest Service wrong about the legality of federal clearcutting.[46]

This was a stunning turn of events, and its national repercussions were immediately felt. As Glen Robinson and others had foreseen, the upheld appeal brought the Forest Service's timber harvest program crashing to a standstill. By 1975 nearly all national forest timber harvesting involved clearcutting or other even-aged harvest methods, and the Monongahela decision outlawed these methods. As a result, tree cutting on national forestlands across the country screeched to a nearly complete halt. Four years after USFS Chief Cliff disdained them as self-interested whiners, the West Virginia turkey hunters had brought his agency to its knees. Retired western North Carolina forester Bob Padgett remembered how the Forest Service had been "cornered and stopped by [this] alert conservation group." The Monongahela decision was "not only a severe inconvenience to the Forest Service but also a great embarrassment," he wrote. The agency had tangled with Appalachian hunters' commons brand of forest conservationism and lost, with landmark results.[47]

Neither conservationists nor the Forest Service quite knew how to react in the wake of the Monongahela decision. Conservationists had not anticipated such unalloyed victory, and the Forest Service had not expected such resounding defeat. The court of appeals recognized the monumental nature of its decision. "We are not insensitive to the fact that our reading of the Act will have serious and far-reaching consequences," wrote the court, "and it may well be that this legislation enacted over seventy-five years ago is an anachronism which no longer serves the public interest. However, the appropriate forum to resolve this complex and controversial issue is not the courts, but Congress."[48]

The National Forest Management Act of 1976

To Congress all interested parties accordingly went. Timber-industry and Forest Service lobbyists scrambled to introduce legislation that would repeal or amend the Organic Act. Conservationists lobbied to leave the act intact. A number of grassroots lawsuits on the Monongahela model waited to go to court, but national groups urged plaintiffs to hold off, fearful that more victories would only add fuel to repeal-minded fires. A series of bills were crafted: timber wanted legal support for maximum harvesting, the Forest Service wanted legal support for maximum agency discretion, and conservationists wanted legal support for meaningful forest protection. In limbo in the meantime, timber and the Forest Service wanted quick results so that they could once more roll trucks.[49]

Western North Carolina congressman Roy Taylor introduced a stopgap bill that would have allowed timber harvesting to continue for two years while Congress crafted new legislation to govern national forest management. Democrat Taylor was a commons-style conservationist who had helped design the 1964 Wilderness Act. Forest activists Esther and Jim Cunningham were among his staunch supporters. Taylor also believed in timber harvesting and recognized the importance of the industry to his mountain district. In the wake of Monongahela, western North Carolina timbermen issued dire warnings that many in their industry would go belly-up if national forest harvesting did not resume quickly. Taylor the timber-area representative was concerned about jobs in the region. Taylor the conservationist wanted good legislation to protect the national forests. He recognized the impossibility of drafting careful and deliberate legislation in the atmosphere of hysteria that surrounded the post-Monongahela ban on timber harvesting. He hoped to use his interim bill both to allay immediate industry fears and to create a calmer atmosphere for conservationist legislation. But his bill was trampled underfoot in the congressional scuffles that followed Monongahela.[50]

When the dust settled in D.C., two bills remained standing. One, sponsored by Minnesota senator Hubert Humphrey, a Democrat, had more environmental protections and included provisions for long-range forest planning based on science rather than politics. The second, a House bill, had fewer environmental protections. A third bill, sponsored by West Virginia senator Jennings Randolph, also a Democrat, was especially ambitious in terms of conservation and had the approval of several environmental groups but lost out to Humphrey's bill. When the House-Senate conference committee hammered the two final bills into one, the planning process remained. But conservationists lost some of Humphrey's restrictions, and they divided over whether to support the final version. Interestingly, none of the organizations that had participated in the Monongahela lawsuit supported the final bill. The Izaak Walton League, the Sierra Club, and the Natural Resources Defense Council all went on record against it. Some other conservation organizations supported it, as did the Forest Service. Lumber lobbyists also opposed the bill.[51]

In a heated atmosphere and by a handful of votes, the bill passed, becoming the National Forest Management Act of 1976. It repealed the 1897 Organic Act and replaced it as the central legislation governing national forest management. Though conservationists helped craft NFMA, its initial results proved disappointing to them. In fact, some conservationists who worked on the legislation later expressed extreme bitterness and a sense of betrayal. Reacting in 1987 to the minimal restrictions guiding a planned clearcut timber sale on the Nantahala Forest near his home, forester Walton Smith expressed the dismay many conservationists felt in similar situations. "Although all this may be technically within the law," Smith wrote, "it violates the principles of the National Forest Management Act of 1976." The act legalized clearcutting as a national forest harvest method, but it sought to restrict the use of the controversial practice. It limited the size of eastern clearcuts to forty acres, for instance. Significantly, it also curtailed the practice of replanting pine stands where hardwood forests had been. This practice "had irritated many sportsmen," forester Bob Padgett recalled. NFMA also stipulated that clearcutting should be used "only where it is determined to be the optimum method" and "only where" consistent "with the multiple use of the general area."[52]

Conservationists hoped this "only where" language would put the brakes on clearcutting. Their intent was to require the Forest Service to shift from routine clearcutting to routine use of other, less controversial timber harvest methods. The initial net effect of NFMA, however, was precisely the opposite. In practice, the Forest Service used the legislation as a sort of license to clearcut. "Eight years since passage of the National Forest Management Act," Bob Padgett noted in 1984, "national forest timber management practices are essentially the same as they were before Izaak Walton League filed its lawsuit." The agency effectively ignored the "only where" language and easily overcame the "optimum method" bar. It made silvicultural arguments to support clearcutting as nearly always the "optimum method" of timber harvest. In western North Carolina, for instance, Forest Service officials used the history of previous forest abuse as an argument for clearcutting. Other methods did not properly regenerate the forest, they contended.

Specific silvicultural justifications varied from region to region, but the end result was the same. The Forest Service used NFMA as the legislative underpinning for policies favoring wholesale clearcutting. Only the hard and fast rule against eastern clearcuts larger than forty acres functioned as conservationists intended.[53]

Though its initial impact proved disappointing to forest conservationists, over the long haul the National Forest Management Act enabled greater environmental protection through increased citizen and scientist participation in forest decision making. Its forest-planning provisions required opportunities for citizen response and provided an appeal mechanism for grievances. Across the nation, citizen groups used individual forest plans as means through which to influence national forest policy. Over time they helped bend the agency away from its commodity forestry emphasis and toward a more ecologically grounded forestry. The Western North Carolina Alliance joined the ranks of these citizen groups. The organization built an effective anticlearcutting movement linked to the Nantahala and Pisgah NFMA forest plans.[54]

Legislating Wilderness

The first major initiative carried out under the National Forest Management Act's new rules was a wilderness designation study undertaken by the administration of President Jimmy Carter. The program, called Roadless Area Review and Evaluation II, or RARE II (it was the second such federal survey), came in the wake of an ongoing push for wilderness designation throughout the country. The booming national economy after World War II spurred increased timber harvests and mineral extraction and prompted environmentalist fears that unprotected natural areas were continuously at risk of devastation by industrial exploitation. These fears spurred a series of wilderness initiatives, including the landmark 1964 Wilderness Act, which created the National Wilderness Preservation System (NWPS).

The Wilderness Act adopted a "zoning" strategy of land protection and targeted especially lands held by the Forest Service. The USFS had played a pioneering role establishing wilderness areas in the 1920s and 1930s, but after World War II environmentalists feared that national forestlands faced particularly acute risk of development. Since its inception, the Forest Service, unlike the National Park Service, had been conceived as a utilitarian rather than a preservationist agency. Its mandate could include recreation and some preservation, but it emphasized commodity production, especially timber. Under what came to be known as multiple-use management, timber production theoretically stood as one among several equally important uses, but as budgets, training, and decision making demonstrated, in practice timber trumped all other concerns.[55]

In the postwar period, the USFS stepped up timber harvests. Logging roads pushed ever deeper into the national forests, and timber cutting increased nearly every year. At the same time, demand for outdoor recreation—camping, hiking, fishing, and the like—also skyrocketed. In an effort to address these conflicting demands, Congress passed the Multiple-Use Sustained-Yield Act of 1960. The act listed outdoor recreation, watershed protection, livestock range provision, and wildlife and fish management alongside timber as central to the Forest Service's mission. Legislators intended to move the agency away from timbering as first priority, but in the long run the 1960 act failed to have this effect.[56]

Some agency limits on timber harvest did exist. The Forest Service did not allow logging in areas it labeled "primitive," "wild," "wilderness," and "canoe." But these administrative designations could be undone and the path cleared for timber harvesting simply through a stroke of the secretary of agriculture's pen. Administrative wilderness areas shrank or even disappeared altogether in response to harvest pressures. To wilderness advocates, this seemed too fragile a system of protection, especially given the agency's seemingly endless postwar appetite for timbering. By removing discretionary control from the Forest Service and siting it with Congress, Wilderness Act architects aimed to permanently protect undeveloped lands.[57]

With the 1964 Wilderness Act, Congress immediately protected 9.1 million acres of national forestlands by including them in the new National Wilderness Preservation System. In its inaugural version, the system included only these national forestlands, though the act made provisions for National Park Service and Fish and Wildlife Service lands to join the system eventually. The original NWPS included all tracts the Forest Service had administratively identified between 1939 and 1964 as wild, wilderness, and canoe areas. The Wilderness Act effectively zoned these areas for permanent protection from development.[58]

Nearly all the newly designated federal wilderness lay well west of the Mississippi River, beyond the one hundredth meridian. Western North Carolina hosted two of the East's scant three exceptions and accounted for more than 80 percent of the East's total designated wilderness acreage. Pisgah's Linville Gorge and Shining Rock tracts, both of which had previously been "wild areas," joined New Hampshire's Great Gulf as lonely eastern units in the new wilderness system. Together these three areas included only about 26,500 acres, less than three-tenths of 1 percent of the total National Wilderness Preservation System.[59]

Many other potential wilderness sites in both East and West remained outside the system, their status to be determined in future. In North Carolina's mountains, the Joyce Kilmer–Slickrock Creek Primitive Area was one such site. The Forest Service had identified "primitive" areas since 1929, ten years before it began its wild, wilderness, and canoe designations. The agency followed similar management guidelines for both types of areas and had gradually been reviewing "primitive" areas and moving some into the other three categories. The Forest Service acquired Kilmer-Slickrock in 1936, three years before the agency began its "wild" designations. It had managed the tract as "primitive" ever since.

The Wilderness Act temporarily protected primitive sites such as Kilmer-Slickrock nationwide and required the Forest Service to study them within ten years and make recommendations to Congress about whether or not they should be included in the National Wilderness Preservation System. Designated primitive areas comprised some fourteen million acres of national forestland. Decisions about their status, then, had important ramifications for the size and variety of the federal wilderness system.

In the years after 1964, a piecemeal process emerged as the USFS reviewed primitive areas. Some reviews moved forward with little controversy, but others faced hot challenges from conservationists and commodity interests. Wilderness advocates charged the Forest Service with attempting to minimize wilderness designation and maximize timber production. The agency argued that it had to keep in mind its other responsibilities under the 1960 Multiple-Use Sustained-Yield Act. From the fray emerged some additions to the NWPS, as Congress passed bills addressing individual land parcels, always in the West.[60]

Though struggles over USFS primitive areas continued, by the early 1970s the question of undesignated de facto wilderness in the national forests loomed far larger. For wilderness advocates, these areas had special urgency. They used the term "de facto wilderness" to describe undeveloped lands left unaddressed in the Wilderness Act, especially national forestlands neither designated "primitive" by the USFS nor contiguous to areas that were. Under the 1964 act, designated USFS primitive areas had temporary protection from development. Questions lingered about undeveloped lands immediately adjoining primitive areas, but by 1970 they too earned similar protection. This protection came through the Parker case, a USFS timber-sale challenge brought by citizens of Colorado with support from the Sierra Club.[61]

With logging temporarily prohibited on these USFS lands, wilderness advocates turned their attention to millions of undeveloped national forest acres with no legal protection, their de facto wilderness. Some of these areas adjoined existing units of the National Wilderness Preservation System, while others stood separately. The Forest Service began addressing these tracts in 1967, when regional foresters received instructions to review road-less areas under their jurisdiction for wilderness potential. By 1971 this effort had developed into the Forest Service's first Roadless Area Review and Evaluation initiative, or RARE I, as it eventually came to be known.[62]

When the USFS surveyed almost exclusively western tracts in RARE I, frustration mounted among advocates for wilderness in the East. The RARE I inventory included some 55.9 million roadless acres in 1,449 parcels, again almost all of them west of the one hundredth meridian. Only two eastern tracts and one unit in Puerto Rico stood as exceptions. The Forest Service released its report in 1973, just as furious debate over two competing eastern wilderness bills raged in Congress. The agency's parsimonious approach to eastern wildlands in RARE I added fuel to the legislative fire.[63]

The Forest Service, advocating what came to be known as the "purity doctrine," argued that eastern parcels were too small and too heavily marked by human history to qualify as wilderness. Nearly all the East had been logged and much of it burned over, the agency noted, and these developments had forever marred its wilderness quality. Designating these damaged eastern lands as "wilderness" diluted the concept too far.[64]

Forest Service critics rejected the purity doctrine, countering that the Wilderness Act provided definitional flexibility, that the National Wilderness Preservation System needed to be truly national in scope, and that eastern lands could recover wilderness qualities. The huge American population east of the Mississippi deserved access to wilderness resources, they argued. They also pointed out that precedent for eastern wilderness existed not only in the three USFS units already in the system but also in National Park Service and Fish and Wildlife Service proposals for NWPS additions. All these lands had suffered logging and fire damage but had recovered sufficiently to become worthy of congressional wilderness designation.[65]

Between 1972 and 1975 there was an upsurge in the lively political and tactical debate about eastern wilderness, and the Forest Service and Wilderness Society championed competing legislative initiatives. The Forest Service bill, introduced as the Wild Areas Act of 1972, essentially ratified the purity doctrine and created a separate system of wild lands for the East. Spokesmen from the Wilderness Society and Friends of the Earth sharply criticized the bill; one called it "anti-wilderness," and another concurred that it was "something we had to kill." Wilderness Society staffers immediately began work on a competing bill, combining eleven eastern wilderness proposals developed by local groups. A revised and expanded version of this bill eventually carried the day, becoming law in early 1975.[66]

The 1975 legislation, known as the Eastern Wilderness Areas Act, created fifteen new eastern wilderness tracts on the national forests.[67] It also designated seventeen additional wilderness study areas. Two western North Carolina tracts—Ellicott Rock and Joyce Kilmer–Slickrock Creek—became part of the National Wilderness Preservation System as a result of the act.[68]

Just a few years later, the RARE II initiative aimed to permanently protect other eastern lands by adding them to the federal wilderness system. In the Blue Ridge, this effort largely failed, turned back by a swelling tide of commons defense.

SIX

Wilderness as Commons Enclosure

RARE II Opposition

AT 5:00 ON THE AFTERNOON of July 11, 1978, downtown Franklin, North Carolina, seemed its typical self. Shops in the Macon County seat closed their doors, and people headed home after the workday. By 5:30, however, it became clear that this would be no ordinary evening. A caravan of vehicles—including big log-loader trucks, tractor-trailer rigs hauling lumber, cars and pickup trucks bearing hand-lettered protest signs, and even the occasional forklift—moved onto Main Street. Between seventy-five and a hundred of these vehicles crowded both lanes of the road the entire length of town, jamming traffic and eventually blocking access to the town center for at least an hour. Caravan participants included wood haulers, loggers, and other timber-industry workers and families from Macon and adjoining counties. They had come to protest the U.S. Forest Service's second Roadless Area Review and Evaluation (RARE II) wilderness designation initiative, and they trumpeted protimber and antiwilderness messages. "Western North Carolina needs more timber sales—not wilderness," read a caravan banner. "We can't make a living by hiking," proclaimed another. "We have given all we can to parks," added a third. "Stop the Sierra Club," urged a fourth.[1]

For Forest Service officials headed to a 7:00 public information session on RARE II wilderness designation that evening, the angry throng occupying Main Street served as a harbinger of things to come. Once inside the packed Macon County Courthouse, agency officials faced an unruly audience several hundred strong. The crowd almost unanimously opposed the wilderness designation proposals. "We got a bunch of protestants here to your wilderness program, and I'm one of them myself. I'll go on record as saying that," Franklin mayor Woodrow Reeves told Nantahala district forester Fred Foster almost as soon as the meeting opened. Accompanied by hearty cheers from the assembly, Reeves then called the information ses-

sion "a kangaroo-type propaganda message" and led a wholesale exodus—
roughly half the audience—from the courtroom. Many people jeered and
shouted as they left, and a few hurled obscenities.

A few minutes later, Forest Service officials attempting to proceed with
the program saw some fifty more people exit the room. "We are not a proponent of the RARE II program. The Forest Service has not endorsed any of
the alternative plans," Walter Rule, public information officer for the National Forests in North Carolina (NFsNC), tried to reassure the remaining
crowd, but he was interrupted by catcalls. As he and his colleagues pressed
forward, audience members demanded to express their views. "You have
had your time, when do we get ours?" they shouted. Audience member
Willie Hayes walked up to Walter Rule and shook his fist in the official's
face. Later Hayes interrupted the meeting, calling for a show of hands in
opposition to wilderness. "Practically everybody in the courtroom either
stood or waved their arms," wrote a journalist covering the session.[2]

The heated opposition expressed on Main Street and in the courthouse
was part of a larger outpouring of fierce antiwilderness sentiment that left
Forest Service officials throughout the southern mountains reeling. Lumber
trucks tied up traffic, and audience members shouted down USFS representatives at meetings throughout the region.[3] At times during the wilderness-
designation debates, USFS information sessions and the Appalachian region
as a whole seemed to hover on the edge of violent eruption. Forest Service personnel repeatedly found themselves facing angry and intimidat-
ing protesters like Hayes, whose behavior threatened physical assault. Pat
Cook, who served in the Atlanta regional office as RARE II coordinator for
the Forest Service's Southern Region, remembered feeling he risked being
"shot at from all sides."[4]

Why did the Forest Service's roadless area study provoke such heated
responses from southern Appalachian residents? One obvious reason is
timber's importance to the regional economy. The RARE II initiative pre-
cipitated a nationwide battle in the ongoing war over national forest management, with timber and other extractive-industry interests in one camp
and environmentalists in the other.[5] Timber-dependent communities across
the nation fiercely opposed RARE II on economic grounds. Wilderness resistance in the southern mountains was unquestionably part of this larger
national story.

Concerns about the timber economy, however, cannot wholly account
for the ferocity of southern Appalachian wilderness opposition. The region
was not as dependent on timber as some other affected regions—the Pacific
Northwest or the Northern Rockies, for instance. Nor did federal forests

represent as dominant a presence as in some of these other areas. Yet the southern mountains proved a national hotbed of RARE II resistance. Sierra Club spokespeople said they encountered greater wilderness resistance here than anywhere else, and USFS historians echoed this assessment. Like a bright blue flame in a larger fire, Appalachian antipathy to wilderness stood out from the national picture. Timber alone could not adequately explain this phenomenon.[6]

Though timber played a critical role, wilderness opposition in the Appalachians drew crucial force from its ability to tap the powerful wellspring of commons defense. Passionate regionwide attachment to the commons forest fueled antiwilderness fires. Many rural Appalachian residents fought against RARE II because they saw it as a threat to the forests they used not only as a harvest ground for timber but also for fish, game, firewood, herbs, berries, roots, and the like. Wilderness designation would take lands from the pool of accessible multiple-use forest enjoyed by local residents, they argued, and set them aside as inaccessible single-use recreation sites for the benefit of well-off visitors. In other words, RARE II threatened the commons with enclosure.

Timber-industry supporters understood the power of this enclosure analysis, and they actively promoted it. Here as elsewhere in the country, timbermen organized and channeled opposition to additional wilderness designation. Industry spokesman Charles Woodard, for example, remembered putting many days' work into the Franklin demonstration. In the southern mountains, however, timber's success depended on its ability to rally not only woods workers but also commons-style forest users to the antiwilderness cause. Industry supporters did this brilliantly.

It was not a foregone conclusion that mountain residents would flock to the anti–RARE II banner. In fact, early in the wilderness designation process, western North Carolinians expressed widespread support for some additional wilderness. On the whole, wilderness advocates failed to convert this support into congressional protection. Wilderness opponents, on the other hand, succeeded in changing widespread support into widespread opposition by skillfully playing a complicated cultural as well as economic game. They cast wilderness supporters as outside elites aiming to enclose the forest commons, and they painted themselves as defenders of that commons.[7]

On the whole, the timber industry won the battle over RARE II in the North Carolina mountains. Wilderness advocates did achieve some modest victories, most notably, the successful creation of the new Southern Nantahala Wilderness Area. They also gained protection for a number of extensions to existing wilderness.[8] But timber emerged as the primary victor in western North Carolina as throughout the country. The industry's efforts to portray itself as part and parcel of the region's cultural as well as economic fabric largely succeeded, as did its efforts to portray prowilderness environmentalists as foreign and threatening to both. In this first of the post-NFMA showdowns over the fate of western North Carolina's million acres of Forest Service lands, wilderness opponents played most aggressively for the commons card. They essentially took it, and overall they carried the day.[9]

The Carter Administration Launches RARE II

The administration of President Jimmy Carter, elected in November 1976, hoped finally to settle lingering national forest wilderness questions with a second inventory of federal roadless areas, quickly dubbed "RARE II." The administration planned to survey over 50 million qualifying acres (this number grew in the course of the study to around 65.7 million) in the course of a year. This fast-paced survey would determine which tracts should become official wilderness, which should be "released" for commodity development, and which should be left in the "further planning" category. Neither conservationists nor industry interests were prepared for the survey when it was announced, and both scrambled to influence its outcome on the very tight timeline.[10]

Because RARE II was the first large USFS undertaking to occur under the rubric of the 1976 National Forest Management Act, public participation in the process carried a great deal of weight. The mandate to survey Forest Service holdings came down from Washington, and final recommendations for wilderness designation went from the secretary of agriculture to Congress. Between these starting and ending points, however, the RARE II process would be intimately shaped by the political jockeying of pro- and antiwilderness advocates in communities and states affected by the surveys.[11]

In the southern Appalachians, the timber industry was better organized than the wilderness lobby and thus had a leg up. The regionwide Southern Appalachian Hardwood Producers Association, established in 1975 at about the time of the Eastern Wilderness Areas Act, quickly went to work opposing new wilderness designations. No prowilderness counterpart with similar breadth existed.

The Sierra Club and the Wilderness Society had growing presence in the East, but neither had established regional influence comparable to that of the Southern Appalachian Hardwood Producers Association. Both organizations, rooted in the West, stepped up prowilderness efforts in the East during the 1970s. As we have seen, Wilderness Society activists spearheaded work on the Eastern Wilderness Areas Act. Earlier, around the time of RARE I, a North Carolina chapter of the Sierra Club formed and within it a western North Carolina group calling itself Wenoca. Among its national initiatives in the 1970s, the Sierra Club included an effort to halt roading near the Joyce Kilmer area of the Nantahala National Forest.[12]

Despite these efforts, neither organization was prepared to do the kind of grassroots organizing that served the Southern Appalachian Hardwood Producers Association so well in Franklin. The national groups had proved extraordinarily effective in legislative and judicial arenas, and they focused limited resources there. But the National Forest Management Act of 1976 had shifted the political ground under the national forests substantially in ways that did not become altogether clear until years later. The act gave to grassroots participants unprecedented power to influence national forest policy. During the RARE II period in western North Carolina, timber interests mobilized the grass roots and tapped this new power more effectively than did wilderness advocates.[13]

The Forest Service began the RARE II process by accepting nominations from the public for areas to consider for wilderness designation. In North Carolina, the Forest Service hosted three public workshops in July 1977, then continued a series of open participation sessions through September. By November George Olson, NFsNC supervisor, had announced that his office had received nominations for 207,000 acres in twenty-four different pieces. More than three-quarters of this area, over 160,000 acres, lay in nineteen tracts in western North Carolina's Nantahala and Pisgah National Forests. Eastern North Carolina's Croatan included four additional areas, and the piedmont's Uwharrie contributed one.[14]

Olson explained that collecting nominations completed the first step in a four-part process. Next, the Forest Service would evaluate nominations, and then it would make recommendations to the Department of Agriculture. The final step in the RARE II initiative would occur when the secretary of agriculture submitted a list of recommended wilderness areas to Congress. Areas not included in the legislative proposal either would become immediately available for multiple uses, including timber harvest, or would go through the Forest Service's regular planning process and be considered for various uses, including wilderness. Final decisions about wilderness designation would be made by Congress, since only that body had the authority to mandate additions to the National Wilderness Preservation System.[15]

Olson's initial announcement emphasized that the Forest Service had not yet taken a position on any of the proposed wilderness areas. Perhaps anticipating controversy, Olson worked to make his statements as balanced as possible. RARE II aimed to provide the country with a quality wilderness system, he explained, but not at too high a price. The Service planned to identify which areas should be included in an "ideal" wilderness system and "then measure the potential social and economic impacts of designating them as wilderness." The USFS "welcome[d]" and "desired" public input "at any point during the process," Olson noted. After evaluating proposed areas, the agency would present a draft environmental impact statement for public review, including alternatives allowing for more and less wilderness designation. Olson expected this draft to be ready by May or June 1978. During the summer the Forest Service would give the public time to visit the proposed areas and make its own judgments, and in the fall it would hold a series of workshops on the process.[16]

Despite Olson's attempts to use balanced language, speculations about the Forest Service's position on RARE II abounded. In its headline for the story on Olson's announcement, the *Asheville Citizen-Times* asked a question that had doubtless entered many minds: "Is Forest Service Neutral on Wilderness Issue?" Wilderness advocates believed the agency was largely averse to the RARE II process. Key phrases in Olson's careful announcement underscored this belief. The areas were "not a Forest Service recommendation," Olson emphasized. The supervisor's insistence that his agency "must fully consider what the American people would lose, as well as gain," from wilderness designation seemed unpromising, as did his portrayal of wilderness and social and economic welfare as competing interests. Wilderness advocates may also have seen antiwilderness bias in Olson's language differentiating lands recommended for wilderness classification from lands "available" for multiple uses.[17]

The *Asheville Citizen-Times*, on the other hand, doubted Forest Service neutrality from the other direction. Like most local papers, it generally sympathized with area business interests, and it was typically a timber booster. The *Citizen-Times* worried that environmentalists had seized the Forest Service's reins and were steering it down an anti-industry course. Timber-industry spokesmen shared these concerns and complained publicly that the Forest Service was beholden to environmental interest groups.[18]

In fact, wilderness advocates came closer to the truth. Forest Service employees were divided in their enthusiasm for the RARE II initiative, but the agency overall was at best lukewarm toward it. Gifford Pinchot had founded the USFS as a technocratic utilitarian agency, its guiding principle that trained professionals were best suited to manage public lands. Despite various challenges, in the late 1970s that core belief was still very much in place. Wilderness preservation represented an entirely different vision for public lands management, one most Forest Service personnel did not share. Though "ologists"—biologists, archaeologists, and other natural and social scientists—had joined Forest Service ranks, foresters and timber road engineers still dominated its payrolls. These more traditional employees typically thought of themselves as the most competent possible forest managers and of public participation—and wilderness, wildlife, and recreation initiatives—as unwelcome intrusions.[19]

Moreover, RARE II and other wilderness initiatives represented a direct challenge to Forest Service management as it had been carried out. Agency personnel typically felt coerced by the RARE II mandate, resenting the way it sought to restrict the Forest Service's land-management autonomy. Pat Cook, who headed the RARE II program in USFS Region 8, the Southeast region, which included North Carolina, remembered how hostile many of his coworkers had been to the program. He recalled having to drag some agency personnel "kicking and screaming" through the RARE II process.[20]

The battle lines were drawn: national environmental groups warmly supported additional wilderness designation through the RARE II effort; timber and other industry groups adamantly opposed it. A reluctant and wilderness-wary Forest Service found itself caught in the middle, feeling coerced and accused by both sides of being in cahoots with the other— positions it did not relish. "We may not like it," Pat Cook remembered telling Region 8 forest supervisors, "but we've been given this job and we have to do it."[21]

Public Opinion in the Blue Ridge

And what of public opinion, so crucial under the 1976 National Forest Management Act? In North Carolina's mountains in 1977, it seemed generally prowilderness. U.S. representative Lamar Gudger—a Democrat from the state's Eleventh Congressional District, its westernmost region—took his constituents' pulse and found broad support both for additional wilderness and for multiple-use management. Three thousand western North Carolinians responded to a RARE II questionnaire he circulated.

Gudger's survey included a query about current national forest management, and here his constituents expressed general satisfaction. Nearly half the respondents, 47 percent, endorsed the Forest Service's "multiple-use approach" to forest management. About 19 percent wished for a decrease in timber production, and about 24 percent preferred an increase. The remaining 10 percent offered no opinion. Even more than multiple use, however,

Gudger's constituents seemed favorable toward wilderness. A clear majority—55 percent—expressed support for new wilderness designation as long as it did not include more than 10 percent of western North Carolina's million national forest acres. A tiny 7 percent opposed new wilderness altogether. Gudger's office did not report the opinions of the other 38 percent; presumably, they either had no opinion or favored new wilderness for *more* than 10 percent of western North Carolina's national forestlands.[22]

Thus, Gudger's opinion poll revealed no indications of a looming antiwilderness tidal wave. If anything, it seemed to promise a prowilderness groundswell. Moreover, if even a quarter of the unreported 38 percent favored designation for more than 10 percent of western North Carolina's national forestlands, then Gudger had a nearly two-to-one prowilderness mandate. After he conducted the survey, however, Representative Gudger staked out a cautious middle position. He pledged to preserve "true wilderness areas" but vowed continued support for the Forest Service's traditional multiple-use management program, which had little wilderness emphasis.[23]

Besides the low level of outright wilderness opposition and the clear prowilderness majority, the most eye-popping data from Representative Gudger's survey came when he asked constituents how they used the forests. Only 10 percent of respondents reported deriving income from national forestlands. But nearly all—a whopping 90-plus percent—reported personally using national forestlands on a recurring basis. Gudger did not ask for specific information about how his constituents used the woods, and certainly there were wilderness-loving backpackers among them. Many, however, would have been nonindustrial forest harvesters and nonwilderness forest recreationists—people who cut personal-use firewood in the forests or drove to campsites, hunting grounds, berry patches, fishing streams, and swimming holes. In fact, Gudger's three thousand respondents seemed at least as concerned about hunting and fishing issues as about wilderness and national forest timber management. By a two-to-one margin (56 percent to 28 percent, with 16 percent expressing no opinion), they registered dissatisfaction with the quantity of fish and game and the quality of angling and hunting in western North Carolina.[24]

Representative Gudger's survey revealed with crystalline clarity how his constituents had a stake in the region's national forests. A few made a living from them; almost all used them regularly. Though the forests had economic value, their social and cultural significance held far greater importance. In western North Carolina's forest politics, commons-style woods users made up a powerful "swing voter" constituency. During RARE II the region's timber-industry supporters recognized the critical importance of this bloc, and so too did many local wilderness advocates. Both camps worked to tap the deep local reservoirs of commons-based forest concern and channel it toward their own cause.

Antiwilderness Arguments

Throughout the RARE II debates, opponents in western North Carolina cast wilderness as an enclosure threat to the commons. Timbermen and their political allies led the charge. Tom Thrash, a businessman who owned one of western North Carolina's largest woods-products operations, put the case directly. He described proposed wilderness as "a land grab by hikers and backpackers, mostly from Florida and the Midwest, for their exclusive use."[25] Unpacking Thrash's rhetoric underscores the power of his analysis in the context of the forest commons. Thrash described enclosure, pure and simple. He cast wilderness supporters as outside elites aiming essentially to privatize the forest, to "grab" lands from locals "for their exclusive use." His "hikers and backpackers" language painted wilderness advocates as idle recreationists; they wished to wrest away productive forests only to convert them into elite pleasure grounds.

Versions of this analysis appeared throughout the RARE II process. Wilderness proponents, defined as an elite "minority" made up of wealthy and greedy outsiders, sought to "take" mountain lands to "set aside" for their "exclusive" or "private" use. Mere recreationists, they were determined to prevent all other forest uses, including all forms of harvest. Their self-serving actions would deny forest access to "the majority." Wilderness opponents, portrayed as "ordinary" people of middling means and as insiders with long ties to the mountains, sought to defend the democratic multiple-use forest from this elite "land grab."

Like most antienclosure thinking, this line of argument clearly included a strong class dimension. In its opening salvo on RARE II, an editorial entitled "Not for Just a Few," the *Franklin Press* offered its version of wilderness class analysis. Similar interpretations quickly became standard antiwilderness fare. "Macon County, you and I, cannot afford to give up this land for the use of a small minority," *Press* editors wrote. "Let them go to the park." Again, wilderness advocates became elite privatizers, "a few" seeking to force ordinary Macon County folk to "give up" the forest. This "small minority" sought land sacrifices that local residents could not "afford."[26]

Wilderness opponents also argued that the exclusive leisured few who would enjoy wilderness expected the larger, shut-out, working majority to finance their experience. Mitchell County tree farmer Howard Beidler remarked that only a small portion of the population used wilderness areas, and he advocated fees for those who did. As it was, he argued, the nation's taxpayers effectively subsidized the recreational experiences of a privileged handful. Echoed another RARE II detractor, "They say one percent of the people would use it, but the rest of us ninety-nine percent would pay for it."[27]

Beneath this few-versus-many rhetoric, there was also a locals-versus-outsiders argument. The *Franklin Press* put the case forthrightly. "It is not just the logger and the timberman who have an interest in this proposal," wrote the *Press* in a second RARE II editorial. "You and I, the everyday folks who like to spend a weekend camping, but don't have time to back pack into the area, will give up millions of acres to a fanatical few." Here again, the newspaper cast Macon County residents, "you and I," as "everyday folks," while wilderness enthusiasts became "a fanatical few." Ordinary mountain people camped with vehicles; half-crazed outsiders backpacked. Using language that underscored this perceived distance, the *Press* argued that the "back packing cult" already had "ample land" in the eastern states, including the Great Smoky Mountains, Shenandoah, and Everglades National Parks. "Everyday folks" still had access to millions of national forest acres and should not agree to give them up.[28]

Wilderness opponents, including the *Franklin Press*, cast the Sierra Club in particular as an outside agent of enclosure. They saw the club as a political instrument of well-off outsiders who coveted prime western North Carolina forestlands. "Write your Congressman," urged the *Press* in its second RARE II editorial. "The Sierra Club members already have." Reporting for Raleigh's *News and Observer*, Ted Vaden explained that many people in the Franklin area "see wilderness as a soft-headed proposal cooked up by Sierra Club types to create playgrounds for elitist backpackers." As Vaden observed later in his piece, "The Sierra Club [was] felt [to be] an outsider in the mountains."[29]

RARE II opponents also framed the current wilderness study as part of an *ongoing* enclosure process. Here, too, *Franklin Press* editorialists took a typical antiwilderness position. According to the Macon County newspaper, a prowilderness "small minority" had already commandeered vast forests through the Great Smoky Mountains National Park. Of course, the park was not part of the National Wilderness Preservation System, and rules governing NPS land did not match those governing USFS wilderness.[30] Nonetheless, wilderness opponents often equated the two. "We think when the government set aside the Smoky Mountain Park for what might be classified as virtual Wilderness development they took as much of Western North Carolina land as we should be called on to give," *Press* editorialists wrote in an analysis typical of the pattern. Ever insatiable, wilderness enthusiasts now returned to demand more recreational pleasure grounds. They sought 23,000 additional acres in Macon County alone, the paper noted. These too would be "set aside for the exclusive use" of "a small percentage of people." In other words, for all intents and purposes, they would be privatized.[31]

Most of the lands under consideration in Macon County "are much too adaptable for a multiple use classification to be set aside" as wilderness, the paper continued. Restrictions on camping, fishing, and timber harvesting would bring economic hardship to the community, the *Press* argued, as would reductions in the money the county received from the federal government in lieu of taxes. In effect, wilderness designation would transfer the benefits of forest resources from the modest-means local majority to a well-off absentee minority. It would turn into playgrounds for the rich the hard-working forests that local people relied on to meet basic needs. Thus, though neither the paper nor other wilderness opponents ever used the term, RARE II became a question of commons enclosure.[32]

Press editorials called on all Macon residents—hunters, anglers, and campers as well as loggers—to oppose RARE II wilderness designation. The paper glided easily from commons-style issues of access to timber harvest questions. "This land would not be accessible by any type of vehicular road—no campers, trailers," editorialists wrote. "No timber could ever be cut." Anyone who had reaped the benefits of multiple-use national forest management should act now. "We hope those who have enjoyed using the above designated areas in their present state for outdoor recreational purposes and those who have earned a livelihood working in the woods . . . will express themselves," the paper concluded. Commons users as well as timber harvesters should answer the call.[33]

In fact, intertwined worries about job and commons-resource loss ran through much of the debate over RARE II. The *Asheville Citizen-Times* voiced them in one of its early pieces on the wilderness issue. "Timber cutters of Western North Carolina have creases on their foreheads to match the terrain from which they wrest their living these days," wrote reporter Clyde Osborne for the daily paper. If the nineteen areas under study became designated wilderness, warned the *Citizen-Times*, "the timber cutters will be facing unemployment." In a passage emblematic of the sorts of timber-commons ties that wilderness opponents routinely drew, Osborne moved effortlessly from timber-industry job loss to wider commons concerns. "The timber cutters are not alone in their concern," he wrote. "Wilderness designation would also ban mining, harvesting of galax leaves and other mountain industries from which thousands of Western North Carolina citizens receive a major portion of their income."[34]

Some RARE II detractors, pointing to the kinds of issues Osborne discussed, charged wilderness supporters with callous disregard for local people's needs. A man from Marble, North Carolina, in far-western Cherokee County, suggested that people in urban centers did not understand how central forest production was to work and life in the mountains. He intertwined economic with commons concerns. "People in Raleigh and Washington, D.C., they don't have to make their living here," he explained to a team from CBS News. "They don't have to heat with wood. Where we going to get heater wood? Where's these men going to work over here?" In a letter to the *Franklin Press*, Walter T. Buchanan echoed these concerns, asking what wilderness advocates expected local people to do for a living if they could not cut timber.[35]

As the CBS News crew learned, firewood took a place alongside timber as a central concern among wilderness opponents. While timber work put bread on the table, commons firewood cutting put heat in the stove. Clay County Rural Development Authority chairman Tom Day expressed fuel concerns to reporter Clyde Osborne. "We can't even cut firewood between Standing Indian and Fire Creek," Day noted. Standing Indian rose on the western boundary of the proposed Chunky Gal Wilderness area, and Fire Creek marked its eastern boundary. Both were familiar local landmarks. Since law required that areas under consideration for wilderness designation be managed as if they were already wilderness, the Chunky Gal tract was off-limits to would-be local firewood cutters. Had Chunky Gal become wilderness, firewood cutting in the area would have come to a permanent halt.[36]

In sum, RARE II supporters had little concern for the well-being of local people, antiwilderness spokesmen argued. Focused only on expanding their luxurious Appalachian playgrounds, wilderness advocates either could not see or did not care about these recreation sites' effects on local residents. They cavalierly dismissed pressing economic concerns and ran roughshod over cultural traditions that bound many mountain residents to the local woods. Like other outsiders before them, RARE II opponents implicitly argued, wilderness enthusiasts planned to impose their visions on Blue Ridge landscapes and cultures with or without longtime residents' endorsement.[37]

Perhaps no one captured the full constellation of regional concerns about wilderness better than Woodrow Reeves and Verlon Swafford. Reeves, the fiery mayor of Franklin who led the walkout of the Forest Service RARE II information session, issued an antiwilderness declaration together with Swafford, chairman of the Macon County Board of Commissioners. The two wrote a letter to President Jimmy Carter asking for a halt to the wilderness study. They sent two thousand copies of this letter nationwide to state and local officials and to press outlets. The *Franklin Press* carried this lengthy letter—some eight hundred words' worth—in full, beginning on the front page.[38]

Reeves and Swafford agreed with the *Franklin Press* that adequate public lands had already been set aside for wilderness-style recreation. Nationally, they wrote, the wilderness system already included 14.7 million national forest acres. Western North Carolina already contained 32,000 acres of wilderness, and together with eastern Tennessee, the region hosted the 595,000-acre Great Smoky Mountains National Park.[39] In effect, the Forest Service now proposed to designate as many as 123,000 additional western North Carolina acres. Reeves and Swafford argued that the system of national parks, together with the existing wilderness system, already offered ample opportunity for wilderness recreation. They admitted some regulation differences between Department of the Interior lands and USFS wilderness tracts but drew a rough equivalency between these "set aside" parcels nonetheless.[40]

Reeves and Swafford's enclosure analysis could hardly have been more directly stated. For them, the possibility that more western North Carolina tracts might become wilderness represented a "continuing encroachment, upon the now open access and usable land of the Forest Service." If it was allowed to go on, "then only the hard core wilderness oriented pressure groups or clubs . . . would control the use of these public lands for virtually their own private benefits." This was clearly an antienclosure argument. The democratic commons—"usable," "open access," "public" lands—came under siege from the "continuing encroachment" of elite outsiders bent on securing "private benefits."[41]

Reeves and Swafford also saw wilderness as effectively *removed* from the national forests. They contrasted "present wilderness" to "present Forest Service lands," as if the two were mutually exclusive. In fact, of course, all western North Carolina tracts in the National Wilderness Preservation System were part of Nantahala or Pisgah National Forest. But Reeves and Swafford's language suggested the degree to which they saw wilderness designation as a removal of commons lands from commons use. Average citizens used USFS lands "extensively" but wilderness "very little or not at all." With congressional wilderness designation, they implied, lands lost their commons character and their local appeal.[42]

Moreover, Reeves and Swafford wrote as if the multiple-use forest were endangered, a tiny and shrinking island in a rising sea of wilderness. They urged that timber harvesting should continue to take place "on the remaining non-wilderness areas" under Forest Service jurisdiction. Their language seemed to imply that only a small amount of "non-wilderness" land existed, when in fact the reverse was true. Over a million acres of national forestlands came under multiple-use management in western North Carolina, while only thirty thousand acres had become part of the National Wilderness Preservation System.[43]

Like many wilderness opponents, Reeves and Swafford held a producers' view of the forest. They opened by casting RARE II as dangerous to North Carolina's timber economy, and they charged that productive lands became "Frozen Forever" under the Wilderness Act. They touted judicious forest use and cast wilderness designation as wasteful nonuse. "We believe in Conservation," wrote the two officials. "We do not believe in Waste." Under RARE II, they argued, valuable public lands became "un-useable." Timber "should be harvested when it is mature like any other crop," the two stated. "It should not be allowed to rot in the forest." They also pointed out that timber was a renewable resource, and they argued that the United States could "no longer afford to waste its natural resources."[44]

These producers' arguments—comparing trees to agricultural crops, painting wilderness designation as nonuse, portraying mature forests as decadent, and casting wilderness as "wasteful"—were standard antiwilderness fare. "Timber is a crop, don't let it rot!" read a sign at the Franklin protest. "Millions of board feet . . . rots each year," charged Walter Buchanan. The Macon County acreage "being considered for wilderness classification is good timber growing land," opined the *Franklin Press*. "To use our forests otherwise is wasteful," editorialists charged.[45]

Beneath this constellation of ideas lay not only support for the region's timber industry but also a general philosophy of forest *use*. If one thought of the forest as a productive site, the idea that timber was a "crop" that could be "wasted" if not properly "harvested" and "used" made sense. To mountain residents who shared this view, the idea of wilderness could seem shockingly wasteful. Larry Davis, a young former forest ranger from Franklin, nicely summarized this perspective as he talked with a reporter. "The wilderness concept is waste, pure and simple," Davis told the *News and Observer*'s Ted Vaden. Vaden described Davis as genuinely baffled by the wilderness movement. Davis conceded that wilderness was "beautiful to look at," but he found an attractive aesthetic insufficient justification for taking large tracts out of productive use. Reeves and Swafford echoed Davis's assessment. "A wilderness area is of no material use to mankind," they declared.[46]

Some wilderness opponents saw the RARE II controversy in religious terms. To them, wilderness designations seemed to threaten a God-given order. Larry Davis raised this question with Ted Vaden. "You just stand there and look at it [wilderness] and you wonder, is this the way God meant for it to be?" Davis's language implied that for him, the answer was no.[47] Davis's congressman, Democrat Lamar Gudger, went a step further. "God created the earth to bring forth its fruit in its season and he gave man dominion over it to till it and to tend it—not to neglect it and ignore it," Gudger told reporters. "A certain amount of wilderness may be all right," Gudger continued, "but the land [under wilderness management] does not bear fruitfully." Gudger explained that he had forest products in mind as the principal "fruits" of western North Carolina's woods. Only areas too steep or inaccessible to make good timberlands should be designated wilderness, he argued. Larry Davis's description of forestry as "production, not waste," fit nicely with Lamar Gudger's "till and tend, not neglect and ignore," theology. On the other hand, language such as the *Franklin Press*'s "backpacking cult" established religious distance between wilderness supporters and RARE II opponents.[48]

The Hunting Issue

Even with questions of class, economy, region, and religion in the RARE II mix, hunting may have been the single most important political issue to emerge in the wilderness debates. As we have seen, for local residents, hunting was one of the important distinctions between the Great Smoky Mountains National Park, where it was banned, and western North Carolina's national forests, where it was welcomed and encouraged. Rules governing wilderness areas permitted hunting and fishing, but countless local residents thought they did not. On the RARE II beat in Franklin, *News and Observer* journalist Ted Vaden asked people he met questions about wilderness restrictions. "A number of residents interviewed randomly," he reported, "were under the impression that hunting, fishing, and camping would be forbidden in wilderness areas."[49] These residents almost certainly would have opposed wilderness designation on grounds that it would make favorite hunting grounds and fishing holes off-limits.

Probably part of the local misunderstanding about hunting stemmed from residents' tendency to equate national forest wilderness areas with the Great Smoky Mountains National Park and to see both as recreation areas designed with outside visitors in mind. One observer wrote that "there was a false but unshakable belief that once a wilderness was established, the next step would be to outlaw hunting." This observation suggests that mountain residents feared wilderness designation as only one step in an ongoing process of commons enclosure.[50]

Wilderness opponents actively abetted local residents' fears. "[During RARE II] the politicians and the logging companies had done an excellent job around here scaring people to death that they were going to be shut out of the forest, that these environmental groups were opposed to hunting," Madison County resident and forest activist Mary Kelly remembered. "You wouldn't be able to camp. You wouldn't be able to hunt. You wouldn't be able to fish. All they were about was shutting people out of the forest and they were no good." Local wilderness supporters' letters to the *Franklin Press* editor supported Kelly's assessment.[51]

One crucial example of the sort of misinformation wilderness opponents spread appeared in Woodrow Reeves and Verlon Swafford's widely circulated letter to President Carter. Reeves and Swafford included a list detailing how a change from multiple-use management to wilderness classification would affect various forest activities. The first three entries on the list read as follows:

	Present Uses [Multiple-Use Management]	Uses Under RARE II [Wilderness Management]
Harvesting of Timber and Pulpwood	Yes	No
Harvesting of non-marketable or uprooted trees for Firewood or Fuel	Yes	No
Open use of lands for hunting, fishing, or other recreational purposes	Yes	No

A lay reader scanning this list would almost certainly come away believing that wilderness regulations prohibited timber harvesting, firewood cutting, and hunting, fishing, and camping. The reader would be correct on the first two counts and entirely mistaken on the third. Hunting, fishing, and camping were permissible uses of wilderness.[52]

Reeves and Swafford constructed their list in a way designed to mislead sportsmen and swing them toward the antiwilderness camp. The two men had become thoroughly familiar with the rules governing wilderness, as many of the detailed entries farther down their list demonstrated. They had to know that wilderness regulations permitted hunting, fishing, and camping. Their misleading trick lay in the "open-use" language they used to introduce the hunting category. If their third entry had simply said "Hunting and fishing," they would have had to put "Yes" under wilderness. By muddying things with the phrase "open use," Reeves and Swafford could lead people to believe what many already feared—that hunting would be prohibited in designated wilderness just as it was in the Great Smoky Mountains National Park.[53]

Reeves and Swafford wrote that their eleven-point chart "fairly" made a multiple-use versus wilderness comparison. Except for their third entry, this was a reasonable claim, as the rest of their list was scrupulously accurate. This meticulous precision on other points—obscure points, about electronic communications installations, for instance—underscored the disingenuousness beneath Reeves and Swafford's handling of hunting and fishing. By lumping all recreation into one giant category, Reeves and Swafford gave readers the impression that *all* hunting, fishing, and camping would be banned in wilderness areas. From their antiwilderness point of view, this was a useful misconception for readers to have.[54]

Had the two men allowed themselves a straightforward "motorized vehicle" category, they could have clarified things considerably. The vehicles were at issue, not the rods and guns. One could hunt on foot in a designated wilderness, but one could not drive one's hunting party into the area in a pickup truck. Reeves and Swafford's list included entries treating aircraft and motorboats, neither of which frequented western North Carolina forests with anything approaching the regularity of ordinary automobiles. Yet their eleven-point chart failed even to mention the everyday cars and trucks in which thousands of western North Carolinians routinely drove into the national forests. If they had put "vehicles" and "hunting" in separate categories, they could have explained the issues more accurately. But they did not seek accuracy; their antiwilderness efforts were better served if hunters saw through a glass darkly. The chart artfully painted hunting and fishing as more threatened by wilderness designation than they actually were.[55]

Woodrow Reeves was himself an avid hunter. He appeared regularly at local North Carolina Wildlife Resources Commission meetings, and he had long been active in Macon County hunting circles. He knew how strongly his neighbors felt about their hunting and fishing. Reeves wanted to harness that energy for the antiwilderness cause, and he constructed his chart in such a way as to maximize its ability to do so. He and Swafford could argue that their language was technically accurate, but it was nevertheless deliberately misleading.

Evidence suggests that these tactics worked. *News and Observer* reporter Ted Vaden canvassed Franklin residents about the same time Reeves and Swafford's letter appeared in the *Franklin Press* and reported that many of his interviewees were under the impression that hunting, fishing, and camping were banned in designated wilderness areas. It might well have been because they had recently read their newspapers.[56]

The town of Boone's *Watauga Democrat* went Reeves and Swafford one better. It actually told readers in straightforward (and straightforwardly inaccurate) language that wilderness regulations prohibited hunting and fishing. In an editorial entitled "Ah, Wilderness . . . When Is Enough Enough?," the *Democrat* wrote: "There will be no hunting, fishing, or other recreational use of the [wilderness] lands." This piece appeared just under a month after Reeves and Swafford sent their letter to presses and officials nationwide, probably including the *Democrat*. Boone's editorialists may have picked up their inaccuracy from the letter's misleading language. In any case, Watauga County's antiwilderness effort probably got a boost from the incorrect story.[57]

Antiwilderness Campaigning

Antiwilderness stalwarts used organizing as well as rhetoric to turn back the RARE II initiative. In western North Carolina, a number of antiwilderness groups emerged. Jack Brettler, a Franklin-based minerals developer with interests in olivine and uranium deposits in two of western North Carolina's proposed wilderness areas, founded and became president of the Save America Club. The club enlisted other businessmen in the anti–RARE II effort, and Brettler began building a political career on his antiwilderness credentials. He boasted that the half-mile road his mining company built into the Chunky Gal Wilderness Study Area made Appalachian Properties, Inc., a pioneer in wilderness commodity development. He made a 1978 bid for a North Carolina Senate seat on the Republican ticket. Woodrow Reeves joined Brettler's club and succeeded him as its president. Timber lobbyist and Baptist minister Jimmy Rogers also organized an antiwilderness coalition across western North Carolina and north Georgia. Rogers's group produced "Stop RARE II" bumper stickers, which quickly became a fixture on mountain roads. And a group billing itself as "mountain counties' citizens who have organized against the RARE II Wilderness proposal" announced a meeting in the *Franklin Press*.[58]

RARE II opponents also took aim at the opposition. They targeted Forest Service personnel, whom they saw as agents of RARE II enclosure. They targeted Sierra Club members, whom they cast as instigators of enclosure. And in a classic commons-defense move, they also threatened the forests themselves.[59]

RARE II anger occasionally spilled into gestures of attack on USFS personnel. The most famous local incident targeted George Olson, NFsNC supervisor and the highest-ranking USFS official in the state. Though he himself was not a RARE II enthusiast, Olson found no immunity from antiwilderness ire. He "got hit over the head a couple of times at some of those meetings," remembered RARE II coordinator Pat Cook. During a talk Olson tried to give in Hayesville, an audience member raised and lowered a "Stop RARE II" sign on a long pole in such a way that the sign bumped the speaker's head repeatedly. A timber-industry lobbyist remembered trying to calm the Hayesville crowd but reported that he too was shouted down. More than twenty years later, this incident—the time "somebody whacked [George Olson] over the head with a 'Stop RARE II' sign"—was still legendary among western North Carolina Forest Service personnel.[60]

Members of western North Carolina's Wenoca Sierra Club group also faced bullying. Wenoca members had actively participated in the RARE II process since its beginning, nominating roadless areas for consideration and lobbying NFsNC offices on behalf of plans favoring more wilderness. Wenoca Sierrans testified that they had met with threats of violence on backpacking and hiking trips near wilderness study areas. When they returned from such hikes, they reported, members sometimes found their car windows smashed and their tires slashed. Responding to these attacks, Wenoca Sierrans charged that wilderness opponents preferred threats and violence to responsible argument. Sierrans played leading RARE II wilderness advocacy roles nationwide, but the Nantahala and Pisgah battles stood out. Members reported confronting more ferocious wilderness-designation opposition in western North Carolina than anywhere else in the country.[61]

Threats to the woods, too, trickled in. "Put it in wilderness and we'll put it in ashes," a hand-lettered sign in north Georgia announced forthrightly (see figure 11). "Do you want to walk on ashes?" echoed an anonymous note that the Forest Service's North Carolina offices received. A rash of forest fires in western North Carolina in the spring of 1978 prompted an arson-minded editorial from the *Asheville Citizen-Times*. The newspaper called some of the fires deliberate and linked them to vengeful frustration with government forestry. Woodrow Reeves and Verlon Swafford's letter to President Carter also contained a barely veiled threat of arson. "Here in Western North Carolina we have an excellent relationship between the United States Forest Service and the people in our rural communities," the two wilderness opponents wrote. "Forest fires have been held to a minimum and a good working relationship now exists. With discontent among our mountain people it will be difficult to continue this relationship." If the Forest Service pressed forward with its plans for enclosure through RARE II, these pieces suggested, commons users might reach for the age-old weapon of fire.[62]

Antiwilderness Campaign Results

Taken together, the antiwilderness campaigns proved quite effective. The series of demonstrations around the Forest Service information sessions, in particular, became RARE II opponents' crowning achievement. And among these, the timber industry's carefully orchestrated Franklin demonstration especially proved a master political stroke. Until then the wilderness designation study in western North Carolina had percolated along in relatively uneventful fashion. Occasionally it cropped up in the local press, and certainly it preoccupied Forest Service officials, but it had not caused stir in the streets or in the careers of local politicians. "You know, they about had this thing through before we knew what was happening," former logger, timber-industry lobbyist, and Baptist preacher Jimmy Rogers later remembered about the wilderness designations.[63]

After the July 11 demonstrations in Franklin, everything changed. At 6:00 the morning of July 12, U.S. representative Lamar Gudger telephoned Charles Woodard, timber manager for Hammermill Hardwood Company, spokesman for the regional timber-industry group the Appalachian Hardwood Producers Association, and demonstration organizer. Woodard later told a reporter he had spent twenty-hour days coordinating the Franklin demonstrations and other similar protests. Congressman Gudger, impressed by the July 11 results, offered Woodard his support. The spokesman told the representative that timbermen wanted a more active role in the wilderness designation process. Gudger now shifted his position from limited wilderness support to outright wilderness opposition. Later, when Gudger lost his 1980 reelection bid to Republican challenger William Hendon, a staunch RARE II opponent, Charles Woodard attributed the defeat to Gudger's "liberal stance" on wilderness. Hendon landed a seat on the House Committee on the Interior, where he continued to fight against wilderness initiatives and where he played a supporting role in the Reagan administration's public lands revolution.[64]

Despite Hendon's success, antipathy to wilderness did not bedrock western North Carolina politics. Lamar Gudger's prowilderness questionnaire responses and his early wilderness support demonstrated this verity. In fact, Gudger's Eleventh District predecessor, Democrat Roy Taylor, made a name for himself as a prowilderness conservationist while representing western North Carolina in Congress for eight terms between 1961 and 1977. He even helped craft the 1964 Wilderness Act, which first created the National Wilderness Preservation System. Taylor's popularity in western North Carolina remained high at least through the early 1980s—so high that Republican representative Hendon sponsored successful legislation to name one of the region's national forest tracts after him.

In a powerful tribute to wilderness opponents' successful organizing, after the Franklin demonstrations even Roy Taylor went on record opposing RARE II. He did express some reservations as he took this position, saying he believed further wilderness designations might be justifiable. But the Forest Service's "broadside approach" to the wilderness study convinced him of "the need for broadside opposition at this time." Thus, by bringing the weight of public opinion to bear on their side of the issue, western North Carolina's wilderness opponents won not only lukewarm wilderness advocates such as Lamar Gudger to their cause but also conservationist standard-bearers such as Roy Taylor.[65]

Local wilderness opponents recognized an important fact that many national-level wilderness advocates seem to have overlooked. Though RARE II was a national program, local opinion had a profound impact on how it was implemented. At every stage of the wilderness study process, USFS officials actively sought local input—under NFMA they were legally required to do so. The Forest Service's initial list of roadless areas was developed in concert with local citizens. Its recommendations for which areas should become wilderness, which should be managed for nonwilderness multiple use, and which should receive further planning attention took local opinion into consideration. The mammoth national RARE II project entailed, in effect, a series of concrete decisions about how specific local tracts of public land would be allocated.[66] Local efforts to lay claim to particular pieces of the undeveloped public lands pie were critically important to the eventual fate of those lands.[67]

Western North Carolina's timber-industry supporters understood the power of local opinion to affect RARE II outcomes. They would not have spent long days organizing street demonstrations if they had not thought these protests would significantly strengthen their hand in the timber-versus-environmentalist struggle over roadless areas. The Franklin caravan and other demonstrations effectively shifted the political ground beneath

RARE II, turning a national-level initiative into a local crusade. By demonstrating in the streets and disrupting Forest Service information sessions, wilderness opponents took control of the RARE II process. They stopped playing by Forest Service rules and started calling the shots themselves. Congressman Lamar Gudger's 6:00 a.m. call to timber spokesman Charles Woodard demonstrates just how well this strategy worked.

To build local support, timber-industry leaders painted themselves as champions of the popular multiple-use forest, the wooded harvest grounds. In one telling move indicative of this effort, the Southern Appalachian Hardwood Producers Association changed its name to the Southern Appalachian Multiple-Use Council midway through the RARE II battle. With this name change the organization portrayed itself as a principled defender of the forest commons rather than as a straightforward, self-interested industry group.[68]

The furious groundswell of wilderness opposition in western North Carolina testified to the industry's success in drawing commons users to its cause. Residents took to the streets and to the forests to defend not only their timber but also, as Walter Buchanan put it, "our way of life."[69] If RARE II was an enclosure move, then it represented a threat not only to timber interests but also to anyone who harvested the forests or participated in forest culture. Whether or not you had ever felled a tree or sawed a log, if you enjoyed hearing Grandpa's bear stories, eating Mama's cold berry pies, or listening to the hounds run on a frosty night, then wilderness designation threatened you. Fighting against wilderness thus meant not only—in the case of timber workers—protecting one's job but also defending one's community, one's heritage, and one's cultural legacy. By using populist anti-enclosure rhetoric and casting themselves as defenders not only of western North Carolina's economy but also of its multiple-use commons, wilderness opponents drew commons-style forest users to their cause. And as a result, they carried the day.

SEVEN

Wilderness as Commons Defense

The Southern Nantahala

FOR ALL ITS FEROCITY, commons-inspired opposition to RARE II in western North Carolina was not inevitable. In fact, commons-inspired support for wilderness designation could also be powerful—and in at least one instance it was. According to local advocates for the proposed Southern Nantahala Wilderness Area, wilderness designation need not be an elitist tool of the privileged outsider backpacking few. It could be a populist instrument of the workaday resident pickup-truck-camping many. Armed with this commons-friendly line of argument, Southern Nantahala advocates won designation for the only entirely new wilderness created in western North Carolina in the aftermath of RARE II.[1]

The Southern Nantahala tract began just ten miles southwest of Franklin, where the region's most heated antiwilderness demonstrations took place. The northeastern edge of the eventual wilderness area spread through Franklin's own Macon County. Thus, the most impressive RARE II victory in western North Carolina came practically within spitting distance of the region's most dramatic antiwilderness protests. Mobilized commons defense lies at the root of this apparent paradox.

Like antiwilderness timber industry supporters, local advocates for the proposed Southern Nantahala Wilderness cast themselves as defenders of the forest commons. To do so, they turned the antiwilderness argument on its head. Timber claimed wilderness as an enclosure threat and multiple-use designation as a means of commons defense, but local Southern Nantahala supporters pointed to *timbering*—specifically, clearcutting—as a looming enclosure threat and argued for wilderness designation as an effective means of commons protection in the face of this threat.

Thus savvy organizers on *both* sides understood the latent power of commons protectionism and worked to harness this power for their own position. In a sense, commons users functioned as swing voters in the RARE II tug-of-war. The side that persuaded them most effectively to its standpoint emerged victorious. On the whole, antiwilderness advocates did so, and triumphed accordingly. In the case of the Southern Nantahala, however, wilderness proponents garnered important commons-based support and by doing so scored western North Carolina's biggest RARE II wilderness victory.

Like wilderness opponents, local Southern Nantahala Wilderness advocates actively courted commons users and advanced commons-friendly arguments. Indeed, area hunters led the local wilderness charge. They recognized the political power of commons culture and tried to recruit fellow hunters, fishers, and other commons-style forest users to prowilderness positions. If local people did not protect some of their beloved forestlands by designating them wilderness, these advocates argued, then timber barons would destroy the woods. In the hands of local people, wilderness designation became a way to protect the multiple-use forest commons from single-use exploitation by rich timbermen bent on clearcutting. According to this line of argument, then, wilderness designation—not wilderness opposition—represented the populist commons-defense tool of choice. Wilderness opposition and clearcutting, not RARE II and wilderness designation, became enclosure tools wielded by a privileged elite.[2]

Significantly, local wilderness advocates chose different battles than national groups. They focused their efforts on areas such as the Southern Nantahala that were particularly beloved to local residents. Where national groups saw remoteness from human history as a prime wilderness attribute, local wilderness supporters used human history as a central prowilderness justification. If you had camped at Standing Indian with your kids or fished the Nantahala with your father, they wrote, then you understood why the Southern Nantahala should become designated wilderness. This was a commons-based protectionist argument that essentially turned conventional ideas about wilderness upside-down. The Southern Nantahala should be protected not because it was removed from human events but precisely because it was—and had long been—an integral part of the fabric of ordinary local life. Where Cheoah Bald's vast roadlessness made it attractive to national wilderness groups, Southern Nantahala's ready accessibility made it the focus of local effort.[3]

National Wilderness Advocacy

The arguments local wilderness supporters advanced also stood in marked contrast to those proffered by wilderness advocates from national groups.

These groups advanced rationales that had served them well in the fight for the 1975 Eastern Wilderness Areas Act but that may actually have undermined their RARE II efforts. In fact, while local wilderness supporters aimed to debunk wilderness opponents' antielitist, insider-versus-outsider arguments, mainstream environmentalists sometimes unwittingly reinforced those arguments.

The key to national wilderness advocates' tactics during RARE II lay in the immediate history of wilderness politics. The Eastern Wilderness Areas Act of 1975 had gathered local wilderness proposals into an omnibus bill. Thus, by definition, each proposed wilderness area already enjoyed significant local backing. The strategic challenge was how to build *national* support for these local initiatives through the package bill. As we have seen, advocates from the Wilderness Society and other groups met this challenge largely by advancing an "eastern population centers" fairness argument. They pointed out that nearly all NWPS units lay in the West, while much of the nation's population inhabited the East. Simple fairness required this population to have access to nearby wilderness through a truly national system.

Both the structure of RARE II and especially the public participation requirements of the 1976 National Forest Management Act represented enormous shifts in the earlier political ground. By advancing local proposals, the Eastern Wilderness Areas Act had essentially come from the bottom up. The RARE II initiative, however, originated with the executive branch—it came from the top down. And NFMA, which mandated public inclusion, insured that local input would carry weight. Thus, the strategic challenge became building *local* support.

The extremely tight RARE II timetable and the vast amount of land included in the survey made it impossible for national wilderness groups to build grassroots support under many wilderness units, even if they did realize how vital that support could be. And the ink on NFMA had barely dried. The degree to which that legislation empowered grassroots input would not become completely evident until much later. Under the circumstances, it is not surprising that national-level wilderness advocates, making the best of a difficult situation, reached for tools that had served them well in the past.[4]

Yet in western North Carolina, unbeknownst to most Sierra Club and Wilderness Society spokespeople, these tools actually worked to hamper the wilderness effort by dampening local support. During RARE II, when they emphasized the importance of accessible wilderness for people in "eastern population centers," wilderness advocates inadvertently bolstered antiwilderness arguments and may have unwittingly helped send mountain commons users to the antiwilderness cause. An emphasis on public input in the decision-making protocols outlined by NFMA magnified the negative results of this error.[5]

According to "eastern population center" logic, prime western North Carolina forest tracts should be declared wilderness largely for the benefit of Atlantans, Washingtonians, Charlotteans, and other urbanites. This argument alienated many mountain residents because it seemed to privilege outside interests over local need, implying that Blue Ridge people should once again ante up for the nation's city folk, whether or not they saw area wilderness designations as in their own best interests. At best, this line of argument appeared to dismiss local concerns in cavalier fashion. At worst, it seemed to threaten mountain residents' prized woods with enclosure.[6]

Wilderness opponents also cast wilderness advocates as wealthy outsiders, and here too mainstream environmentalists sometimes accidentally reinforced opponents' arguments. Regional Sierra Club vice president Edward Easton III and Wenoca chair Preston Brown, for example, spoke with reporters about RARE II. These men's names may have implied social distance from many western North Carolinians, and their addresses certainly did. Easton made his home in Charlotte, one of the "eastern population centers" to whose needs rural mountain residents felt they were once again being asked to defer. Brown lived in Pisgah Forest, an incorporated community on onetime Vanderbilt estate lands just outside Asheville that enjoyed a reputation as one of the region's swankiest addresses.[7]

Moreover, Easton may have inadvertently fanned the antiwilderness flames of class resentment when he dismissed the vocal protests of July 1978 by telling a reporter, "All of that hurrah out there is just so much uninformed hurrah." If western North Carolinians understood RARE II properly, they would not object to it, he implied. Certainly, the Sierra Club spokesman had a point. Misunderstandings about wilderness abounded, and RARE II did enjoy more support in places where the issues were better understood. Easton's frustration is also understandable. The RARE II misinformation campaigns must have maddened wilderness advocates, who found themselves forced to play defense rather than offense, to spend time countering falsehoods instead of building support for the wilderness initiative. But Easton's language risked inflaming the cultural politics that wilderness opponents tapped so effectively. Rural mountain residents, bruised by a century-long barrage of popular stereotypes portraying them as barely civilized rubes and drunkards, often bristled at any hint of condescension. Easton's "uninformed hurrah," though not equivalent to "ignorant hillbillies" name-calling, might have struck mountain residents as cut from the same galling bolt. Though it had basis in truth, Easton's language was unlikely to win local support for the wilderness cause.[8]

Mainstream wilderness advocates made critical contributions to the RARE II effort, just as they had to every wilderness initiative that came before. Sierra Club advocacy helped the Forest Service identify areas in the North Carolina mountains to include in the roadless area survey, including the locally beloved Southern Nantahala. Sierra Club organizing also built impressive nationwide support for additional wilderness in the region, particularly for the Chunky Gal tract, where unusual geology supported a variety of rare plant species. Letters supporting Chunky Gal wilderness designation poured into USFS headquarters from around the nation. At the end of the survey, the Forest Service announced that Chunky Gal received higher favorable ratings than any other western North Carolina boundary, including the Southern Nantahala.

Moreover, when the Forest Service circulated its North Carolina RARE II alternatives for public comment and Sierra Club members realized the list included no realistic alternative for substantial wilderness protection, they drew up and submitted their own alternative. Forest Service Alternatives A through I minimized wilderness designation. None, for instance, included the Southern Nantahala as designated wilderness. Only the final Forest Service option, Alternative J, included that area. Under Alternative J *all* surveyed roadless tracts became designated wilderness. Players on all sides knew it would be politically impossible to add every surveyed acre to the National Wilderness Preservation System. Thus, the original Forest Service list offered the Southern Nantahala no viable path to protection. Sierra Club members offered another option, Alternative W, which provided protection to the Southern Nantahala and other tracts without requiring the politically impossible feat of designating every available roadless area as wilderness.

By targeting its members, wilderness opponents bore eloquent testimony to the Sierra Club's effectiveness as a wilderness advocate. The timber industry and its supporters sought to discredit the Sierra Club precisely because that organization had become a visible and effective wilderness proponent in western North Carolina. Though it had organized in the region only a few years before RARE II, the club had already built itself into a prowilderness force to be reckoned with. Wilderness opponents' concerted efforts to discredit the organization and its membership, alongside actual attacks on club members' property, underscore how fully its opponents appreciated the Sierra Club's real potency.

Thus, Sierra Club members and other mainstream environmentalists made enormous contributions to the RARE II effort in western North Carolina. Any tactical missteps the organization or its members may have made cannot detract from this legacy. In fact, without the dogged prowilderness efforts of mainstream environmentalists, local commons users would almost certainly not have had the opportunity to protect their beloved Southern Nantahala woods through RARE II.

At the same time, national groups' wilderness brand of environmentalism could not attract the widespread local support needed to heave ambitious new western North Carolina wilderness designations over the finish line. Commons environmentalism had that potential. Wilderness environmentalists had pried open the door to permanent forest protection. It remained for commons environmentalists to usher their neighboring woods through that door.

Taylor Crockett Leads the Southern Nantahala Commons-Defense Effort

Particularly in the Southern Nantahala area, commons defenders set about doing precisely that. Taylor Crockett, a renowned Macon County bear and boar hunter and a retired logger, led a locally based wilderness designation effort centered on the proposed Southern Nantahala tract. Huge by eastern wilderness standards, this boundary originally included roughly 43,000 acres in North Carolina and Georgia. The area had the highest rainfall east of the Pacific coast and contained the southernmost Appalachian peaks over five thousand feet. The proposed wilderness included both high- and low-elevation lands that together hosted a dazzling array of plant and animal species. After visiting parts of the Southern Nantahala with Crockett, *Atlanta Journal* reporter Russ Rymer described a breathtaking landscape of giant trees. "The treetops met above us in a soaring vault," Rymer wrote. "We climbed into a land of exaggerated scale, of cherry trees two feet wide in the trunk and birches as stately and gnarled as oaks."[9]

The area Rymer hiked—the forest surrounding Laurel Creek and other headwaters of the Nantahala River—provided a favorite retreat for local campers, anglers, and hunters. Standing Indian Campground near the edge of the proposed wilderness served as a local landmark, very popular with Macon County and surrounding area families. The campground supported vehicle-based camping, which most local families preferred over backpacking. Nantahala fishing enjoyed a reputation as among the best in the region, as did Nantahala hunting. Local recreationists favored the area, Macon resident J. S. Waldroop wrote in a letter to the *Franklin Press* editor, "because of its recognized values for fishing, hunting and a great variety of scenery."[10]

Crockett had become intimately familiar with much of the vast Nantahala tract. He grew up near Black Mountain, where as a boy he spent many hours in the woods with an "old-timer," trapping, hunting, and collecting herbs and semiprecious stones. As a young man in 1928, Crockett came to the Nantahala area, and he roamed the surrounding forests for the next fifty years. Part of that time he worked as a logger, employed with the 1930s crews that first cut great swathes of the Nantahala woods. Years later he remembered the logging scenes and tales of his youth with evident enjoyment. Crockett had served as a commons law enforcer too, a Nantahala game warden trekking the woods in search of poachers. He had also worked as a sort of commons gatekeeper, a popular Nantahala hunting guide introducing sporting tourists to the forest. He spun a good yarn about greenhorns hunting bear. Also, before the Forest Service closed the grazing range in the 1940s, Crockett had run hogs in the Nantahala woods. Throughout his five Nantahala decades, he spent countless days in the forest fishing for trout and hunting boar, bear, and turkey. Hunting was "in his nature," Crockett explained. When he was a young man, he headed to the woods for days at a time between logging jobs. "If I'd worked as hard as I hunted and fished," Crockett told interviewers, "I'd be a millionaire now, I guess."[11]

Thus, Crockett's personal history was entwined with the history of the Nantahala forest. As he led Russ Rymer up the trail to Scream Ridge, Crockett helped the journalist see the woods through the lens of this braided past. "This was virgin forest when we came in and logged it in the thirties," Crockett told Rymer as they headed into the trees. "Some of these north slopes had stands of hemlock on them so thick that sunlight never hit the ground, and when you walked, you sunk up to your knees in the moss." The elder man moved easily from this forest history to his own past. "I was a young man then, a logger," he remembered. "I had spikes on my boots and jumped from log to log, feeling as big as a cowboy with a six-gun." Then Crockett twined both histories together. "We cut the big hemlocks," he told Rymer, "and they never came back."[12]

This was not a "wilderness" view of the forest, though Crockett served as North Carolina's central advocate for the proposed Southern Nantahala Wilderness. Crockett saw clearly how human hands—including his own—had shaped the woods. He led Rymer along a trail etched with peopled history. Beneath the party's feet lay an old narrow-gauge logging railroad bed.

Memorials of the "Great Forest" lined the route. "Shoulder-high stumps of the large hemlocks that had been sawed half a century ago stood like vacant pedestals beside our diminutive parade," Rymer wrote; "powdery green moss lay on them like tarnish on brass." Crockett remembered the loggers who had peopled the lumber camps, how they had worked the old landscape and created the new. "Oh, we'd work 'til our eyes popped out just to see that big trip of logs start. It was a sight," he recalled. Crockett recognized the ghostly stumps as monuments to the people and woods he had known. He relished his memories, but he did not mystify his role or its consequences. "We cut the big hemlocks, and they never came back."[13]

Crockett's long forest experience told in his narratives of forest change over time and in his detailed knowledge of Nantahala plant and animal life. He remembered the ancient forest as a rich feeding ground for wildlife. "There was oak grass and wild legumes, like peavine and beggar lice, that kept the animals fat," he explained to interviewers. "High-bush blueberries and blackberries would grow in the openings where one of the big trees had died and fallen out of the crown. Mast was plentiful at that time as well. Probably 20 percent of the forest was chestnut." Residents used the rich forests as an open range for livestock. "In those days people virtually replaced the native wildlife with cattle, hogs, and sheep," Crockett recalled. The bears had all but disappeared from Nantahala in the 1920s, nearly exterminated by trapping and hunting. He occasionally saw bear sign when he was way back in the roughest upper Nantahala thickets, but the bear population did not begin making a comeback until the Great Smoky Mountains National Park was established in the 1930s, he said.[14]

For Crockett, this history of human interaction with the Nantahala provided a central reason for protecting it. The bear hunter read in the history of local bear populations a compelling case for wilderness designation. Since the death of the American chestnut, beech and especially oak had become mainstays of bear diet, particularly in the fall, when bears needed rich, hard mast to fatten for winter. Crockett knew it could take roughly a human lifetime for oak and beech trees to reach mast-bearing maturity. Heavy cutting rendered an area essentially useless as bear habitat for decades. Bear also needed rugged terrain where they could range unmolested by humans. His observations about the Great Smoky Mountains National Park's happy effect on bear populations fueled Crockett's wilderness designation efforts. By the late 1970s, Nantahala bears had rebounded nicely from their pre-Smokies low, but Crockett worried that increased roading and clearcutting spelled new danger for them.[15]

Taylor Crockett's commons experience propelled his commitment to

Nantahala wilderness designation. His decades spent harvesting the woods taught him to value their productivity and their beauty and to take measures to preserve both. "When I was hunting and looking after my stock, and all, I'd go through these pretty places, you know, and as a logger that tree had a dollar sign on it to me," Crockett told interviewers. "But I'd see places and I'd think, well, now it's a pity that this has got to be done with. That ought to be left for people to enjoy." The elderly hunter saw in RARE II an opportunity to protect remaining forest gems. "There are places up here that are climax forest, almost like you would have seen 50, 70 years ago," he told Russ Rymer. "That's why it should be protected. That's why it should be put in wilderness."[16]

Franklin Press Letter Writers Campaign for Southern Nantahala Wilderness

Other local forest users joined Crockett's commons-based crusade to protect the Southern Nantahala as wilderness. Taken together, letters local Nantahala wilderness advocates wrote to the *Franklin Press* editor outlined a different wilderness rationale than did national-style pro–RARE II arguments. The Franklin letters came from writers who touted insider and commons credentials and who sometimes distanced themselves from mainstream environmentalists. Writers emphasized the value the Southern Nantahala had to local people rather than to visitors from far away. They cited its superiority as hunting and fishing ground, and they carefully underscored the fact that hunting and fishing opportunities would continue under wilderness management. They also emphasized that Standing Indian Campground would remain open to vehicle camping and that wilderness designation would not compromise current Nantahala access. Nantahala wilderness supporters often addressed economic concerns and worked economic arguments into their advocacy. Almost all mentioned the Forest Service's plans to allow clearcutting in Nantahala. They cast timber interests as dangerous elites threatening commons enclosure, and they argued for wilderness designation as a populist tool of commons defense.

Southern Nantahala wilderness supporters writing to the *Franklin Press* emphasized local roots and forest-harvest histories. "I am not a trail hiker or hippie, I am 88 years old and have used the woods and streams of Nantahala since I was old enough to fish and hunt," wrote Macon resident J. S. Waldroop in the opening line of his ringing commons call for Nantahala wilderness. In a single sentence Waldroop succinctly distanced himself from wilderness-advocate stereotypes and established both his lifelong commons credentials and his ties to Nantahala. He had harvested wildlife—"used the woods"—in the proposed wilderness area all his life. Lyman Ledbetter echoed Waldroop. Ledbetter began by listing insider and timber credentials. "I was born and raised here in Macon County," he wrote. "I have farmed and worked in the woods most of my life." Like Waldroop, Ledbetter emphasized his commons-style ties to the potential wilderness. "Nantahala has always been my favorite place to go to camp out and do a little hunting or fishing," Ledbetter wrote.[17]

These writers argued that the Southern Nantahala should become designated wilderness precisely because it was so important to "average" local people. Lyman Ledbetter thought most of his neighbors had wildlife-commons Nantahala relationships similar to his own. "I would venture to guess that a majority of the people of Macon County have gone there for the same purpose at some time or other; some of them many times over," Ledbetter remarked. "The average man in Macon County cannot find the time or afford to take his family out West for a mountain trip or even to the Smokies," Ledbetter explained. "I know I couldn't when my children were growing up," he remembered, "but we did find time to go to Nantahala." Ledbetter cast Nantahala as a commons-style vacation spot available to modest-means locals such as himself.[18]

Now Lyman Ledbetter moved from detailing local relationships with Nantahala to using these relationships as a reason the tract should be protected as wilderness. "If the Forest Service puts Nantahala under Wilderness Management," he wrote, "the natural conditions that now obtain will be protected for the use of hunting, fishing, camping, horseback riding and hiking." In other words, wilderness designation would preserve this popular forest site for the benefit of local users. Ledbetter even listed recreational forest activities in descending order of typical local importance—first hunting, fishing, and camping, then horseback riding, with hiking bringing up the rear. J. S. Waldroop constructed a similar list, adding nature study and herb gathering after fishing, hunting, and camping. For these writers, local people stood as the biggest potential beneficiaries of Southern Nantahala Wilderness designation. "As I see it the people of Macon County would benefit greatly if the part of Nantahala that is proposed for Wilderness management were kept in its present natural state," Waldroop wrote.[19]

Southern Nantahala advocates also directly attacked the idea of wilderness as a public lands set-aside for the elite few. "A wilderness area is not for just a few but for all," Howe Crockett argued. "Everyone would reap the benefits." Other *Franklin Press* letter writers concurred. Wilderness opponents claimed that "wilderness study areas would be locked up and their use denied to all but a privileged minority," Lester C. Waldroop Sr. wrote. "This is far from the facts." Only activities such as road building and timber harvesting—undertakings that would compromise or destroy the woods—would be prohibited, Waldroop explained. The point of wilderness designation was not to enclose for a minority but to protect some commons forests "for the great majority of us who would use them for many phases of outdoor recreation." Where opponents painted wilderness as a danger to "us," "the many," and a benefit only to "them," "the few," Southern Nantahala advocates such as Waldroop claimed wilderness "for the great majority of us."[20]

Franklin Press letter writers advocating for the Southern Nantahala Wilderness also carefully addressed commons-style concerns about wilderness-area restrictions on forest access, hunting, and fishing. They accused RARE II opponents and the media of misrepresenting the facts on these all-important points. The "general public" following the wilderness controversy in the local media would come away with "a misleading picture," charged Lester C. Waldroop Sr.—especially on access and hunting questions. Howe Crockett went a step further. He accused timber interests and other wilderness detractors of deliberately cultivating misunderstanding. "There are those who are exploiting this issue for whatever purpose, be it political gain, public face, or the dollar made from another felled tree," Crockett wrote. "They would spread falsifications to the public for their own gain."[21]

Crockett, Waldroop, and other writers worked to set the record straight. "Contrary to belief and to rumors spread," wrote Howe Crockett, "a wilderness area does not mean man is barred." Camping, hunting, fishing, and hiking could all continue in designated wilderness, Crockett explained. Nor would popular Standing Indian car camping come to an end. "Standing Indian Campground would remain as is for mobile units," he noted. "From there it would be a short walk into the wilderness area." J. S. Waldroop also addressed the access issues so important to commons users. "The road to Standing Indian campground and on up the river is not included in the proposed area," Waldroop noted, "therefore access would remain the same."[22]

Nearly all prowilderness local letter writers noted that hunting and fishing could continue in designated wilderness. Lester C. Waldroop Sr.'s letter addressed not only this general point but also an important specific one. Waldroop debunked "the statement that has been widely circulated to the effect that the sportsman cannot use his dogs in any wilderness area." "Not true," he announced. Waldroop had contacted his local wildlife commissioner for clarification on this question. He could report authoritatively that state game laws for wilderness areas did not differ from those on any other

Forest Service lands. If hunting with dogs was currently legal on a given tract (as it was in Southern Nantahala), then wilderness designation would not change that fact.[23]

Local letter writers also took care to address economic concerns about wilderness designation. In fact, Taylor Crockett devoted his whole letter to economic questions. He and other writers argued three main points. First, they noted that wilderness designation would not affect the minimum revenues county governments received from the Forest Service. The 1976 Payments in Lieu of Taxes Act mandated the USFS to make minimum annual payments of seventy-five cents per acre to counties hosting federal forestlands. This act replaced an earlier system that had tied county receipts more directly to USFS timber harvests by allotting local governments 25 percent of Forest Service sales receipts. The new system intended to assure host counties steady revenue (timber-based numbers had fluctuated wildly from year to year) and to compensate them for the lost potential tax base national forestlands represented.[24]

Taylor Crockett and other Southern Nantahala Wilderness advocates pointed out that wilderness designations would not affect minimum per-acre payments to counties. In 1978, when the RARE II debates reached their height, the new system had been in place only two years. The former system had made wilderness-area hosting an unattractive economic prospect for local governments, and it probably still lingered in public memory. With county revenues tightly linked to Forest Service timber receipts, removing large tracts from the available local timber base threatened to cause genuine financial hardship to area governments. Under this old system, wilderness designation was a difficult local sell partly for legitimate economic reasons. Letter writers underscored the fact that this hardship no longer threatened. "The county collects a per acre tax so there is no loss there," Taylor Crockett wrote. Lyman Ledbetter and Howe Crockett also made this point.[25]

Local writers made a second economic argument, that the local tourism industry stood to benefit from the Southern Nantahala Wilderness. Lyman Ledbetter pointed out that visitors from far away "come to Nantahala because it is like it is, and a lot of them spend money in Macon County." J. S. Waldroop made a similar point. Howe Crockett predicted that as officially designated wilderness, the Nantahala would become an even bigger draw. "I think a wilderness area would attract more tourists to our county, which means more motel rooms filled, more business for our stores and shops, and more work for builders," he wrote.[26]

Taylor Crockett launched an all-out tourism pitch, using *Franklin Press* editorials, the Great Smoky Mountains National Park, and Forest Service research as evidence. The *Press* had tirelessly voiced its RARE II opposition, but Crockett argued that its protourism stance provided an argument *for* Southern Nantahala Wilderness designation. A recent editorial had noted that tourism was Macon County's largest industry and had applauded a new golf course because it would draw more tourists and boost the area economy. "It follows that anything that attracts tourists is good for our local economy," wrote Crockett, "a wilderness area for instance." He cited Forest Service studies indicating that designated wilderness tracts saw increased use. "Anyone can see that there is business and jobs created because of tourists attracted to the Smoky Mountains Park," Crockett continued. "If the Southern Nantahala's area were put under Wilderness Management you would get the same effect." Wilderness designation represented a potential tourism bonanza, "so why turn it down," Crockett concluded.[27]

Local letter writers' third economic argument had to do with timber. Designating the Southern Nantahala Wilderness would not sound a death knell for the region's timber industry, they wrote. Taylor Crockett used the industry's own numbers to refute claims that wilderness designation threatened its health. Recent figures from both the Southern Appalachian Hardwood Producers Association and the Forest Service estimated that the region's forests were growing at six or more times the rate they were being harvested. The industry anticipated it would be several years before the annual cut matched the annual growth. "These figures would indicate an expansion in forest products production, and an increase in jobs rather than a loss," Crockett noted. Industry and USFS representatives used numbers like these to justify higher annual harvest rates and more clearcutting. Crockett wanted to make sure they did not play it both ways—at once touting the forests' increasing productivity and lamenting the industry's imminent demise at the hands of RARE II. Wilderness designation would barely blip the robust expansion graphs industry outlined, Crockett argued.[28]

Other letter writers underscored the fact that proposed wilderness represented only a small proportion of the region's national forests. "There would still be millions of acres in North Carolina and thousands in this area left for timber harvest," Howe Crockett pointed out. Martha Fort Prince agreed. "More than enough land exists for justifiable lumbering," she argued. "The lands involved [in the RARE II study] are a very small percentage," she continued, giving Region 8 figures. Carl A. Reiche noted that even if conservationists' most ambitious dreams came true, and they won wilderness designation for all the western North Carolina RARE II areas they supported, 85 percent of Nantahala and Pisgah lands—some 750,000 acres—would still remain available for timber harvest. Lyman Ledbetter echoed this point. All local people urged was protection for "a little small fraction" of the forest they enjoyed. Sawmills would not stop running nor log trucks stop rolling for want of this tiny bit of woods. "Big sawmill operators" would still "have the rest."[29]

Here Lyman Ledbetter hinted at the timber enclosure threat he and other letter writers saw looming over Nantahala. In their view, timber barons rather than wealthy hikers posed the greatest danger to Macon residents' beloved commons forest. Elite timber interests aimed to enclose the woods, to reserve publicly held forest resources for their own exclusive private benefit. Specifically, they planned to transform the multiple-use commons into a single-use clearcutting site. "Big sawmill operators and lumber dealers" wished to "make more millions," Lyman Ledbetter wrote, and would clearcut everything in the forest if they had their way. Howe Crockett agreed with this analysis. "A few 'lumber kings' will have more money to fatten their wallets," Crockett wrote, if they were allowed to "clearcut a game sanctuary and watershed" such as the Southern Nantahala. Crockett conceded that "the working man will have a little money in his pocket," but fat timber cats would be the real winners. And everyone would pay a high price—in devastated forests and muddied streams—for the lumber kings' bonanza.[30]

According to these local letter writers, commons mountain woods needed defending from clearcutting, not wilderness designation. "I believe all this clearcutting and permanent road building the Forest Service is doing is hurting our hunting and fishing," J. S. Waldroop wrote. Waldroop remembered a day when Nantahala sport was better than at present. "That was before any timber was cut and roads built up the river." Lester C. Waldroop agreed. "Every hunter knows what happens in most cases to the hunting and fishing when an area is cut over the way it is done with modern machinery; it will be a long time before that area is much good to hunt on again," he reminded readers. "Look at the Little Tennessee River after a brief shower," Howe Crockett suggested. "Do you want the Nantahala to look the same?" Crockett referred to the mud and silt that clouded good fishing streams after road construction.[31]

Local advocacy on behalf of the proposed Southern Nantahala tract gained urgency from the fact that road building and clearcut timber harvest plans for the area already existed in Forest Service books. If Nantahala "is subjected to (as scheduled) intensive even aged timber management which means much road construction and clearcutting," wrote J. S. Waldroop, its "high recreational values will almost certainly be severely and forever degraded." Lyman Ledbetter echoed Waldroop. "I believe it [Nantahala] would be worth more to a big majority of the people of Macon County to keep it like it is rather than for the Forest Service to cover it with roads and clear cuts as they propose to do in Unit Plan 22," Ledbetter argued. Wilderness designation might not seem a natural tool for commons defense, but it could keep the Nantahala forest commons "like it is" and preserve its value for "a big majority" of local people. It could be wielded to protect the commons from the imminent threat of clearcutting enclosure.[32]

Thus, for the longtime commons users who wrote on behalf of Nantahala, wilderness designation represented a populist tool of commons defense. They urged their many fellow commons users to reach for it. Lester C. Waldroop exhorted brother hunting and fishing enthusiasts to move quickly to protect their grounds. "The sportsmen here in Western North Carolina have the best and last opportunity they will ever have to save some of their best hunting woods in their present state. Act now," he wrote. Martha Fort Prince echoed this call. "The [RARE II] publications are hard to read and understand," she warned, "and the F.S. gives us little time." Prince explained how each particular area had a number—the Southern Nantahala was #08025. It and other specific tracts "should be defended by all people who care." Prince and Waldroop urged readers to press for RARE II Alternatives J and W, the only two alternative plans under which the Southern Nantahala would become wilderness.[33]

J. S. Waldroop stated the commons case for wilderness designation directly and succinctly. "It seems to me that if fairness and justice is of any consideration at all," he wrote, "the great number of people who use Nantahala for its recreational value rather than to make a personal money profit are entitled to have some of it kept in an unspoiled state." Here was the commons vision in a nutshell. Waldroop had lingered over Nantahala's superior attractions as a commons-style forest. "This area is the best turkey, bear, coon, and wild boar woods that I know of," he wrote. He had explained how commons uses would continue under wilderness designation, and he had emphasized that current access would not be compromised. Now he drove home the point. The question was whether a "great number of people" would continue to "use Nantahala" or whether a few rich timbermen out to "make a personal money profit" would successfully privatize it with clearcutting. Along with the trees, "justice" itself was at stake.[34]

RARE II Results

When the Forest Service announced the results of the public commentary it had solicited, the Southern Nantahala numbers must have gratified

Taylor Crockett and other local letter writers. Ninety-four percent of the responses were favorable. Only Middle Prong, essentially an uncontested extension of popular Shining Rock, and Chunky Gal, which was the subject of a nationwide letter-writing campaign, had higher favorable ratings. At the same time, the overall western North Carolina numbers must have gratified Woodrow Reeves and other wilderness opponents. Sixty percent of the letters that came from the region's residents opposed wilderness designation for any more area lands. Both numbers testified to the power of commons-based forest politics.[35]

In the end, however, commons-style Southern Nantahala advocates, like other wilderness supporters, came away disappointed. When the Forest Service released its RARE II recommendations in January 1979, wilderness advocates expressed great disappointment in North Carolina as throughout the country. Partly because the Forest Service was itself timber-minded, partly because extractive industry wielded great political clout both locally and at the federal level, and partly because RARE II opponents had drawn public opinion to their side, the recommendations tilted away from wilderness.

In spite of the outpouring of support for the Southern Nantahala, the Forest Service cut in half the acreage it recommended for wilderness designation. It "released" the other half, meaning planned road building and clearcutting would go forward. The Southern Nantahala recommendation typified a nationwide pattern. The Forest Service removed low-lying acreage, the richest timber grounds, from the parcel. It recommended the higher and less timber-productive ridges for protection. The *Franklin Press* commended this decision. "It is our understanding that particularly in the Southern Nantahala a great effort was made to include mostly areas of steep higher elevations and exclude the better timber growing areas," the *Press* wrote approvingly.[36]

Nationally, the Forest Service's January 1979 recommendations meant that 36 of the 62 million roadless acres surveyed would be opened for commodity development. The agency recommended some 15 million acres for congressional designation as wilderness and set aside 11 million for further study. Agriculture secretary Bob Bergland planned to allow forty-five days for public comment on the proposals. At the end of that period, he would forward the recommendations to President Carter and begin releasing non-wilderness acreage to multiple-use development.[37]

Environmental groups considered the Forest Service recommendations a defeat for the wilderness preservation effort. Since all the lands surveyed were undeveloped, and since all enjoyed protection as long as the study continued, an end to the study meant de facto loss of wilderness. Only a most unlikely scenario—that the USFS recommended every inventoried acre for wilderness designation—would prevent this loss. Because any change in the status quo represented a setback for wilderness, some disappointment was inevitable. But the particular recommendations in the Forest Service's final plan left environmentalists feeling acutely aggrieved. They pointed out that more than two-thirds of the nation's remaining USFS roadless areas could be opened to development under the agency's proposal and that less than a fourth would receive permanent wilderness protection.[38]

Moreover, over a third of the wilderness recommendations, 5.6 million acres, lay in Alaska. Since wilderness advocates expected to protect much of this area through the pending Alaska Lands Bill, they did not consider the RARE II recommendations a substantive wilderness victory.[39] The Forest Service merely acquiesced to the unavoidable, proposing wilderness designation for lands that would almost certainly soon earn legislative protection in any case. Thus, wilderness advocates considered the Alaskan third of the proposed RARE II wilderness essentially meaningless.

Only 20 percent of the surveyed roadless areas in the lower forty-eight states received wilderness recommendation, and much of this land too "was already safe." Environmental groups charged, moreover, that the Forest Service had consistently favored commodity interests. It had "excluded some of the best wilderness areas from protection and [had] left mostly ice and rocks for wilderness," they accused.[40]

Where environmentalists universally expressed frustration, timber-industry reaction was mixed. Timber spokesmen charged that significant timberlands would be removed from the available harvest pool if the agency's recommendations went through. In their analysis, the Forest Service proposal would reduce the national forests' annual potential yield by about 1.2 billion board feet. This could be significant, the industry argued, given that the nation would likely face a woods-products shortage in the coming years. But the American Forestry Association opined that "in general the RARE II recommendations look pretty good."[41]

In North Carolina, the Forest Service recommended 66,000 of the 200,000 surveyed acres for wilderness designation. About half this acreage came from the wilderness-poor piedmont Uwharrie and coastal Croatan National Forests. The USFS inventoried roughly 40,000 eastern North Carolina acres and recommended over three-quarters of these lands for wilderness designation. In the mountainous Pisgah and Nantahala National Forests, where the agency surveyed 160,000 acres, it recommended a little less than 34,000 acres for wilderness classification. This number represented just over a fifth of the roadless acreage included in the inventory but would double the amount of designated wilderness in the western counties. The Forest Service recommended around 18,000 western North Carolina acres for further planning, which made them off-limits for immediate commodity development but did not afford them permanent protection. Most of the roadless lands surveyed in western North Carolina, some 111,000 acres, would be released for commodity development.[42]

In general, the agency's recommendations favored extending existing wilderness areas over creating new ones. Each of western North Carolina's established wildernesses picked up between two and five thousand acres. The agency proposed creating two new wilderness areas but only one out of whole cloth. Since the eight-thousand-acre Middle Prong stood directly adjacent to Shining Rock, it too could be considered a sort of existing-wilderness extension.[43]

The Southern Nantahala emerged as the only completely new wilderness area recommended for the North Carolina mountains. Taylor Crockett and his allies had managed an astonishing achievement. Even at its reduced eleven-thousand-acre size, the area remained the largest western North Carolina tract to earn Forest Service approval and accounted for nearly a third of the area's wilderness recommendation. Crockett and other North Carolinians had worked closely with Georgia advocates for the Southern Nantahala, and together Nantahala supporters had won recommendation for 21,000 acres in the two states. Given the overall national and regional results of RARE II, this represented a huge victory.[44]

The Forest Service recommended that most of western North Carolina's surveyed acreage, including all the proposed tracts over 11,000 acres, be classified as nonwilderness multiple use. The 12,000-acre Chunky Gal tract, the 13,500-acre Balsam Cone tract, the 16,500-acre Tusquittee tract, and the 21,000-acre Cheoah Bald tract should all become available for commodity development. Each of these areas contained riches in timber, minerals, or both. Cheoah Bald and Chunky Gal were especially mineral-rich. Franklin minerals developer Jack Brettler had his eye on a massive olivine outcropping at Chunky Gal and expressed satisfaction that the USFS had recommended that piece for nonwilderness classification. The agency had done so in spite of a nationwide outpouring of protectionist support for that tract in particular.[45]

Wilderness advocates charged that the Forest Service had in effect handed most of the region's best de facto wilderness areas to commodity interests. North Carolina's Joseph LeConte Sierra Club group announced that the agency's recommendation "confirms the Sierra Club's fears about the RARE II program and every suspicion about the Forest Service's bias against wilderness." Timber interests might as well have written the proposal, it was so friendly to the industry. "It proposes little more than the uncontested areas for wilderness and gives the bulk of the reviewed areas back to timber cutting," the LeConte group charged. Like Charles Woodard and other timber lobbyists, the LeConte club pointed to the torrent of regional opposition as a major force in the Forest Service's decision, though of course the club did so disapprovingly. LeConte chairman Garland Lieberman accused the agency of allowing itself to be steamrolled by timber. The Forest Service "significantly surrendered to the hysteria engendered by the timber industry in Western North Carolina," he wrote in a press release.[46]

In particular, the LeConte Sierra Club group took issue with the Forest Service's decision to allocate most of the proposed wilderness areas to multiple use and to make major acreage cuts in the areas it did recommend for wilderness designation. The LeConte club considered the agency's cursory assessments of Cheoah Bald, Tusquittee Mountain, Balsam Cone, Big Creek, and Snowbird Creek and its hasty decisions to classify these for multiple-use management "unacceptable." It also wondered about the large acreage cuts in the Middle Prong, Shining Rock, Linville Gorge, and Southern Nantahala tracts.[47]

Timber interests too expressed dissatisfaction with the Forest Service proposals. Charles Woodard wrote a letter to the editor on behalf of the Southern Appalachian Multiple-Use Council (the former Southern Appalachian Hardwood Producers Association). The wilderness recommendations confirmed the council's fears that the Forest Service was beholden to the environmental lobby, he wrote. "As we feared they have given in to these small Special Interest Groups by recommending 32,000 acres of additional National Forest lands for designation as additional Wilderness Areas."[48] Retired forester Alexander L. Setser echoed Woodard's analysis. "Why must our Forest Service be brow-beaten with a Wilderness Club at the expense of the local taxpayers?" he asked. Setser took some comfort in the fact that a relatively small amount of land had been recommended for wilderness, and he credited *Franklin Press* editorials and citizen opposition with keeping the size down. Without local opposition, he said, "I honestly believe that a much larger acreage of Nantahala and Pisgah lands would have been recommended as Wilderness."[49]

The *Franklin Press* responded to the Forest Service recommendation by reiterating its support for multiple-use management, worrying that wilderness advocates would continue to encroach on multiple-use lands, and commending the Forest Service for doing a good job under difficult circumstances. "We still wish that the RARE II program would be dropped," the *Press* noted. The paper suspected that the USFS also remained unenthusiastic. "We believe they too would like to scrap the RARE II program, but they carried out their orders as directed by Congress and came up with as equitable a program as possible." Still, the *Press* did not relish the prospect of some 34,000 more wilderness acres nearby.[50]

Controversy over RARE II continued to rage after the Forest Service made its recommendations in January 1979. In April the Carter administration acted on the agency's proposals and released 36 million acres nationally, including 110,000 acres in western North Carolina, for multiple-use development. The areas the agency had proposed for wilderness and for further study remained in limbo until Congress finally decided their fate. In the meantime, the Forest Service continued to manage these lands as if they were wilderness.[51]

Aftermath

For North Carolinians, the RARE II battle finally ended in June 1984, when Congress passed the North Carolina Wilderness Act of 1984. This act essentially ratified the Forest Service's earlier recommendations. Southern Nantahala advocates breathed a sigh of relief. For six years they had kept the pressure on, unsure which way Congress would finally go.[52]

Though the creation of the Southern Nantahala Wilderness stood as the most impressive victory for western North Carolina wilderness supporters in the wake of the RARE II debates, Taylor Crockett felt defeated. "It was the worst mistake we made not getting it," Crockett told interviewers a year after Congress designated the wilderness. He and his allies had asked for forty thousand acres so they could protect both low- and high-elevation plants and animals, Crockett explained to *Wildlife in North Carolina* interviewers. "What we got is just lip service. It doesn't serve the wildlife or the aesthetics, but it served the purpose of the timber people." The interviewers were doing a "Carolina Profile" piece on Crockett's lifetime of woodsmanship. They printed his forest tales of hog driving and timber cutting on the Nantahala and included one of his signature bear stories. But they ended the article on a poignant note. Crockett had helped to work one of the few protectionist miracles to come out of the RARE II process. He and his allies had won wilderness designation for all the lands Russ Rymer described. The trail to Scream Ridge, the majestic beech and cherry forest, the hemlock monuments—all these received permanent protection. Nonetheless,

Crockett felt he had lost the Nantahala he loved. "She's all gone now," he told the interviewers.[53]

On the other side of the RARE II aisle, the *Franklin Press* sounded a re-vealingly similar note. Throughout the RARE II debates, the paper based much of its wilderness opposition on a commons-style populist view of the multiple-use forest. It touted the good management Forest Service officials had provided in the past and used current forest beauty and health as an argument for continuing these policies in the future. After the USFS made its recommendations, however, a new edge of concern crept into the paper. It reprinted a piece on mineral development in Crested Butte, Colorado. A new molybdenum mine on the local ranger district threatened spectacular scenery and the best wildlife valley in the state. Macon County might an-ticipate a similar situation, the *Press* wrote. The Chunky Gal tract that had been proposed for wilderness designation included one of the largest oliv-ine deposits in the United States. Local minerals businessman Jack Brettler made no secret of the fact that he wanted that olivine. Now that the Forest Service had released the tract for multiple-use development, Brettler could move forward. "Let's be thinking what will be best for the whole area," wrote the *Press*.[54]

The *Press*'s last RARE II editorial, "Still Like to Drop It," remained as ada-mantly antiwilderness as ever. But here too the paper sounded a new, more anxious note. As it always had, the *Press* anticipated that "the wilderness people will continue to nibble away at our national forest." But now it also predicted that as more Forest Service land became wilderness, the timber industry would intensify its harvesting on nonwilderness areas. The rest of the forest "will not be as attractive for multiple use." The *Press* worried that Macon County's commons woods would be caught in the squeeze between wilderness and clearcutting. If backpackers and sawmill owners had their way, enclosure would claim ever more of the national forests. "There will be no great 'outdoors' for the majority," the *Press* feared.[55]

EIGHT

Mobilizing Commons Defense
"Oil Fever" Threatens the Forests

TIMBERMAN CHARLES WOODARD, minerals developer Jack Brett-ler, and other western North Carolina RARE II opponents welcomed the widespread opposition to the Forest Service's 1970s wilderness designation mandates. They saw in this opposition evidence of broad support for their own position: that public lands were best used as raw materials for industrial development. They hoped to ride the antiwilderness tide all the way to full-scale extractive exploitation of the region's national forests. Some wilderness-model environmentalists also read local opposition to RARE II as evidence that rural mountain residents were hostile to environmentalism and sympathetic to industrial exploitation of the Nantahala and Pisgah. The lenses of their own ideologies effectively blinded some industrialists and some preservationists to the real force behind wilderness opposition, a commons-based approach to public lands management. Many commons users were hostile to *both* wilderness and large-scale industrial development of the national forests. Events in the early 1980s underscored the strength of this commons philosophy and proved that both camps had fundamentally misread the meaning of the wilderness battles.[1]

The Ronald Reagan administration, elected in 1980, fell squarely into the industrialists' public land-use camp. Republican Reagan and his secretary of the interior, James Watt, the cabinet member most closely and visibly associated with public lands, believed that the best use of federal landholdings was industrial development if not privatization. The Reagan administration also believed in cutting taxes and reducing the size of the federal government. These two policies meant that many federal agencies, including the Forest Service, would come under increasing pressure from the executive branch both to slash costs and to generate more revenue. For the Forest Service, selling resources, especially timber and mineral rights, represented the easiest way to increase revenue. Such sales dovetailed nicely with the Reagan administration's views on the proper use of federal lands. Thus, the Forest Service in the early 1980s faced both financial and ideological demands from the White House to sell the timber and mineral resources under its management.[2]

Eventually, these twin pressures, combined with an urgent push to discover new domestic petroleum reserves, brought oil and gas exploration to western North Carolina's Nantahala and Pisgah National Forests. Industrialists in the region welcomed this development, and most environmental groups tolerated it. Jack Brettler, for instance, added a petroleum company to the list of extractive-industry corporations in his portfolio, and he publicly touted the benefits an "oil boom" would bring to the region. Environmentalists sometimes decried oil and gas development but did not formally oppose it. The North Carolina Conservation Council and the state chapter of the Sierra Club, for example, officially stated they would not object to petroleum development as long as it did not threaten wilderness areas.[3]

Their readings of the wilderness designation battles probably led both camps to expect that rural mountain residents would embrace—or at least acquiesce to—petroleum development in the national forests. But they did not. A group of commons-inspired Macon County citizens mounted a fierce and unrelenting campaign of opposition to oil and gas exploration in the Nantahala and Pisgah. For them, the question of whether or not drilling would affect wilderness areas was at best secondary. The damage that petroleum exploration could do to *all* the region's forests, together with the negative consequences exploration could bring to surrounding communities, proved central. In effect, this group argued, petroleum development would turn the public forests from multiple-use commons to single-use extractive sites, with big business reaping nearly all the rewards and local residents paying most of the price.

The mountain residents who rallied to oppose oil and gas leasing in western North Carolina's national forests included housewives, hunters, farmers, students, fishers, and hikers. They had leadership from the Carson Community Development Association and its president, Esther Cunningham, and assistance from David Liden and his associates at the Appalachian Alliance. Cunningham and Liden recognized what industrialists and preservationist environmentalists had not: that widespread Blue Ridge opposition to wilderness designation did not necessarily indicate laissez-faire attitudes toward the region's environment or a general embrace of the industrialists' approach to public lands management. Rather, the multiple-use commons ethic made many rural residents hostile to any single-use forest designation, whether preservationist or industrialist. This ethic led many western North Carolinians to oppose set-asides of the public forests for extractive corporations just as they had opposed set-asides for recreational hikers. They would fight perceived enclosure threats in whatever guise these threats appeared. Cunningham and Liden understood the protectionist potential of mobilized commons environmentalism, and in the oil and gas fights of the early 1980s, they set about harnessing this potential.

"Overthrust Belt" Oil Fever

For all Americans, the 1970s Organization of Petroleum Exporting Countries (OPEC) oil embargo meant high energy prices and long lines at the gas pump. The "energy crisis" of 1973 propelled a national drive to make the United States more energy self-sufficient. A massive push to locate and tap new domestic petroleum reserves emerged, and companies probed nearly every nook and cranny in the nation. In the second half of the decade, their explorations brought oil and gas outfits to the Blue Ridge.

U.S. geologists had long recognized and exploited the extractive potential of the Appalachian basin, which included lands just to the north and west of western North Carolina. The basin—eastern Tennessee and Kentucky, southwestern Virginia, West Virginia, and hill-country Pennsylvania—had earned fame as coal country. The petroleum industry had also tapped it successfully, beginning in 1859, when "Drake's well" in Pennsylvania became the nation's first commercial oil operation. Between 1859 and 1979, some 40 trillion cubic feet of gas and 3.1 billion barrels of oil came out of the region. In 1977 Amoco Production Company, the domestic exploration wing of international hydrocarbon giant Standard Oil Company of Indiana, hit natural gas pay dirt with a major well near Snowshoe, Pennsylvania. The Amoco/Standard strike fired speculation about the possibility of an "overthrust belt" existing in the Appalachians that could profitably be explored further.[4]

The term "overthrust belt" refers to a geologic structure in which older, harder igneous and metamorphic rock has been pushed over younger, softer sedimentary rock capable of containing hydrocarbons. The complicated "mix-and-match" geology that results from this pattern makes overthrusts difficult and expensive to explore, but persistence can yield big results. Industry fascination with the overthrust idea dated to the early 1970s. Using sophisticated new seismic mapping techniques and cutting-edge computer analysis of underground rock formations, Standard of Indiana had located an overthrust belt in the Rocky Mountains. Industry analysts had long suspected that there might be potential hydrocarbon deposits in the region, but for decades their efforts to locate these deposits had proved futile.[5]

On the heels of Standard's Rocky Mountain discovery followed a string of other important strikes and spectacular drilling successes in Wyoming and Utah. On the Canadian side of the border, overthrust exploration in the Rockies rewarded wildcatters with discoveries of some of the world's largest gas fields. By mid-decade oil and gas prospectors considered the Rocky Mountain overthrust belt one of the top onshore "frontier area" exploration prospects in the contiguous United States. In 1977, propelled largely by its new-field wildcat successes in the Rockies' overthrust belt (and helped by its Pennsylvania strikes), Amoco Production Company replaced competitor Shell Oil Company as the top U.S. exploratory driller. By early 1978 at least eight hydrocarbon discoveries in the western mountains had been reported, and wildcatters had moved into the overthrust belt "with new purpose and interest," hoping to cash in on the region's "major oil and gas potential." The U.S. Geological Survey estimated this undiscovered potential between 0.6 and 3 billion barrels of oil and 4 to 12 trillion cubic feet of gas. Industry analysts offered a higher estimate: between 1.5 and 8.8 billion oil barrels and 6 to 51.5 trillion cubic feet of gas. Proven success in the Rocky Mountain overthrust made the late-1970s prospect of an Appalachian overthrust tantalizing to industry explorers.[6]

After Amoco/Standard's 1977 Snowshoe gas discovery, the pace of oil and gas exploration in the Appalachian basin quickened. In the spring of 1978, drilling in southeastern Kentucky's Bell County yielded a "prolific" gas discovery that some industry analysts said "proved the potential of another overthrust belt with some similarities to the active Utah-Wyoming play." Just over a year later, Columbia Gas Transmission Corporation—a 10 percent partner of Exxon U.S.A.—announced a "major natural gas discovery" south of Keyser, West Virginia, and identified its find as part of the "eastern overthrust belt." Even Virginia, the "most nonproductive state in the Appalachian basin empire," boasted three gas strikes in its mountainous southwestern corner by the fall of 1979. Energy prospectors and investors pricked up their ears. "Should you invest in natural gas drilling in the Appalachian basin?" the *Washington Post* asked its Sunday readers in August. "Stockbrokers at Butcher and Singer, a major brokerage house in Philadelphia, think so." The firm had put $31 million into the basin in 1978 and was on track for a 40 percent larger figure in 1979.[7]

By the end of the decade, the Appalachian basin produced approximately 24 million barrels of oil and about 400 billion cubic feet of gas each year. Geologists believed only between 10 and 12 percent of the region's potentially oil- and gas-rich sedimentary deposits had thus far been tapped. The eastern overthrust belt, a band of sedimentary rock running a thousand miles along the Appalachian mountains in a northeast–southwest line from

Vermont to Alabama, was now an established fact and a hot commodity in petroleum industry quarters. "Eastern Overthrust Belt Grabs Major's Interest" trumpeted a 1980 headline in the industry's *Oil and Gas Journal* as it reported on "a concerted frontal exploratory campaign . . . in parts of nine eastern states."[8]

In early 1980 the *New York Times* described how "oil fever" swept through the hills of Pennsylvania, West Virginia, Kentucky, Maryland, Virginia, and Tennessee. In a hectic "lease play," land agents for a dozen major companies raced to secure exploration and hydrocarbon rights from "backwoods" mountain landowners. Geophysical mapping crews out to diagram underground rock formations swarmed over the region. As much as ten million acres had already been leased by March, though exact numbers were impossible to obtain because "much of the work [was] cloaked in secrecy," with players reluctant to release details about their activities. "Everyone is trying to keep his competitors in the dark just like a high-stakes poker game," U.S. Geological Survey official Wallace DeWitt explained to the *Times*. "You really couldn't say that this is a frontier area yet," DeWitt added, noting that "lease plays" often proceeded pell-mell on only scanty evidence because no company wanted to be left out if a major discovery were made. Still, "it certainly has potential," he concluded.[9]

The first public sign that eastern overthrust oil fever was headed for the hills of North Carolina came in October 1979. USGS researchers Leonard Harris and Kenneth Bayer informed a gathering of the eastern section of the American Association of Petroleum Geologists that the rich eastern overthrust belt likely extended more than one hundred miles farther east than geologists had realized. Scientists had divided the Appalachian mountains into "two main parallel parts," Harris explained, "an eastern part—the Blue Ridge and Piedmont—composed of crystalline rocks (metamorphic and igneous) and [a western part,] an Overthrust Belt composed of sedimentary rocks." The sedimentary rock was younger and softer than crystalline rock, and, unlike its older counterpart, it was capable of containing hydrocarbons. Western North Carolina was part of the crystalline Blue Ridge and had long been considered an unlikely petroleum prospect.[10]

But data gathered in seismic surveys conducted in North Carolina, Tennessee, and Georgia suggested that large segments of sedimentary rock similar to that in the exposed overthrust lay buried thousands of feet beneath the crystalline rock of the Blue Ridge and Piedmont. Scientists theorized that 250–450 million years ago immense pressures from the east had forced the hard older rock west and buried the soft, younger rock in the process. The overlying crystalline "thrust plates" seemed to be about five thousand feet thick at their western edges and more than ten thousand feet thick in the east. Underneath this layer, the sedimentary rock appeared to range between ten thousand and more than twenty thousand feet thick.[11]

If correct, Harris and Bayer's analysis meant a revolution in geologic and industry thinking about the eastern Appalachians. Petroleum producers had paid little attention to the Blue Ridge and Piedmont areas because their crystalline rocks had been considered basement rock and the presence of oil or gas "a geologic impossibility." If Harris and Bayer were right about the existence and approximate size of the concealed sedimentary layer beneath the crystalline rock, then this buried treasure was potentially as important as the exposed band it bordered. The sedimentary rock layer the two USGS geologists described was approximately the same size as the known Appalachian overthrust. Thus, with one stroke, the scientists doubled the size of the eastern U.S. region that could, at least in theory, yield energy bounty. Though Harris and Bayer were careful to point out that their data were insufficient to assess the likelihood of hydrocarbon deposits in the area, the implications were clear: the same rock that had drawn scores of corporate land agents and seismic mapping crews to the Appalachian basin lay buried deep beneath the Blue Ridge.[12]

Petroleum Prospectors Turn to Nantahala and Pisgah

The rush began. Prospectors and speculators raced for the Blue Ridge. Early in the summer of 1980, the *Oil and Gas Journal* reported that "considerable interest in the deep potential of the belt" had spurred companies to plan eight-thousand-plus-foot wells in parts of eastern Tennessee, southwestern Virginia, and eastern West Virginia—considered "new eastern overthrust action." Geologists believed that any oil deposits that might once have been present in the region would have been "cooked off" in high heat millions of years ago. But they had high hopes for the eastern Appalachians' natural gas potential. Industry scientists theorized that the movement of thrust plates over sedimentary rock might have created fissures through which natural gas could move and that this gas would likely accumulate in structural traps that seismic mapping could identify. Wildcatters therefore aimed their drills at the undersides of thrust plates, thousands of feet beneath the ground.[13]

The rush to acquire exploration rights within the newly discovered Appalachian overthrust brought petroleum prospectors to the Forest Service, one of the principal landholders in the region. In western North Carolina alone, the Forest Service managed nearly a million acres of public lands.

Industry strategists recognized the difficulties of working on national forestlands. They had to navigate a series of bureaucracies, wait out the lengthy permit approval process, and comply with complicated regulations governing federal holdings. Obtaining leases on private lands was often a speedier and less cumbersome process, and there were usually fewer environmental guidelines to which companies would have to adhere once they commenced operations.[14]

But corporations also appreciated significant advantages to public lands leasing. Petroleum exploration was costly and risky, especially in the Appalachian overthrust, where potential reserves were miles deep. One industry geologist described drilling in the area as "a very high risk proposition." Most wells, like one that Exxon and Consolidated Gas drilled twenty miles northwest of Perry, West Virginia, which went sixteen thousand feet deep and cost $4 million, came up dry. Companies wanted to insure that when they did get a gusher, there would be no legal entanglements over rights to it, so they preferred to work in areas where they had clear title to mineral rights on large, contiguous tracts of land. On private property, obtaining such rights often involved piecing together a patchwork of leases negotiated with scores of different landowners. One holdout could sour a deal. Through the Forest Service, companies could gain access to just the sort of extensive tracts they wanted, and they only had to work with a single landholder.[15]

Also, national forest leases often cost significantly less than leases on private lands. The standard lease payment on both public and private lands was one dollar per acre per year. But companies usually enticed private landowners with signing bonuses that could raise costs significantly. Even small bonuses of three dollars per acre quadrupled the initial cost of obtaining leases, and in hot prospect areas, bonuses of fifteen dollars and twenty dollars per acre were common. In Appalachian overthrust spots they considered most promising, petroleum producers paid private landowners as much as $3,000 per acre. Thus, the one-dollar-per-acre, no-bonus-necessary price of public lands leases fell considerably below market value even in risky areas and plunged dramatically below it in the hottest spots.[16]

Politics provided one further potential advantage for public lands leases over private lands. If a private landowner proved intransigent and refused to lease mineral rights, the industry could usually do little beyond offering better terms. But the Forest Service answered to the federal executive branch and received funding through Congress. It proved sensitive to directives from these quarters. Petroleum companies enjoyed connections and clout in Washington, and they could leverage their political muscle to influence USFS decisions.[17]

All this meant that soon after the USGS announced in October 1979 that the overthrust might be larger than previously suspected, George Olson, National Forests in North Carolina (NFsNC) supervisor, "got signals" that his office would be receiving requests for exploration permits. The sense of national urgency attending energy issues meant that the Forest Service came under pressure, even before Reagan's election, to cooperate with petroleum exploration efforts. Olson's office initiated a study of the likely effects of exploratory oil and gas work on the Nantahala and Pisgah forests, and within months lease requests began pouring into NFsNC's Asheville headquarters. By June 30, 1980, the office had received 103 applications for exploration rights in 228,000 national forest acres. The applications came from exploration leader Amoco Production Company, and they affected lands in Buncombe, Clay, Graham, Henderson, Cherokee, and Transylvania Counties. The Asheville National Forest office announced on July 1 that it planned to recommend to the Bureau of Land Management (BLM) that the oil and gas lease requests be granted.[18]

The BLM controls all mineral rights on federal lands, so it has ultimate authority to grant or deny lease applications. On national forestlands, however, the USFS has responsibility for surface resources and authority over surface activities. It is the Forest Service's job to predict the likely impact of mineral, oil, or gas exploration and extraction on these resources. Charged with a multiple-use mission and with protecting all forest resources from the destructive consequences of any one use, the Forest Service must weigh competing interests and decide what uses best serve the nation. The BLM routinely honors—rubber-stamps, really—USFS recommendations.[19]

Asheville's Forest Service officials explained that their office's planned recommendation would be the first step in a long and complicated process. Besides getting the green light from the BLM, oil companies would also need to submit exploration plans to the U.S. Geological Survey for that agency's approval. Initial permits would allow only exploration. Forest Service officials had determined (and most contemporary observers agreed) that modern seismic mapping projects would create only "minor disturbances" in the forests. Any more significant surface disruption would need Forest Service go-ahead. If Amoco or any other company decided to drill, it must go through another permit round with the Forest Service and the USGS. For each proposed drilling site, the two agencies would produce assessments of likely environmental impacts. Once a well struck oil or gas, another round of environmental studies would be required before the company could build the necessary extraction and distribution facilities.[20]

As he announced his office's proposed recommendation to proceed with oil and gas leasing, Karl Tameler, assistant supervisor of the NFsNC, emphasized the nation's need for an accurate inventory of its energy resources. "We need to know what is there," he commented. Should exploratory work uncover significant oil and gas fields, there would be important repercussions for the forests. Scenery, recreation, water quality, soil, air quality, vegetation, and wildlife would, "for short periods," feel the effects of hydrocarbon development. Local communities would see results too, especially in new employment, broader tax bases, higher personal incomes, wealthier economies, and higher demands on government services. Tameler invited the western North Carolina public to review his office's draft proposal at local ranger stations and public libraries or at the Asheville headquarters of the NFsNC. In his July 1 speech he asked the public to submit comments by month's end, a deadline later extended by two weeks.[21]

Public Opinion in Western North Carolina

Reaction to Tameler's announcement reflected the full spectrum of public lands philosophy in western North Carolina. A spokesman for the Sierra Club and the Conservation Council of North Carolina said the two groups would not oppose the leases because they did not affect designated wilderness areas or proposed wilderness areas. The wilderness "zoning" strategy these mainstream groups embraced could accommodate petroleum exploration in the national forests. Commons users expressed more concern. A Macon County member of North Carolina's Wildlife Resources Commission, for example, told reporters that he was "not real comfortable" with the forest supervisor's decision. "Our only hope," he continued, is that Forest Service regulation of the process "will be enough to preserve the environment and not affect wildlife too drastically." The wildlife commissioner's language—"only hope," "drastically"—suggested profound concern.[22]

Local reaction in Franklin reflected the controversy over proposed olivine mining in the nearby Buck Creek section of the Nantahala National Forest, controversy that had raged for years. The Macon County Board of Commissioners had long supported the olivine mining initiative, and after Tameler's announcement it passed a resolution supporting oil, gas, and mineral exploration on USFS lands. One version of the resolution the commissioners passed on August 5, 1980, had been submitted by minerals developer Jack Brettler, the central figure behind the Buck Creek proposal. Brettler was an undiluted industrialist who believed the public lands' potential for economic development should be fully exploited. The board combined Brettler's resolution with a similar one presented by Commissioner

Bob Carpenter; the final document largely accorded with industrialists' ideas about public lands use. It noted the need to develop domestic energy sources, commented favorably on recent hydrocarbon strikes in nearby Tennessee, and emphasized the potential benefits to county coffers in case of similar local discoveries. Even the probusiness commissioners, however, put limits on the industrial model and encouraged sound conservation and immediate reclamation of affected lands.[23]

Franklin Press editorial writers issued stronger cautions about the dangers of petroleum exploration. The paper ran two apprehensive editorials before the public comment period ended in mid-August. The first piece appeared August 7, the same day the paper gave front-page coverage to the commissioners' resolution. The second ran in its next edition, August 11. In both columns, *Press* writers eyed the leasing issue warily. "Unless we exercise extreme care [and] unless the operations are well regulated and controlled we could regret [these] actions," editorialists warned. The smell of big money too often induced individuals and corporations to proceed with little regard for a community's future, to "commit actions that others suffer from for years." The *Press*, which had long worried about the Buck Creek olivine scheme, reminded Macon residents of a local exploratory mining operation that had come up empty but "left a scarred and gutted mountainside." This worry about the destructive potential of mineral and petroleum exploration on the public lands reflected, among other things, the multiple-use commons forest philosophy shared by many *Press* readers. Oil and gas exploration threatened to effectively transform public forests into single-use extractive sites and leave local residents with "gutted mountainsides" where once there had been commons forests.[24]

The *Press* editorialists singled out for praise only the least proindustry clause of the commissioners' resolution: its call for conservation and reclamation. "We are glad . . . that the [commissioners' resolution] requires that 'the environmental disturbance to the land is completely repaired immediately,'" editors wrote. "We would hate to see one of the most beautiful and livable spots on earth literally destroyed." The writers ended with yet another note of caution. The commissioners should continue "to keep an eye on [this] program," the August 7 piece concluded. "It will bear watching."[25]

The second editorial took an even more emphatic stand, especially on minerals development. *Press* writers almost certainly had Buck Creek olivine in mind as they warned against the potential devastation that extraction could cause. "We are greatly concerned about the manner in which the exploration of the National Forest lands in this area may be carried out," editors wrote under a headline enjoining readers, "Don't Wait Too Late!"

Extraction could be very destructive and its damage hard to contain, as anyone familiar with strip mining well knew. "Our beautiful mountainsides [could be] denuded, eroded, and gutted, [and] unless great care and precaution are exercised our streams could be filled with silt and our fish life in both Nantahala Lake and Nantahala River destroyed," the *Press* continued. The editorial's attention to silted streams and endangered fish populations reflected local concerns about threats to the wildlife commons. The *Press*'s first-person plural possessives also reflected the commons philosophy it drew on—"*our* mountainsides," "*our* streams," and "*our* fish life" could be lost to industrial extraction. "*Our forests* deserve more than paper protection," the paper concluded.[26]

Leasing Begins and Parties Debate Likely Consequences

"I made the decision today that we should consent to leases," George Olson announced on September 16, 1980, just over a month after the period for public input had ended. The leases would be granted for ten years, and companies would pay one dollar per year for each acre under lease. Olson explained that his office realized that some forest degradation might result from the exploration, but it also recognized the "national interest" in energy development. "The task then becomes ensuring that this development is done with sensitivity and care so that the other multiple uses assigned to and enjoyed on national forest lands are not significantly compromised." Olson's office seemed to believe it possible to enable petroleum development without compromising other uses of the forest and essentially offered a full-scale embrace of leasing proposals. No leases could be granted within a half mile of the Chattooga River, which Congress had designated as a Wild and Scenic River. And the chief of the Forest Service ultimately had the authority to decide whether leases could be granted in tracts designated as wilderness areas, wilderness study areas, experimental forests, and municipal watersheds. But Olson recommended that leasing be allowed on all Nantahala and Pisgah territory, including lands holding those designations.[27]

Once Olson had made his recommendation, oil and gas exploration in western North Carolina's national forests became all but a certainty. The Asheville office anticipated receiving lease requests that would affect nine hundred thousand acres—nearly all its Nantahala and Pisgah holdings. Most observers agreed that the initial seismic exploration phase would have little impact on the forests beyond bringing some $900,000 into NFsNC coffers. If seismic testing came up empty, the "leases will expire and that will be that," wrote the *Asheville Citizen* in a front-page article. Oil fever would pass over the region and leave little trace.[28]

Amoco spokesman Dave Tayrien thought this scenario most likely. In a 1980 interview with Murphy's *Cherokee Scout*, Tayrien described his company's lease push as a "rank, wildcat-type operation." Amoco had made a specialty of just such operations over the past several years, and its string of successes had catapulted the company to the elite front ranks of domestic hydrocarbon exploration. But "the odds are slim to none of finding oil or gas in your part of the country," Tayrien told the *Scout*, apparently without further explanation. Other industry spokesmen also described the eastern overthrust as unlikely to yield giant oil fields or huge gas deposits. And unlocking the secrets of the belt's complex geology would require a great deal of drilling. Yet high energy prices gave companies incentive to go forward with exploration, even given these conditions and limitations.[29]

Local residents remained unconvinced by disclaimers such as Tayrien's and continued debating the petroleum question. They pointed to Amoco's eagerness to lease 230,000 national forest acres, nearly the maximum allowed any single company under the law, as evidence that the corporation considered its Blue Ridge prospects better than Tayrien indicated. "The huge acreages which are involved in the proposed exploratory leases on area National Forest lands have convinced many local residents that the interest of the oil companies is more than passing," the *Cherokee Scout* commented.[30]

The North Carolina Energy Institute proved sanguine about the prospect of discovering gas reserves in the state's mountains. Most scientists agreed that the region likely did not contain significant oil deposits, but as University of North Carolina at Chapel Hill geologist John M. Dennison explained, "We're fairly optimistic about the possibility of finding natural gas." With North Carolina Energy Institute funding, Dennison spent the summer of 1981 compiling data about sedimentary rock formations in the western part of the state. Dennison opined that the sedimentary layer three to eight thousand feet below the North Carolina mountains could contain "important amounts" of natural gas. He pointed to active and successful exploration in neighboring Virginia and Tennessee and described scientists as "quite confident" that western North Carolina's geology was similar. Dennison called the western counties part of "one of this country's real frontiers for gas exploration." "Far below the black bears, the moonshine stills and the towering pine trees," a stereotyping wire report on Dennison's work read, "may be significant reserves of natural gas."[31]

Other oil companies may have shared the North Carolina Energy Institute's hopefulness; at least, domestic exploration giant Amoco did not have the field to itself for long. By April 1981 Weaver Oil had applied for national forest leases on nearly 80,000 acres in Graham, Haywood, and Madison Counties, and Texas-based Mid-Continent Oil and Gas Inc. had requested leases affecting 44,000 acres in Jackson and Cherokee Counties. In June the Atlantic-Richfield Company (ARCO) joined the ranks with ten applications for leases involving 15,700 acres in Macon, Swain, and Clay Counties. Mid-Continent Oil settled representatives Ralph and Sarah Rivers in Cherokee County to pursue private leasing options. The Riverses expressed more optimism about their chances of discovering gas and oil near Murphy than had Amoco's Tayrien. The couple noted that Cherokee's location within the eastern overthrust belt made it part of "one of the hottest oil and natural gas prospects in the United States," and Sarah Rivers explained to the *Cherokee Scout* Mid-Continent's hopes "to make Cherokee County a very prosperous place."[32]

But what would this new prosperity mean for western North Carolina? The *Asheville Citizen* asked this question in a November 1980 piece. Suppose black gold did flow from the Blue Ridge. "This seems to be the worry of most persons interviewed," the paper reported. "There is little question but that the discovery of gas or oil in Western North Carolina would change the region and perhaps the life of everyone living in the area." Concerned residents mentioned heavy machinery, noise, stream siltation, litter, loss of wilderness, loss of hunting and fishing grounds, rising land values, increased road building, "mountains cluttered with oil wells," and "mountainsides cluttered with houses" as consequences they feared. Reporter Clyde Osborne fired off a list of pressing questions raised by the prospect of petroleum discoveries in the area: "Will the influx of humanity following such a discovery create social chaos, change the economy of the mountains from recreation and tourism to industry, create camps of workmen with brawling saloons and wild women, place burdens on schools, hospitals and other institutions?" "Will there be a drilling tower on every hillside?" And what about the forests? "Will the roads needed to handle heavy equipment for drilling and pumping destroy [them]?" "Will [they] become acreages of machines dripping oil, sandwich wrappers, noisy with grinding equipment, and lose wildlife, flora, and their natural quiet?"[33] Osborne's final question reflected the commons concerns of the people he interviewed. Local residents placed a high value on the wildlife, flora, and quiet of the forest, as all three were central to the commons experience.

George Olson offered his assessment of petroleum development's likely consequences in the final impact statement he included with his September 1980 proleasing recommendation. If oil or gas were discovered, Olson noted, extensive drilling would likely follow, with important repercussions for local economies and communities. The forest supervisor predicted "boom conditions" that would alter the "traditional living patterns," transforming agricultural and recreation-based communities to industrialized towns. More job opportunities would result, and youth out-migration patterns might slow. The employment boom would lure more newcomers to the region, further altering local communities. County governments might eventually benefit economically by reaping more money in petroleum royalties than the seventy-five-cent minimum per public acre they currently received under federal law. Surveyors and lawyers would see increased demand for their services as mineral-rights issues grew in importance and prospecting began on private lands. State roads would need upgrading in order to handle increased traffic demands.[34]

In the forests, recreation opportunities in drilling areas would decrease, Olson noted. Areas without drilling would have to absorb greater recreational burdens, and the USFS would build more access roads. The supervisor cited road development as a potential benefit to the Forest Service and forest users; wilderness proponents would disagree. Wildlife species that cohabited well with humans and thrived around forest canopy openings could benefit, Olson continued. Species sensitive to human intrusions and preferring unbroken canopy could suffer. Petroleum companies and the Forest Service could disagree about site-specific environmental assessments and rules governing the drilling process. Finally, Olson noted, drilling and road construction could have further unspecified impacts on the mountain environment, though the USFS would closely supervise development to keep environmental damage minimal.[35]

Some Nantahala and Pisgah residents welcomed the leases. Franklin minerals developer Jack Brettler, who had ties to lease applicant Mid-Continent Oil, served as one example. Reaching for the economic and cultural arguments he and others had used against RARE II, Brettler wrote a letter to the *Franklin Press* accusing "left-wing environmentalists" of preventing a Macon County oil boom. Brettler noted that by April 1981, ARCO and other companies had filed over 200 requests for leases, affecting 150,000 national forest acres in Macon—nearly the county's entire Nantahala holding. He noted that if these lease requests received approval, Macon County could claim 25 percent of the lease fee of $150,000 collected by the USFS and would receive between 12.5 and 16.66 percent of royalties should oil or gas be discovered. "The key to solving our energy crisis is development of our own energy resources," Brettler wrote. "Environmentalist delays" and "the freezing of federal lands" were preventing this development and "costing the American tax-payer dearly." "The closing of our National Forest can only be construed as a left wing tactic to destroy our national economy," Brettler opined. "If you are tired of giving money to OPEC, perhaps you should take an active interest in the management of our public lands, and support the natural resource industry in their fight against environmentalists," he concluded.[36]

Brettler approached the oil and gas question as a straight-up industrialist, and he cast "left-wing environmentalists" as the principal obstacles to commercial development of the public forests. Environmentalists aimed to "freeze" public lands where possible and to delay development if their "freezing" efforts failed. Brettler painted environmental activists as unpatriotic, short-sighted, and downright dangerous. They were out to destroy the American prosperity industrialists were working hard to insure. There was a commons echo even here, as Brettler argued that environmentalists would like to "close" the national forests.[37]

Franklin Press editors parted company with Brettler and expressed much less enthusiasm about the prospect of a Macon County "oil boom." When they learned in early July 1981 that ARCO had applied for national forest leases affecting Macon County, *Press* writers ran an editorial urging the county to respond quickly to this development. They entitled the piece "Our Land's Great; Let's Keep It That Way." Where Brettler had emphasized the potential financial benefits that would accrue to the county from petroleum exploration and development, *Press* editorialists highlighted likely drawbacks. They wanted county commissioners to "begin now to develop controls which will prevent the despoliation, contamination, or overcrowding of our land." Oil and gas wells in Macon County would "undoubtedly . . . create problems we're not accustomed to." Editors urged commissioners to appoint a study committee "right away" and to "begin now to take action to control those problems." "Let's not wait until the well runs dry or until the roof leaks to start to work," they advised. "We don't want to lose what we have!"[38]

As it had during the RARE II debates, *Press* editors again adopted a position that squared with the commons views held by many Macon citizens. The *Press* did not object to petroleum development on preservationist grounds: it did not advance arguments about unspoiled wilderness, and it did not advocate "freezing" the public lands. Rather, the *Press* took a commons position, arguing that Macon citizens should make sure they were good long-term stewards of their utilitarian lands. Development should go forward, but it should be controlled to assure that it did not destroy the common "house" that Macon residents inhabited. And again the *Press* peppered its editorial with first-person plurals and possessives. "We" Maconians should work now to prevent industrial abuses of "our lands."[39]

Oil companies did not let these concerns go unaddressed. In early December 1981 ARCO spokesperson Marjorie Davis responded to the *Press* editorial. In reply to editors' worries about "despoiling, contamination, or overcrowding," Davis referred them to existing state and federal statutes governing resource extraction. She assured the *Press* that ARCO "and most other responsible oil exploration and production companies have strictly adhered to all applicable environmental protection standards." Companies had incentive to do so, Davis wrote, because "failure to comply results in rather severe penalties"; because disregarding these protections led to "friction with landowners and local communities" that made a corporation's job more difficult; and because ARCO "[took] pride in our reputation as a responsible corporate citizen that acts with complete awareness of local requirements and sensitivities." ARCO Exploration looked forward to working with the people of Macon County and would be happy to receive their comments and suggestions, Davis concluded.[40]

Appalachian Land Ownership Task Force Releases Study

Just as Macon County stakeholders debated the petroleum exploration issue, a monumental study of landownership and land use in the southern mountains made national news. The Appalachian Land Ownership Task Force's findings had far-reaching implications for Blue Ridge energy development. Task force participants and landownership study results would also prove to have enduring effects on environmental politics in western North Carolina.

In April 1981 the Appalachian Land Ownership Task Force released its seven-volume, eighteen-hundred-page study of landownership patterns in eighty counties in West Virginia, southwestern Virginia, eastern Kentucky and Tennessee, western North Carolina, and northern Alabama. The study, conducted over a two-year period with funding from the Appalachian Regional Commission, found that large absentee landowners controlled nearly half the surface area in the eighty counties. Coal, timber, steel, and petroleum companies ranked among the largest landholders.[41]

The survey traced a direct link between large corporate landholding and local community impoverishment. Residents of the southern Appalachian region battled chronic poverty even as they inhabited an area immensely rich in timber and minerals. The study found a correlation between absentee corporate ownership and widespread poverty. "We've found that this kind of [corporate] control translates into land shortages, high prices, housing crises, stifled economies, loss of farmland, outmigration, environmental disturbance, resistance to tax increases, and inadequate public services like education," task force spokesman David Liden told a UPI reporter. Liden cited the example of Randolph County, West Virginia, where corporate interests owned 69 percent of the surface and 58 percent of the minerals but provided only 9 percent of the county's tax revenue. In places like Randolph County, corporate landowners controlled the tax structure and contributed only paltry sums to government coffers—as little as two cents per acre, the study found. This system forced small landholders to shoulder a disproportionate share of the tax burden, and it limited communities' abilities to afford crucial public services. Randolph County, for example, fell 46 percent below the state average in spending per public school student. The task force reported that equitable tax administration, which it defined as assessing corporate holdings at market value and taxing them accordingly, would generate a total of $16.5 million for the eighty counties in the study.[42]

The Appalachian Land Ownership Task Force also reported that petroleum companies had made "dramatic" incursions into the region in the 1960s and 1970s. They had bought tens of thousands of acres and had leased mineral rights to hundreds of thousands more. The West Virginia segment of the survey found that eight oil companies owned more than 50,000 surface acres and more than 340,000 acres of mineral rights. Altogether, eleven oil and gas companies owned a total of more than 1.2 of the 20 million acres of surface and mineral rights in the eighty counties. The study underscored the significance of extensive leasing, reporting that it amounted to "such a control of options for the use of land as to be de facto ownership."[43]

The task force summary also noted that energy development and its attendant consequences had begun extending out of the coal-country Appalachian "core" and into non-coal-bearing "fringe" areas. This pattern threatened broad new sections with the troubles that had long plagued coalfield residents, it warned. North Carolina's Blue Ridge appeared among the report's "new areas" likely to feel the effects of such development.

The land-use study summarized the history of the strip-mining controversy, commenting that "perhaps no issue in Central Appalachia has been more emotion-laden." "In the past ten to fifteen years," it continued, "strip mining for coal has met with citizen resistance through every possible means." It also pointed to recent scientific studies confirming residents' long-standing contentions that strip-mining methods caused severe land damage and contributed to devastating floods and groundwater contamination.

Where energy development extended, the report concluded, strip mining would likely follow. "Our study suggests that in the future," battles such as those over strip mining "will have to be fought with new protagonists (big oil companies as well as independent coal companies, for example) . . . over new environmental impacts . . . and in new areas," the task force wrote. Moreover, these battles would take place "in a national political context in which the need for energy often is given more weight than the social and environmental costs of energy development."[44]

John Gaventa, who had coordinated and coauthored the study with Bill Horton, soon brought the task force's conclusions directly to North Carolinians. Gaventa, a research analyst with the Highlander Research and Education Center in New Market, Tennessee, spoke at a conference of the Western North Carolina Minerals Association in November 1981. Gaventa noted that petroleum companies were actively pursuing leases on North Carolina lands. Citing the eighty-county study, he warned that exploitative mining with most benefits going to outside interests could result. Mining could become a net drag on the area economy, he cautioned, as it had in sections of Kentucky and Tennessee where monies spent on health, environmental, and other mining-related problems outpaced tax revenues from the industry. Unless local officials taxed mineral rights at market values, western North Carolina could suffer the same fate.[45]

Franklin Press editors heard with concern Gaventa's warnings that coal-country troubles might loom in western North Carolina's future. They summarized Gaventa's arguments in an editorial entitled "It's Not Too Late to Plan Our Fate." The piece called the Highlander analyst's cautions "warnings that the people of Western North Carolina . . . would do well to heed." It urged action to prevent the gloomy economic, social, and environmental outcomes Gaventa described. "Areas like the Cumberland Valley of Tennessee and regions of Kentucky lost their farms, their environment, and the good life," *Press* editors wrote. Macon County must not follow suit. Local officials should take steps to ensure that developers could not speak honeyed words about progress and riches, then cut and run with the region's wealth, leaving behind impoverished communities. "The hour is late, but not too late," the *Press* opined. "Western North Carolina [still] has the opportunity not to lose itself."[46]

Esther and Jim Cunningham Organize in Carson

Esther and Jim Cunningham, residents of Macon County's small community of Carson, were among those who followed the oil and gas issue with concern. Responding to news about the likely consequences of petroleum development in western North Carolina, the Cunninghams added forest defense to slates already crowded with community and regional commitments. Esther Cunningham, in particular, emerged as a key leader in the fight against oil and gas development on the Nantahala and Pisgah. With Jim's support and in partnership with David Liden, who had worked with the Appalachian Land Ownership Task Force, she pioneered a staunch forest defense effort rooted in the region's commons culture.

A retired beautician and schoolteacher, beloved Sunday school leader, and lifelong resident of Macon County, Esther Clouse Cunningham was hardly an archetypal environmentalist. But she proved to be a formidable defender of western North Carolina's woods. Cunningham was a gifted and tireless organizer, a tiny dynamo of a woman with an infectious "can-do approach."[47]

In 1980, when petroleum exploration in the region's national forests first became a public issue, Esther and Jim Cunningham had retired and were living on his longtime family lands in the Carson neighborhood. Carson was an unincorporated community of two hundred families just outside Franklin. Both Cunninghams had lived in Macon County nearly all their lives, and both were homegrown leaders who had long been active in local and regional affairs.

Esther Cunningham had earned a reputation as one of her community's most accomplished organizers. This was no small feat, as women's activism suffused Carson's civic life and shaped community dialogue and decision making. Sex-segregated associations in Cunningham's neighborhood and throughout Macon County nurtured a vibrant culture of female leadership. These groups incubated women's organizing, which then spread beyond them. As a result, both men and women in Carson recognized and granted legitimacy to skilled female leadership.[48]

Since her girlhood Esther Cunningham had moved in these activist female circles. When she was barely out of her teens, neighborhood women began tapping her to lead them. Cunningham's parents had died when she was just nineteen, and she had become a self-supporting beautician with responsibilities for two siblings. When she married Jim Cunningham in her early twenties, she was already an established businesswoman. Soon after her marriage, the women of Carson Chapel Methodist Church asked her to serve as president of their Wesleyan Service Guild. A national Methodist women's missionary organization, "the Guild" had chapters in most local churches. Esther Cunningham had always identified as an active Methodist, but she hesitated to accept this invitation. "When they first began calling on me to do things," she remembered, "I was very shy. . . . I remember just sitting back there saying, 'I can't do this.'" Though by this time she had confidence in her ability to run a business, presiding over the annual Guild banquet seemed different. She felt nervous to be in so public a role—standing up in front of so many women, speaking to them, leading their meetings.[49]

Cunningham recalled how a Guild member she admired—a woman who was about ten years older than she and whom she had known all her life—took her aside. When the younger woman said, "I can't do it," the older woman replied, "Yes, you can, Esther. We will all help you. And we know you can. You are the one we want, and we will help you." For Cunningham, this proved a pivotal moment. "You have to see yourself as a leader before you can become a leader," she later explained. Cunningham credited the older churchwoman with launching her leadership career. This mentor "showed me an image of myself that I hadn't seen before," she reflected. The older woman also offered her protégée crucial support while the young woman tested and tried this new vision.[50]

This first leadership encounter set the tone for Cunningham's decades of activism. Again and again female mentors offered challenges accompanied by support. The Carson Chapel Guild presidency was only the first of many leadership roles these mentors encouraged. In the church and in her Eastern Star chapter—a companion organization to the Masons she joined at her sister-in-law's urging—Cunningham gradually overcame her initial fears of public speaking and presiding. Among these women friends, family, and neighbors, she learned to arrange and lead a meeting, to speak in public, and to facilitate discussion. Later, in PTA and Extension Homemakers, she learned to organize on county and regional levels and to connect local affairs to regional, state, and national developments. Especially through PTA and Extension work—first with the Homemakers, later with 4-H, and later still through Community Development—she also gained a set of far-reaching regional connections.[51]

Esther Cunningham thrived under her neighbors' tutelage, and in a few years she began to envision and carry out her own ambitious endeavors. The Carson Cloggers 4-H group she coordinated in the 1950s danced its way onto the cover of a national 4-H magazine and onto stages with the Everly Brothers and the Carter family. In the 1960s she served on the first board of directors for the county's North Carolina Fund antipoverty organization, Macon Program for Progress, and she helped to develop its Headstart and Homestart initiatives.[52]

Also in the 1960s Esther Cunningham organized the Macon County PTA Council. She and her friend Nell Jones visited each local PTA in the county's segregated school system. All responded positively, including Chapel School, the county's lone African American school. Esther Cunningham wrote to the state PTA announcing the new county council and listing participating schools. In its reply the state board informed Cunningham that North Carolina PTA could not admit an integrated council to its membership. If the Macon County PTA Council wished to receive recognition from the state organization, it would have to drop Chapel School. Cunningham found herself in a quandary. After all her hard work she hated to see the council die, but neither did she want to renege on her agreement with Chapel School. She fretted about the right course of action and talked the situation over with a close female friend. The next morning she wrote back to the state board. "When a baby is ready to walk you don't tell it to go back in the crib," she declared. Macon County stood ready for an integrated PTA council, and it would have one. If the state PTA refused to recognize the Macon County PTA Council, that was the state's prerogative. But Macon would not change its plans. A few months later Cunningham received another letter, this time asking her to serve on the state PTA board.[53]

Through all these undertakings, female friends and relatives provided Cunningham with critical support. Fellow churchwomen nudged her toward the racially egalitarian vision behind the PTA controversy. Female colleagues helped her launch the county organization and offered supportive counsel when the state board issued its ultimatum. An aunt nominated her for the Macon Program for Progress position. Neighbors helped sew costumes for the Carson Cloggers. A phalanx of activist women stood behind everything Esther Cunningham organized.[54]

Jim Cunningham also had a history of committed organizing. After he retired from Nantahala Power and Light in 1977, Cunningham founded an association of NP&L retirees, served as chairman of the Macon County Council on Aging, and took leadership roles in local and county community development work. He involved himself with a number of area associations, among them the County Extension Advisory Council and the fledgling Macon Coon Hunters Club. He served as president of his local Wildlife Club, and in the late 1970s he chaired the Macon County Democratic Party. Cunningham was also a Mason, an active Methodist churchman, a dairy farmer, and an avid bear hunter.[55]

Both Cunninghams had been longtime staunch supporters of their neighborhood's Carson Community Development Association and the Western North Carolina Community Development Program of which it was a part. The regional program was a joint effort of the Western North Carolina Development Association, the North Carolina Agricultural Extension Service, area businesses, and local sponsors. It had begun in 1949 and was widely recognized as one of the nation's pioneering rural "self-help" projects, "an outstanding example of a locally financed and locally operated effort of people working together to help themselves," wrote the *Franklin Press*. By 1980 nearly one hundred communities from North Carolina's eighteen westernmost counties and the Qualla Boundary Cherokee Indian Reservation participated in the community improvement program. Local clubs typically constructed or renovated a central community building and encouraged residents to cooperate on other community improvement projects. They provided neighbors with opportunities to hear from speakers on various aspects of community development, to travel to other clubs, and to socialize at picnics, barbecues, raffles, and the like.[56]

Since his retirement Jim Cunningham had served as president of both the Carson club and the countywide council of neighborhood clubs and had held a seat on the program's WNC Area Steering Committee. He had twice won the county's community development leadership award. During his tenure as president of the local club, Cunningham had overseen renovation of Carson's community building, which had deteriorated badly since it was first completed in 1955, three years after the club formed.[57]

A trio of activist Carson women had leaned on Jim Cunningham to undertake the renovation project. All were longtime community club members and Extension Homemakers. During the 1970s, the Carson club had gradually lost members, and the three women feared it might die altogether. As Jim Cunningham approached retirement age, he and Esther considered a move to Florida. The three women urged him to substitute their club rebuilding project for his Sunshine State retirement project. Jim Cunningham demurred, but Laura Waldroop, Leona Moore, and especially Esther Greene—whom Esther Cunningham described as "a self-appointed nominating committee of one"—continued urging. Finally he allowed himself to be persuaded, and the Florida idea was tabled.[58]

Esther Cunningham had supported her husband's renovation campaign by shepherding the Carson club through not-for-profit incorporation paperwork that enabled it to accept building grants and other monies. She had also served as secretary of the Macon County Community Development Council. Both Cunninghams had attended regionwide community development meetings in Asheville.[59]

When oil and gas leasing news began breaking in western North Carolina, the membership had elected Esther Cunningham president of the Carson Community Development Association. Her club presidency would focus on the leasing issue much as Jim's had centered on the renovation campaign. And just as Jim had led the building effort with her support, so she would spearhead the antileasing endeavor with his.

The Carson Community Launches Oil and Gas Opposition

Esther Cunningham saw "a natural stepping-stone" between community development work and environmental activism. "The environment was just another step in the same thing we were working in," she explained. "We were already organized to work together for the betterment of our community. And that just seemed a natural place for us to start with an environmental movement." The move from community development effort to regionwide environmental organizing "was easy for us."[60]

The connections Cunningham drew between community development and environmental work hinted at the cultural roots of her approach to environmentalism. Carson had a history of "working together for the benefit of our community," and its environmentalism grew from this context. Firmly grounded in connections to neighbors and to local utilitarian lands, Cunningham and the Carson community held a commons environmentalist ethic.

Oil and gas leasing developments spurred Carson residents to include explicit environmental concerns on their community agenda. Carson residents followed local petroleum exploration news with growing alarm from the moment the Forest Service first began considering leases in spring 1980. Early information came from local newspaper coverage—which often spotlighted the issue with front-page reports—from hunters who met surveyors out in the woods and from neighbors employed by the Forest Service.[61] Esther Cunningham began laying the groundwork for organized regionwide leasing opposition with a one-woman letter-writing campaign. She sent newspaper clippings along with personal notes to an extensive western North Carolina network, requesting support. "I already sort of had an organization going when [Appalachian Alliance associate David Liden] came," she remembered.[62]

The Carson club actively encouraged and supported its president's efforts. In 1981, a year after leasing news first reached the community, Esther Cunningham received an Extension Service invitation to attend the "Future of Appalachia" conference at Lincoln Memorial University in Harrogate, Tennessee. She remembered feeling initially reluctant to accept the invitation. She recalled how fellow Carson Community Development Association members, including her indomitable aunt Esther Greene, eventually convinced her. Greene considered the conference important and helped sway Esther Cunningham by persuading the Carson club to underwrite Jim Cunningham's expenses, enabling him to accompany his wife. This conference at Lincoln Memorial University proved a turning point for the two Cunninghams. "Neither one of us was very interested in going," Esther Cunningham remembered. "But then when we got there it was such an excellent conference that we just became motivated to be activists, both of us ... and we became leaders in western North Carolina in this environmental movement."[63]

The Appalachian Alliance, a regional coalition of citizens' organizations, sponsored the Harrogate gathering. The alliance had come together to coordinate a response after major floods devastated the coal country mountains in the spring of 1977, leaving thousands homeless. The organization aimed to expose and address root causes of mountain poverty and environmental degradation, and it had quickly established a task force on land. Scholars from the newly formed Appalachian Studies Association soon joined with this task force, and the resulting larger group became the Appalachian Land Ownership Task Force, which conducted the immense land-use study released in 1981.[64]

The Appalachian Alliance's Harrogate forum was the first gathering of its kind. It brought together activists from dozens of citizens' groups across the southern mountains as well as representatives from the Cooperative Extension Services of Kentucky, Tennessee, Virginia, West Virginia, and North Carolina. The conference featured the Highlander Research and Education Center's John Gaventa, and it highlighted pressing environmental issues from across the region.[65]

Esther and Jim Cunningham found the conference's small group sessions especially chilling. These roundtables chronicled environmental devastation in the Appalachians, and Esther Cunningham remembered them as "most impressive." She and Jim listened in near disbelief to dramatic firsthand accounts from coal-country residents who described how strip mining, flooding, and displacement had ravaged their communities and despoiled their mountains. This desolate testimony from neighboring states made a powerful impression on the Cunninghams. With petroleum leasing already a reality in western North Carolina, they found these tales of suffering at the hands of the energy industry extremely alarming.[66]

From John Gaventa and his book *Power and Powerlessness*, which the Cunninghams bought at Harrogate, they took new inspiration for organizing. "We saw that the powerless, in essence, could become powerful just by uniting and working together," Esther Cunningham explained. "And that people could be involved in the decision-making process that ultimately made a difference in their future." Thus, the couple came away from the Appalachian Alliance conference deeply worried about energy development's possible dire consequences but also armed with an idea for how to ward off those consequences.[67]

The two Carson representatives returned home from Harrogate "furious" and "determined to do something," Esther Cunningham remembered. As a first step, she wrote to Bill Horton of the Appalachian Alliance: "I'm so afraid they're going to drill for gas and oil, they're going to clearcut all over our beautiful mountains in Western North Carolina. I need to help and I don't know what to do." Horton responded with a key introduction, launching a partnership that would help to sculpt western North Carolina's unfolding forest history.[68]

David Liden Comes to Carson

Bill Horton put Esther Cunningham in touch with David Liden, an Appalachian Alliance veteran who had recently relocated to the Murphy area of Cherokee County, Macon's western neighbor. Cunningham invited Liden to attend a mid-1982 picnic meeting of the Carson Community Development Association, now more than a year into its antileasing campaign. Liden accepted this invitation and traveled for the first time what would become the familiar road to Carson. Longtime forest activists credit this meeting of local and regional minds—this coming together of Cunningham, Liden, the Carson club, and the Appalachian Alliance—with giving birth to an effective new regional environmental group, the Western North Carolina Alliance.[69]

Though David Liden spent his childhood far from the North Carolina mountains, his family ties and deep respect for mountain cultures made him seem less an outsider than some migrants to the region. Liden's wife, Martha Owen, had grown up in western North Carolina, and the couple moved to Cherokee County to be near her family. When he began to organize in this new setting, Liden's local kinship ties provided him some protection against the "outsider" charges so often hurled against the region's environmental activists. Through his relationships with his wife and her family, his years organizing in West Virginia, and his academic studies, Liden also had developed a thorough familiarity with and respect for mountain cultures.[70]

Moreover, David Liden brought firsthand experience in the coal country to his work on western North Carolina's oil and gas leasing issue. He participated in the Appalachian Alliance's mammoth land-use survey, serving as coordinator for its West Virginia portion. During his years in the coal fields, he had seen bulldozers strip-mine land to within a few feet of residents' houses. He remembered Appalachian families powerless to stop their fruitful farms and verdant yards from becoming slashed cliffs of naked earth. He repeatedly witnessed environmental and social carnage, watching as the energy industry destroyed farms, obliterated orchards, razed forests, clogged rivers, and rendered families and entire mountain communities destitute. He believed that effective organization offered the Appalachian region's best hope for preventing and turning back this kind of wholesale devastation.[71]

As they fought against oil and gas leasing, Liden and Cunningham quickly formed a fruitful working partnership. "We had this strong bond, and this strong commitment from the time we met, that never varied," Esther Cunningham remembered. "There was a lot of difference in our age; our formative backgrounds were so different, our educational backgrounds were so different—none of that seemed to matter," she explained. "We had the common interest of saving the environment." Cunningham brought to the collaboration a thorough familiarity with the local scene, decades of experience in local and regional organizing, a vast personal network, and what Liden described as an infectious "can-do approach." Liden contributed his strengths as a writer, his expertise on leasing and land-use issues, his own local and regional networks, his academic credentials, and considerable grassroots organizing experience.[72]

The Carson Community Development Association extended critical support to Cunningham and Liden's early partnership, as did the Appalachian Alliance. "I was working through Carson Community Club. And therefore [David] did too," Cunningham remembered. Throughout the early days, "the Community Club was backing us up," she explained. Liden and Cunningham began organizing open meetings designed to educate the public about the leasing issue. Carson offered its building as a location, its name as an organizational sponsor, and its "community news" column in the *Franklin Press* as a publicity venue. The club also awarded Cunningham and Liden a small but important early grant. The Appalachian Alliance lent its support as well, serving as organizational recipient for such monies and then channeling the funds to the pair.[73]

Liden and Cunningham's open meetings garnered significant press coverage and cautioned Macon residents about the potential dangers of petroleum exploration. "We were trying to tell the people, 'we can save ourselves if we get in here early,'" Esther Cunningham explained. The two activists drew on each other's strengths to publicize the meetings. "When we wanted to hold a public meeting and alert people," Esther Cunningham recalled, "I'd lived here all my life, and my husband had too. We knew the leaders of the community. We knew who to send the letters out [to]. And David had a small portable typewriter and he just sat down in my living room and he'd just type out all these [letters]. He was an excellent writer." Both Cunningham and Liden recognized the importance of press coverage. "The press was interested" in Carson's campaign, Cunningham explained, "because if you make news they will print news. . . . The bottom line is, we got their attention, and we got their attention probably through the open meetings."[74]

Carson Hosts Its First Public Meeting on Leasing

The Carson club hosted a series of five open meetings in 1982, and Esther Cunningham used the weekly Carson column she wrote for the *Franklin Press*'s Community News section to publicize them. Community News was a women's space in the local paper, its columns written by "in the know" women from Macon County's several rural neighborhoods. Typical columns included news about neighbors' travels, illnesses, deaths, births, home construction, awards, weddings, and visitors; announcements of neighborhood meetings, church doings, and carry-in suppers; and occasional discussions of local concerns such as firefighting and water supplies. Alongside such updates and announcements, Esther Cunningham included detailed reports on forest policy. "To be silent when our once protected natural resources are being leased to rich oil companies for $1 per acre . . . is to be indifferent to our future," she wrote in January.[75]

Here as throughout her efforts, Esther Cunningham issued a commons rallying cry. "Our natural resources" risked being sold, and cheaply, to "rich oil companies." Wealthy outsiders threatened to reserve commonly held resources for their own private benefit. Simply stated, oil leasing represented an enclosure threat. Quoting a USFS official who underscored the "commons" status of the public forests when he said, "Forest Service lands belong to the people," Cunningham concluded that it was "therefore the responsibility of the people to let their voices be heard." "Come and enjoy the food and fellowship," she encouraged Macon citizens as she invited them to a February covered-dish supper at which deputy North Carolina forest supervisor Karl L. Tameler would discuss the future of the national forests in western North Carolina. "To be present and to ask the right questions is to have in-put on the Forest Service [proposed ten-year land-use management] plan which will have direct affect on our decisions for generations to come."[76]

Some sixty people responded to Cunningham's invitation and came to Carson's February 25 meeting. They included commons-defense scouts from the Macon County Coon Hunting Club and the North Carolina Wildlife Commission as well as representatives from the Nantahala Hiking Club, Western Carolina University's WNC Tomorrow program, Franklin High School's science classes, neighboring community development clubs, and local church groups. Carson residents, USFS employees, *Franklin Press* reporters, a Macon County commissioner, and Jack Brettler, the local developer with national forest mining and petroleum interests, also attended. This diverse group came prepared with questions for the deputy supervisor. Tameler's talk focused on the "serious economic problems" and "tight governmental budgets" currently facing the Reagan era Forest Service. But many in his audience "were present due to their concern over the possibility of oil and gas exploration taking place on government lands in Western North Carolina," reported the *Franklin Press*, which made the Carson meeting its front-page lead.[77]

Esther Cunningham presided over this heated meeting and recalled that minerals businessman Jack Brettler seemed determined to disrupt it. Cunningham remembered seeing Brettler's hand raised repeatedly; she recognized him once but then ignored his efforts to regain the floor. Finally, he blurted, "I want to speak." Carson club member Florence Sherrill, a lifelong Macon resident and respected local figure, came to Cunningham's aid. "We've already heard from you, and we don't want to hear any more," she told Brettler. "We want to hear from some of the others." Sherrill had worked for decades in the county's Home Extension office and had close ties with scores of area families. At least one neighbor believed she had contributed more to the welfare of Macon County than any other single person. She also enjoyed a wide reputation as a tactful and gracious lady. According to Cunningham, her uncharacteristic outburst silenced Brettler and everyone else, and after it the meeting proceeded in an orderly fashion.[78]

Brettler proved to be one of the few people who had come to Carson to speak in favor of petroleum development. "Several people at the meeting voiced opposition to granting leases for oil and gas," the *Press* reported. Esther Cunningham "seemed to speak for many when she said, 'The need for drilling in this part of the state needs to be looked into carefully.'" "Our forests are a drawing card for hunters, fishermen, and hikers," Cunningham reminded her audience, referencing Macon County's tourism economy. "We don't want the natural beauty of the land destroyed." She acknowledged the legitimacy of the energy search but balanced it against the benefits the rich Nantahala Forest provided to Macon County. Local residents reaped a host of advantages from the multiple-use forests, economic as well as aesthetic, Cunningham argued, and these needed to be weighed against the benefits of single-use extraction. Hunting and fishing figured prominently in Cunningham's utilitarian framework.[79]

When he spoke, Tameler forthrightly addressed the wilderness concerns he anticipated. "We are a long way from putting drilling rigs in Joyce Kilmer," he assured his audience. Under the Wilderness Act, minerals development could go forward on federal wilderness until 1984, and Amoco had applied for leases in Graham County's Kilmer Wilderness. But the Forest Service had issued a lease-processing moratorium for wilderness areas, so petroleum development did not immediately threaten Kilmer's rare primeval forest stands. Tameler's audience probably found his comments less reassuring than he hoped, however. Doubtless, the gathering included Kilmer fans, but many in attendance had forest concerns that went well beyond wilderness. The coon hunters, farmers, housewives, and anglers who showed up at Carson probably held more trepidation about the vast expanses of multiple-use forest than about the relatively small and better-protected wilderness tracts. Petroleum companies had applied for leases on some 315,000 nonwilderness acres in the Nantahala and Pisgah, including 12,000 acres in Macon County. All these leases fell outside the wilderness moratorium and overshadowed its temporary protection for Kilmer's roughly 15,000 acres.[80]

Hunting and fishing organizations' visible presence at the Carson meeting suggested the potential for a commons-based campaign against oil and gas leases. These groups feared damage to prized wildlife harvest grounds, just as they feared lost access to those grounds. Their attendance at Carson represented a first step along the road to a mobilized commons-based forest stewardship campaign.

Carson Continues Its Antileasing Campaign

After its first public gathering, the Carson club continued its antileasing efforts. It appointed a committee to evaluate the meeting's implications and to "determine what steps to take as a follow-up," Esther Cunningham reported. In March 1982 Carson gained statewide publicity when it hosted *Raleigh News and Observer* reporter Monte Basgall, who was in the mountains conducting research for a series on western North Carolina's environmental troubles. In April Basgall devoted one of four pieces to the leasing issue. The state capital's paper also published an antileasing "Point of View" piece by Esther Cunningham and a letter to the editor she wrote as a follow-up to Basgall's series.[81]

Also in April, George Olson accepted a Carson Community Development Association invitation to speak in Franklin. Addressing a group that a *Franklin Press* headline story described as "concerned Maconians," Olson reported that his office had recently received additional lease requests affecting 538,000 acres of the Nantahala and Pisgah. Total USFS holdings under application in the region now came to 900,000 acres. If the Forest Service granted all requested oil and gas leases, these leases would "essentially blanket" western North Carolina's national forestland. A week after Olson's April 19 appearance in Macon, his office announced that the Bureau of Land Management had granted its first approvals for oil and gas leasing on North Carolina's national forests. These first leases allowed Amoco rights to explore 4,770 Nantahala acres in Cherokee County, Macon's westernmost neighbor, and 8,879 Pisgah acres in Transylvania County, which lay just five miles to Macon's east.[82]

In May 1982 Esther Cunningham wrote a Carson community news column that stitched together forest policy, local economic concerns, environmental issues, and neighborhood updates in a seamless web. "A covered dish supper is being planned for the next community meeting, (May 27 at 6:30 p.m.) prior to hearing a progress report on the 36 leases which have been approved by the Bureau of Land Management of Washington, D.C. to permit drilling explorations for gas and oil by Amoco, Weaver, and Atlantic Richfield in WNC National Forests," she wrote. "Atlantic Richfield Oil Co. has filed leases to drill on Forest Service land in Macon County at Wayah Bald, north of Nantahala Lake, and near the Swain County line. These leases are granted at $1 per acre per year for 10 years with option by companies to renew leases for duration of time oil and gas are available. Very few jobs for local people and minimum revenue payments will be released from the drilling activities. Yet, extensive damage may be done to the environment." Then, without missing a beat, she continued, "Heather Wallace, Myra Setser, and Renee Williams presented a lovely rendition at Memorial Church last Sunday, titled 'Mothers are a Gift of God.'... Special greetings are sent to our loved ones who are sick and/or hospitalized: Mrs.

Norman Boyle, Mrs. Burton C. Boesser. . . . Welcome back home to Mr. and Mrs. Charles Lennon and others who have been away."[83]

Though leases had now become a reality, Cunningham and Carson kept up their opposition. In August Esther Cunningham announced that Lewis Kearney, ranger on the local Wayah District of the Nantahala National Forest, would visit Carson and offer a USFS update. She used her Community News column to remind readers that the Forest Service owned 48 percent of Macon County and that ARCO had applied for eight leases within county borders. Cunningham also publicized a new controversy: she informed Macon citizens that the Bureau of Land Management had designated a sixty-day period to allow the public to respond to news that "Arab oil interests in Kuwait are seeking to explore and drill on our public lands in Western North Carolina. Kuwait Petroleum Corp. now awaits approval of BLM to lease 235,000 acres in Pisgah National Forest." Knowing that the prospect of an OPEC-affiliated company drilling in their forests would infuriate western North Carolinians, Cunningham advised that "public outcry is all that can stop it." She urged Maconians to write to the BLM and to come out to Carson with a covered dish and "guests or neighbors who are interested in the future of Western North Carolina." "This is our opportunity to unite and *save our mountains* from the Shieks of Araby!" she concluded.[84]

Here Cunningham turned one of the industrialists' most powerful arguments against them. The need to pursue national energy self-sufficiency had long served as a prime justification for petroleum exploration on U.S. public lands. But now the national forest commons—"our public lands in Western North Carolina"—faced potential destruction at the hands of the very same "Arab oil interests" that had held the nation hostage during the 1973 oil embargo. Now Macon citizens were asked to sacrifice their local commons forests not for the greater national good but to enrich wealthy foreign oil kings. Esther Cunningham's choice to use "Shieks of Araby" language reflected the anti-Arab cultural stereotypes she shared with many Americans. This language also indicated her sense that elite outside interests threatened to corral important commons resources: rich Kuwaitis sought to enclose the Nantahala. Maconians should come to Carson and let the Forest Service know that they would not agree to mortgage their forests' and communities' futures for the sake of fabulously wealthy foreign oil barons.

The *Franklin Press* reported that on August 26 "Kearney became the latest in a long line of high-ranking Forest Service personnel to present a [natural resources] program to residents of this Macon County community." Kearney's audience's "most immediate concern," the report continued, "was the possibility of major oil companies drilling for oil and gas on area government property, and how this drilling, if it takes place, might affect the surrounding ecology." The "ecology" phrase would certainly have included commons issues, such as questions about game populations and fishing streams. The Macon County Coon Hunting Club, for example, regularly sent representatives—including Jim Cunningham—to oil and gas meetings. Kearney would not have made it through his evening at Carson without questions from concerned hunters responsible for carrying the latest updates back to the club's two hundred members.[85]

Kearney informed the assembled citizens that leases affecting 10,200 Wayah District acres, including 8,000 acres in Macon County, had received final approval. ARCO held the five leases involving Macon County lands, most of which lay north of scenic local landmark Wayah Bald in an east–west band, though leases included parts of the Bald itself. "Talk then turned" to the question of Santa Fe Minerals, a wholly owned subsidiary of OPEC company Kuwait Petroleum Corporation, which had applied for leases in the Pisgah National Forest, the *Press* reported. "The idea of Arabs prospecting for resources on American [public] lands has caused more than a little controversy," *Press* reporter Scott McRae noted. Kearney assured his audience that federal restrictions made the Kuwait Petroleum possibility most unlikely.[86]

After Kearney's presentation, David Liden took the podium to inform Macon citizens about how oil and gas discoveries could affect private landholders. He noted that if oil prospecting in the region proved fruitful, most early wells would go on private land. He warned that private owners in the past had faced difficulties if they inadequately understood the terms of lease agreements.[87]

Carson Community and the Appalachian Alliance Host Oil and Gas Conference

In November 1982 the Carson Community Development Association, together with the Appalachian Alliance, hosted another open meeting on the oil and gas issue. Though publicity for the event made no mention of the Western North Carolina Alliance, an early newsletter later referred to this gathering as "the first Western North Carolina Alliance Forum on natural resource issues." For the November assembly, Carson and the Appalachian Alliance brought a number of other local and regional organizations on board, including the Conservation Committee of the Highlands Biological Foundation, the North Carolina Land Stewardship Council, the Social, Economic, and Political Issues Committee of the Commission on Religion in Appalachia, and the Wenoca Sierra Club. The gathering these organizations cosponsored had a conference format and featured not only Forest Service personnel but also a slate of other experts. David Liden and Bill Horton of the Appalachian Alliance spoke, as did two local academics and two representatives from the Agricultural Extension Service.[88]

At this conference the local campaign Carson had spearheaded took on regional significance. Nearly one hundred people from six different counties turned out for the November 9 meeting. Like the "Future of Appalachia" conference the Cunninghams had attended, the two-and-a-half-hour "Oil and Gas Development" session featured both academic expertise and first-person accounts. Opening speaker Tom McKinney began his discussion of potential social and community costs by promising to be "quick and gruesome." He described worst-case "boomtown" conditions in which rapid population growth led to deterioration and overcrowding of roads, schools, and medical facilities, increases in crime, divorce, and consumer prices, clashes of values between longtime permanent residents and transient newcomers, strains on government services, and potential changes in the local power structure.[89]

Other panelists, reported the *Asheville Citizen*, "painted equally depressing pictures." David Liden described the massive equipment necessary to extract oil from the region's miles-deep potential reserves. Bill Horton recounted his firsthand experience witnessing mining operations carried out on a West Virginia farm, where bulldozers leveled orchards worth thousands of dollars. He described how a state road became impassable and a farm pond disappeared, and he charged that reclamation efforts had not materialized. Conference organizers also showed a videotape produced by the Blue Ridge Sierra Club that illustrated the destruction caused by mining in several West Virginia counties. Groundwater contamination, erosion, oil spills, and surface destruction were common, the panelists concluded.[90]

With the November 9 forum, Cunningham, Liden, Carson, and the Appalachian Alliance had indeed "made news." Local press gave the conference and its message extensive coverage. "Experts Portray Gloomy Picture of Oil Drilling," announced the *Asheville Citizen* in its regional story, and the *Franklin Press* carried a similar front-page headline. "The people of Western North Carolina may very well have a hard road ahead of them," the *Press* cautioned. The paper reminded readers that there was still no proof that oil and gas deposits even existed in western North Carolina, but it also observed that "oil companies are showing a great deal of interest in the area." Panelists painted a "grim picture" of "the very negative effects that could ultimately result" from oil and gas exploration, the *Press* warned.[91]

Though more ambivalent in its reaction than the *Press*, the *Asheville Citizen* also gave the conference message careful thought. A few days after the meeting it ran an editorial arguing that carefully controlled drilling might be the best available option, given the nation's need for energy and the importance of avoiding destructive "crash" emergency drilling. Even here, however, the *Citizen* admitted that "oil and gas drilling is, at best, a messy, often destructive process" and that western North Carolinians faced "some unpleasant choices about the future." The paper's coverage of the Franklin meeting called "the hypothetical picture" of a petroleum-producing Blue Ridge "scary" and "bleak."[92]

Hard on the heels of this conference, the Carson club hosted its last public meeting of 1982 before "a large crowd" at the Carson Community Building on November 15. This forum featured Clarence Moore, Stanton District ranger for the Daniel Boone National Forest, sixty miles east of Lexington, Kentucky. Moore's district included between a thousand and fifteen hundred active oil wells. As local Wayah District Ranger Lewis Kearney noted, "Clarence probably has more active wells on his district than any other ranger in the 13-state Southern Region of the Forest Service." The USFS cooperated with Carson to bring Moore to Macon County, and Forest Service officials apparently hoped his talk would allay the community's fears about leasing. But the ranger's presentation had the opposite effect.[93]

Moore illustrated with dramatic slides his talk about the effects of drilling on lands he supervised. "The visual impact of these wells and their support apparatus is tremendous," reported Scott McRae in a front-page story for the *Franklin Press*. "Ridge lines are criss-crossed by roads leading to well sites, numerous man-made lakes have been created to provide the water necessary to force oil from the ground, catchment basins have been built to catch the oil in case of spills, power lines cut through the forests, pipelines cross the terrain, and old cable-related powerhouses dot the landscape." Nor did the effects end there. "Other related facilities, such as water injection wells, storage tanks, separation tanks, and equipment storage yards, are much in evidence throughout this Kentucky ranger district," McRae continued. The scale of this forest destruction must have alarmed both citizens who attended the meeting and those who read the *Press* story.[94]

Moore's audience also heard how oil wells represented only part of the story and only part of the problem in his district. The Kentucky ranger estimated that Stanton had as many water injection wells as oil wells, bringing the total number of man-made structures in the district to over two thousand. Injection wells pumped water into the earth to force oil to the surface. Chemicals added to these wells surfaced in recovered oil and made their way to area streams, where they raised levels of sodium, magnesium, and calcium sometimes thousands of times. Eventually, oil field chemicals wound up in nearby municipal water sources, and officials suspected they contributed to rising cancer rates. Stanton oil extraction also produced brine as a by-product, sometimes at rates as high as forty or fifty barrels per single barrel of oil. When the salty water entered local creeks, it destroyed all life. According to the *Press*'s McRae, Moore finished his talk by warning listeners that "past drilling operations have been able to build and not become a noticeable problem until it's too late."[95]

Years later, Moore's talk and his listeners' reactions remained etched in audience memories. Moore had described and vividly illustrated petroleum development's wholesale destruction of the multiple-use forest in Stanton. Esther Cunningham and David Liden both remembered Moore's graphic slides and the scenes of fish kills and other "extreme devastation" the photos depicted. Liden recalled how Moore frankly confessed that he and other rangers in the Daniel Boone National Forest were "sorry they ever let this happen." Liden also remembered noticing local Forest Service employees' growing discomfort as Moore's talk progressed. These officials had hoped the Kentucky ranger would calm Carson's fears, and Liden could almost hear an occasional "oh no" from them as the dramatic presentation went on. Esther Cunningham remembered hearing the *Franklin Press* editor respond to Moore's discussion by leaning over and saying to his neighbor, "Well, where is our state legislator? He lives in this community. Why isn't he present?" One Forest Service employee later opined that even the *possibility* their neighboring forests could see developments such as those Moore described so alarmed Macon residents that they rallied to organize a forest watchdog group, the Western North Carolina Alliance (WNCA).[96]

Cunningham and Liden Found the Western North Carolina Alliance

In their fight against petroleum development, Cunningham and Liden had tapped a powerful vein of commons-inspired frustration with national forest policies. Oil, gas, and mineral exploration posed the most ominous enclosure threat. Petroleum development could transform large tracts of the public lands from healthy multiple-use forests to heavily damaged single-use extraction sites. In the oil and gas controversy, Forest Service officials repeatedly found themselves on the receiving end of commons-defense concern.

Cunningham, Liden, and other sensitive observers recognized that just as commons thinking had been successfully mobilized against wilderness designation, so too could it be harnessed in opposition to industrial exploitation of the forests. They understood that most rural western North Carolinians' opposition to wilderness designation did not stem from any fundamental antipathy to environmental concern but rather from a philosophical difference with wilderness environmentalism. Build an environmentalist platform on the multiple-use commons ethic rather than on the wilderness ethic, and many longtime residents might take a stand there. Broad public participation in the antileasing open meetings demonstrated the power of this vision.

Indeed, many Macon County commons users rallied to Carson's antipetroleum banner. Hunters and anglers in the region were especially well organized and accustomed to discussing concerns with public officials. Their hunting, fishing, and wildlife clubs played active roles in North Carolina Wildlife Resources Commission policymaking. These organized commons users showed up in force at Carson. Western North Carolina's District 9 wildlife commissioner attended at least one forum. The two-hundred-member Macon County Coon Hunting Club regularly sent representatives to the Carson meetings. So concerned were the coon hunters about oil and gas exploration, in fact, that they listed this issue first among recent community service projects in a *Franklin Press* club profile.[97]

The sportsmen's groups also brought bipartisan political clout and far-reaching networks to the antipetroleum campaign. Jim Cunningham, for instance, had long been a leader in local Democratic Party politics as well as an active member of the Macon County Coon Hunting Club. His fellow members included prominent local Republicans as well as other prominent Democrats. When the club plunged into the antileasing campaign, then, it brought a long political reach. It also contributed ties to other sportsmen and community groups, and antipetroleum alerts doubtless traveled quickly among these. Word-of-mouth alarms almost certainly played a key role in packing the house at the oil and gas summit and graphic slide show that capped Carson's antipetroleum campaign.[98]

The overwhelming response to their public meeting series convinced Liden and Cunningham that the region needed an organization that could mobilize local people around their commons environmentalist concerns. This group would serve as watchdog over natural resource issues, educate the public, offer opportunities for citizens to express their ideas and concerns, and facilitate coordinated responses. It would respond to the needs of western North Carolina residents and would take its cues from their environmental stewardship priorities. It would be a broad-based regional effort that could unite diverse constituencies, just as the petroleum fight had. Cunningham and Liden set about building such a group, which became the Western North Carolina Alliance. They had help from the Appalachian Alliance, which offered consultations with seasoned mountain organizers such as its own Bill Horton and Kentuckians for the Commonwealth's Joe Szakos. The Appalachian Alliance also served temporarily as a funding clearinghouse for the fledgling western North Carolina organization.[99]

As they worked to launch the new group, Cunningham, Liden, and other early organizers carefully differentiated it from the national environmental organizations that had figured so prominently in the wilderness designation controversies. As former WNCA organizer Mary Kelly explained, mainstream environmentalists "were viewed as city folks, tourists coming in from the outside and all they want to do is make fun of us and cut the collars off our bear dogs and shut down our hunting." "Environmental groups had gotten a bad name," Kelly remembered, "by being caught on the wrong side of a lot of very popular issues in the mountains, [including] the wilderness debates of the seventies. . . . So if you said the Wilderness Society, people would just want to toss you out on your fanny. Sierra Club, same way."[100]

David Liden remembered a concrete example of the pattern Kelly described. He recalled attending a local turkey hunters' club gathering and making an announcement inviting the hunters to come to a meeting of the newly launched WNCA. One hunter came up to him afterward and said, "You're part of that Sierra Club, aren't you?" Liden replied that he was not and that in fact the new organization had no connections to the Sierra Club or to any other national environmental organization. Skeptical at first, the hunter finally became convinced and made an appointment to talk about the new group.[101]

Liden, Kelly, and other WNCA organizers recognized and respected the fact that the environmental label immediately conjured images of mainstream national organizations that were anathema to many rural residents. Liden even declined to call the WNCA an "environmental" group; instead, he talked in terms of natural resources. He described the young WNCA as a coalition of ordinary citizens concerned about the future of the forests. Liden also responded sensitively to other local concerns. He valued the participation of area hunters, for instance, noting that "they police the forest. We wouldn't know what's going on back there if those people didn't get out there and use the forest."[102]

Cunningham, Liden, and other organizers succeeded in making their vision for the WNCA a reality. They brought together diverse constituencies from across the region, united by a shared concern for the health of Blue Ridge forests. By 1984 the organization was fully launched, complete with officially recognized status as a nonprofit, a fully developed organizational structure including a steering committee, task forces, local chapters, paid staff members, and some grant monies. It was a "homegrown" regional association actively engaged in debates over forest use in western North Carolina. As Mary Kelly put it, "It wasn't some outside agenda that came in and created the Alliance. It really was the brainchild of the people of the region. It was created by and for the people of western North Carolina for the purposes that they saw fit."[103]

Changes in the international energy economy and the prohibitive costs of reaching western North Carolina's miles-deep potential reserves eventually brought an end to "oil fever" in the region. Though the young WNCA continued its petroleum-exploration education campaigns at least through 1985, the sense of urgency surrounding the issue had largely dissipated by early 1984. Oil fever had come and gone without leaving many marks on western North Carolina's physical landscape. It had etched permanent imprints on the region's political landscape, however. The petroleum scare had stirred the depths of mountain residents' commons brand of environmental concern. It had given local activists an issue around which to mobilize this concern, and it had enabled Cunningham, Liden, Carson, and the Appalachian Alliance to lay the groundwork for organized resistance to further forest threats. With the oil and gas issue safely behind them, western North Carolina forest activists turned nearly complete attention to clearcutting. And here they unleashed the full force of commons environmentalism.

NINE

Clearcutting Returns

Timber Enclosure Threatens the Forests

ON A FALL DAY IN 1965, western North Carolina district ranger Bob Padgett stood staring in near disbelief at a research site on the Mead Experimental Forest in Ohio. The seasoned forester had a hard time wrapping his mind around what he was seeing and hearing. Padgett and his fellow Nantahala and Pisgah district rangers had piled into a chartered bus and headed to Ohio with their boss, Peter J. Hanlon, supervisor of National Forests in North Carolina (NFsNC), who had organized and required this training trip. Once arrived, the group toured a series of clearcutting study sites, guided by Ben Roach, a leading Forest Service researcher. Padgett reacted to the tour, he remembered two decades later, with something akin to shock.[1]

"On first seeing the expansive clearcut hillsides on the Mead Forest," Padgett wrote, "one was reminded of the shocking pictures of similarly denuded forests in the reports which led to passage of the Weeks Act." Padgett probably had in mind Secretary of Agriculture James Wilson's 1902 report to President Theodore Roosevelt on the condition of the southern Appalachian forests. The famous "Wilson report" included striking photographs graphically illustrating the devastated conditions Wilson's research team found in the region. To Bob Padgett, the experimental clearcut sites he saw in 1965 resembled nothing so much as these powerful photos from six decades earlier. "It was very strange, then," he recalled, "to hear a Forest Service research forester explaining how this same timber harvesting technique, once anathema as 'destructive exploitation,' was now the recommended way to cut timber in the eastern hardwood forests."[2]

In the ensuing decades, countless viewers would experience shock parallel to Padgett's. The 1965 tour proved a harbinger of things to come. "Lands controlled by the Forest Service are never clearcut," the agency wrote unequivocally in a 1940 pamphlet about its work in the southern Appalachians.[3] But that was about to change, and on a large scale. Ben Roach's experiments and demonstrations helped to bring clearcutting, which was an established practice on western national forests by the late 1950s, to the eastern forests. Bob Padgett wrote that Roach "largely 'fathered' clearcutting in eastern hardwood forests." Roach had experimented with clearcutting as a method of regenerating hardwood stands, Padgett recalled. Paper products company Mead Corporation had underwritten much of Roach's research, and many of the studies had taken place on Mead lands.[4]

The Mead Corporation's close involvement with Roach's research is telling. Mead needed pulpwood, and lots of it, for paper manufacture. The paper industry had wrestled with raw material supply issues throughout its history, and it continued to do so. Clearcutting offered an easy, cheap, efficient method for harvesting pulpwood, and the national forests represented a significant potential source. Mead therefore had a vested interest in convincing national forest managers that clearcutting was good silvicultural practice. If Ben Roach's experiments proved favorable, he could proselytize from within the agency. Bob Padgett described a Forest Service meeting, a gathering exclusively of USFS personnel. But he also remembered Mead Corporation's looming background presence.[5]

The 1965 visit illustrates a larger nationwide pattern of growing agency-industry cordiality in the postwar period. Increasingly, the Forest Service developed close ties with woods-products industries on both national and local levels. On both scales the Nantahala and Pisgah rangers' visit serves as an example. Mead, a huge company with operations in many parts of the United States, had midwifed the clearcutting research Roach introduced. The results from that research would have national implications, helping change the face of forestry throughout eastern national forests. Mead also had particular interests in western North Carolina and thus reason to court NFsNC personnel. Since 1928 the corporation had operated a paperboard plant in Sylva, a Jackson County town nestled in Nantahala National Forest country. Mead held forestland of its own in the area but stood to benefit considerably if Nantahala rangers took up clearcutting. For its part, the Forest Service encouraged personnel to support local forest-products industries. Hanlon's Mead-friendly trip exemplified contemporary agency policy. This cordiality stood in marked contrast to patterns sixty years previously, when Gifford Pinchot considered most timber operators his sworn enemies.[6]

Bob Padgett's account of the 1965 tour nicely captures his sense that agency ground was shifting beneath his feet, that a new era in USFS history was beginning. Of course, he had the benefit of hindsight when he wrote about the trip, and as a result he could clearly see how pivotal the introduction—or reintroduction—of clearcutting had been to eastern forestry. And though he had continued working for the Forest Service well into its new proclearcutting phase, he wrote his account after he retired and became an outspoken critic of national forest clearcutting. In fact, when he penned his description of the Ohio tour, Padgett was actively engaged in a pitched battle against his former employer. In an anticlearcutting speech a few years later, he described the USFS as "the agency that would destroy our stands of trees we worked so hard to create."[7]

Despite the particulars of Padgett's position, his account captures important broad realities. The shocked response to clearcutting he described repeated itself over and over—among foresters, hunters, hikers, and anyone else who used or viewed the southern Appalachian national forests. The sense that extensive clearcutting represented an important and disturbing departure from earlier USFS practice was also widely shared. A sea change was in fact under way. Its results would be far-reaching—for the agency, for the law, for forest neighbors, and for the forests themselves.

The Reagan Administration Embraces Industrial Development of Public Lands

Though its framers intended the National Forest Management Act of 1976 to limit large-scale clearcut timber harvesting on the national forests, in the short term the legislation cleared a legal path for the practice. A few years later, the Reagan administration raced down that path. The 1980 presidential election, which sent Republican Ronald Reagan to the White House, ushered in a new era of public lands management. The Reagan administration expressed ambivalence about the very existence of federal lands and launched a short-lived early effort to sell off many lands or hand them over to the states. Given that wholesale privatization could not be achieved, as quickly became apparent, the administration's approach to public lands management sought to mimic private patterns. Reagan's philosophy of public lands management emphasized industrial development, held that public lands should be financially self-supporting, and considered environmental legislation to be what Interior Secretary James Watt memorably called "paralysis by analysis."[8]

Taken together, these ideas put heavy pressures on the Forest Service to sell resources—particularly timber but also minerals where available. Such sales were practically the agency's only way to raise revenue internally and abide by the "pay-your-own-way" plank. The administration encouraged resource sales as appropriate public land use and facilitated them with a staff of environmental regulators committed to rolling back rather than enforcing protective legislation enacted in the previous fifteen years. The Reagan administration proved especially friendly to extractive industry, including timber, which of course welcomed increases in USFS sales.[9]

Increased clearcutting on western North Carolina's national forests, then, followed a nationwide pattern. The effects of this pattern were regionally expressed, however. Like every other eastern national forest, the Nantahala and Pisgah forests had ragged, snaking boundaries that reflected the piecemeal nature of their original acquisition from private property owners. As a result of this convoluted-boundary inheritance, thousands of rural smallholdings adjoined Blue Ridge national forests. Where western timber harvests could go on in relative isolation, largely invisible behind the "beauty strips" Forest Service officials learned to leave, eastern clearcutting almost inevitably meant irate neighbors. The fact that many mountain residents spent time in the woods hunting, fishing, and the like made it even more difficult for the Forest Service to clearcut unnoticed.[10]

Western North Carolina's environmental mobilization also followed a larger national pattern. The Reagan administration's approach to public lands management and environmental issues sparked unprecedented nationwide organizing and fund-raising around these issues. Within six months of Reagan's inauguration, for example, the entire catalog of national conservationist organizations had gone on record against his policies. They took aim especially at Interior Secretary James Watt, whom one historian described as the president's "public lands alter ego." Three months after Reagan took office, the Izaak Walton League, a moderate sportsmen's organization that considered itself representative of "mainstream America," charged that "piece by piece, acre by acre, principle by principle, our natural resource legacy is being eaten away." Delegates to the league's 1981 convention unanimously asked Reagan to fire Watt. A 1981 Audubon Society drive opposing Watt garnered nine times more money from eight times more members than any previous organization fund-raiser. Some 70 percent of the National Wildlife Federation's membership voted for Reagan in 1980, but in 1981 the organization broke a long neutrality tradition to condemn the administration's public lands policies and join the chorus clamoring for Watt's resignation.[11]

The Western North Carolina Alliance's campaign against clearcutting was at once part of this national movement and a particular regional expression. The organization was launched during Watt's controversial tenure at Interior, and its anticlearcutting activism began in earnest with the 1984 release of a draft management plan for the Nantahala and Pisgah. As secretary of the interior, James Watt was not responsible for the Department of

Agriculture's national forest policies. Thus, WNCA did not appear in direct response to Watt, and it never battled him head-on. However, the WNCA did challenge the Reagan administration public lands policies that Watt symbolized for most conservationists. Yet the specific brand of environmentalism propelling the WNCA was particular to the organization.[12]

In many instances, the Reagan administration's environmental policies represented radical departures from established patterns, but for USFS timber harvesting, this was not the case. Until 1970 national forest timber harvest levels had risen—usually dramatically—under every president since World War II. Ever-increasing timber sales and straitened congressional budgets for everything but timber and timber-related road building had become facts of Forest Service life during this period. Though Democratic presidents typically supported recreation initiatives more enthusiastically than did Republicans, both parties' postwar administrations largely steered national forest policy down a course that emphasized timber production. Between 1970 and 1975 environmentalists had begun to change this pattern, and national forest harvest levels dropped precipitously to pre-1960 levels, largely due to the Monongahela lawsuit and a series of new environmental laws. But the administration of Democrat Jimmy Carter, Reagan's immediate predecessor, had already begun reversing this downward trend. The 1976 National Forest Management Act reopened the clearcutting floodgates, and as recession gripped the national economy, Carter put significant pressure on the Forest Service to raise revenue and to harvest more timber. As a result, timber harvest levels climbed again between 1975 and 1980. The Reagan administration simply accelerated this returned upward trend. But the acceleration was important. Reagan era cuts in Forest Service budgets and raises in "allowable sale quantities" of timber had far-reaching consequences for the national forests.[13]

In fact, no Forest Service unit, except for those tracts congressionally designated as wilderness or wilderness study areas, remained untouched by presidential timber policy. Because the Forest Service answered to the Department of Agriculture, the policies of a sitting president had profound effects. Congress controlled the agency's purse strings, but the president set its agenda.

Rising Timber Harvest Targets and the Pulpwood Industry Encourage Clearcutting

The case of national forest timber harvest goals provides one telling example. The president's Agriculture Department set national timber harvest goals for the Forest Service. The Washington office of the Forest Service chief then assigned portions of the national timber target to each region. Western North Carolina was part of Region 8, the Southeast Region, which had headquarters in Atlanta. The Forest Service chief's orders came to Atlanta and other regional offices, and regional supervisors then divvied the numbers among states. Atlanta sent numbers to NFsNC headquarters in Asheville, for example. Then state offices doled out target shares to specific forests, and forest supervisors handed numbers down to local district rangers. In North Carolina, the Asheville office allotted targets to the mountains' Nantahala and Pisgah forests and also to the piedmont's Uwharrie and the coast's Croatan. The Nantahala National Forest divided its target number quota among the Cheoah, Tusquitee, Highlands, and Wayah Ranger Districts. The local ranger district was the basic building block of the national forest system, so the buck stopped there.[14]

Thus, the district ranger had responsibility not to determine how much timber should be harvested in his district but rather to consider how best to harvest the amount of timber higher-ups (and ultimately the president) demanded. When Washington raised overall target numbers, every ranger district felt the effects. Rangers found themselves expected to meet the quotas they had been handed, whether or not they approved of these numbers. Institutional incentives such as raises and promotions were routinely tied to a ranger's success in meeting the district's timber harvest goals. When the numbers went up, rangers had little choice but to come up with ways to cut more timber. Bob Padgett described the plight of "beleaguered rangers who were trying to make their annual timber sale quotas with limited operating funds."[15]

Target harvest levels increased with nearly every postwar administration, and they rose again under Reagan. Timber industry lobbyists were always anxious to have national forest harvest targets climb higher, and they had an ally in the Reagan White House. They also had allies in Congress, which in the mid-1980s set separate timber harvest targets for the Forest Service, numbers even higher than the already high administration goals. As target harvest goals rose through the postwar period, it became increasingly difficult for local rangers to use anything but clearcutting techniques to meet them. Bob Padgett remembered how in the mid-1960s western North Carolina's district foresters had embraced clearcutting because "it spelled the end to long years of agonizing over how to meet timber sale quotas by difficult selective cutting." They were "delighted with this new, easy way to make timber sale quotas," he recalled.[16]

The Appalachian national forests were shielded from the worst effects of the first decades of high postwar federal target numbers because they had already been logged once. The northern Rockies and especially the Pacific Northwest, which after World War II still had vast stands of never-cut forest, bore the brunt of USFS harvesting throughout the period. But by the 1960s and increasingly through the following decades, forests in the Appalachians and much of the rest of the South became once again commercially valuable. The eastern "lands nobody wanted" had become maturing forests everybody wanted—recreationists, commons harvesters, and timber operators especially. Heavy harvesting continued in the Douglas fir regions, but as these last ancient old-growth tracts dwindled, national timber interests increased their attention to the East's—and especially the South's—recovering forests. As one USFS employee explained to interviewers in the 1980s, the Appalachian forests were once again "ready for harvest."[17]

Eventually, even-aged management replaced all-aged as the Forest Service's preferred technique in the Appalachians as elsewhere. Some established USFS foresters resisted this change, while others embraced it with varying degrees of eagerness or reluctance. Bob Padgett, as we have seen, worked as a district ranger at the time Nantahala and Pisgah forest managers began advocating clearcutting. He first reacted with shock to clearcutting demonstrations, but it was probably difficult for him to avoid clearcutting in his district. Assured by Forest Service researchers that the technique was silviculturally sound, encouraged by his supervisors to use it, faced with his district's high annually assigned timber harvest targets, and pressured by the agency's incentive structures to meet these targets, he likely arranged clearcut timber sales on his district. When retirement liberated him from agency constraints, Padgett vocally expressed the opposition he had originally felt.[18]

It is no coincidence that in 1965, when Bob Padgett and other western North Carolina district rangers visited Mead Experimental Forest to learn about clearcutting, the southern Appalachian pulpwood industry was booming. Pulp mills had operated in the region for decades, but they expanded enormously in the 1960s and 1970s, and they looked increasingly to the national forests as a supply source. The all-aged management techniques familiar to Padgett and his generation aimed to produce quality sawtimber, the most valuable forest product. Only mature hardwoods, which for mountain species generally meant trees some sixty or more years old, made good sawtimber. As long as pulpwood demand remained low, lumbermen aimed primarily to harvest sawlogs. Younger trees had economic value mostly for their sawtimber promise. With the pulpwood market unreliable, cutting juvenile growth meant risking immediate economic losses.

By providing a ready market for small logs—indeed, creating burgeoning demand for these logs—the growing pulpwood industry helped change the region's timber harvest economics and propel it toward clearcutting. An operator could cut everything, haul the big logs to his sawmills, and rely on selling smaller growth to local pulp mills.[19]

Though political and economic pressures largely fueled the Forest Service's move away from all-aged and toward even-aged techniques, the agency justified this move in silvicultural terms. Clearcutting was the best method for bringing back hardwood stands, its supporters argued. Selective cutting failed to regenerate hardwoods because it left only small holes in the forest canopy. Valuable timber species such as black cherry, oak, and yellow poplar failed to thrive in the shade left by selective harvesting techniques. Shade-tolerant trees such as maple, dogwood, and sourwood, which were not valuable timber species, crowded out the more valuable sun-lovers.[20]

Foresters Divide over Clearcutting

Some foresters—especially older foresters—criticized clearcutting. Walton Smith, a USFS retiree and practicing private forester who became an outspoken opponent of Nantahala and Pisgah clearcutting, serves as one example. Smith did not reject the method altogether, but he did think that when it was used indiscriminately, it amounted to bad forestry. To his mind, the Forest Service had taken a wrong turn when it shifted emphasis from uneven-aged to even-aged management. Smith managed his family's private tract, Waldee Forest, using uneven-aged techniques, and he readily displayed his woods to anyone interested in discussing silviculture. In fact, Waldee often served as Smith's "exhibit A" in debates about clearcutting. He pointed out the beauty of the woods, its compatibility with other uses such as hunting and camping, the health of young growing trees, the variety of commercially desirable species, and the ongoing timber productivity of the tract. "I'm growing them faster than I can cut them," Smith told visitors. He contrasted Waldee to tracts harvested by clearcutting, which he described as unattractive, incompatible with other uses, and harvestable only every six or seven decades. Smith argued that clearcutting wasted years of growth in promising young trees and resulted in fewer desirable species and less high quality hardwood timber.[21]

Smith's early Forest Service experiences informed his approach to forest management. Foresters of his generation had seen the devastating aftermath of turn-of-the-century Appalachian harvests. They had worked to restore the lands that loggers, fires, and erosion had left in ruins—the huge tracts of smoldering, muddy mess the Forest Service had acquired under the Weeks Act.[22]

Repairing these heavily damaged lands proved a central job for Walton Smith's cohort of USFS foresters. Earlier foresters were mostly in the business of land acquisition and planning, and postwar foresters would emphasize timber cutting, but forest rehabilitation provided the 1930s generation's chief mission. This group participated in one of the great conservationist triumphs of U.S. history as they helped spoiled Appalachian hillsides transform into productive and beautiful woodlands. The story of West Virginia's "Great Burn" wasteland, become by the 1960s the majestic Monongahela, illustrated the larger pattern. Most western North Carolina forests had not been quite so heavily devastated, but the effects of industrial timber harvest had nonetheless been enormous. Destructive logging and the repeated fires that followed it left the slopes of Mount Mitchell and many other western North Carolina tracts fully denuded and dangerously eroded. Walton Smith and his generation presided over the near-miraculous renewal of these desertlike areas. For them, wholesale clearcutting was a destructive harvest method whose results they had spent careers working to overcome. Among Forest Service personnel in the southern Appalachians, at least until the 1950s, "anything like clearcutting was heresy," Smith recalled. His colleague Bob Padgett put the date later but agreed with the basic analysis. Until the mid-1960s, Padgett wrote, "clearcutting . . . was simply a bad word in management of eastern national forests."[23]

The Appalachian forests had enormous regenerative power. The Forest Service that employed young Walton Smith nurtured this capacity for renewal, actively assisting the forest's own recovery efforts. The agency's fire suppression program, for instance, proved crucial to its success. Repeated fires damaged the soils of logged tracts and made it all but impossible for seedlings and root sprouts establish and grow. By fighting fires and fire starters and encouraging fire prevention with missionary-like zeal, the Forest Service broke the destructive fire cycle that had prevented recovery in many Appalachian tracts.[24]

When Franklin Roosevelt's New Deal made a large labor pool available by sending thousands of Civilian Conservation Corps workers to national forest camps, the USFS added other rehabilitation programs to its fire suppression centerpiece. The CCC men performed much of the work that made the forests what they are today. Their most visible legacy is in the trails, overlooks, shelters, bridges, fire towers, campgrounds, buildings, and roads that are still in use throughout the national forests. But the CCC workers also left their mark on the woods themselves. They did timber stand improvement work such as thinning crowded juvenile trees, pruning established trees, and fighting tree diseases. In especially degraded areas, they mounted soil erosion control programs and planted tree seedlings. And, of course, CCC crews served as the first line of forest fire defense. World War II both took this workforce and brought increased demand for lumber, but until then the Forest Service continued to play a largely custodial and rehabilitative role in the Appalachian national forests.[25]

Walton Smith came to the Nantahala National Forest in 1936, during the active woods restoration period. In his first assignment, he helped assess the value of a Graham County tract Gennett Lumber Company had offered to sell. The tract included rare, never-cut Appalachian woods, and part of it later became the Joyce Kilmer Memorial Forest. "I spent three months in a government camp making the volume tables for those big trees," Smith remembered. He and his colleagues managed to find timber numbers high enough to enable the Forest Service to justify paying twenty-eight dollars per acre for the Gennett tract. "That was the most expensive land we'd ever bought at that time," Smith later recalled. This first assignment, which required Smith both to be a timber-minded professional forester and to be sensitive to nontimber values, would set the tone for his long forestry career.[26]

In the 1950s and 1960s, Smith remembered, the Forest Service in the southern Appalachians increased its emphasis on timber production. This shift was part of a nationwide trend that began during World War II. Before the war, Forest Service officials and timber operators typically had an uneasy relationship, each group regarding the other with some suspicion. Appalachian forester Inman Eldredge summed up the foresters' point of view: "You produced the timber and cared for it, and then you turned it over to the roughnecks to cut it up and ship it around. There wasn't any science or art to [lumbermen's work]." In their turn, timbermen saw foresters as frivolous. Forest Service personnel did not do real work, they charged, and professional forestry amounted to little more than "a parlor game." After the war, relations between the two camps became more cordial, and by the 1960s they were closely intertwined. Industry and Forest Service foresters trained in the same schools and held memberships in the same professional organizations. They moved with relative ease between public and private sectors—USFS foresters took industry jobs, and timbermen joined the Forest Service. The increasing professional emphasis on even-aged management techniques meant that by the 1960s most Forest Service as well as industry personnel had schooled as even-aged forest managers.[27]

The shift in emphasis from all-aged to even-aged management techniques represented a sea change in professional forestry. "Just as 'clearcutting' was once the bad word in management of eastern national forests," Bob Padgett wrote in 1985, "'selective cutting' is now the bad word." The shift often pitted younger foresters, who generally supported even-aged strategies, against older foresters, who typically favored all-aged management. Walton Smith remembered a series of 1960s era discussions among Forest Service personnel in western North Carolina, and he described them as divided along generational lines.[28]

Forest Management Becomes a Desk Job

Walton Smith's hands-on approach to forestry stood in marked contrast to away-from-the-woods trends in national forest management. By the late 1970s Forest Service employees spent more time at their desks than ever before. Greater regulation and demand for paper trails contributed to this shift, as environmental legislation required extensive documentation of agency plans and decisions. The four-hundred-page, fifty-year draft plan for the Nantahala and Pisgah released in 1984, for instance, would have been unthinkable twenty-five years earlier. In those days, remembered USFS forester Pat Cook, forest management was a very seat-of-the-pants affair. District rangers managed the woods largely according to their own lights, with few documentary requirements. They seldom pushed much paper. In the early 1960s, Cook recalled, young men like himself often chose forestry as a career because they enjoyed spending time in the woods and wanted to do so on a daily basis. Fifteen years later, they frequently found that weeks went by without their ever setting foot in the forest.[29]

The rise of computer technology also fueled the Forest Service movement from woods to desk. Computer analysis had become a fact of Forest Service life by the late 1970s, as personnel routinely used computer models to strategize forest management. Such models physically removed foresters from the woods by shifting the site of analysis and planning from the ground to the office. The language computer models used also distanced foresters from trees. One example suffices to illustrate the pattern. "Linear program systems," wrote one analyst in 1975, "will allow the planner to examine the effect of various decisions on the resource base (the forest) and on the product output levels (e.g., timber, wildlife, and recreation)." This sentence transformed concrete and specific entities—the forest, timber, wildlife—into abstract generalizations—the resource base, product outputs. It encouraged planners to distance themselves mentally as well as physically from the immensely complicated material web of a forest.[30]

The question of distance from the forest proved a bone of contention between advocates of even-aged and uneven-aged management. Foresters like Walton Smith, who believed in all-aged management, thought that good forestry required a great deal of time spent in the woods. One could not plan a responsible selection harvest without intimate knowledge of the tract in question. The forester had to walk the woods and pay attention to individual trees. Which ones should be harvested, which culled, which encouraged to provide later harvest? Foresters like Walton Smith and fellow Forest Service retiree Bob Padgett also believed that timber managers should keep in mind other forest uses. Which stands provided important wildlife food, which groves would make good picnic areas, which snags were animal den trees? It was impossible to answer these sorts of questions without a sophisticated hands-on knowledge of the particular forest under one's management, these older foresters contended.[31]

By contrast, Bob Padgett charged, even-aged techniques encouraged desk work rather than woods work. They privileged computer analysis over on-the-ground site analysis, and the forest suffered as a result. Padgett was one of Walton Smith's central anticlearcutting partners, another former employee of the Forest Service who spent his retirement working a tree farm of his own. He believed clearcutting had agency approval partly because it was a computer-friendly technique that used designated tracts rather than individual trees as basic timber-harvest units. Single-tree complexity proved too much for computer technology to handle, but a list of tracts was tailor-made for computer analysis. This was especially true if all trees within a given tract were the same age. "The theoretical objective [of even-aged management]," Bob Padgett wrote, "is to have even-aged timber stands ranging in age from one to eighty years, with equal acreage in each age class, throughout the general forest area." A computer program could simply store information about when a given tract had been harvested and then calculate the next harvest date by adding eighty years. Foresters would never have to venture into the woods to know which sites were ready for harvest; their computers would tell them. "All a ranger of the future will need do is punch his computer buttons to locate all stands of trees reaching age 80 that year, and schedule that timber for clearcutting," Padgett explained. In managing the woods by computer, forestry became a desk job.[32]

Padgett might also have noted that the agency's linear computer programs distanced planners from forests because their design was ill suited to model the interdependent workings of forest ecology. Physical forests frequently defied the predictions of abstract models, yet in Forest Service offices, the models sometimes trumped the forests. One western case revealed that local planners had built impossibly high minimum timber harvest numbers into their model. Despite evidence that the physical forests could not produce timber at the jerry-rigged level the model demanded, managers stuck with their artificially inflated numbers for years. This 1986 example supported Bob Padgett's 1985 concern that easily computerizable even-aged management distanced forest managers from their woods to the detriment of forest health and sustainability.[33]

Mountain Opposition to Clearcutting Grows

As timber harvesting and especially clearcutting in the southern Appalachians increased during the 1960s, 1970s, and 1980s, so too did public concern. Just as it had in the Monongahela area, clearcutting drew fire across the region. High clearcut visibility, regional soil fragility, and local traditions of forest use combined to give the issue particular urgency. Observers noted that the southern Appalachians became a hotbed of clearcutting antipathy. "Forest Service officials found themselves in constant defense of their newly-adopted even-aged management," Bob Padgett recalled. In western North Carolina, clearcutting proved to be an important issue in the debates over RARE II wilderness designation, and it surfaced again in the conflict over petroleum development.[34]

Because it took whole forest stands, clearcutting especially provoked opposition from anyone interested in using the public forests as commons. Madison County hunter Haze Landers explained to Appalshop filmmakers his theory that commons users would even mount financial defenses of the public forests if allowed. He offered the example of a local clearcut timber sale that had recently gone for $3,500. Hunters like himself would have paid the Forest Service at least as much not to have cut it, he said. "I'd have made up thirty-five hundred dollars and give it to them if they'd have left it there," Landers declared. "I'd have took up a collection, and I'd have soon got it off of these hunters here." In Landers's analysis, the forest held a higher commons value—even in dollar-for-dollar monetary terms—than the timber value Forest Service officials assigned to it.[35]

But the rural people like Haze Landers, who opposed clearcutting on commons grounds, were scattered across hundreds of miles and more than a dozen western North Carolina counties. They had no central channel through which to express their opposition. The obvious possible channel, the Forest Service itself, seemed determined to suppress rather than coordinate local opposition. During earlier wilderness fights, the Forest Service had encouraged local residents (who typically opposed further wilderness designation) to visit district offices and have secretaries transcribe verbal comments for inclusion in the all-important written record. It apparently offered no parallel service to clearcutting opponents. Antipathy to clearcutting in western North Carolina was probably at least as widespread throughout the 1970s and 1980s as antipathy to wilderness, but the agency did little to record or respond to this situation.[36]

Nor did national environmental groups help western North Carolinians express their opposition effectively. Communities in the region poured time, energy, money, and other resources into contesting particular timber sales, for instance. At Little Laurel, Roaring Hole, Craggy Gardens, Little Prong, Big Rocky, and other sites, local citizens and groups fought national forest clearcutting acre by acre. They filed formal appeals, circulated petitions, and organized public meetings. Throughout the 1980s, however, Sierra Club policy was not to oppose individual sales in the region. The club filed its first appeal of a western North Carolina timber sale in June 1990, more than a year after the Western North Carolina Alliance held its massive Cut the Clearcutting! campaign. Other national groups followed a similar pattern.[37]

Of course, the Sierra Club and other national groups had limited resources and had of necessity to pick their battles. Wilderness was a cornerstone of their strategy. They resolutely defended wilderness areas and worked to gain protection for more acreage. In general, however, if an area was not wilderness or potential wilderness, they did not contest Forest Service management decisions for it. One result of these national-level priorities was that local commons users, whose highly valued forest places did not necessarily overlap with roadless wilderness, had to mount defenses largely on their own.[38]

With its years of dedicated clearcutting opposition and especially with its well-orchestrated Cut the Clearcutting! campaign, the WNCA stepped into the breach left by Forest Service and national environmental groups' unresponsiveness to local concerns. The 1989 campaign, in particular, finally provided a central channel for the political expression of the widespread and long-standing but dispersed regional antipathy to clearcutting.

Walton Smith Leads WNCA Clearcutting Opposition

Since its founding, the WNCA had steadily fought clearcutting and always with an emphasis on the method's destruction of commons forest. Shortly after the petroleum issue prompted Esther Cunningham and David Liden to found the Alliance, the fledgling organization began attracting activists concerned with other dangers to the region's national forests, including clearcutting. These activists formed the Forest Management Task Force within the WNCA, and for years that group spearheaded the organization's anticlearcutting efforts.[39]

Walton Smith quickly emerged as a central figure in the WNCA's Forest Management Task Force. Smith and his wife, Dee Leatherman Smith, resided in the Cowee community in Macon County, near the Swain County border. Nantahala National Forest lands stood a stone's throw from Cowee. Neighborhood landmarks bore Dee's family name: Leatherman Gap, Leatherman Knob, Leatherman Bald. The Smiths lived on a 150-acre tract that Dee Leatherman Smith's family had held for generations. Walton and Dee Smith called their land Waldee Forest, and Walton managed the property for timber production using selection harvest methods. He operated a small sawmill on the tract and kept it busy cutting Waldee logs.[40]

The Smiths numbered among Esther and Jim Cunningham's friends, and Walton Smith soon became active in the new regional organization Esther Cunningham and David Liden worked to form. Cunningham remembered how people with a variety of environmental concerns showed up in the early days of Alliance organizing, before the embryonic group had a name or an organizational structure. Walton Smith emerged as the central figure around whom a group concerned with clearcutting and other forest issues coalesced. "Here was this bunch over here, and they were upset about clearcutting. And Walton was the main one of those," Esther Cunningham recalled.[41]

Walton Smith became the chief architect of WNCA's forest management platform, which included strong opposition to clearcutting. Where wilderness opponents had used commons-friendly multiple-use arguments to turn back proposed wilderness designations, Smith used the same arguments to combat clearcutting. He described clearcutting as a single-use threat to the multiple-use commons forest. Addressing the crowd at a 1985 WNCA fund-raiser, for instance, Smith criticized the USFS for embracing "wholesale clearcutting at the expense of watershed protection, hunting, recreation, and the continuous production of high quality hardwood trees which make the area so unique," the organization's *Accent* newsletter reported.[42]

If RARE II was an important issue for Walton Smith, he did not mention it in his many writings. Smith was friendly with Taylor Crockett and no friend to clearcutting, so he might have supported Crockett's efforts to protect the slated-for-clearcutting southern Nantahala tract by having it designated wilderness. But in general he was not a wilderness enthusiast. "Unlike most of the environmental organizations," he wrote in a 1989 forest management newsletter, "we are not asking for special treatment of forest lands to suit the special interests of our members." With this language Smith almost certainly meant to distance himself from the Sierra Club and the Wilderness Society. He also carefully differentiated the Forest Service from the Park Service and expressed strong support for making USFS lands "available to the people at large for multiple uses." None of this was wilderness-friendly language—in fact, it edged close to antiwilderness rhetoric: "special treatment" for "special interests" who wanted the forests to become more like the parks. The implicit contrast Smith drew between single-use exclusivity and multiple-use availability also echoed wilderness opponents' refrain.[43]

During the hot RARE II summer of 1978—in fact, just two weeks after antiwilderness demonstrations convulsed the town—Walton and Dee Smith helped to host a Franklin meeting of the North Carolina Society of Consulting Foresters. Participants studied cable logging (which typically involved clearcutting), pine beetle control, and new techniques for building timber access roads. It is hard to imagine this group offering a full embrace to RARE II wilderness designation.[44]

Walton Smith's ideal model of Forest Service management mirrored his practices at Waldee and departed from the wilderness model. He firmly believed that as a renewable resource trees could and should be harvested; the trick was to do so responsibly. He was committed to multiple-use management, and he had faith in the Forest Service as a trustworthy lands manager—faith that remained unshaken until the mid-1980s.

Walton and Dee Smith's Waldee Forest lay nearly surrounded by Nantahala lands, so it was all but inevitable that clearcutting would eventually show up at their doorstep. In 1984, faced with rising timber harvest targets, Wayah District Ranger Steve Davis turned to Waldee's Cowee Mountains neighborhood. Davis put together the Little Laurel timber sale, which called for eleven separate clearcuts totaling 329 acres. Another nine acres would be cleared for an access road. Davis also planned to clear eight to ten tracts ranging from twelve to fifty-seven acres, areas he did not consider to be producing merchantable timber. The agency would clear and burn all the trees in these tracts, and then it would plant white pine seedlings. The "gross sale area"—the tract over which these projects spread—encompassed 2,922 Nantahala acres.[45]

Walton Smith objected to the sale and appealed it through Forest Service channels. The new WNCA, the Cowee Community Development Association, and Alarka Laurel Ltd. joined his appeal. The Cowee Community Development Association was the Smiths' neighborhood club—the Cowee parallel of the Carson Community Development Association, which had backed Esther Cunningham's antipetroleum and early WNCA work.[46]

In June 1985 the young WNCA held a barbecue fund-raiser in Franklin for a new Educational and Legal Fund, which was designed to support the Little Laurel timber sale appeal and other anticlearcutting work. Two hundred people from six mountain counties purchased tickets and showed up. Esther Cunningham—now WNCA steering committee chair—played a central role in this fund-raiser, which took place in the Macon County Community Building. It was just the sort of event she had spent years organizing through various church and community groups and most recently through the Carson Community Development Association. Rally participants ate local barbecue, bid for homemade cakes, listened to live music, and bought "Conserve Our Natural Resources" T-shirts designed and produced by local residents. The front page of the Alliance newsletter, *Accent*, carried a photograph of Cunningham displaying one of the shirts, which featured a mountain scene. Area merchants contributed door prizes, and a local auctioneer ran the cake sale.[47]

Jackson County residents Margie and Clarence Hall, friends of the Cunninghams and anticlearcutting stalwarts, participated actively in the rally. Clarence was an avid bear hunter, and Margie was a homemaker. She contributed to the fund-raiser "luscious cakes far above and beyond the call of duty," *Accent* reported. With help from cake, T-shirt, and barbecue sales, the event raised a total of nearly $800 for the WNCA fund. Walton Smith later commented that Esther Cunningham's fund-raising efforts on behalf of the WNCA's Forest Management Task Force had "been tremendous." He also appreciated her tireless letter writing, her work building and strengthening the organization, and her many constructive suggestions on anticlearcutting strategy. Both Esther and Jim Cunningham were "a continuous source of inspiration and information" in the struggle against clearcutting, Smith wrote in a newsletter he circulated to fellow forest activists. "Sometimes when I feel a little low about the entire matter," the retired forester remarked. "I telephone Esther and before long she has me on cloud 9 again and going strong. She is superb!"[48]

WNCA Volunteers Step into the Woods with Walton Smith

While Esther Cunningham coordinated fund-raisers, Walton Smith trained WNCA members as lay foresters. To prepare for the Little Laurel timber sale appeal, Smith took a team of twenty Alliance activists to the sale site and taught them how to assess its timber value. Some volunteers probably had timber experience, but many were greenhorns. Men and women who had never even seen one before headed to the woods armed with a Biltmore stick. The sticks were standard professional foresters' tools, developed nearly a century earlier at the Biltmore School of Forestry on George Vanderbilt's vast western North Carolina estate.[49]

Under Smith's tutelage, these amateur foresters performed a professional-quality timber survey, calculating the timber value of two sample quarter-acre plots and measuring the promising timber growth on a sample strip across the site. Smith's volunteers worked their way down his sample strip, marking all the young timber trees six to fourteen inches in diameter. At their current sizes these trees could be sold only as cheap pulp, but in ten to twenty years they would become valuable sawtimber.[50]

One of Walton Smith's primary objections to clearcutting was that it wasted "years of investment in young hardwood growth." Smith wanted to make the case that Little Laurel clearcutting would destroy promising growth, and he needed good estimates of just how much young timber would be affected. Since he needed a knowledgeable labor force to gather this information, he created it. The team of volunteers worked with Smith over the course of three weekends to do the Little Laurel site survey. Under Smith's tutelage, rank amateurs learned to identify valuable timber species and use Biltmore sticks to measure tree sizes and estimate timber volume. They practiced taking the measurements and making the calculations that enabled timber cruisers mentally to transform living trees into numbers of sawlogs and boards. Before the session ended, Smith had his team estimating board-foot yield and taking core samples to determine a tree's age. He had every promising young timber tree in the sample strip marked, and he had the hard evidence he needed to craft appeal arguments.[51]

The training session Walton Smith conducted in 1985 was one of many similar workshops he led as part of the WNCA's anticlearcutting effort. Time and time again Alliance volunteers took to the woods, carrying notebooks, pencils, and Biltmore sticks. Smith developed a sophisticated hands-on curriculum in forestry, complete with photos, video, diagrams, and basic explanations of different silvicultural techniques. In effect, he trained a core group of citizen foresters.

Eventually, Smith's volunteers toted "Waldee" instead of "Biltmore" sticks. Walton Smith held ideas about mountain forestry more complicated than the standard Biltmore stick could accommodate. He believed the slope of a given site should be factored into timber harvest decisions, for instance, so he modified the Biltmore stick, adding a feature designed to help timber cruisers estimate the percent slope of a plot. He called the new instrument a "Waldee stick" and designed it to be easily replicated—he could quickly turn out copies in his own woodworking shop. One by one, the sticks made their way into WNCA members' homes. And gradually Smith's students developed the timber knowledge they needed to talk confidently about woods management with Forest Service officials.[52]

Antiwilderness and Anticlearcutting Overlap

A number of western North Carolina observers noted that determined clearcutting opposition often came from some of the same quarters as wilderness opposition. WNCA staffer Mary Kelly remembered that some of her best anticlearcutting allies sported "Stop RARE II" bumper stickers. The *Asheville Citizen* also recognized this pattern. "Some groups that were so adamantly against wilderness and who stood for additional logging," wrote the *Citizen* in early 1985, "have now turned against clear-cutting." The newspaper did not name these groups, but it seemed to imply that hunters dominated their ranks. A Forest Service official the *Citizen* interviewed traced clearcutting opposition to residents' dislike of what they had seen in recent cuts and to concerns over "what they have read in wildlife magazines."[53]

In western North Carolina, "wildlife magazines" typically meant hunting and fishing publications such as the North Carolina Wildlife Resources Commission's *Wildlife in North Carolina*. Though this magazine carried some nongame stories—features on songbirds and the like—it focused on fish and game. *Wildlife in North Carolina* covered hunting and fishing regulations, state game harvest totals, gun and water safety issues, and wildlife enforcement developments. Rod and gun features crowded its pages, including historical retrospectives, hunting tales, sportsmen's reminiscences, and tips for anglers and shooters. Just as "wildlife clubs" were not Audubon groups but hunting and fishing organizations, so "wildlife magazines" in local parlance were sportsmen's rather than birdwatchers' publications. Thus, clearcutting opponents upset about "what they have read in wildlife magazines" were almost certainly hunters and anglers and their families.

"Several hunting groups, hiking groups and individuals—in some cases organizations that do not see eye to eye—have gone on record against clear-cutting," the *Asheville Citizen* continued. Again, the newspaper did not name the groups it had in mind, nor did it specify in what ways some of these groups disagreed with one another. In recent forest politics, however, "not seeing eye to eye" almost certainly meant taking opposite sides on the wilderness issue. Though some hunters did fight for certain wilderness areas, RARE II had generally pitted hikers against timber harvesters, with hunters usually taking the timber side. Yet now, just six years after going head-to-head over wilderness, hunters and hikers both rallied against clearcutting.[54]

WNCA records contain subtle but suggestive evidence of this trend among hunters. The most telling example came from Macon County's Harold Corbin, an avid boar hunter and the Republican Party chair for North Carolina's eleventh congressional district. Corbin was a longtime resident of Macon County, likely related to the old area family for whom Corbin Knob was named. He loved boar hunting and mounted a decades-long crusade to bring wild pigs to Macon County. Corbin made himself a fixture at western North Carolina meetings of the Wildlife Resources Commission, where he repeatedly lobbied for boar stocking. Graham County hunters had wild boar in their forests, he argued; it was time to "get some pigs in Macon."[55]

The boar issue was a hot forest topic in western North Carolina in the 1970s and 1980s. Boars were not native to the Appalachian forests. A few European wild boars, imported to a private hunting preserve in the early twentieth century, had escaped and mingled with domestic pigs roaming what was then the open-range forest commons. Late twentieth-century boars were likely the descendants of these imported game and grazing-commons forebears. Very popular with hunters, they were fierce-looking animals with long, sharp tusks. Harold Corbin was not the only western North Carolina boar hunter who aspired to get a piece of the Graham County action for his neighborhood. The North Carolina Wildlife Resources Commission heard proboar arguments from western North Carolina hunting enthusiasts for roughly fifteen years.[56]

While boar hunters lobbied determinedly for boar stocking in the western North Carolina mountains, environmentalists lobbied with equal determination against these proposals. Boars wreaked ecological havoc, they argued, destroying the forest floor and threatening the hundreds of plant and animal species living there. The forest looked as if it had been plowed and harrowed after a group of wild boars passed through, leaving practically every square inch of soil disturbed. Rooting snouts uprooted plant communities, and hungry boars depleted the forests' snail and salamander populations. Boars also wallowed in mountain streams, destroying streambanks and raising bacteria counts in local waters. In sum, argued environmentalists, boars were a destructive force, not an asset. It was bad enough that any boar population existed, and certainly the animals should not be deliberately cultivated.[57]

Official Great Smoky Mountains National Park policy reflected this view. The park considered its boar population an undesirable nuisance. Park officials waged ongoing boar wars to control and reduce boar populations within park boundaries. They trapped the animals and released them on Nantahala National Forest lands in North Carolina's Graham County.[58]

Harold Corbin rejected environmentalists' arguments, saying that local residents knew more about habitat issues "than these hippie backpackers who walk through the park." For Corbin, the boar question pitted ordinary hunters against various elites. As he saw it, outsider backpackers arrogantly claimed to know more about forest ecology than local residents. Corbin rejected these claims and demanded that the Wildlife Resources Commission do likewise. He was tired of the commission's "gathering information," he said in January 1984; it had studied the boar question for a decade and a half. It was time for the commission to make a move and to do so unintimidated by environmentalist worries about habitat.[59]

Harold Corbin also expressed frustration with the limited boar-stocking program in the Nantahala forest. Boars trapped in the Smoky Mountains park were released on the Cheoah Ranger District in Graham County. This Park Service arrangement required cooperation from the Forest Service and the North Carolina Wildlife Resources Commission. Corbin charged that it amounted to a bonanza for Graham County hunters. Its end result was that "a bunch of rich hunters in Robbinsville" got to hunt boar, while Macon hunters—presumably less rich—did not. Since hunters from all over the United States made boar pilgrimages to Graham County, the exclusive Great Smokies arrangement also meant a unique boost for the county's economy. In Corbin's view, this amounted to preferential treatment.[60]

It is unclear how actively the Wildlife Resources Commission participated in managing, financing, and carrying out the Smokies-to-Cheoah boar program. It likely collaborated with the Park Service and the Forest Service to some degree, however. Since all sportsmen paid for Wildlife Resources Commission activities through license purchases and taxes on hunting and fishing gear, any apparent boondoggle favoring a select few rankled. In Harold Corbin's mind, Graham County boar represented such a boondoggle, and he "took the Wildlife Commission to task" for not making boar more accessible.[61]

Harold Corbin's comments about "rich hunters" and "hippie backpackers" at the January 1984 Wildlife Resources Commission hearing in Franklin were part of an all-out boar offensive he and his supporters had launched. Corbin chaired the Republican Party in North Carolina's mountainous eleventh congressional district. He had a close political alliance with Bill Hendon, the Republican candidate who won the eleventh district's congressional seat in 1980. Hendon was firmly antiwilderness. Supporters identified his strong RARE II opposition as one of the crucial factors in his 1980 victory over Democratic congressman Lamar Gudger, who had initially supported some additional wilderness in western North Carolina. Though Gudger changed his position after the 1978 anti–RARE II demonstrations and went on record against further wilderness designations, RARE II opponents saw Hendon as the true antiwilderness candidate. As the district's Republican Party chair during the 1980 campaign, Harold Corbin played a central role in engineering Hendon's election, and he helped the congressman win reelection in 1982 and 1984. Hendon expressed his political gratitude by endorsing Corbin's Macon boar-stocking proposal. The congressman pressed both the state Wildlife Resources Commission and the Forest Service to embrace boar.[62]

By January 1984 the tenacious proboar campaign was beginning to have an effect. District 9 Wildlife Commissioner Dan Robinson, who represented much of the mountain region, told Corbin and other Franklin sportsmen that unless someone could present him with some "pretty darn good reasons not to, I'm going to vote in favor" of boar stocking in Macon. Interestingly, Robinson was an active Democrat, not one of Corbin's Republican allies. Later in 1984 the commission gave the nod to the Macon boar-stocking proposal. Together, Representative Bill Hendon and the newly proboar state Wildlife Resources Commission convinced NFsNC supervisor George Olson to back the boar-stocking plan. In February 1985 Olson announced that his office would allow stocking on a 4,600-acre tract in the Nantahala area of Macon County and on a 5,100-acre tract in neighboring Cherokee County.[63]

Corbin appeared finally to have won his long battle, but it was not over yet. Environmental groups quickly appealed Olson's decision to expand the boar's range. They persuaded John Alcock, the Forest Service regional supervisor in Atlanta, to overturn the plan. Explaining his July 1985 decision to overrule Olson, Alcock cited scientific evidence and possible adverse environmental effects. In fact, just a month before Olson released his boar-expansion decision, a Forest Service environmental assessment had recommended against extending the animals' range. As he explained his decision, John Alcock also expressed concerns about potential dangers the boars posed to people and property.[64]

Harold Corbin reacted to Alcock's antiboar decision with dismay. Years of effort had finally brought Corbin right to the brink of his "pigs in Macon" goal, and now Alcock had swept his victory away. "You can bet [this decision] will be appealed," Corbin told reporters. "Bill Hendon's not through with this thing yet. He went to a lot of trouble to help us." Corbin rejected Alcock's concerns about people and property, stating that boars attacked only when cornered. He also dismissed Alcock's environmental concerns, saying it looked as if "tree-hugging, flower- and butterfly-looking environmentalists influenced this decision."[65]

Harold Corbin's rhetoric and political history proved he was no environmentalist. From railing against "hippie backpackers" and "tree-hugging environmentalists" to shepherding a staunchly antiwilderness Republican candidate into Congress, he had all the markings of an antienvironmental political activist. Yet in June 1985, just five months after expressing scorn for "hippie backpackers" and one month before excoriating "flower- and butterfly-looking environmentalists," Corbin cooked barbecue for the Western North Carolina Alliance's anticlearcutting fund-raiser. Rally attendees munched Harold Corbin's food as they listened to Walton Smith explain why the Forest Service's proclearcutting policies must go. WNCA staff and steering committee members—meaning Esther Cunningham and David Liden, among others—publicly thanked Corbin and his restaurant staff "for the fine food" that helped make the event "such a success."[66]

Commons Concerns Inspire Clearcutting Opposition

How did local Republican Party chair and antiwilderness boar hunter Harold Corbin end up playing such a central role in the anticlearcutting fund-raiser organized largely by local Democratic Women's chair Esther Cunningham? Part of the answer lay in the clearcutting issue itself and part in the savvy organizing strategies WNCA activists used to fight the practice.

Alliance organizers kept a tight focus on key goals and refused to take positions on secondary questions. They did not take a stand on the boar issue, for instance, though they must have been under significant pressure to do so. Harold Corbin was a man on a mission. He certainly would have tried to enlist WNCA support for his proboar campaign. On the other hand, many ecology-minded forest activists adamantly opposed the boar-stocking proposal. The Alliance risked alienating these potential supporters if it supported Corbin's pet project. By keeping its vision focused on clearcutting and by remaining neutral on the boar question, the WNCA pitched a tent big enough to hold both wildflower enthusiasts and the fiery Macon hunter. Heated debates about bear size limits also roared through western North Carolina in the 1980s. These debates too proved deeply divisive, and again the Alliance stayed out of them.[67]

Also, as we have seen, clearcutting provoked opposition from anyone interested in using the public forests as commons, and Harold Corbin fell into this category. He wanted to intervene in the commons by introducing nonnative boar, but his boar vision rested on an understanding of the forests as accessible public harvest grounds. Esther Cunningham, David Liden, Walton Smith, and other leaders of the WNCA's early campaigns against clearcutting understood the importance of the forest commons. From the beginning they made their organization's clearcutting opposition inviting even to antiwilderness commons users such as Harold Corbin. A petition they circulated in response to the fifty-year Pisgah and Nantahala management plan, for instance, opposed both clearcutting and gated roads. Its demand for increased forest access made it clearly a commons-inspired rather than a wilderness-inspired document. Antiwilderness commons users such as Corbin could sign it comfortably because it carried no whiff of RARE II.[68]

By coupling clearcutting opposition to concerns about forest access, WNCA strategists broke new and commons-friendly protectionist ground. A few years later, they married their commons-based anticlearcutting position to a broad grassroots organizing campaign. In doing so, they harnessed the full power of commons environmentalism.

TEN

Commons Environmentalism Mobilized

Western North Carolina Alliance's Cut the Clearcutting! Campaign

"THE PEOPLE HAVE SPOKEN with a loud voice," Mary Kelly declared as she and other Western North Carolina Alliance (WNCA) activists delivered an enormous petition to the U.S. Forest Service's Asheville office on Cut the Clearcutting! Day in 1989. "Wow," responded forest supervisor Bjorn Dahl, staring at the giant document. Fully unfurled, the petition stretched over four city blocks. It contained no fewer than 15,500 signatures. More than two hundred people representing at least twelve mountain counties marched the massive ribbon of names through the streets of Asheville to National Forests in North Carolina (NFsNC) headquarters. Armed with hand-lettered signs, banners, and a large American flag, they had spent the last two hours listening to speeches and traditional mountain music in the plaza downtown. Hunters, loggers, fiddlers, foresters, biologists, potters, and organizers took turns at the microphone, some with mountain accents and some without. Despite overcast skies and chilly weather, their mood was jubilant.[1]

This April 15 street demonstration built on years of anticlearcutting activism in Appalachian North Carolina. The petition and rally carried local forest watchdogs' best hopes for reversing Forest Service policy in the region, which here as elsewhere favored large-scale clearcut timber harvesting above all other methods. The WNCA had organized Cut the Clearcutting! Day as the culmination of an intense four-month campaign of public opposition to clearcutting on the Nantahala and Pisgah National Forests. The enormous petition served as a campaign centerpiece. With it, organizers intended to showcase the breadth and depth of hostility to clearcutting in the region. They gathered the signatures in a coordinated multicounty effort, knocking on doors and setting up signing stations at convenience stores, supermarkets, and tire shops.[2]

Organizers planned Cut the Clearcutting! Day's spirited events to maximize publicity for the petition's delivery and for the larger anticlearcutting effort. Through the rally, they also showcased WNCA's trademark brand of commons-friendly environmentalism. In the crowd, protesters carried posters reflecting harvest relationships with the woods. "Stop clearcutting says Forester," read one such sign. "Bearhunters against clearcutting," trumpeted another. "We oppose clearcutting NOT Logging," proclaimed a third. Much of the rhetoric from the stage echoed these messages. "We can put those logs on those trucks," thundered WNCA member Bob Padgett in his anticlearcutting speech. Padgett, a Forest Service retiree and active private forester, delivered one of many addresses emphasizing the productive value of Appalachian forests.[3]

As these signs and speeches demonstrated, the WNCA's anticlearcutting campaign drew its central strength not from wilderness environmentalism but from a different source. The idea of wilderness, emphasizing as it did an absence of people and of human work in the woods, failed to resonate with many longtime mountain residents. It often seemed to them elitist, economically unsound, and historically dishonest. Thus, wilderness-inspired environmental campaigns typically gained little traction among mountain people.

Yet as the boisterous WNCA rally and the eventual total of over twenty thousand petition signatures clearly proved, mountain people could be passionate, effective, and ambitious defenders of Appalachian forests. In western North Carolina, they fought clearcutting with remarkable vigor and tenacity. In the Cut the Clearcutting! campaign, WNCA members championed forest protection goals so far-reaching that national environmental groups were unwilling to support them. Yet the Alliance won widespread backing for these bold initiatives from a diverse array of mountain residents.

With its Cut the Clearcutting! campaign, the WNCA tapped the latent power of commons culture for an environmentalist cause. The WNCA framed its opposition to clearcutting as a form of commons forest defense. The organization decoupled the issue of forest protection from the question of wilderness preservation and hitched it instead to widely shared concerns about the wooded mountain commons. This strategy succeeded in making the Alliance's anticlearcutting position attractive even to many mountain inhabitants who did not ordinarily consider themselves environmentalists. Moreover, with its petition drive, the WNCA provided rural mountain residents with an organized political channel through which to express their protectionist stance. Presented with this opportunity, residents leaped: "Give me that. I'll take it home and get my folks to sign that."[4]

In effect, though they never used the term, WNCA activists pioneered a form of commons environmentalism. As a result, what Mary Kelly told Bjorn Dahl on Cut the Clearcutting! Day was no exaggeration: "The people have spoken with a loud voice. They do not like what clearcutting is doing to our mountains."[5]

The Fifty-Year Draft Management Plan Spurs Clearcutting Opposition

Organized opposition to clearcutting in western North Carolina began in earnest after the NFsNC office released—in October 1984—its fifty-year draft management plan for the Pisgah and Nantahala forests. The 1976 National Forest Management Act required forest supervisors to prepare such long-range forest management plans periodically. The legislation also called for public input into the planning process. The 1984 draft was the first plan produced for western North Carolina forests under NFMA. Five years in the making, it ran some four hundred pages long and challenged ordinary readers with what one critic described as "technical jargon."[6]

The Forest Service allotted the public ninety days to comment on the draft. Forest activists found small agency announcements soliciting public input buried deep in the pages of area newspapers, often in the legal section. "It became clear to those of us who saw [the legal notice]," Mitchell County clearcutting opponent Will Ruggles remembered, that "they didn't actually want any public response." WNCA coordinator Mary Kelly concurred. "I don't think they ever really intended [the draft plan] for public consumption," she later reflected. Other Forest Service decisions underscored this point. Perhaps remembering ardent protests at its wilderness information sessions a few years earlier, the Asheville office arranged no public hearings on the fifty-year plan.[7]

Walton Smith obtained a copy of the plan and deciphered its contents. He grew alarmed when he realized the document called for 389,000 acres—over a third of the national forestlands in western North Carolina—to be harvested by clearcutting during the next five decades. Access restrictions on two hundred thousand acres would also be eased to allow mineral and petroleum development, and more than seven thousand miles of new roads would be built. Placed end to end, the proposed Forest Service roads would stretch from the North Carolina mountains to the California coast and back, with plenty to spare. "I was jolted into action," Smith remembered.

"In spite of public opinion, in spite of legislation, and in spite of the feeling of many in the forestry profession, my prided Forest Service had come up with a plan for almost 100 percent even-aged management with clearcutting as the method of harvesting."[8]

Smith and the WNCA scrambled to organize a public hearing on the plan in Franklin. Esther Cunningham and David Liden arranged the meeting and announced it on radio spots and in the *Franklin Press*. They invited North Carolina forest supervisor George Olson to address the gathering, and he accepted the invitation.[9] When he reached Franklin in early 1985, Olson found himself once again in an all-too-familiar position. An angry overflow crowd, gathered from Macon and surrounding counties, confronted him. He and Bob Cunningham, the Asheville office's planning director, explained the fifty-year plan's origins and defended its merits. Speaking on behalf of the WNCA, Walton Smith and David Liden raised a series of concerns. Smith argued that clearcutting destroyed Appalachian hardwood diversity and undermined western North Carolina's recreation economy. Liden advocated greater USFS responsiveness to local interests and warned against a too-hasty commitment to mineral and petroleum development in the absence of adequate protections.[10]

During the discussion period that followed these presentations, audience members poured out their concerns about forest management. Hunters, loggers, anglers, retirees, real estate agents, hikers, and merchants—old-timers and newcomers—turned out for the Franklin meeting and others like it. They expressed a broad range of concerns sparked by the plan. Some worried about wildlife, others about water quality, others about effects on area businesses. Long-simmering resentments also came to the surface. Speakers spoke of frustrations about gated Forest Service roads, about "harassment" over firewood gathering, about timber contracts that had gone to big companies rather than small local operators.[11]

Many of these were commons concerns. Gated roads, for instance, meant reduced access to the forest, a critical issue in any commons system. Closed Forest Service gates symbolized "shutting people out" of the woods and served as lightning rods for commons-inspired worries and resentments. Similarly, firewood gathering represented a classic commons activity: the securing of fuel. In western North Carolina firewood gathering had become increasingly urgent during the oil crises of the late 1970s. Forest Service offices made free and low-cost firewood permits readily available, but some restrictions did apply, and unlicensed firewood gathering could be prosecuted. Complaints of "harassment" probably had to do with the permit process, gathering guidelines, or (most likely) no-permit enforcement. Finally, charges that timber contracts too often bypassed small outfits also rang true to commons patterns. Petty producer access to significant resources is one hallmark of a functioning commons system. Accusations that large companies received the lion's share of timber contracts reflected concerns about potential loss of commons.[12]

Of course, not all gripes were commons inspired. Concerns about effects on area businesses might or might not represent commons anxieties, for example. Insofar as business owners fretted about small-producer access, their concerns were consistent with commons patterns. But other worries could be traced to different sources. For instance, many business people noted particularly the detrimental effect ugly clearcuts could have on the tourist industry. In a sense, these were concerns about a scenic commons, but they were categorically different from the extractive-resource commons worries expressed by gated-roads opponents and firewood gatherers. The scenic commons was not extractive. It was compatible with gated roads and wilderness designation; in fact, it was potentially furthered rather than threatened by these.[13]

Clearcutting attracted enemies from across a broad local spectrum. It offended both extractive commons users and those who valued nonextractive forest goods such as scenery. It drew fire from nearly everyone who gathered in Franklin and other locations to discuss the Forest Service's proposed fifty-year management plan. Though the people who showed up for these meetings represented a large cross-section of the community and voiced various gripes and diverse concerns, their message on clearcutting was unequivocal. They hated it, they excoriated the Forest Service for using it, they demanded that it stop.[14]

The Forest Service responded by acknowledging the method's ugly aftermath but emphasizing its usefulness as a forestry tool. Effective hardwood regeneration required clearcutting and other even-aged management techniques, North Carolina USFS personnel stated repeatedly. "I don't look out there and see devastation—I see the rebirth of the forest," commented forester Don Beck in a typical defense. This kind of statement implied that clearcutting opponents lacked adequate understanding of forest science. Their aesthetic concerns, though reasonable, were shortsighted. "Armchair biologists" should not question the authority of genuine forestry professionals. Timber industry spokesmen typically echoed this refrain. "Let's let the experts do their jobs," a procurement officer for Champion Paper told Appalshop filmmakers in reference to the question of national forest clearcutting. If the Forest Service embraced clearcutting, the public should defer to its expertise and respect the science behind the embrace.[15]

But the western North Carolina public did no such thing. Some speakers flatly rejected silvicultural arguments, countering Forest Service officials' statements with evidence "from their own eyes," as the *Asheville Citizen* put it. To foresters' claims of expert professional knowledge they responded with knowledge claims of their own. These claims were often grounded in the everyday familiarity of long forest use, of years spent working the woods. Loggers and hunters proved especially outspoken, not at all deferential to USFS authority. They mounted claims to an alternative, experience-based brand of woods expertise.[16]

McKinley Jenkins, a retired logger and hunter from Graham County, "summed up much of the feeling at the Franklin meeting" when he tackled USFS expertise head-on. "I've worked in the woods almost all my life and one of the worst things I've ever seen is this clearcutting," Jenkins told the crowd. "If they don't stop it there won't be anything in the woods over four inches round." Jenkins used a lifetime of logging and hunting as grounds for making expert claims of his own. He could compare clearcutting to innumerable other human interventions he had witnessed and performed. If he pronounced it "one of the worst" woods practices he had ever seen, the condemnation could not be taken lightly by anyone who granted the authority of his experience. Much of his audience, a substantial number of whom had also spent countless hours working the woods harvesting timber, game, firewood, and other forest products, doubtless respected this authority.[17]

Jenkins directly challenged foresters' contention that clearcutting regenerated the forest. He rejected this contention outright and forwarded his own thesis instead: clearcutting destroyed the forest. If the Forest Service did not stop clearcutting, he charged, "there won't be anything in the woods over four inches round." The experienced forest users that Jenkins addressed knew that "nothing over four inches round" meant no harvestable forest commons. Though it could be used as firewood, juvenile four-inch growth was all but useless for timber and wildlife purposes. Since the passing of American chestnut, oak trees had become the primary source of "hard mast" many native animals—including popular game species such as bear and turkey—needed to survive mountain winters. Oaks required roughly sixty years to reach acorn-bearing age. A tree "four inches round" could be decades away from producing hard mast. Similarly, to make good sawtimber a tree had to be about twenty inches in diameter. Again, a four-inch sapling was decades from this mark.[18]

McKinley Jenkins's challenge went on. "I know north-facing coves that will never come back," he charged. "And I can take you there." Here the hunter and retired logger unequivocally laid down a forest-expertise gauntlet, frankly telling Forest Service officials they did not know what they were talking about. The agency argued that clearcutting regenerated hardwoods, but Jenkins claimed to know of instances where this was simply not true. He challenged Forest Service officials to come with him to see the evidence themselves. He seemed to feel confident that foresters would be unable to refute his charges if they saw the tracts he had in mind.[19]

McKinley Jenkins was not an educated man, but his language reflected a nuanced forest knowledge earned through years of working the woods commons-style. To counter Forest Service statements about the regenerative value of clearcutting, he pointed specifically to "north-facing coves" where hardwoods had not come back. Beneath this phrase lay a world of forest knowledge. Jenkins could distinguish north-facing coves from slopes facing other directions, probably without recourse to a compass. He likely walked familiar ground, and when he was in unfamiliar territory, he "read" the landscape. Differences in elevation, exposure, and soil type made the Appalachian forest a place of seemingly endless variety. To experienced forest users, the patterns in this variety often functioned as a sort of woods-mapping tool. Long hours spent in the forests taught some loggers, hunters, herb diggers, and the like to notice a drier soil, a distinct concentration of tree species, a predominance of certain understory plants, or a characteristic trick of wildflower or moss. Awareness of these forest subtleties was a material help to commons hunters and gatherers. The wooded landscape offered clues about where ginseng or turkeys or rattlesnakes might lurk. Like other experienced commons users, Jenkins probably read these forest signs as he worked his way through the woods. He knew which combinations of plants, moisture, growth patterns, and the like typified north-facing coves.[20]

As he observed clearcuts, Jenkins noticed that forest tracts responded differently after harvest: some began to recover relatively quickly, others slowly or not at all. Jenkins used his forest familiarity to analyze these differences and noticed that hardwoods on north-facing slopes seemed particularly hard-pressed to regenerate. He concluded that clearcutting was not a good harvest technique for these locales. Jenkins was prepared to subject his conclusions to professional scrutiny—he welcomed peer review. He invited Forest Service officials to do site inspections, to analyze his evidence themselves.

But Forest Service officials did not see Jenkins as a peer forest expert, and they rejected his offer to take them to the north-facing coves he had observed. Rumor had it that some foresters in the Asheville office made Jenkins the butt of jokes after the Franklin meeting, ridiculing his mountain accent and what they saw as his "hillbilly" demeanor. Whether or not these rumors were accurate, it was clear that Forest Service officials rebuffed Jenkins's claims to woods expertise. They dismissed his critique and turned away from the gauntlet he threw down.[21]

By denying Jenkins's claims to forest expertise, however, Forest Service officials effectively rejected the experiential pool of forest knowledge shared by many local residents and highly valued in rural commons culture. McKinley Jenkins made a powerful and positive impression on some of his hearers. The WNCA prominently featured his photo in a front-page story for its newsletter, *Accent*. At least two people who were present at the Franklin meeting had vivid memories of Jenkins almost fifteen years later. They described him as a particularly eloquent and compelling speaker. Jenkins was a lay preacher, one recalled, and it showed—he knew how to connect with an audience. These hearers saw McKinley Jenkins as a sort of forest spokesperson. To them it seemed that the logger, hunter, and preacher had powerfully expressed views and concerns shared by many others in the room. They read Forest Service officials' dismissive reaction as evidence of agency arrogance. To them this response stood as a sign of USFS unwillingness to listen and respond not only to a single speaker but to a whole array of widely shared local concerns.[22]

Other events surrounding the release of the fifty-year management plan draft underscored the depth of local concerns similar to those McKinley Jenkins expressed. Other hunters also participated actively in the Macon County meeting, and sportsmen's groups in other mountain counties soon followed the WNCA's example and organized their own local public hearings. Robbinsville, Bakersville, Andrews, and Waynesville hosted sessions similar to the one in Franklin. At each there was a "surprising turnout," though they took place in the dead of winter and were plagued with bad weather. "I'm real concerned about it [the plan]," a Cherokee County coon hunter commented, understatedly summing up views shared by thousands of western North Carolinians.[23]

Hunters overwhelmingly opposed wholesale clearcutting, even though not all game species suffered as a result of the practice, and some even benefited in its aftermath. Deer, quail, grouse, and rabbit populations could expand in old clearcuts, as young green growth and early-succession blackberries, grapes, and the like offered food and cover these animals favored. In fact, grouse hunters often sought out former clearcut sites. The Forest Service touted these wildlife benefits, but there seems to be little evidence that hunters responded favorably. And other key game animals—raccoon, bear, squirrel, and turkey—fared less well after clearcuts, as the harvest method removed all mature trees, these species' preferred sources of food and shelter. These animals typically rejected clearcut sites until the trees grew back decades later. Also, even if they did harbor some game species, the tangles of briary brush that followed a clearcut operation made for uninviting hunting. As Madison County's Haze Landers explained, "If you go out in that place they cut—that clearcut and stuff—you can't go through there. You'd just as well go back."[24]

Haze Landers summed up the widespread opposition to clearcutting when he told interviewers, "The timbermen's about the only ones I know that's for it." Hunter Raymond Williams, of Graham County, echoed Landers. He told Forest Service officials he believed 90 percent of Graham County residents wanted a halt to clearcutting. The Graham County commissioners apparently agreed. On February 4, 1985, a month before the public comment period officially ended, they unanimously passed a resolution calling for an end to clearcutting in the county and putting the commission on record as opposed to the Forest Service's proposed fifty-year plan.[25]

"Somehow—and no one is really sure how," wrote the *Asheville Citizen*, the Forest Service's draft fifty-year plan "touched off the anti-clearcutting movement." The plan's release sparked an astonishing public response that snowballed to include petitions, letters to the editor, letters to the Forest Service, letters to U.S. Representative Bill Hendon, and newspaper editorials. At one point Congressman Hendon's office reported receiving roughly one hundred anticlearcutting letters a day. In spite of its buried legal notices, nearly two thousand written responses had reached the Forest Service by the end of its comment period, and these were overwhelmingly opposed to clearcutting. Area newspapers printed a steady stream of anticlearcutting letters to the editor and ran editorials calling for revisions to the plan. Thousands of people signed anticlearcutting petitions circulated by the WNCA and other concerned organizations and individuals. Twenty-six different petitions made their way to Forest Service headquarters.[26]

This public uproar and the level of emotion it involved came as a surprise to Forest Service officials. George Olson was so upset by the flood of opposition he faced at the Franklin meeting that he accused Esther Cunningham and David Liden of setting him up for an "ambush," and he vowed never to come to another of their meetings. Cunningham and Liden protested that they had not meant to ambush Olson, only to offer area residents a chance to learn about the plan and express their views and concerns. They had not known how vehemently those concerns would be expressed. Nevertheless, Olson kept his promise and steered clear of Franklin during the rest of his North Carolina tenure.[27]

Clearcutting emotions ran so high that they reminded some observers of RARE II passions. The *Asheville Citizen* reported that some USFS employees "believe the public's sentiment against the Forest Service is nearly as strong as it was during the RARE II controversy in 1978 and 1979." Forester Pat Cook identified the RARE II wilderness designation controversy and the debates over clearcutting as the two most emotional issues to have faced the agency during his three decades with it.[28]

The WNCA Circulates a Petition Opposing the Fifty-Year Plan

The petition WNCA leaders circulated in response to the fifty-year Pisgah and Nantahala management plan drew on commons understandings of the forest and opposed both clearcutting and gated roads. Also important and again reflecting a commons standpoint, neither the official WNCA platform nor the organization's petition objected to national forest timber harvesting per se. On the contrary, both documents explicitly listed timber harvesting as a legitimate use of the public forests. Platform and petition did not even object absolutely to clearcutting as a USFS timber harvest method. In fact, in its forest management platform the WNCA pointedly recognized "the need for even-aged management (clear-cutting) on some sites under some conditions." The Alliance and petition signatories opposed "indiscriminate" clearcutting and argued that the Forest Service "now practiced" this wholesale abuse of a valid technique. According to the WNCA and petition signatories, extensive clearcut timber harvesting prevented other rightful uses of the national forest. Large-scale clearcutting was unacceptable because it was incompatible with true multiple use.[29]

A wilderness-inspired position would have argued against timber harvesting altogether, since lumbering meant consequential human manipulation of the forest. Timber harvesting by any method threatened wilderness values, as timber prohibitions in federally designated wilderness areas attested. Of course, these restrictions reflected conservationists' concern to protect some lands from the devastating effects of industrial-scale timber harvests, effects that had already become abundantly clear by the time activists began working toward wilderness legislation in the 1950s. But wilderness ideology had the effect of lumping all harvesting together with industrial timber harvesting. It therefore left little room for legitimate tree cutting, and it seemed hostile to other types of forest harvest as well. Wilderness preservation inevitably alienated those who relied on timber for a living, but it could also repel commons users for whom the forest was often more important as a cultural than as an economic site.[30]

The WNCA, by contrast, argued that clearcutting was categorically different from other forms of forest use, including other methods of timber harvesting. By drawing a careful distinction between timber harvesting, including limited clearcutting, on the one hand, and wholesale clearcutting, on the other, the WNCA staked out environmentalist ground that could be comfortably, even enthusiastically, inhabited by many longtime mountain residents. The timber industry had been a central pillar of North Carolina's highland economy for many decades. Dismissing the industry's economic importance (as many wilderness advocates seemed to do) or failing to grant timber harvesting environmental legitimacy (as wilderness terminology and regulations seemed to do) meant alienating most rural western North Carolinians. By recognizing timber's importance and granting its legitimacy as a use of the forest, the Alliance made environmentalism safe for many of these same rural residents. "You'd come up with petitions, you'd have people grabbing them out of your hand," Mary Kelly remembered.[31]

The WNCA Appeals the Nantahala and Pisgah Plan

When local citizens poured out their objections to the large-scale clearcutting called for in the draft fifty-year plan, the Forest Service indicated a willingness to listen. "We were told that our voices were heard," Walton Smith wrote. "We were thanked for our input; and we were assured that the Final Plan would give full consideration to our comments." But when the agency released its final plan, now scaled back from fifty years to fifteen, clearcutting opponents felt they had received only lip service. The new plan included small amendments, but it still overwhelmingly favored clearcutting.[32]

Many groups were dissatisfied with the final plan, called "Land and Resource Plan for the Nantahala and Pisgah Forests, 1986–2000." Walton and Dee Smith and WNCA activist Taylor Barnhill met with representatives of the Sierra Club, the Wilderness Society, and the Southern Environmental Law Center to discuss the possibility of filing a joint appeal. The parties found some agreement, and the Sierra Club and Wilderness Society joined forces. Eventually, the North Carolina Wildlife Federation also enlisted in these groups' appeal. Though they concurred with some of these organizations' objections, the Smiths and Barnhill noted important differences in emphasis, and they decided to move the Alliance forward independently.[33]

The WNCA hired the Washington, D.C., law firm of Wilson and Cotter to help it craft an independent appeal of the fifteen-year final plan. The WNCA's Forest Management Task Force worked closely with this legal team to develop the appeal. To document widespread local opposition to clearcutting, the WNCA hurriedly gathered sixteen hundred signatures for an anticlearcutting petition it appended to the text.[34]

All appeals went to the Forest Service on September 7, 1987. The WNCA had asked twice for a stay on clearcutting and burning while the agency considered its appeal, but these requests were "summarily denied," Walton Smith wrote. "Clearcutting and burning will go on as usual or maybe be increased while we bite our fingernails." The full WNCA appeal was an immense document two inches thick. WNCA coordinator Mary Kelly described it as "beautifully crafted." But on February 5, 1988, the regional forester's office in Atlanta denied the appeal. He "did not give an inch," Smith reported.[35]

Smith circulated a fifteen-page commentary on the regional forester's forty-page response to the appeal. The Forest Management Task Force planned to resubmit the appeal, this time to federal headquarters—the D.C. office of the Forest Service chief. Walton Smith and other WNCA activists raced to fortify the original appeal with further evidence before the May 2 filing deadline. Smith took one of his amateur forester teams to the woods to do timber assessments on two tracts, one clearcut in 1963–64, and one selectively harvested in 1972. The team's study refuted the Forest Service's claim that clearcutting was the best method for regenerating Appalachian hardwoods. There was more growth on the old clearcuts, the WNCA survey showed, but of less species diversity and lower timber quality. The task force appended formal results from this study to its D.C. appeal. It also appended statements from local citizens, including area scientists and locally renowned bear hunter and forest expert Taylor Crockett.[36] After the WNCA turned in this final appeal, nail-biting began in earnest. As Smith had predicted, clearcutting continued at full speed.

WNCA chapters fought at least three timber sales while the appeal sat in Washington. Bear hunter Clarence Hall, chair of the Jackson County chapter, led the charge against the Forest Service's Roaring Hole timber sale in that area. Hall had participated in one of Smith's timber surveys, and Smith worked with another volunteer team to study the Jackson County site.[37]

WNCA newcomers Mary and Rob Kelly assisted Hall and Smith with the Roaring Hole survey. The Kellys had recently moved to the Hickey Fork area of Madison County, near the Pisgah National Forest. Mary Sauls Kelly was a PhD ecologist and Rob Kelly a trained forester; both were angling enthusiasts and musicians in the old-time mountain style. Mary joined the WNCA staff as coordinator, and Rob came aboard as a volunteer forester.[38]

Clay County resident Darry Wood organized local opposition to another proposed USFS clearcut, this one on the Clay-Swain county line. Wood arranged a public hearing with Forest Service personnel, and Walton Smith, David Liden, and Mary Kelly spoke at the meeting. Wood also wrote a series of Timber Targets columns for the *Clay County Progress*. These columns discussed silviculture in layman's terms, explaining current USFS policy and why Wood and other local residents objected to it. Like other WNCA members, Wood made commons-friendly arguments. Clearcutting "wastes good timber and tax-payer dollars, and it destroys hard mast supplies for wildlife," he wrote.[39]

At roughly the same time, residents of the North Fork Valley near Black Mountain fought a clearcut harvest project approved by the Asheville-Buncombe Water Authority. The Water Authority controlled the Asheville watershed, a vast tract that many North Fork families had once called home. The families had been forced to leave when Asheville condemned the land in the 1920s for a dam project to provide the city with water, and displacement resentments still lingered. In 1988 residents noticed clearcut scars on the watershed property and learned that the Water Authority had put a USFS-style timber program in place. It had made one clearcut timber sale already and had plans for more on a rotating basis. Watershed restrictions prevented local residents even from visiting their families' old homesites on grounds that human activity in the area threatened water quality. The Water Authority's decision to allow massive timber-harvesting equipment to come in and clearcut while forbidding area residents to walk or hunt in the woods infuriated local people. They formed Citizens Against Clearcutting in the Asheville Watershed (CACAW) and joined the WNCA as a chapter. Though not a national forest fight, the controversy over watershed clearcutting raised many of the same issues. Walton Smith came to Black Mountain and spoke at a public hearing CACAW sponsored.[40]

WNCA members fought these and other clearcutting projects, and they waited with growing impatience for an appeal decision from Washington. By late 1988 participants in the organization's Forest Management Task Force were fed up. Mary Kelly remembered one meeting at which "everybody had the same story. 'We're not getting anywhere. We're not getting anywhere.'" They had painstakingly crafted timber sale appeals, but "the Forest Service had just turned them down, flat out, everywhere around." Years of working on a case-by-case basis, mounting technical challenges to Forest Service proposals, and protesting through official USFS channels had earned the organization's volunteers professional respect but had achieved few concrete results. In fact, clearcutting on the Nantahala and Pisgah increased almost every year, even as the task force gained supporters and momentum and stepped up its opposition efforts. By 1988 the group had concluded that technical arguments alone would never turn the Forest Service away from clearcutting. "So we sat around the table and the people just said, 'What we're doing is not working. We've got to jack it up. We've got to do something else,'" Kelly recalled.[41]

The WNCA Launches Cut the Clearcutting!

The WNCA now upped the ante, supplementing its technical opposition with a publicity and grassroots organizing campaign. This campaign, which became Cut the Clearcutting!, benefited from the expertise of Monroe Gilmour, a Black Mountain resident and crack organizer who had been a central figure in the Citizens Against Clearcutting in the Asheville Watershed fight.[42]

Gilmour brought vast organizational experience to the WNCA. For decades he had worked on a host of social justice causes in the United States and abroad, including racial discrimination in western North Carolina and South Africa. Gilmour was a relative newcomer to environmental work. As he later explained, he had seen environmental concerns as a luxury compared to issues of hunger and discrimination. The watershed fight and his WNCA work on clearcutting led Gilmour to see environmental issues in a new light. "It became more and more a social justice issue for me," he explained.[43]

Plans for a four-month Cut the Clearcutting! campaign grew out of task force discussions and a memo Monroe Gilmour circulated. The campaign aimed to use publicity and grassroots organizing to put pressure on the Forest Service just as its D.C. chief was deciding how to rule on the WNCA's appeal. Task force members heard from the chief's office that he would likely pass judgment on the appeal in the first half of 1989. As the Alliance newsletter, *Accent*, explained to members, the Forest Management Task Force hoped to use "the sheer weight of numbers of voters opposed to clear-cutting" to influence the chief's decision.[44]

The WNCA launched Cut the Clearcutting! on January 25, 1989, with a press conference in front of NFsNC headquarters. The campaign wedded Monroe Gilmour's organizing and publicity vision to the commons-friendly anticlearcutting platform Walton Smith and other Forest Management Task Force members had developed. The street theater was Gilmour's, the rhetoric Smith's. The call for Forest Service responsiveness to local communities belonged to both.

As she kicked off the initial press conference, WNCA Steering Committee chair Judy Williamson proclaimed, "Clearing in our National Forests has gotten out of hand." Western North Carolinians loved their national forests, she continued, and used them for a variety of purposes, including hunting, fishing, sightseeing, and recreation. "We are concerned that clearcut harvesting will ruin large areas of our forest for these other uses," Williamson explained. Current policy called for unacceptable levels of clearcutting. The WNCA did not demand a halt to timber harvesting, Williamson emphasized; it did call on the Forest Service to switch to harvest methods more compatible with multiple uses.[45]

Mitchell County's Douglass Rankin echoed these sentiments when she spoke with reporters. Clearcutting wasted taxpayer money, destroyed wildlife habitat and food supplies, blemished the tourist-attracting mountain landscape, and damaged prime trout streams, Rankin explained. She told reporters that the Alliance was "made up of a real cross-section of folks in Western North Carolina including loggers, hunters, farmers and business people. We don't want to tie up the forest resources; we just want to see them used for the benefit of all in the long run." Rankin's language distanced the WNCA from wilderness environmentalism. Wilderness opponents' frequent charge that wilderness designation "tied up forest resources" resonated with commons users concerned about enclosure threats. By specifically rejecting this language, Rankin made the WNCA's position more attractive to these same commons users.[46]

Press conference participants also unrolled a ninety-foot-long anti-clearcutting petition, and Dick Heywood of Jackson County announced the petition drive. Heywood pledged that by the time the Alliance campaign finished in April, the petition would be long enough to wrap around the Federal Building in Asheville, which housed NFsNC headquarters. "Only Santa Claus may have a list of names longer," wrote one reporter covering the story.[47]

This opening press conference set the tone for the rest of the campaign. It showcased the WNCA's multicounty breadth, it emphasized the organization's protimber but anticlearcutting position, and it provided drama. Walton Smith's protégés played leading roles. Dick Heywood was a regular member of Smith's timber survey teams. Douglass Rankin was a longtime Forest Management Task Force activist who had worked closely with Smith for years. She and her husband, Will Ruggles, were stalwarts on Mitchell County's anticlearcutting front lines. Monroe Gilmour's work was also on display. The handmade signs around the stage, the unfurled petition, the promise of more later—all were signature Gilmour publicity strategies. To dramatize their concerns, Alliance members had even hauled dozens of heavy logs and stumps to the streets and placed them beneath a poster reading "Your Forest, Compliments USFS."[48]

In the months after its campaign kickoff, the WNCA busily continued getting the word out. Monroe Gilmour, Mary Kelly, and other staffers and volunteers put long hours into the campaign. A letter-writing campaign poured letters into editors' offices, and local newspapers around the region covered petition drive progress. "Anti-Clear-Cut Drive Picks Up Some Steam," read one typical headline. Organizers photocopied that article and put it on the back of their circulating petitions. Regional media, including the *Charlotte Observer* and Tennessee's *Greeneville Sun*, also covered the campaign. Participants widely posted flyers for the campaign's Ugliest Clearcut Photo Contest ("this one will be tough to judge!"). The contest carried a cash prize and generated yet more press coverage.[49]

The Cut the Clearcutting! campaign also featured other events designed to attract media attention. In March the WNCA brought Project Lighthawk, a group billing itself as "The Environmental Air Force," to Asheville. Independent pilots with the organization volunteered their planes and services to fly media representatives, politicians, and activists over various environmental sites to view, photograph, and film them. Lighthawk had helped to document dramatic clearcuts and dam projects in the West, but the WNCA-sponsored trip was its first mission in the East. Pilot Ed Coffman flew several trips over the Pisgah National Forest, carrying reporters, photographers, and activists. Area newspapers and Asheville's television news team covered his visit and ran striking footage from his flights.[50]

Meanwhile, on-the-ground organizers set up petition-signing stations inside and outside local businesses. Monroe Gilmour worked with Clarence Hall and some of his fellow Jackson County bear hunters in role-play exercises designed to help them gather signatures. Black Mountain volunteers sat in front of their local Roses department store beside a poster bearing a clearcut photo and a "Stop Clearcutting in WNC Forests" message. More than a dozen Yancey activists came to a petition-drive meeting called by local organizer Lisa Loveday. Several were hunters, Loveday reported, and all left carrying copies of the petition. The Yancey team planned to work three weekends in front of the Ingles grocery and Carolina Tire store in Burnsville. "The people who came to the meeting tonight are energized to collect signatures," Loveday reported. "Most of them have spent a lot of time in the woods, they know where the clear-cuts are, and they don't like them," she added.[51]

Petitions seemed to fly off the tables. "At first we were scared," Mitchell County activist Will Ruggles told reporters, "but everywhere we've gone the store owner has been the first one to sign." He and other county volunteers had collected one thousand signatures in two weekends at a station in front of the Roses department store in Spruce Pine. The Mitchell chapter aimed to have two thousand signatures before the drive was over at the end of March, and they were pleased to be halfway to their goal early in the month. Mary Kelly reported that over one hundred people in her small rural community of Hickey Fork in Madison County signed the petition the first day she and Rob left it in the local convenience store. "Everybody had some—or several—big timber sale that they were fighting and could get mad about," Kelly explained. "It was an issue that was deeply felt. It was broad-based." This profound concern translated into ever growing numbers. By the end of the drive—in a matter of weeks—WNCA volunteers had collected over sixteen thousand petition signatures. "These signatures were collected with ease," Mary Kelly told Bjorn Dahl on Cut the Clearcutting! Day. "We could get tens of thousands if we kept going."[52]

The Campaign Proves Effective

The Cut the Clearcutting! campaign proved to be a political masterstroke. It marked a crucial turning point in the decades-long debate over clearcutting on the western North Carolina national forests. Opposition to clearcutting in the region had long been widespread; it had emerged practically the moment the Forest Service introduced the timber harvest technique, and it had surfaced in nearly every public discussion of forest policy since. Yet levels of clearcut timber harvesting on North Carolina's national forests continued to rise through the 1980s, as they had more or less steadily since the early 1960s.[53]

The WNCA Cut the Clearcutting! campaign helped finally to reverse this upward trend. In September 1989 Forest Service chief Dale Robertson finally issued his long-awaited decision on the WNCA's appeal of the "Land and Resource Management Plan, 1986–2000." The document he released also addressed appeals filed by other organizations. Robertson remanded the plan to the Asheville office and ordered important changes. He cited below-cost timber sales as a major problem, and he also ruled that planners had not adequately considered "the large public opposition to clearcutting."

"The public has won quite a victory with this decision," Mary Kelly announced on behalf of the WNCA. "It has taken a lot of hard, hard work by our foresters and volunteers, but we have finally convinced the chief of the Forest Service that the public has rejected extensive use of clearcutting on our public forests."[54]

Partly this victory reflected national trends. A federal policy shift occurred with the inauguration of a new president in January 1989. The George H. W. Bush White House, though in many ways similar to that of its fellow Republican predecessor, was not so hostile to environmental concerns nor so adamant about industrial uses of the public lands as the Reagan administration had been. And the USFS began to shift away from wholesale clearcutting partly because mobilized environmentalists nationwide forced it to do so. National-level work on below-cost timber sales, in particular, helped expose the skewed economics behind much of the Forest Service's timber program. Timber sales on North Carolina's national forests, for instance, lost $2.5 million in 1988 alone. The Wilderness Society spearheaded an effort to carefully scrutinize Forest Service accounting and bring to light the true costs of timber sales. This work uncovered striking numbers nationwide and revealed that taxpayers paid staggering sums to have their publicly owned forests mowed down and hauled off. Amid growing concerns about federal budget deficits, this massive public funding for the timber industry became increasingly difficult to justify. Forest Service chief Dale Robertson noted these concerns in his 1989 ruling on the Pisgah and Nantahala appeals.[55]

Yet important as these national developments were, they could not fully account for all the changes in western North Carolina. When Robertson cited "large public opposition to clearcutting," he referred to the outpouring through the Cut the Clearcutting! campaign. Mary Kelly recalled forest supervisor Bjorn Dahl's calling her office when the chief announced his ruling. "The Alliance was the first person I had to call because you were the ones that got it," Kelly remembered Dahl saying.[56]

For the WNCA, the chief's decision represented an important victory. Esther Cunningham, David Liden, Bob Padgett, Walton and Dee Smith, Mary and Rob Kelly, and Dick and Gill Heywood celebrated at the Carson Community Center, where the Alliance had been born (see figure 16). Mary Kelly rejoiced that Robertson had "told his folks that they'd better listen [to local people], and go back and redo their harvest plans." Walton Smith took a cautious approach. "We may have won a little on paper," he said, "but we haven't won in the woods yet."[57]

It was not until 1994 that NFsNC offices issued a fully revised long-range plan for the Nantahala and Pisgah. This document proved far different from the original fifty-year plan it replaced. The new plan represented a clear victory for conservationists.

The WNCA was jubilant. "PUBLIC OPINION MAKES A DIFFERENCE! REVISED FOREST PLAN 'CUTS THE CLEARCUTTING!'" trumpeted its newsletter. A cartoon of smiling animals—a raccoon, bear, and deer (all popular game species)—dancing above a gravestone accompanied the article. The tombstone read "Here lies Clearcutting, Died 1994" (see figure 19). Forest Management Task Force chair Bob Gelder thanked everyone who had helped bring about this happy result. "None of this would have been possible unless the vast majority of people in our region felt very strongly about this, and were willing to stand up and be counted," he announced. "Everyone who signed a petition, came to a meeting, wrote a letter, or challenged timber sales in their community shares the credit!"[58]

This new plan was part of a larger trend toward more ecologically sensitive national forest management. Democrat William Jefferson Clinton's presidential administration, which began in 1993, was friendlier to environmental interests than the Bush administration had been. Under Clinton, for the first time, a biologist—not a forester or an engineer—headed the Forest Service.[59]

Here again, national developments could not fully account for regional particularities, however. The 1994 plan for the Nantahala and Pisgah was one of the most environmentally sensitive USFS regional management plans in the nation. It stood out as a model even among the new wave of more ecologically grounded plans. This was no accident. It was a direct result of the Western North Carolina Alliance's dozen years of tireless forest activism. By wedding Walton Smith's commons-friendly brand of professional forestry to a grassroots campaign tapping powerful regional veins of commons protectionism, the Alliance had reshaped its region's national forest management landscape. It had brought technical credibility to rural residents' brand of forest protection and political credibility to Walton Smith's version of professional forest management. It had unleashed commons environmentalism.[60]

The forests felt the results. The 1994 plan cut allowable timber harvest levels on the Nantahala and Pisgah forests by more than half, from 72 million board feet per year to 34 million. It nearly eliminated clearcutting as a harvest tool. Clearcutting levels dropped from 4,500 acres per year under the old plan to fewer than 300 under the new plan. The plan removed over 252,000 acres from the 586,000-acre "suitable timber base," declaring these areas too costly, too ecologically sensitive, or too overcut for logging. It made pathbreaking provisions for the first full-scale assessment of bear habitat, forest interior bird habitat, and old growth forest across the USFS's western North Carolina holdings. And it protected 32,500 acres as "Semi-Primitive Non-Motorized" areas, a status similar to wilderness.[61]

This victory did not belong only to commons users, but it could not have been accomplished without them. Trained foresters, biologists, ecologists, and botanists lent their expertise to the fight. Wilderness-style environmentalists joined the effort. Ultimately, however, the campaign's success rested on its ability to mobilize commons users in defense of the region's forests. A handful of "outsiders" could be dismissed, but the signatures of twenty thousand local voters could not.[62] This was especially true because the voters were Republicans as well as Democrats, natives as well as newcomers, housewives and hunters as well as mainstream environmentalists. Western North Carolina commons users gave the pivotal Cut the Clearcutting! campaign the cultural credibility and political clout it needed to succeed.

The Cut the Clearcutting! campaign therefore offers lessons to anyone who cares about the future of mountain forests. As the most diverse temperate forests on Earth, the southern Appalachian woods are among the world's critically important ecological treasures. The need to protect these forests gains urgency as concerns about species diversity loss and global climate change—and the deforestation that contributes to both—mount. The WNCA's 1989 Cut the Clearcutting! campaign provides a compelling example of how mobilized commons defense can be a powerful means through which to protect these rich forest ecosystems.

An American Commons in the Blue Ridge

AN AMERICAN COMMONS thrived in the Blue Ridge for centuries and continues into the present day. The long-standing presence of rich and widely accessible forests has had far-reaching effects on the region's history and culture and has shaped its ties to the rest of the nation and to the world. In every period, a commons history of the southern Appalachians waits to be unearthed. The deerskin, ginseng, livestock, and chestnut trades, while important, remain only a beginning.

Reams of evidence attest to the power of commons traditions in the southern mountains and to residents' stalwart determination to defend the woods against perceived enclosure threats. Commons defenders repeatedly trespassed and poached on would-be private lands belonging to absentee landowners, timber companies, and wealthy part-time residents. They also used classic commons defense weapons, including arms, fence cutting, and fire, to resist enclosure. Local communities regularly supported commons defenders by declining to assist efforts to capture or punish them—that is, by refusing to help enforce privatizing laws.

By enabling the federal government to purchase eastern forestlands, the 1911 Weeks Act marked a watershed in Blue Ridge commons history. When the U.S. Forest Service created national forests in the southern Appalachians, it ushered in a new era: much of the region's long-standing de facto wooded commons became de jure commons. Federal ownership brought official forest managers, an elaborate formal governance structure, and a new fee system to the traditional commons. These developments changed the contours of that commons even as they enabled it to endure and flourish.

For decades, Forest Service philosophy and governance dovetailed fairly well with Blue Ridge commons tradition and practice. Though the agency stressed timber production above all else, its emphasis on forest productivity and its multiple-use mandate served to legitimize commons harvest. Its close cooperation with sportsmen's organizations, including the North Carolina Wildlife Resources Commission, enabled the hunting and fishing commons to maintain vigor. Its routine sales of low-cost firewood permits buttressed the fuel-gathering commons, and its readiness to issue other plant-material permits further sustained gathering-commons practice.

Commons vitality also received a boost thanks to the Forest Service policy of acquiring lands only from willing sellers. This USFS commitment made possible relatively cordial relations with local communities, in marked contrast to agencies such as the National Park Service and Tennessee Valley Authority, which forcibly displaced many residents. Though USFS personnel had their own public relations challenges to face, their agency's gentler land-acquisition history made it easier for them to forge community partnerships. Through much of the twentieth century, forest neighbors could accept Pisgah and Nantahala managers as at least relatively benign commons caretakers.

The willing-sellers-only legacy also appeared on the ground, where national forestlands entwined intimately with local communities. The piecemeal nature of willing-seller acquisition left a public-private land mosaic, as the Pisgah and Nantahala forests' irregular boundaries wound through scores of Blue Ridge neighborhoods. Thousands of western North Carolinians owned land adjacent to the federal forests, and thousands more lived only minutes away. These patterns—and the impossibility of policing such sprawling patchwork borders—insured widespread access to the national forests, bolstering their ongoing use as commons.

By requiring public participation in USFS decision making, the 1976 National Forest Management Act brought another sea change to the Blue Ridge forest commons. It substantially strengthened western North Carolina residents' hands, enabling them to have significant input into Pisgah and Nantahala forest management plans. Mountain residents began wielding their new power almost immediately, especially to defend the woods against perceived enclosure threats.

Savvy organizers on both sides of the 1978 wilderness debates cast themselves as antienclosure defenders of the commons forests. Timber industry spokesmen successfully used commons-defense arguments to turn back most proposed wilderness designations during RARE II. At the same time, western North Carolina hunters used strikingly similar arguments to win wilderness protection for the locally beloved Southern Nantahala, the only entirely new wilderness area created in the state's mountains in the wake of RARE II. In effect, commons users functioned as "swing voters" in the wilderness debates—the side that lured them most effectively carried the day.

The Forest Service's postwar embrace of industrial forest development put it on a collision course with Blue Ridge commons users bent on resisting enclosure. Shortly after the wilderness controversy, the young Western North Carolina Alliance spearheaded a series of ambitious commons-defense efforts to curtail industrial exploitation of the Pisgah and Nantahala. In the early 1980s, the fledgling organization used commons-based arguments to combat petroleum leasing and to advocate forest protection on a sweeping scale more ambitious than national organizations embraced.

The WNCA also used commons-defense arguments to mount a vigorous anticlearcutting effort in the mid-1980s, culminating in its masterly 1989 Cut the Clearcutting! campaign. In this case, especially with its enormous petition drive, the organization provided mountain residents with a vehicle to express their long-standing aversion to clearcutting as a timber harvest method. Even as it took a firm stand against clearcutting, however, the WNCA carefully expressed support for forest harvest, including other forms of timber harvest. Organizers drew a distinction between clearcutting and other methods because it destroyed the woods for other uses, effectively enclosing the commons.

By championing a harvest-friendly brand of forest protection in these campaigns, the WNCA pioneered a form of commons environmentalism. And like the earlier wilderness debates, the organization's antipetroleum and anticlearcutting crusades demonstrated the power of organized commons defense. The vigorous, commons-based Cut the Clearcutting! campaign helped turn back clearcutting and paved the way for exemplary Pisgah and Nantahala forest management plans in the 1990s, plans that served as models for the rest of the nation.

These Blue Ridge examples demonstrate the enduring power of one American commons. And while Blue Ridge forests are unique in their richness and diversity, the centrality of commons to their history is assuredly not unique. Other examples abound throughout the nation, from its plains to its fisheries and through all its public lands. In every period, a commons history of the United States of America waits to be unearthed. The Blue Ridge story, while important, remains only a beginning.

A Call to Commons

AS SEA LEVELS RISE, biodiversity shrinks, invasive species explode, and ozone depletes, it becomes increasingly clear: all the world's a commons. Anyone who cares about the health of our planet is involved in commons defense.

In the last quarter of the twentieth century, western North Carolina's forest activists crafted positions and mobilized effective campaigns that drew strength from their region's commons history and culture. They conceived a form of commons environmentalism. The example of these commons-inspired woods protectors has something to teach us all.

The U.S. environmental movement has always been complex, and commons environmentalism has been one of its powerful, if largely invisible, forms. Wilderness environmentalism has been far more visible and much better understood—though even there plenty of work remains to be done. That more widely recognized form of environmentalism held little attraction for many Nantahala and Pisgah neighbors, however, and even drew substantial outright opposition. Nevertheless, western North Carolinians proved to be robust forest guardians on their own commons grounds. By mobilizing commons users, highlands activists achieved greater forest protection, even greater wilderness protection, than would otherwise have been possible in the Blue Ridge.

Their example offers lessons for both historians of the environmental movement and contemporary activists at work in the movement. For historians, this southern highlands story can serve as a reminder to think of the movement as plural rather than singular—as a series of "environmentalisms" growing out of particular, on-the-ground contexts.[1] It may also nudge movement chroniclers to pay attention to longer histories and to the role of cultural politics. Centuries of forest use and a widely (though by no means universally) shared commons culture sculpted western North Carolina forest politics in ways not immediately apparent to some activists. Contests over national forest management in the region simply cannot be understood outside this context.

Nantahala and Pisgah controversies offer parallel lessons to present-day environmental activists. These contests can remind grassroots environmentalists to study local and regional history and to listen for the ways residents talk about lands and waters. Which places do local people especially value? Why do they choose these places, and how do they express the value they see? What environmental anxieties do they have? How can these priorities, values, and anxieties be incorporated into campaigns for protection? Which "environmentalisms" fit this context? Of course, many environmental activists already ask these and similar questions, but this study underscores their importance. Beyond the grassroots level, this case history suggests that insights and tactics from particular locations might be fruitfully incorporated into larger regional, national, and even international strategies.

Finally, and perhaps most importantly, this Blue Ridge story can remind both historians and environmental activists to notice the commons. Despite its long history and centrality to American thought and experience, in the United States the commons remains all but invisible. When it is recognized at all, it is usually treated as an archaic holdover rather than a vital presence in today's world.[2]

Once we have the language to talk about commons systems and the tools with which to recognize their pattern, I predict we will begin to see them in many places. Whether we know it or not, such systems certainly affect all our lives. Though this history focuses on a particular region's forest commons, its implications reach far beyond the Blue Ridge. Similar commons woods exist in many other places across the North American continent and the rest of the globe. Moreover, there are striking parallels between forested and wetland commons. The world's fisheries—its bayous, lakes, swamps, river systems, floodplains, and oceans—have rich commons histories and cultures attached to them. There are also commons grasslands, groundwater commons, the commons of breathable air, and doubtless many other forms. And all these forms face threats of enclosure.[3]

When I started this project, only a small group of pioneering scholars, almost none of them U.S. historians, had published studies on the commons.[4] Recently, that has begun to change, and the commons has become increasingly visible. Among other indicators, it now boasts its first Nobel Laureate. A 2009 Nobel Prize in Economics went to Elinor Ostrom, one of the important early trailblazers in commons research. Peter Linebaugh, and Herbert Reid and Betsy Taylor, respectively, have published illuminating recent works on commons history and commons political theory, with an emphasis on the U.S. context. Discussions of commons have appeared in a variety of academic periodicals aimed at social and natural scientists, folklorists, and theorists. Today, the idea of the commons enjoys a higher profile than it did even a decade ago.[5]

The concept of the commons is not a panacea, as this growing body of scholarship makes clear. Commons systems are messy, fraught, and complicated and can destroy ecosystems as well as protect them. Though Garrett Hardin's famous article—as he later acknowledged—exaggerated the potential "Tragedy of the Commons," it was not entirely baseless. Commons systems can and do fail. In fact, the Nobel Prize committee particularly noted Laureate Elinor Ostrom's work examining and comparing commons systems and her efforts to discover patterns explaining why some such systems worked and others did not. The list of possible commons frailties stretches long. Governance can be fragile. Systems can fail to recognize limits, adapt to change, or respond effectively to threats. Inadequate policing and lack of rule enforcement can bring ruin. Insufficient clarity in regulation can topple a system, as can ecological stress or resource collapse. And even the most robust commons systems face near-constant threats of enclosure. These threats adapt and evolve, and therefore so must the systems' efforts to repel them.[6]

Despite these and other imperfections, the idea of the commons has great forest protection potential. The concept brings with it a variety of useful adjuncts. First, it offers recognition of natural systems' material value and a sense of this value's continuation over extended periods. Commons sensibility often reaches deep into the past, and it can project well into the future. It represents ongoing relationship with a given ecosystem and therefore the possibility of commitment to that ecosystem's long-term health. And it does this on quite pragmatic grounds of material well-being rather than appeals to less concrete ethical, spiritual, or emotional terrain.

The idea of the commons also offers a sense of ownership. This can be beneficial, as people are more likely to defend something they think of as theirs. By recognizing the claims of many potential owners, however, commons systems can also exercise a kind of braking effect, preventing any single owner from gaining a monopolistic and potentially destructive upper hand. At its strongest, the commons can offer the best of both worlds—the sense of investment that can come with property ownership without the unchecked power that too often also accompanies it.

Finally, the idea of the commons can inspire real passion and commitment, especially around efforts at commons defense. Commons twines into basic human needs: livelihood, family, place. It also affords opportunity to experience other key aspects of human existence: exploration, observation, teamwork, solitude, storytelling, knowledge and skill acquisition, awareness of nature, appreciation of beauty, and many more. It wraps into memory, tendrils through community, and interlaces with reverence. Since commons sites can braid so powerfully into fundamental human experiences, they can also inspire vigorous commitment grounded in those experiences. Macon County coon hunters, for instance, did not see themselves as a caricaturist might—as defending a frivolous or even cruel form of entertainment, expending tremendous energies out of all proportion to the unworthy object of that effort. Instead, they saw themselves as torchbearers for a rich tradition, a tradition of great power, beauty, and dignity. This tradition had roots many generations deep, and they aimed to pass its knowledge, skills, and pleasures to generations yet to come. Far from being unworthy of their efforts, the hunting tradition eminently deserved every bit of exertion they could muster. This expansive perspective lent force to hunters' work defending the forests on which their cherished tradition depended.

The power of commons, mobilized as commons environmentalism, offers a potent tool for addressing forest issues on every level, from local to global. This tool cannot be hefted too soon. Issues of forest conservation become more critical every day, with no end in sight. Deforestation currently contributes between 17 and 20 percent of the world's carbon emissions, more than the globe's entire fleet of automobiles, buses, and planes. Thus, forest protection and management are crucial to issues of global climate change. The planet's forests also contain a great deal of its biodiversity, so for species conservation as well, forest protection is critical.[7]

Commons environmentalism might also be wielded on behalf of other ecosystems—of grasslands, swamps, rivers, and sounds. It might also assist groundwater conservation efforts and policy development around oceans, air, and even the night sky. Though it cannot solve all environmental problems, it will have a role to play in many.

The point of this book is simple: remember the commons. I have tried to show how one historical commons has worked and how commons politics rooted in history have played out in one important American region. My hope is that this example will not only offer useful lessons itself but also inspire others to study the phenomenon of the commons and to recognize its potential to contribute to present-day environmental problem solving.

For environmental historians, a parting message. The commons are crucial, and there is much work to be done, as their story remains largely unwritten. The current near-invisibility must change, and the commons must take a place on our discipline's center stage. The study of commons systems, commons enclosures, and commons defense should become for environmental historians what the study of the rise and fall of empires has long been for political historians—a central mission, the very heart of the enterprise.

For environmental activists, a parting message. Environmentalist efforts to sculpt the future are crucial, and the commons can be a powerful ally. As you work to bend humanity toward choices the planet can sustain, listen and watch for the presence of commons. They may be there not only on a vast global scale but also on more local, particular scales. Other forms of environmentalism will continue to have value, and it will always be imperative to pay attention to environmentalisms growing out of particular contexts. But much of the environmentalist future, far more than we currently realize, lies with the commons.

NOTES

INTRODUCTION. Of Forests and Commons

1. Morley, *The Carolina Mountains*. Elizabeth Giard correspondence in author's possession.

2. It is possible that the woman had not harvested in the woods, but this fact does not diminish the power of Morley's image as an expression of the relationship between Appalachian commons users and their forests.

3. One example of such oversimplification comes from the brilliant landscape architect Frederick Law Olmsted, who criticized stockmen for failing to feed their animals properly but admired the quality of their product. He did not understand that animals could thrive in the commons forests without supplementary feeding. See Olmsted, *A Journey*, 22, 223.

4. The Great Smoky Mountains National Park All Taxa Biodiversity Inventory, undertaken by Discover Life in America in 1998, had by 2009 documented over nine hundred species new to science. See the Discover Life website; see also "Nearly 900 Species Discovered in Smokies," *Asheville Citizen-Times*, July 22, 2008; "Inventory of Smokies Flora, Fauna Important," *Asheville Citizen-Times*, April 28, 2009.

5. Martin et al., *Biodiversity*; Hsiung, "Geographic Determinism"; Gale, "Scent of Hickory"; Bolgiano, *Appalachian Forest*, 3–5.

6. See the Discover Life website; see also "Nearly 900 Species"; "Inventory of Smokies Flora"; National Park Service, "Great Smoky Mountains National Park" website; Gale, "Scent of Hickory"; Johnson, *Ready for Harvest*; United Nations Educational, Scientific, and Cultural Organization, "World Heritage" website.

7. See Southern Appalachian Man and the Biosphere, "SAMAB Reserve" website. Great Smoky Mountains National Park, Mount Mitchell State Park, Grandfather Mountain, and Coweeta Hydrological Laboratory are Blue Ridge units. Oak Ridge National Environmental Research Park is in the Valley and Ridge province, and the Tennessee River Gorge is in the Appalachian Plateaus. For history of the Southern Appalachian Man and the Biosphere program, see Van Sickle and Turner, "The Southern Appalachian Man." For the Southern Appalachian Biosphere Reserve, see United Nations Educational, Scientific, and Cultural Organization, "Biosphere Reserve" website. For World Heritage, see National Park Service, "U.S. World Heritage Sites" website; United Nations Educational, Scientific, and Cultural Organization, "World Heritage" website.

8. Portions of five states: north Georgia, northwestern South Carolina, western North Carolina, eastern Tennessee, and southwestern Virginia. See Clark, "Geology."

9. See Blue Ridge National Heritage Area website. See also Public Law 108-108, Title I, sec. 140, 117 STAT 1241.

10. In September 2009, together the Nantahala and Pisgah National Forests encompassed 1,043,866 acres. This is more than 1,630 square miles, or 4,224 square kilometers, an area significantly larger than Rhode Island, even including Narragansett Bay, and more than twenty-five times the size of the District of Columbia. Nearly a third of the world's recognized sovereign nations—some 75 of 249—encompass smaller land areas than the combined Pisgah and Nantahala National Forests. See United States Central Intelligence Agency, World Factbook website. No formal history of the Nantahala and Pisgah National Forests currently exists. For a well-researched USFS introduction to Appalachian National Forest history, see Mastran and Lowerre, *Mountaineers and Rangers*. For a classic brief introduction to the region's national forests, see Eller, *Miners*. For a USFS land-use overview history, see Yarnell, *The Southern Appalachians*. For an overview of national forests in the East, see Shands and Healy, *Lands Nobody Wanted*. For fine explorations of Blue Ridge Virginia's Jefferson National Forest history, see Sarvis, "An Appalachian Forest," "Fisheries and Wildlife," and "Mount Rogers."

11. For a discussion of state and commons, see McKay and Acheson, "Human Ecology."

12. The USFS shared responsibility for these lands with other federal and state agencies. The North Carolina Wildlife Commission held authority over fish and game; the federal Bureau of Land Management held authority over minerals. For examples of Pisgah and Nantahala forest use and fees in the early 1980s, see Clyde Osborne, "Moss Thieves," *Asheville Citizen*, March 26, 1981; "Fraser Cones to Be Available This Fall," *Franklin Press*, August 20, 1981; "Fish Hides Constructed through Joint Effort," *Franklin Press*, October 22, 1981; "Sutton on Sports," *Franklin Press*, March 4, 1982; "Sale of Green Standing Firewood Is Not Offered," *Franklin Press*, June 3, 1982; "Save Money if You Purchase Lifetime State Hunting License," *Franklin Press*, July 28, 1982.

13. For discussion of another national forest as commons, see Geores, *Common Ground*. For the Appalachian national forests as commons, see Bolgiano, "National Forests."

14. For an excellent discussion of the critical importance of the NFMA, see Hays, *Wars in the Woods*.

15. For a fine history of forest use in the southern Appalachians, see Davis, *Where There Are Mountains*. For a sweeping case study of one Appalachian range, see Silver, *Mount Mitchell*. For histories of the Great Smoky Mountains National Park, see Brown, *Wild East*; and Pierce, *The Great Smokies*.

16. Here I am fortunate to build on the work of fine scholars of Appalachian environmental history. See Brown, *Wild East*; Davis, *Where There Are Mountains*; Lewis, *Transforming*; Pierce, *The Great Smokies*; Silver, *Mount Mitchell*.

17. Some mountain residents viewed wilderness in ways similar to those explored in William Cronon's essay "Trouble with Wilderness."

18. A complete list of works treating American commons traditions would be long indeed. Among the most important and insightful of those works are Catton, *Inhabited Wilderness*; Donahue, *Reclaiming the Commons*; Geores, *Common Ground*;

Hahn, "Hunting, Fishing, and Foraging"; Jacoby, *Crimes against Nature*; Johnson, "Conservation, Subsistence"; Judd, *Common Lands*; Linebaugh, *Magna Carta Manifesto*; Reid and Taylor, *Recovering the Commons*; Schneider, "Enclosing the Floodplain"; Steinberg, "Down to Earth"; Warren, *The Hunter's Game*; Watson, "'Common Rights.'"

19. There is a rich literature on the history and current outlines of commons systems across the globe. For an excellent introduction to common property resources, see Feeney et al., "Tragedy of the Commons." For a thoughtful series of reflections on commons systems, see McKay and Acheson, *Question of the Commons*. For a brief introduction to the idea of the commons, see Nonini, *Global Idea*. See also Baden and Noonan, *Managing the Commons*. For an outstanding exploration of commons governance, see Ostrom, *Governing the Commons*. For an exploration of the global context, see Goldman, *Privatizing Nature*. For a classic consideration of the commons in British history, see Thompson, *Whigs and Hunters*. For an illuminating recent exploration of commons in Anglo-American law and history, see Linebaugh, *Magna Carta Manifesto*. For examples of commons property systems in world history, see De Moor, Shaw-Taylor, and Warde, *Management of Common Land*; Fritzboger, *Windfall for the Magnates*; Maurer, "Colonial Policy"; Castro, "Njukiine Forest"; Bauer, "Economic Differentiation." For ocean commons discussion, see Heidbrink, "The Oceans." For a widely influential but no longer current theory of the commons, see Hardin, "Tragedy of the Commons." Hardin's theory predicted dangerous resource depletion as the inevitable result of commons. But as Elinor Ostrom and others demonstrated, many historical commons prevented resource depletion, and some lasted for centuries; they rarely allowed the unfettered open access of Hardin's model. Hardin himself conceded that he might better have titled his piece "The Tragedy of the Unmanaged Commons." See McKay and Acheson, "Human Ecology." Nobel Laureate Elinor Ostrom has supplanted Hardin as the standard model on issues of commons governance. See Ostrom, *Governing the Commons*, and Nobel Prize, press release website.

20. Pioneering folklorist Mary Hufford has done critically important work documenting a rich set of commons cultures in contemporary West Virginia. Parallel cultures thrived in mountainous North Carolina. See Hufford, "American Ginseng," and American Folklife Center, Library of Congress, "Tending the Commons" website.

21. For deforestation and global climate change, see Stern, *Economics of Climate Change*.

22. Among the important pioneering works on the history of the American conservation and environmental movements are Nash, *Wilderness and the American Mind*; Hays, *Conservation* and *Beauty, Health, and Permanence*; Bullard, *Dumping in Dixie*; Gottlieb, *Forcing the Spring*; Merchant, *Earthcare*; Judd, *Common Lands*; and Rothman, *Greening of a Nation?* Illuminating case studies include Donahue, *Reclaiming the Commons*; Sutter, *Driven Wild*; Merrill, *Public Lands*; Jacoby, *Crimes against Nature*; Marsh, *Drawing Lines*. One indicator of the field as still in its early stages comes from the 2010 Organization of American Historians' annual meeting program, which featured a plenary roundtable on environmental history but nothing else from the field and nothing on the history of the environmental movement.

23. For more on mountaintop removal's environmental, social, and cultural destruction, see the periodical *Appalachian Voice*, which has covered it extensively. See also the Appalachian Voices website and Yale Environment 360, "Leveling Appalachia" website.

24. For one example, see Larry Gibson's Keeper of the Mountains Foundation website.

25. See, for example, Howell, "Mountain Foragers."

26. See, for example, Reid and Taylor, *Recovering the Commons*.

27. These comments have come from conferences of the Oral History Association, the American Society for Environmental History, and the Berkshire Conference on Women's History and from colleagues in the 2005 and 2006 National Endowment for the Humanities Landmarks of American History Workshops for Community College Faculty titled "Working the Woods: Economies and Cultures in the Southern Blue Ridge, 1650–1950."

28. Scholars whose commons-resonant work has influenced my own include Jacoby, *Crimes against Nature*; Schneider, "Enclosing the Floodplain"; Spence, *Dispossessing the Wilderness*; Judd, *Common Lands*; Donahue, *Reclaiming the Commons*; Montoya, *Translating Property*; Catton, *Inhabited Wilderness*; Warren, *The Hunter's Game*; Cronon, *Nature's Metropolis*; Keiner, *The Oyster Question*. Some of these works use the term "commons," while others do not, but all illuminate aspects of North American commons history.

29. Insightful histories treating national forests include Marsh, *Drawing Lines*; Langston, *Forest Dreams*; Kosek, *Understories*; Merrill, *Public Lands*; Geores, *Common Ground*; Johnson, "Conservation, Subsistence." I am also fortunate to have fine southern Appalachian national forest histories by agency historians, including Mastran and Lowerre as well as Sarvis.

30. Perceptive scholarship exploring international commons includes Nguiffo, "In Defense of the Commons"; Diegues, "Social Movements"; Lu, "'The Commons'"; Ostrom, *Governing the Commons*; Castro, "Njukiine Forest," 160–68; Guha, *The Unquiet Woods*; Brownhill, "Gendered Struggles."

31. Norman, "Notes," 329.

ONE. "The Custom of Our Country"

1. Dale Neal, "Lost in the Dark Forest of a Strange and Unforgiving Economy," *Asheville Citizen-Times*, March 21, 2010. For Walker Evans photographs, see Agee and Evans, *Let Us Now Praise*.

2. Jeanine Davis quoted in Neal, "Lost in the Dark Forest." In recent decades, the Latino presence has increased in Blue Ridge commons forests, especially as galax pickers. For an excellent account of one Latino community in the region, see Fink, *Maya of Morganton*.

3. Arguably, these patterns have a far longer history. This chapter addresses the period of documented intercontinental exchange that began in the seventeenth century, but forest products also sustained prehistoric Appalachians and probably linked them to distant North American markets.

4. In this book I use the word "commons" to refer both to the Appalachian for-

ests themselves and to the systems that governed them. Some scholars differentiate these two, for instance, using "common-pool resource" to describe material commons and "common property regime" to describe commons governance. I respect this approach but find it most helpful to apply the term "commons" to both resource and governance. In my view, the western North Carolina commons is best grasped in total rather than as a sum of component parts; forest resources, local use of these resources, and customs, practices, and regulations governing this use braided together to create Blue Ridge commons. I also use "commons" as both singular and plural. Where multiple commons types overlap, I call them "commons" rather than "commonses."

5. Bonnie McKay and James M. Acheson argued that Garrett Hardin's "inevitable commons collapse" thesis was valid only for "open-access" systems and not for "commons," as actual commons limit access. See Hardin, "Tragedy of the Commons"; and McKay and Acheson, "Human Ecology," esp. 7–9. For limits discussion, see also Geores, *Common Ground*, 8–14.

6. See Nonini, *Global Idea*, especially the introduction, 1–25.

7. Mary Hufford ("American Ginseng") offers a vivid example in her discussion of commons traditions in West Virginia, where strip mining and mountaintop removal have destroyed some long-standing de facto commons.

8. McKay and Acheson, "Human Ecology"; Bromley, "Property Rights."

9. McKay and Acheson, "Human Ecology"; and McKay, "Culture of the Commoners."

10. For commons as activity, see Linebaugh, *Magna Carta Manifesto*, 279.

11. For a description of fishing commons in one Appalachian community, see Davis, *Homeplace Geography*, 9–16.

12. In Cherokee mythology, for example, animals unleashed diseases on humans as a response to overhunting. Animals could also take revenge on specific hunters; deer punished with rheumatism hunters who failed to follow ritual observances in the deer's honor. See Mooney, *History, Myths*, 250–52.

13. The limited success of state efforts is evident in North Carolina Wildlife Resources Commission records, which record cooperation and detected violations and estimate undetected violations. See back issues of *Wildlife in North Carolina* for examples. For present-day regulation, see the website of the North Carolina Wildlife Resources Commission.

14. For a discussion of recent national developments, see Jones, McLain, and Weigand, *Nontimber Forest Products*.

15. See Arthur, *Western North Carolina*, 284–87; Sondley, *Buncombe County*, 619–21. See also Davis, *Where There Are Mountains*, 74–76; Inscoe, *Mountain Masters*, 45–52; Walpole, "Closing."

16. Matthew R. Walpole's fine study of the closing of Watauga County's open range is the best available for highland North Carolina ("Closing"). For range masters, see Medford, *Early History*, 85–86; Sondley, *Buncombe County*, 476–79.

17. Linebaugh, *Magna Carta Manifesto*, 38–39, 50–59.

18. The classic study of commons issues in Britain is Thompson, *Whigs and Hunters*. For an insightful recent exploration of this topic, see Linebaugh, *Magna Carta Manifesto*, 46–68.

19. McKay, "Culture of the Commoners," 196–97. See also Howkins, "Economic Crime."

20. McKay, "Culture of the Commoners," 195–96, 201–2. For American wildlife history, see Lund, *American Wildlife Law*, and Tober, *Who Owns the Wildlife?* For an especially important example of U.S. commons history, see Judd, *Common Lands*. For other examinations of commons traditions in the United States, see Schneider, "Enclosing the Floodplain"; Johnson, "Conservation, Subsistence"; Jacoby, "Class and Environmental History"; Warren, *The Hunter's Game*; Mitchell, *Trespassing*.

21. Quote is taken from Hatley, *Dividing Paths*, 83.

22. Silver, *New Face*, 83–86; Davis, *Where There Are Mountains*, 70–71.

23. See Yarnell, *The Southern Appalachians*, 252; Davis, *Where There Are Mountains*, 106–7.

24. For example, see the bark bucket exhibit at the Museum of the Cherokee Indian. Nearly identical buckets appear in antebellum collections, including collections at the Zebulon B. Vance Birthplace North Carolina State Historical Site and at the Ramsey Center for Regional Studies at Mars Hill College. Fish traps and bear traps similar to those used by Cherokee people also appeared in white communities; for bear trap, see Fears, "Bear Hunting"; for fish basket, see Davis, *Homeplace Geography*, 9–12.

25. See Davis, *Where There Are Mountains*, 11–34.

26. Yarnell, *The Southern Appalachians*, 4; Davis, *Where There Are Mountains*, 11–55; Silver, *Mount Mitchell*, 37–55. For a valuable exploration of Mississippian and Spanish contact, see Hudson, *Knights of Spain*.

27. Hatley, *Dividing Paths*, 32–33.

28. Hill, *Weaving New Worlds*, 37–41, 55–62. See also Hatley, *Dividing Paths*, 33.

29. See Davis, *Where There Are Mountains*, 70–71.

30. Hatley, *Dividing Paths*, 42.

31. Ibid., 42, 252. Lawson quote at 252.

32. Silver, *Mount Mitchell*, 57–59.

33. Davis, *Where There Are Mountains*, 67.

34. Hatley, *Dividing Paths*, 39.

35. The scale of the Appalachian deerskin trade has inspired a scholarly debate and is unlikely to be resolved with any precision. For a useful overview, see Davis, *Where There Are Mountains*, 65–67. See also Hatley, *Dividing Paths*, 164; Crane, *Southern Frontier*, 112, 176–77.

36. Hatley, *Dividing Paths*, 37.

37. Logan, *Upper Country*, 254–55.

38. Crane, *Southern Frontier*, 154.

39. Davis, *Where There Are Mountains*, 64. It seems likely that the Cherokees supplied Charleston with between a quarter and a third of its deerskins in the peak years of the trade. The South Carolina port shipped 160,000 deerskins in 1748; in 1751 Cherokee hunters likely supplied around 50,000 skins.

40. Ibid., 66.

41. Hatley, *Dividing Paths*, 119–40, 163–66; Davis, *Where There Are Mountains*, 61–69.

42. Davis, *Where There Are Mountains*, 71–79.

43. Quote from Williams, *Early Travels*, 139–40. See Davis, *Where There Are Mountains*, 72–77.

44. Davis, *Where There Are Mountains*, 73–74, 108–11.

45. Ibid., 112–13; Marks, *Southern Hunting*; Nickens, "Brief Glance Backwards," 14.

46. Marks, *Southern Hunting*, 30–31; Nickens, "Brief Glance Backwards," 14. Quote from *An additional Act to an Act, entitled, An act to prevent killing deer at unseasonable times and for putting a stop to many abuses committed by white persons, under pretence of hunting* (N.C., 1745), *The Colonial and State Records of North Carolina*, Acts of the North Carolina General Assembly, 1745, vol. 23, 218–19.

47. Nickens, "Brief Glance Backwards," 14; Davis, *Where There Are Mountains*, 112–13; Marks, *Southern Hunting*, 30–31; Tober, *Who Owns the Wildlife?*, xv–xix, 25.

48. Eller, *Miners*, 16–22; Hufford, "American Ginseng," 5, 7–8; Davis, *Where There Are Mountains*, 125–26, 132–33, 144–47.

49. Davis, *Where There Are Mountains*, 179–82; Hufford, "American Ginseng," 7.

50. Jacoby, "Class and Environmental History," 324–42; Davis, *Where There Are Mountains*, 179; Hufford, "American Ginseng," 5, 7–8; Mastran and Lowerre, *Mountaineers and Rangers*, 164–65. For a history of absentee ownership, see Dunaway, *First American Frontier*, esp. 51–86.

51. Inscoe, *Mountain Masters*, 45–52; Davis, *Where There Are Mountains*, 110–15, 130–36, 160; Silver, *Mount Mitchell*, 65–75, 122–26.

52. Inscoe, *Mountain Masters*, 38–39. See also Duncan, "American Ginseng."

53. Michaux quoted in Inscoe, *Mountain Masters*, 40.

54. Gash quoted in ibid., 38.

55. Duncan, "American Ginseng," 210; Inscoe, *Mountain Masters*, 38; Davidson quoted in Sondley, *Buncombe County*, 440.

56. Betsy Calloway reportedly walked countless miles and dug many ginseng roots with her youngest child on her back. Delilah Baird "fought wolves with firebrands" and knit socks while she traveled over the ridge on horseback. See Arthur, *Watauga County*, 188, 191, 199.

57. John Winebarger quoted in Walpole, "Closing," 327.

58. "Incomparable" quote from Bishop I. Spangenberg, quoted in Arthur, *Western North Carolina*, 65. Michaux and Mitchell quoted in Inscoe, *Mountain Masters*, 12, 13. Inscoe discusses the livestock trade on 41–52; for 1800 markets, see 45.

59. Inscoe, *Mountain Masters*, 45–52; Davis, *Where There Are Mountains*, 130–36.

60. Inscoe, *Mountain Masters*, 45, 52.

61. Ibid., 46; Eller, *Miners*, 21; Davis, *Where There Are Mountains*, 130–32.

62. Inscoe, *Mountain Masters*, 48.

63. Walpole, "Closing," 321; Arthur, *Watauga County*, 139.

64. Davis, *Where There Are Mountains*, 131–33; Olmsted, *A Journey*, 22, 223.

65. Walpole, "Closing," 321–22; on range masters, see Medford, *Early History*, 86; for national history, see Tober, *Who Owns the Wildlife?*

66. Walpole, "Closing," 321–22; Medford, *Early History*, 85–88; for a description of marks, see Sondley, *Buncombe County*, 476–79.

67. Walpole, "Closing," 321, 326–27; Hufford, "American Ginseng," 8; Davis, *Where There Are Mountains*, 179. For landholding patterns, see Dunaway, *First American Frontier*.

68. Leander Greene quoted in Walpole, "Closing," 326–27.

69. For a fine exploration of tourism history in western North Carolina, see Starnes, *Creating*. D. B. Dougherty quoted in Walpole, "Closing," 324.

70. *Watauga Democrat* quoted in Walpole, "Closing," 328; McKinney, *Southern Mountain Republicans*, 120–21. For a related discussion of stock-law politics in the upland South, see Hahn, *Roots*.

71. Walpole, "Closing," 330–31.

72. *Watauga Democrat* quoted in ibid., 332. For analyses of range debate class dynamics in the South, see Hahn, *Roots*, especially "Common Right and Commonwealth," 239–68, and "The Contours of Populism," 269–89; and see Durrill, "Producing Poverty," 764–81.

73. Leander L. Greene quoted in Walpole, "Closing," 326–27.

74. John Winebarger quoted in ibid., 327. On fire as commons-enclosure retaliation, see Thompson, *Whigs and Hunters*, 147, 225–27; Jacoby, "Class and Environmental History."

75. *Watauga Democrat* and John Hodges quoted in Walpole, "Closing," 332. For commons uses as rights, see Scott, *Domination*, 189–95; Hahn, *Roots*, 243, 260–62.

76. *Watauga Democrat* quoted in Walpole, "Closing," 332. For poaching as enclosure resistance, see McKay, "Culture of the Commoners," 200–201; Scott, *Domination*, 189–91; Jacoby, "Class and Environmental History," 324–42; Warren, *The Hunter's Game*, 71–105.

77. Crockett, interview by Early and Wooten, 19; Walpole, "Closing," 330–31. See also Jim Cunningham, interview.

78. Stewart, interview, 500.

79. Jim Cunningham, interview; Crockett, interview by Early and Wooten. See also Webb, "Hunting Tales," 276, 283.

80. See Lutts, "Like Manna." See also the American Chestnut Foundation website; Bolgiano, *Mighty Giants*.

81. Davis, *Where There Are Mountains*, 192–94; Bolgiano, *Appalachian Forest*, 209–13.

82. Davis, *Where There Are Mountains*, 194–97; Bolgiano, *Appalachian Forest*, 206–9.

83. Bolgiano, *Appalachian Forest*, 209–11; Davis, *Where There Are Mountains*, 193–94.

84. Davis, *Where There Are Mountains*, 194–95; Crockett, interview by Early and Wooten, 18–22; Bolgiano, *Appalachian Forest*, 208–9.

85. Silver, *Mount Mitchell*, 155–62.

86. *Message from the President*, 97; Silver, *Mount Mitchell*, 159.

87. For a valuable exploration of the chestnut trade, see Lutts, "Like Manna." See also Bolgiano, *Mighty Giants*; Bolgiano, *Appalachian Forest*; "Chestnut Memories" oral histories, the American Chestnut Foundation.

88. Lutts, "Like Manna."

89. Eller, *Miners*, 103–4, 122; Bolgiano, *Appalachian Forest*.

90. Silver, *Mount Mitchell*, 158; Lutts, "Like Manna," 251.

91. Brown, *Wild East*, 25–26; Smith, "Appalachian National Park Movement," 44.

92. Brown, *Wild East*, 25–26.

93. Mastran and Lowerre, *Mountaineers and Rangers*, 55.

94. Billy Long quoted in Cheek, Nix, and Foxfire students, *Foxfire 40th Anniversary Book*, 455.

95. Lloyd Fish photo by Nick Lanier in Southern Appalachian Archives at Mars Hill College. For information on Lloyd Fish, I am indebted to Richard Dillingham, personal communication.

96. Mary Hufford perceptively described timber and coal company purchases in West Virginia as enclosure ("American Ginseng").

97. For absentee ownership, see Dunaway, *First American Frontier*. Ronald L. Lewis aptly describes the timber harvests as transforming the southern mountain region, and his fine book traces these transformations (*Transforming*).

98. Eller, *Miners*, 86–93; Mastran and Lowerre, *Mountaineers and Rangers*, 8–10.

99. Mastran and Lowerre, *Mountaineers and Rangers*, 2–3.

100. Ibid., 1–2; Eller, *Miners*, 101.

101. Eller, *Miners*, 101–4.

102. Ibid., 104–5, 110; Mastran and Lowerre, *Mountaineers and Rangers*, 2–3; Archives of Appalachia, "Harvesting the Hardwoods" website, esp. 2, "W. M. Ritter and Other Logging Companies."

103. Davis, *Where There Are Mountains*, 170; Eller, *Miners*, 103–4; Lewis, *Transforming*, 83.

104. Eller, *Miners*, 103–4; Mastran and Lowerre, *Mountaineers and Rangers*, 2.

105. Eller, *Miners*, 108–9.

106. Lewis, *Transforming*, 45–80; Eller, *Miners*, 44–64; Mastran and Lowerre, *Mountaineers and Rangers*, 3–5.

107. Community Research Center, "A Socioeconomic Overview." For one example of the workings of such a market, see Burnett, "Hog Raising."

108. *Message from the President*, 24; Kephart, *Our Southern Highlanders*, 457.

109. Eller, *Miners*, 54–57; Lewis, *Transforming*, 85–92; Mastran and Lowerre, *Mountaineers and Rangers*, 1–8. For the Cherokee example, see Smith, "Appalachian National Park Movement," 64.

110. Mastran and Lowerre, *Mountaineers and Rangers*, 4–5.

111. Davis, *Where There Are Mountains*, 181–82; Eller, *Miners*, 64; Mastran and Lowerre, *Mountaineers and Rangers*, 4–6.

112. Silver, *Mount Mitchell*, 144–49; Mastran and Lowerre, *Mountaineers and Rangers*, 8–10, 38–39; Lewis, *Transforming*, 263–92.

TWO. Response to Devastation

1. Pinchot, *Biltmore Forest*; Pinchot, *Breaking New Ground*. For information on the Chicago World's Fair, see Burg, *Chicago's White City*.

2. Pinchot, *Biltmore Forest*, 14, 18, 21.

3. Ibid., 21–22.

4. Ibid., 48, 49.

5. There are countless writings about Gifford Pinchot, but Char Miller's nuanced biography is the standard source for his life and career (*Gifford Pinchot*). Pinchot himself left a lively autobiography (*Breaking New Ground*).

6. For an insightful analysis of how native forests resist systematization, see Scott, *Seeing like a State*, 11–84. Pinchot wrote about Biltmore in Pinchot, *Breaking New Ground*, 47–69. Carl Schenck offered his account in Schenck, *Birth of Forestry*. For a compelling account of forest management failures in the Douglas fir region, see Langston, *Forest Dreams*.

7. Pinchot, *Biltmore Forest*, 11–13.

8. See Lewis, *Forest Service*, 11–23.

9. Ibid., 20–21, 34–35.

10. Ibid., 36–42. See also Klyza, *Who Controls*, 70–73; Hirt, *Conspiracy of Optimism*, 31–34; Steen, *U.S. Forest Service*, 7–9; Frome, *The Forest Service*, 12–20; Dan Morgan, "USDA Proposes Options for Usage of Wilderness," *Washington Post*, June 16, 1978.

11. Klyza, *Who Controls*, 73–76; Hirt, *Conspiracy of Optimism*, 30–31, 34; Frome, *The Forest Service*, 19–21.

12. Pinchot quotes from Klyza, *Who Controls*, 73. See also Hirt, *Conspiracy of Optimism*, 31–34; Klyza, *Who Controls*, 68–76. For discussions of the Hetch-Hetchy issue, see Miller, *Gifford Pinchot*, 138–44; Nash, *Wilderness and the American Mind*, 161–81; Rothman, *Saving the Planet*, 55–59. See also Frome, *The Forest Service*, 22–23; Robinson, *The Forest Service*, 155; Gottlieb, *Forcing the Spring*, 28–29.

13. Miller, *Gifford Pinchot*, 118; Hirt, *Conspiracy of Optimism*, 32–34; Frome, *The Forest Service*, 19–24; Klyza, *Who Controls*, 73.

14. For an account of the "Ballinger-Pinchot controversy" that led not only to Pinchot's sacking but also to Interior Secretary Richard Achilles Ballinger's resignation and ultimately contributed to William Howard Taft's losing the White House, see Miller, *Gifford Pinchot*, 206–38.

15. Klyza, *Who Controls*, 73–76; Hirt, *Conspiracy of Optimism*, 32–34.

16. Hays, *American People*; Shands and Healy, *Lands Nobody Wanted*, 42.

17. Pinchot, *Breaking New Ground*, 47–49; Miller, *Gifford Pinchot*, 101–7.

18. Pinchot, *Breaking New Ground*, 3, 5; Miller, *Gifford Pinchot*, 53–54, 78–80, 91–92.

19. For a history of the Biltmore Forest School, see Schenck, *Birth of Forestry*. The U.S. Forest Service's "Cradle of Forestry in America" site in Pisgah National Forest commemorates and interprets the school's history. See Cradle of Forestry website.

20. Eller, *Miners*, 115–17; Mastran and Lowerre, *Mountaineers and Rangers*, 17–18. For Pinchot's role in the Forest Service, see Frome, *Forest Service*, 12, 19–24; Steen, *U.S. Forest Service*; Robinson, *The Forest Service*, 8–11; Klyza, *Who Controls*, 70–76. For Pinchot's role in U.S. conservation generally, see Hays, *Conservation*.

21. Mastran and Lowerre, *Mountaineers and Rangers*, 13; Eller, *Miners*, 102–3.

22. Pinchot claimed he was the first, but this was an exaggeration, as Char Miller demonstrates in his fine biography of the ambitious forester (*Gifford Pinchot*, 105–7).

23. Pinchot, *Breaking New Ground*, 61; Schenck, *Birth of Forestry*, 30.

24. Schenck, *Birth of Forestry*, 30; Pinchot, *Breaking New Ground*, 17.

25. Pinchot, *Breaking New Ground*, 22, 65.

26. Ibid., 22, 61; Pinchot, *Biltmore Forest*, 14. Pinchot also described mountain people with evident pleasure and even admiration. For instance, of his "special pal"

Jimmy Case, he wrote: "He could neither read nor write, but no truer gentleman ever stepped." He recalled appreciatively a tombstone epitaph he found at a little house deep in the mountains: "He left this country better than he found it." Pinchot also remembered spending "a pleasant day" fishing with an accused murderer and concluded of this seemingly "harmless sort of fellow": "Somebody must have picked on him pretty hard." And he fondly described a mountain dinner he attended at which "the banquet was still walking around" when he arrived. He and another guest shot chickens for their supper, then waited through a long preparation time. "No banquet in my honor has ever pleased me more," he concluded (Pinchot, *Breaking New Ground*, 60–63). Schenck, far more than Pinchot, routinely differentiated the "better class," "better element," or "best element" of mountain residents from the "bad element." Into the former group he put religious farming families, even if poor, and into the latter group he put moonshiners. He described himself as "friendly" with the first group (Schenck, *Birth of Forestry*, 63–66).

27. Schenck, *Birth of Forestry*, 30.

28. Ibid., 28.

29. Ibid., 97.

30. Ibid., 65. For a more detailed discussion of moonshine from a slightly later period in nearby counties, see Kephart, *Our Southern Highlanders*, 110–90. Like Schenck, Kephart believed that many people feared moonshiners, but he also thought that many had sympathy for the distillers, largely because they recognized how difficult it was to earn a living in the mountains. For rich discussion of moonshiners see Stewart, *Moonshiners and Prohibition*.

31. Schenck, *Birth of Forestry*, 65–66.

32. Ibid. There are compelling parallels in the Adirondacks around the same time. Residents shot at perceived agents of enclosure, including patrolling state foresters; at least one private estate owner was shot to death (Jacoby, *Crimes against Nature*, 11–78; for shootings, see 37, 41).

33. Schenck, *Birth of Forestry*, 52, 30.

34. Gifford Pinchot had long advocated this move and played a key role in bringing it about (Lewis, *Forest Service*, 34–42).

35. This discussion is taken largely from ibid., 18–42.

36. Smith, "Appalachian National Park Movement," 41–65; Eller, *Miners*, 115; Steen, *U.S. Forest Service*, 123.

37. Smith, "Appalachian National Park Movement," 41.

38. Ibid., 41–42.

39. Ibid., 42–44.

40. Ibid., 44–46.

41. Ibid., 46–48; Whisnant, *Super-Scenic Motorway*, 27–28. See also Brown, *Wild East*, 81; Mastran and Lowerre, *Mountaineers and Rangers*, 16.

42. Brown, *Wild East*, 81.

43. Ibid., 81–82; Mastran and Lowerre, *Mountaineers and Rangers*, 16; Pinchot, *Breaking New Ground*, 238–39. Margaret Brown suggests that timber and railroad lawyer George Smathers likely played a role in shifting the group's emphasis from park to forest reserve. I have no doubt she is correct, but I am convinced Gifford Pinchot also had a hand in the move. He was aware of the proposed organization

before its inaugural meeting and expressed early support. Its legislative strategy has his master tactician fingerprints all over it. After consultations with Pinchot, Appalachian National Park Association lobbyist M. V. Richards worked with Senator Jeter C. Pritchard to develop a strategy that put the Department of Agriculture rather than the Interior in charge of federal investigations into the park proposal. Pritchard introduced an amendment to fiscal 1901's *agriculture* appropriation bill, proposing funding for an examination of southern mountain lands as a preliminary step toward establishing a park. The amendment went to the Senate Committee on Agriculture and Forestry, and in revised form it secured $5,000 for southern Appalachian forest investigations, enabling the pivotal 1902 report on southern forest conditions prepared under Agriculture Secretary James Wilson and sent to Congress by President Theodore Roosevelt. For Richards's and Pritchard's legislative strategy, including Pinchot's role, see Smith, "Appalachian National Park Movement," 51–52, 56–59.

44. *Message from the President*, 13; Mastran and Lowerre, *Mountaineers and Rangers*, 16.

45. Pritchard descriptions from "North Carolina May Cast Republican Vote," *New York Times*, September 28, 1902. For more on Jeter Connelly Pritchard, see Powell, *Dictionary*. See also Brown, *Wild East*, 80–81.

46. "Forest reserve" quote from *Message from the President*, 13; see also Shands and Healy, *Lands Nobody Wanted*, 13–14.

47. Pinchot, *Breaking New Ground*, 238–39; Hall, "To Remake," 321; Mastran and Lowerre, *Mountaineers and Rangers*, 16. The forests Wilson's team viewed from Mount Mitchell would be nearly all liquidated fifteen years later. See Silver, *Mount Mitchell*, 143–54.

48. Steen, *U.S. Forest Service*, 122–29; Brinkley, *Wilderness Warrior*, 667; Mastran and Lowerre, *Mountaineers and Rangers*, 10, 16. See also *Message from the President*.

49. *Message from the President*, 26; Mastran and Lowerre, *Mountaineers and Rangers*, 16.

50. *Message from the President*; Steen, *U.S. Forest Service*, 123–24.

51. Steen, *U.S. Forest Service*, 124; *Message from the President*; Eller, *Miners*, 115.

52. Steen, *U.S. Forest Service*, 124; Mastran and Lowerre, *Mountaineers and Rangers*, 16; *Message from the President*; Eller, *Miners*, 116–17.

53. Steen, *U.S. Forest Service*, 124; Mastran and Lowerre, *Mountaineers and Rangers*, 16.

54. Mastran and Lowerre, *Mountaineers and Rangers*, 16; Steen, *U.S. Forest Service*, 124–25; Smith, "Appalachian National Park Movement," 57–58.

55. Roosevelt quoted in Brinkley, *Wilderness Warrior*, 667. See also Mastran and Lowerre, *Mountaineers and Rangers*, 16.

56. Steen, *U.S. Forest Service*, 124; Eller, *Miners*, 117; "The Nation: Uncle Joe Cannon: Iron Duke of Congress," *Time Magazine*, January 15, 1973.

57. Mastran and Lowerre, *Mountaineers and Rangers*, 16; Pinchot, *Breaking New Ground*, 239; quote from Brinkley, *Wilderness Warrior*, 667, see also 758.

58. Brown, *Wild East*, 92; Steen, *U.S. Forest Service*, 125.

59. Steen, *U.S. Forest Service*, 125–27; Mastran and Lowerre, *Mountaineers and Rangers*, 16–17.

60. Quotes from Mastran and Lowerre, *Mountaineers and Rangers*, 17. See also Steen, *U.S. Forest Service*, 125.

61. Steen, *U.S. Forest Service*, 126.

62. Ibid., 126–27.

63. Shands and Healy, *Lands Nobody Wanted*, 14–15.

64. Mastran and Lowerre, *Mountaineers and Rangers*, 17; quote from Steen, *U.S. Forest Service*, 128.

65. Steen, *U.S. Forest Service*, 125–27.

66. Mastran and Lowerre, *Mountaineers and Rangers*, 17; Steen, *U.S. Forest Service*, 127–28.

67. Weeks Act; Mastran and Lowerre, *Mountaineers and Rangers*, 17–18.

68. Weeks Act.

69. Ibid.

70. Mastran and Lowerre, *Mountaineers and Rangers*, 17.

THREE. Plenty of Trouble

1. R. Clifford Hall to the Assistant Forester, July 8, 1911, Valuations 1911–21, box 2, Examinations New Hampshire–North Carolina, folder NC 1911, DLA, NA.

2. Ibid. In that folder see also Daniel W. Adams to the Forester, July 20, 1911.

3. See *United States v. Hiawassee Lumber Co.*, 238 U.S. 553 (1915). See also Smathers, *History of Land Titles*, 110–11. No mention of anything resembling Holland's proffered testimony appears in available court records.

4. For more on these issues, see Lewis, *Transforming*; Brown, *Wild East*; Eller, *Miners*.

5. R. Clifford Hall to Mr. Clyde Leavitt, Acting Assistant Forester, August 21, 1911, Valuations 1911–21, box 2, Examinations New Hampshire–North Carolina, folder NC 1911, DLA, NA.

6. Bolgiano, *Appalachian Forest*, 106, 110; Mastran and Lowerre, *Mountaineers and Rangers*, 25–29.

7. For a landmark account of the turn-of-the-century timber harvests in West Virginia, see Lewis, *Transforming*. For a classic western North Carolina perspective, see Eller, *Miners*, 86–112. Also see Davis, *Where There Are Mountains*, 166–82; Mastran and Lowerre, *Mountaineers and Rangers*, 1–11. The "multiple-use" concept became law under the 1960 Multiple-Use Sustained-Yield Act. The act aimed to require the Forest Service to place other uses—watershed protection, range management, and the like—alongside its preferred emphasis on timber management. See Hays, *American People*, 14, 54, 56, 92–94.

8. Mastran and Lowerre, *Mountaineers and Rangers*, 23; Eller, *Miners*, 117.

9. Shands and Healy, *Lands Nobody Wanted*, 265–67.

10. Mastran and Lowerre, *Mountaineers and Rangers*, 17, 23; Eller, *Miners*, 117; Pomeroy and Yoho, *North Carolina Lands*, 211.

11. For acreage figures, see Mastran and Lowerre, *Mountaineers and Rangers*, table 2, "The 11 Original National Forest Purchase Units in the Southern Appalachians," 23.

12. Initial gross acreage numbers for the 1911 and 1912 purchase units are as fol-

lows. Entirely in North Carolina: Mount Mitchell, 214,992; Pisgah, 358,577; Yadkin, 194,496; Boone, 241,462. Together these total 1,009,527 acres. Partially in North Carolina: Nantahala, 595,419; Smoky Mountains, 604,934; Georgia, 475,899; Unaka, 473,533. Together these total 2,149,785 acres. Precise state-specific numbers for these initial multistate purchase units are not readily available. I base my estimates on maps available in Mastran and Lowerre (*Mountaineers and Rangers*, 23, 28), which seem to indicate that roughly a third of the total multistate lands lay in North Carolina, or around 700,000 acres. Note that in table 2, "The 11 Original National Forest Purchase Units in the Southern Appalachians," meticulous researchers Mastran and Lowerre made a rare mistake. They list 1,412,952 as the total "initial gross acreage" for all eleven original southern Appalachian national forest purchase units. This number actually represents only the total acreage of the four purchase units established in 1912. The seven units established in 1911 totaled 2,591,205 acres. Thus, the actual total "initial gross acreage" for the eleven original southern Appalachian purchase units is 4,004,157, far greater than the total given in the table.

13. Mastran and Lowerre, *Mountaineers and Rangers*, 17–18, 28–29; Davis, *Where There Are Mountains*, 171–73; Eller, *Miners*, 112–18; Lewis, *Transforming*, 286–88. For a good concise discussion of the origins of national forests in the East, see Shands, "The Lands Nobody Wanted."

14. Mastran and Lowerre, *Mountaineers and Rangers*, 17–18, 28–29. For a recent report of 327 Cherokee acres in North Carolina, see the USFS website, "FY 2009 National Forest Acreage."

15. For a recent report of the still inactive Yadkin purchase unit, see the USFS website, "FY 2009 National Forest Acreage." See also Mastran and Lowerre on Yadkin in *Mountaineers and Rangers*, 23.

16. Mastran and Lowerre, *Mountaineers and Rangers*, 23, 26–27; Brown, *Wild East*, 89–90; Eller, *Miners*, 116.

17. Mastran and Lowerre, *Mountaineers and Rangers*, 26; Silver, *Mount Mitchell*, 144–53.

18. Mastran and Lowerre, *Mountaineers and Rangers*, 23, 25–29.

19. Hall, "To Remake," 322; Mastran and Lowerre, *Mountaineers and Rangers*, 28; *Report of the Secretary*. Rhode Island's land area is 1,045 square miles.

20. Mastran and Lowerre, *Mountaineers and Rangers*, 28.

21. Hall, "Influences," 402–3.

22. Mastran and Lowerre, *Mountaineers and Rangers*, 23.

23. Brown, *Wild East*; Whisnant, *Super-Scenic Motorway*; Perdue and Martin-Perdue, "Appalachian Fables."

24. For an illuminating discussion of government mapmaking, see Scott, *Seeing like a State*, 11–84. Even the most accurate maps left out information that could be important to local people. For instance, USFS researchers Rodney Snedeker and Michael Harmon noted that moonshiners located stills "in coves or ravines that are not evident on U.S. Geological Survey maps" ("Identification").

25. A. L. Hardin to Clyde Leavitt, note on letter from Clyde Leavitt to County Surveyor, March 22, 1911; J. C. Drake to Hon. Clyde Leavitt, March 25, 1911; T. R. Zachary to Mr. Clyde Leavitt, March 29, 1911; all from folder Pisgah 1911–15, box 36, Supervision, DLA, NA.

26. Mastran and Lowerre, *Mountaineers and Rangers*, 25.

27. Percy Ferebee, Boundary Survey Progress Report for Month of June 1914; Boundary Survey Progress Report for Month of July 1914; Boundary Survey Progress Report for Month of August 1914; Boundary Survey Progress Report for Month of February 1915; all in Land Surveys 1911–15, Appalachian Units, box 49, Nantahala Surveys, folder Nantahala Surveys, 1911–15, DLA, NA.

28. Ferebee, Boundary Survey Progress Report for Month of August 1914.

29. Schenck, *Birth of Forestry*, 23, 33; Pinchot, *Biltmore Forest*, "Map of Biltmore Forest," n.p.; James Denman to Assistant Forester, June 21, 1914, Surveys 1911–15, DLA, NA.

30. Mastran and Lowerre, *Mountaineers and Rangers*, 25.

31. U.S. discussions of nontimber forest products were still in their infancy in 2002, when the University of Kansas published the first book-length survey of the topic. See Jones, McLain, and Weigand, *Nontimber Forest Products*.

32. R. Clifford Hall to Assistant Forester, July 8, 1911, Valuations 1911–21, box 2, Examinations New Hampshire–North Carolina, folder NC 1911, DLA, NA.

33. William L. Hall to R. Clifford Hall, July 13, 1911, Valuations 1911–21, box 2, Examinations New Hampshire–North Carolina, folder NC 1911, DLA, NA.

34. L. L. Bishop to Assistant Forester, June 8, 1914; W. W. Ashe to L. L. Bishop, June 12, 1914; table 5, "Stand per Acre of Species and Products and Value per Acre of Tract"; all in Supervision 1913–15, box 36, Mount Mitchell, DLA, NA.

35. Clifford Hall to Forester, telegram, June 6, 1911, Valuations 1911–21, box 2, Examinations New Hampshire–North Carolina, folder NC 1911, DLA, NA.

36. Mr. Diffenbach, telegram, December 10, 1914, Surveys 1911–15, box 50, Appalachian Units, folder Nantahala Surveys, DLA, NA; Harold G. Wood, Report for Month of July 1912, Valuations 1911–21, box 49, Nantahala Surveys, DLA, NA.

37. R. Clifford Hall to Mr. Clyde Leavitt, Acting Assistant Forester, August 21, 1911, Valuations 1911–21, box 2, Examinations New Hampshire–North Carolina, folder NC 1911, DLA, NA.

38. O. D. Ingall, Report for October 7th–31st inclusive, Work Record, enclosure with letter from O. D. Ingall to the Forester, November 4, 1911, Valuations 1911–21, box 2, Examinations New Hampshire–North Carolina, folder NC 1911, DLA, NA.

39. Nantahala Area Report of Field Party for November 1911, Valuations 1911–21, box 2, Examinations New Hampshire–North Carolina, folder NC 1911, DLA, NA. Eventually, a "miscellaneous" category appeared in the reports, and supervisors could conceivably put days such as Ingall described in that catch-all.

40. Wood, Report for Month of July 1912.

41. James Denman, Nantahala Area—Olmstead Surveys, Boundary Survey Progress Report for Month of July 1913, Valuations 1911–21, box 49, Nantahala Surveys, folder Nantahala Surveys 1911–15, DLA, NA.

42. O. D. Ingall to the Forester, November 4, 1911, Valuations 1911–21, box 2, Examinations New Hampshire–North Carolina, folder NC 1911, DLA, NA.

43. O. D. Ingall to the Forester, November 16, 1911, Valuations 1911–21, box 2, Examinations New Hampshire–North Carolina, folder NC 1911, DLA, NA.

44. O. D. Ingall to the Forester, December 2, 1911, Valuations 1911–21, box 2, Examinations New Hampshire–North Carolina, folder NC 1911, DLA, NA.

45. R. Clifford Hall to Mr. Clyde Leavitt, Acting Assistant Forester, August 21, 1911, Valuations 1911–21, box 2, Examinations New Hampshire–North Carolina, folder NC 1911, DLA, NA.

46. Harold G. Wood to the Forester, December 5, 1912, Valuations 1911–21, box 36, Supervision, folder Nantahala 1911–12, DLA, NA.

47. For fallout of the Davis debacle, see O. D. Ingall to the Forester, July 15, 1912; O. D. Ingall to the Forester, July 21, 1912; R. F. Hemingway to the Forester, August 21, 1912; all in Valuations 1911–21, box 36, Supervision, folder Nantahala 1911–12, DLA, NA.

48. R. Clifford Hall to the Assistant Forester, February 6, 1914, Valuations 1911–21, box 36, Mount Mitchell Supervision, 1913–15, folder Mount Mitchell 1913–14, DLA, NA.

49. O. D. Ingall to the Forester, July 15, 1912, Valuations 1911–21, box 36, Supervision, folder Nantahala 1911–12, DLA, NA.

50. O. D. Ingall to the Forester, July 21, 1912, Valuations 1911–21, box 36, Supervision, folder Nantahala 1911–12, DLA, NA.

51. Pinchot, *Breaking New Ground*, 52; Hall, "To Remake," 328.

52. O. D. Ingall to the Forester, October 25, 1911, Valuations 1911–21, box 2, Examinations New Hampshire–North Carolina, folder NC 1911, DLA, NA.

53. O. D. Ingall to the Forester, November 13, 1911, Valuations 1911–21, box 2, Examinations New Hampshire–North Carolina, folder NC 1911, DLA, NA.

54. Daniel W. Adams to the Forester, August 25, 1911, Valuations 1911–21, box 2, Examinations New Hampshire–North Carolina, folder NC 1911, DLA, NA.

55. James Denman to the Assistant Forester, June 21, 1914, Surveys 1911–15, DLA, NA.

56. R. F. Hemingway to the Assistant Forester, April 3, 1915, Valuations, 1911–40, box 2, folder NC 1915 and 1916, DLA, NA.

57. Pinchot, *Breaking New Ground*, 52; Hall, "To Remake," 328.

58. Hall, "To Remake," 328.

59. Quote is from Arthur, *Western North Carolina*, 514.

60. Daniel W. Adams to the Forester, August 25, 1911, Valuations 1911–21, box 2, Examinations New Hampshire–North Carolina, folder NC 1911, DLA, NA. For other examples, see Brown, *Wild East*, 54–55; Eller, *Miners*, 54–64; Lewis, *Transforming*, 87–92.

61. Mastran and Lowerre, *Mountaineers and Rangers*, 26.

62. August 12, 1940, USFS report, "A List of Different Things the Forest Service and Forest Officers Do Which Influence Residents," quoted in Mastran and Lowerre, *Mountaineers and Rangers*, 70.

63. For timber and coal, see Eller, *Miners*, 44–64; Brown, *Wild East*, 54–55. For NPS examples, see Brown, *Wild East*, 92–99; Whisnant, *Super-Scenic Motorway*, 108–55.

64. Clarke-McNary Act, June 7, 1924.

65. Mastran and Lowerre, *Mountaineers and Rangers*, 43.

66. Otto, "Decline of Forest Farming"; Mastran and Lowerre, *Mountaineers and Rangers*, 46.

67. Lutts, "Like Manna"; Davis, *Where There Are Mountains*, 192–98.

68. Mastran and Lowerre, *Mountaineers and Rangers*, 44.

69. Ibid. For a perceptive exploration of the critically important role the CCC played in the New Deal and far beyond, see Maher, *Nature's New Deal*. For an insightful exploration of the New Deal's emphasis on conservation programs and its role in reshaping the contours of rural America, see Phillips, *This Land, This Nation*. The story of New Deal era national forest acquisitions adheres closely to the lines Phillips traces for the nation as a whole.

70. Mastran and Lowerre, *Mountaineers and Rangers*, 71.

71. Ibid., 53. The National Forest Reservation Commission noted the order in its minutes for June 9, 1933. Roosevelt's "Hundred Days" ended June 16.

72. Mastran and Lowerre, *Mountaineers and Rangers*, 53–54.

73. This relocation hope typically went unfulfilled. One of the failures of these programs was their inability to help dislocated people find satisfactory new situations.

74. Pomeroy and Yoho, *North Carolina Lands*, table 49, p. 217. Total Nantahala and Pisgah acreage in 1930: 389,924; in 1940: 791,665.

75. Mastran and Lowerre, *Mountaineers and Rangers*, 54.

76. Ibid., 50–51, 57.

77. Ibid., 54.

78. Ibid., 53.

79. Report quoted in ibid., 61.

80. Pomeroy and Yoho, *North Carolina Lands*, 217; "National Forests in the Southern Appalachians," 25, 30; Mastran and Lowerre, *Mountaineers and Rangers*, 53–57; Shands, "The Lands Nobody Wanted," 21–35.

81. Quote is from "One Function of Forest Service Is to Uphold Laws," *Franklin Press*, March 25, 1982. For USFS history, see Mastran and Lowerre, *Mountaineers and Rangers*, 30, 48, 53–57; Eller, *Miners*, 118–21; Bolgiano, *Appalachian Forest*, 123–230.

82. For an example of commons lost to industrial destruction in West Virginia, see Hufford, "American Ginseng."

83. Mastran and Lowerre, *Mountaineers and Rangers*, 25. See Langston, *Forest Dreams*, for discussions of USFS commitment to harvesting "overmature" or "decadent" forests.

84. Eller, *Miners*, 117–18; Mastran and Lowerre, *Mountaineers and Rangers*, 25, 27–28; Davis, *Where There Are Mountains*, 173. For the Great Smoky Mountains National Park, see Brown, *Wild East*; Pierce, *The Great Smokies*; Dunn, *Cades Cove*; Bramlett and Briggs, *The Road to Nowhere*. For the Shenandoah National Park, see Perdue and Martin-Perdue, "Appalachian Fables." For the Blue Ridge Parkway, see Whisnant, *Super-Scenic Motorway*. For the TVA, see Wheeler and McDonald, *TVA and the Tellico Dam*. For the Mount Rogers NRA, see Sarvis, "Mount Rogers."

85. Bolgiano, *Appalachian Forest*, 110; Mastran and Lowerre, *Mountaineers and Rangers*, 25–28.

86. Shands, "The Lands Nobody Wanted," 19–21; Mastran and Lowerre, *Mountaineers and Rangers*, 15, 25–28; Bolgiano, *Appalachian Forest*, 110. For example, see USFS maps such as "Nantahala National Forest, North Carolina" (see map, page xxiii). Note the blocky outlines on the small "key map." These indicate Nantahala

proclamation boundaries. Compare them to the shaded portions in the large map, which represent the lands actually owned by the USFS.

87. "Everybody's backyard" quote from Mary Kelly, interview.

FOUR. De Jure Commons

1. O. D. Ingall to the Forester, July 18, 1912, Valuations 1911–21, box 36, Supervision, folder Nantahala 1911–12, DLA, NA.

2. William L. Hall to O. D. Ingall, July 19, 1912, Valuations 1911–21, box 36, Supervision, folder Nantahala 1911–12, DLA, NA.

3. For population discussion, see Mastran and Lowerre, *Mountaineers and Rangers*, 30.

4. Ibid., 33–34, 63. Note that fifty dollars monthly was an attractive wage in the region at that time. For more on the importance of agency-local cooperation in fire prevention and fighting, see Sarvis, "An Appalachian Forest," 172, 175.

5. Mastran and Lowerre, *Mountaineers and Rangers*, 34, 61.

6. Ibid., 36.

7. Ibid., 57, 60–61; Sarvis, "An Appalachian Forest," 171, 175. 1940 USFS report quoted in Mastran and Lowerre, *Mountaineers and Rangers*, 61.

8. Eller, *Miners*, 117–18; Mastran and Lowerre, *Mountaineers and Rangers*, 30, 42.

9. See Eller, *Miners*, 118n102.

10. Nicholson quoted in Mastran and Lowerre, *Mountaineers and Rangers*, 30.

11. Adams and Rhoades quoted in ibid., 27.

12. Ibid., 27. For timbering history in the Mitchell area, see Silver, *Mount Mitchell*, 133–54.

13. Mastran and Lowerre, *Mountaineers and Rangers*, 23, 27; Eller, *Miners*, 116–17.

14. Mastran and Lowerre, *Mountaineers and Rangers*, 27; William L. Hall to D. W. Adams, September 15, 1911, Valuations 1911–21, box 2, Examinations New Hampshire–North Carolina, folder NC 1911, DLA, NA.

15. Nicholson quoted in Mastran and Lowerre, *Mountaineers and Rangers*, 30.

16. Verne Rhoades, "Report on the Unaka Area," Examinations, DLA, NA. The quote is on page 9 of the report. For discussions of the tax issue, see Mastran and Lowerre, *Mountaineers and Rangers*, 39, 55–56, 145–46.

17. Mastran and Lowerre, *Mountaineers and Rangers*, 39. For an exposé of hardships resulting from the "25 percent fund" policy, see Kahn, *Forest Service and Appalachia*.

18. Hall, "Influences," 404.

19. Ibid., 55.

20. Ibid., 55–56.

21. Graves quoted in Wallach, "Slighted Mountains."

22. Kahn, *Forest Service and Appalachia*, Fannin County quote, 16, other quotes on 28, 5–6, and frontispiece. Fannin County, Georgia, estimated its lost revenues at $150,000 annually and pointed to "a steady undermining of our tax base" by USFS land acquisition. For discussion of county government issues, see 7–16.

23. Ibid., 7, 11.

24. Mastran and Lowerre, *Mountaineers and Rangers*, 99. In 1941 the Army Corps

of Engineers condemned 59,000 acres in the Oak Ridge vicinity and evicted almost 1,000 families within weeks. The Manhattan Project's urgency prompted the fast-track removals, which left affected families reeling.

25. For land condemnation, see ibid., 27. Excellent explorations of the National Park Service removals have been produced by scholars of the Appalachians. See Brown, *Wild East*; Whisnant, *Super-Scenic Motorway*; Perdue and Martin-Perdue, "Appalachian Fables." For ongoing issues, see Bramlett and Briggs, *Road to Nowhere*. For final road settlement, see "70 Years Later, North Shore Road Dispute Ends in Swain County," *Asheville Citizen-Times*, February 7, 2010; and "$52 Million for NC Road That's Still Going Nowhere," AP report, February 2, 2010. For the TVA, see Wheeler and McDonald, *TVA and the Tellico Dam*. For a discussion of removals and environmental politics, see Williams, "'When I Can Read.'"

26. For a discussion of "friendly condemnation," see Mastran and Lowerre, *Mountaineers and Rangers*, 27, 58.

27. Ibid., 51.

28. Ibid., 56–57, 64–65; Eller, "Land as Commodity," 41; Mary Kelly, interview.

29. Mastran and Lowerre, *Mountaineers and Rangers*, 57. The minutes of the National Forest Reservation Commission for 1935 and 1936 are replete with examples. See National Forest Reservation Commission Minutes, Office of the Chief, Record Group 95, NA. The minutes have separate entries for each purchase unit.

30. Mastran and Lowerre, *Mountaineers and Rangers*, 57, 60–61, 65, 119; Hall, "Influences," 404.

31. Hall, "To Remake," 335–36.

32. Hall, "Influences," 403; Mastran and Lowerre, *Mountaineers and Rangers*, 30.

33. Citizens for Southwest Virginia quoted in Mastran and Lowerre, *Mountaineers and Rangers*, 153, and see also the Mount Rogers NRA discussion on 151–53. For an illuminating examination of the Mount Rogers issue, see Sarvis, "Mount Rogers."

34. O. D. Ingall to the Forester, November 13, 1911, Valuations 1911–21, box 2, Examinations New Hampshire–North Carolina, folder NC 1911, DLA, NA.

35. R. Clifford Hall to Mr. Clyde Leavitt, Acting Assistant Forester, August 21, 1911, Valuations 1911–21, box 2, Examinations New Hampshire–North Carolina, folder NC 1911, DLA, NA.

36. O. D. Ingall to the Forester, November 13, 1911, Valuations 1911–21, box 2, Examinations New Hampshire–North Carolina, folder NC 1911, DLA, NA. Much, though not all, of the crew in question was made up of men from the region. See O. D. Ingall to R. F. Hemingway, December 18, 1911; Rowland F. Hemingway to the Forester, December 20, 1911; Rowland F. Hemingway to the Forester, December 22, 1911; all in Valuations 1911–21, box 2, Examinations New Hampshire–North Carolina, folder NC 1911, DLA, NA.

37. James Denman to the Assistant Forester, June 5, 1913, Valuations 1911–21, box 49, Nantahala Surveys, folder Nantahala Surveys 1911–15, DLA, NA.

38. D. M. Gibson to William L. Hall, June 24, 1912, Surveys 1912–14, box 53, Georgia–Mount Mitchell, folder Mount Mitchell Surveys 1912, DLA, NA. For lumber camp wages, see Lewis, *Transforming*, 169, 172; Davis, *Where There Are Mountains*, 177.

39. O. D. Ingall to the Forester, received November 9, 1911, Valuations 1911–21, box 2, Examinations New Hampshire–North Carolina, folder NC 1911, DLA, NA.

40. Ibid.

41. Hall, "Influences," 404–5.

42. For more on the long history of Appalachian stereotyping, see Billings, Norman, and Ledford, *Backtalk from Appalachia*; and Shapiro, *Appalachia on Our Mind*.

43. For a classic study of this sort of reform, see Whisnant, *All That Is Native*.

44. R. F. Hemingway to the Forester, August 21, 1912, Valuations 1911–21, box 36, Supervision, folder Nantahala 1911–12, DLA, NA.

45. Mastran and Lowerre, *Mountaineers and Rangers*, 23; Daniel W. Adams to the Forester, August 11, 1911, Supervision, 1911–15, box 36, folder Nantahala 1, DLA, NA.

46. Robert J. Noyes to the Assistant Forester, December 30, 1914, Valuations, 1911–40, box 2, folder NC 1915 and 1916, DLA, NA.

47. Daniel W. Adams to the Forester, September 2, 1911, Valuations 1911–21, box 2, Examinations New Hampshire–North Carolina, folder NC 1911, DLA, NA.

48. Verne Rhoades to the Assistant Forester, February 25, 1915, Surveys, 1911–15, box 50, Appalachian Units, folder Pisgah Surveys, DLA, NA.

49. L. L. Bishop to the Assistant Forester, March 15, 1915, Supervision, 1911–15, box 36, folder Mount Mitchell Supervision, 1911–15, DLA, NA.

50. Rowland F. Hemingway to the Assistant Forester, November 20, 1913, Supervision, 1911–15, box 36, folder Nantahala 2, DLA, NA.

51. L. L. Bishop to the Assistant Forester, May 27, 1915, Supervision, 1911–15, box 36, folder Mount Mitchell Supervision, 1911–15, DLA, NA.

52. Robert J. Noyes quoted in Mastran and Lowerre, *Mountaineers and Rangers*, 28.

53. Thomas A. Cox Jr. to the Assistant Forester, August 17, 1914, Surveys 1911–15, box 50, Appalachian Units, folder Mount Mitchell Surveys, DLA, NA.

54. J. A. Allen claim, August 13, 1914; T. A. Dillingham claim, August 13, 1914; both claims attached to Thomas A. Cox Jr., "Claims of T. A. Dillingham et al. on property of Big Ivy Timber Co.," August 31, 1914; all in Surveys 1911–15, box 50, Appalachian Units, folder Mount Mitchell Surveys, DLA, NA.

55. Cox, "Claims of T. A. Dillingham et al."

56. Ibid.

57. Ibid.

58. Dillingham family history comes from Haile, *Dillinghams of Big Ivy:* Thomas Foster Dillingham, 222–25; Albert Gay Dillingham, 230–31; and Job Farris Dillingham, 249–50.

59. Thomas A. Cox Jr. to the Assistant Forester, August 17, 1914, Surveys 1911–15, box 50, Appalachian Units, folder Mount Mitchell Surveys, DLA, NA.

60. Cox, "Claims of T. A. Dillingham et al."

61. For a parallel instance of community solidarity in the face of perceived injustice, this one surrounding construction of the Blue Ridge Parkway, see Whisnant, *Super-Scenic Motorway*, 151–52. In Ashe County's Glendale Springs in 1936, where area families had long awaited payment for lands confiscated for the parkway, resi-

dents "without exception" claimed to know nothing about an incident in which some twenty trees were felled across the new road. Officials never made much headway on the case. It remained unsolved, and no prosecutions took place.

62. Mastran and Lowerre, *Mountaineers and Rangers*, 26–27. The rekindled movement for a national park in the Smoky Mountains emerged partly in response to these developments.

63. Eldredge quoted in ibid., 32; Nicholson quoted in ibid., 30.

64. Hall, "To Remake," 334; Eldredge quoted in Mastran and Lowerre, *Mountaineers and Rangers*, 18.

65. Hall, "To Remake," 334.

66. Ibid.

67. Claude Darnell quoted in Cheek, Nix, and Foxfire students, *Foxfire 40th Anniversary Book*, 466.

68. Stone quoted in Mastran and Lowerre, *Mountaineers and Rangers*, 37.

69. Hall, "To Remake," 334–35, 337.

70. See, for instance, incidents described in Mastran and Lowerre, *Mountaineers and Rangers*, 36–37, 65–67.

71. Quotes in this paragraph come from the fine discussion of relations between the Forest Service and moonshiners in Sarvis, "An Appalachian Forest," 174–76.

72. "National Forests in the Southern Appalachians," 9.

73. Conrad, *Land We Cared For*, chap. 4, "Region 7," section "The Attempt to Promote Grazing," http://www.foresthistory.org/ASPNET/Publications/region/9/history/chap4.aspx.

74. Will Zoellner and Richard Norton quoted in Cheek, Nix, and Foxfire students, *Foxfire 40th Anniversary Book*, 468–69.

75. R. M. "Mack" Dickerson quoted in ibid., 464–65.

76. For Pisgah National Game Preserve, see Mastran and Lowerre, *Mountaineers and Rangers*, 28. For a valuable discussion of wildlife management history on Virginia's Jefferson National Forest, see Sarvis, "Fisheries and Wildlife," 6–8. Pisgah and Nantahala history followed patterns similar to those Sarvis outlines for the Jefferson.

77. John H. Hatton, "Pisgah Fawn and Deer Capturing and Hunting Notes, etc. from Annual and Special Reports or Other Information," November 28, 1940, box #86, W Management R-1-WO, folder R-8 Pisgah Deer Fawn Rearing, Trapping, Transplanting, etc., 1940–41, National Forest Reservation Commission Minutes, Office of the Chief, Record Group 95, NA.

78. Ibid.

79. For a discussion of the "Virginia Plan," see Sarvis, "Fisheries and Wildlife," 6. Richard Norton quoted in Cheek, Nix, and Foxfire students, *Foxfire 40th Anniversary Book*, 468–69.

80. Rhoades, *Federal Forest Purchases*, 6.

81. Hall, "To Remake," 326. The Museum of the Cherokee Indian in Cherokee, North Carolina, includes an example of bark bucket technology in its Mississippian era displays.

82. Stanley Abbott correspondence quoted in Whisnant, *Super-Scenic Motorway*, 152.

83. Hall, "To Remake," 336, 337.

84. Hall, "Influences," 404.

85. Mastran and Lowerre, *Mountaineers and Rangers*, 96.

86. The USFS "Use Book" outlined the parameters of the free-use permit system. See *Use of National Forest Reserves*, 16–20.

87. For a discussion of the postwar Forest Service, see Hirt, *Conspiracy of Optimism*. See also Hays, *Wars in the Woods* and *American People*.

88. Miller, *Gifford Pinchot*, 357–61.

89. For a compelling analysis of the significance of the NFMA, see Hays, *Wars in the Woods*.

FIVE. Contested Forests

1. Ralph B. Sanders, "Feel Law Is Discriminatory," *Franklin Press*, August 3, 1978.

2. Jim Baker, "'Coon Power," *Asheville Citizen-Times*, October 14, 1979; "Local Coon Hunters Club Is Largest in the State," *Franklin Press*, August 11, 1982.

3. For an illuminating account of class dynamics in the history of hunting regulation, see Warren, *The Hunter's Game*. For a portrait of race and class dynamics in eastern North Carolina hunting, see Marks, *Southern Hunting*. For a cultural consideration of foxhunting, see Hufford, *Chaseworld*.

4. "'Coon Power."

5. Sanders, "Feel Law Is Discriminatory."

6. Dillingham did not allow Bolgiano to put words in his mouth. When she asked him if he considered it a spiritual connection, he said no: "That comes in from outsiders, the old hippie thing" (Bolgiano, *Appalachian Forest*, 232). For the importance of shared commons culture in contemporary West Virginia, see Hufford, "American Ginseng."

7. "Definition of Wilderness," 1964 U.S. Wilderness Act.

8. "Permit Is Needed to Harvest Plants," *Franklin Press*, April 2, 1981; "Fraser Cones to Be Available This Fall," *Franklin Press*, August 20, 1981; "Plan Released for Ginseng Sales," *Franklin Press*, September 21, 1978.

9. "Wood—an Economical, but Sometimes Dangerous Source of Energy," *Franklin Press*, December 31, 1981; "Sale of Green Standing Firewood Is Not Offered," *Franklin Press*, June 3, 1982; "The Woodcutters . . . 4150 Permits Issued in Pisgah Area," *Asheville Citizen-Times*, March 5, 1978.

10. "Couple's Battle Provides Inspiration," *Franklin Press*, September 21, 1978.

11. The TVA was a bit more complicated, as it also had regional aims of providing cheap electricity. Still, its toll was real. See Wheeler and McDonald, *TVA and the Tellico Dam*; Whisnant, *Modernizing*, 43–69; Mastran and Lowerre, *Mountaineers and Rangers*, 51–52.

12. Whisnant, *Super-Scenic Motorway*; Brown, *Wild East*; Dunn, *Cades Cove*; Perdue and Martin-Perdue, "Appalachian Fables."

13. Brown, *Wild East*, 92–99; Dunn, *Cades Cove*.

14. Whisnant, *Super-Scenic Motorway*, 108–55.

15. For an overview of the federal role in the Appalachians, see Whisnant, *Modernizing*. For the Great Smoky Mountains National Park, see Brown, *Wild East*;

Pierce, *The Great Smokies*; Dunn, *Cades Cove*; Bramlett and Briggs, *The Road to Nowhere*. For the Shenandoah National Park, see Perdue and Martin-Perdue, "Appalachian Fables." For the Blue Ridge Parkway, see Whisnant, *Super-Scenic Motorway*. For the TVA, see Whisnant, *Modernizing*, 43–69; Wheeler and McDonald, *TVA and the Tellico Dam*.

16. "Park Plan Is Target of Protest," *Asheville Citizen*, July 12, 1978.

17. Bolgiano, *Appalachian Forest*, 145; Bramlett and Briggs, *The Road to Nowhere*; Yarnell, *The Southern Appalachians*, 33; Mastran and Lowerre, *Mountaineers and Rangers*, 88–89.

18. "Interior Department Asks for Swain Settlement Plan," *Franklin Press*, October 12, 1978; Boyd Evison, letter to the editor, *Franklin Press*, August 24, 1978. The controversy finally ended in early 2010, when the federal government and Swain County officials agreed on a settlement of $52 million nullifying the 1943 federal pact to build the access road. See "70 Years Later, North Shore Road Dispute Ends in Swain County," *Asheville Citizen-Times*, February 7, 2010; and "$52 Million for NC Road That's Still Going Nowhere," AP report, February 2, 2010.

19. "Campers, Canoeists Create Problems at Nantahala," *Franklin Press*, September 14, 1978. Eventually, the Forest Service helped solve this problem by purchasing land, providing parking, and building restrooms and a boat ramp. See "Maybe This Would Help," *Franklin Press*, September 21, 1978; "New Access Area Planned," *Franklin Press*, November 30, 1978.

20. Taylor, "The Wilderness Question," 17; "Not Just for a Few," *Franklin Press*, July 6, 1978.

21. Taylor, "The Wilderness Question," 16.

22. Mary Kelly, interview. For hunting and culture, see Hufford, *Chaseworld*; Marks, *Southern Hunting*; Warren, *The Hunter's Game*.

23. Taylor, "The Wilderness Question," 17.

24. Ibid. See also Brown, *Wild East*; Pierce, *The Great Smokies*.

25. For examples of this pattern, see USFS maps such as "Nantahala National Forest, North Carolina." For history, see Shands, "The Lands Nobody Wanted." For a description, see Mary Kelly, interview. For local ill-will toward the Great Smoky Mountains National Park, see Brown, *Wild East*; Pierce, *The Great Smokies*; Dunn, *Cades Cove*; Bramlett and Briggs, *The Road to Nowhere*. For ill-will toward Shenandoah, see Perdue and Martin-Perdue, "Appalachian Fables."

26. Mastran and Lowerre, *Mountaineers and Rangers*, 33–34, 36–37, 63; Cook, interview.

27. The shift reflected a nationwide trend. The nation's timber demands skyrocketed in the postwar period, and between 1945 and 1970 national forest timber harvest levels rose—usually dramatically—under every president. Harvest numbers dipped briefly between 1970 and 1975 but climbed again beginning in 1976 and with accelerating speed in the 1980s. See Hirt, *Conspiracy of Optimism*, xxi–xxv, xliv, 87–93, 113–17, 235–42, 266–67. Also see Clary, *Timber*, chaps. 4–7, and epilogue, 94–199.

28. For discussions of these methods, see Smith, "Green Paper Number 15," March 1, 1989; and Padgett, "Clearcutting the National Forests"; both in Western North Carolina Alliance Archives.

29. For a useful introduction to the clear-cutting issue in western North Carolina, see Johnson, *Ready for Harvest*. For a proclearcutting forester's view, see McGee, "Clearcutting and Aesthetics." For discussion of the method's use in western North Carolina national forests, see Cook, interview. For national critics' views, see Hammond, "Clearcutting"; and Lansky, "Myths." See also Mastran and Lowerre, *Mountaineers and Rangers*, 144; Hirt, *Conspiracy of Optimism*, 131–32, 245–51; Clary, *Timber*, 156–68, 180–94. See also Rymer, "Wilderness Politics."

30. Hall, "To Remake," 338; Mastran and Lowerre, *Mountaineers and Rangers*, 144; McGee, "Clearcutting and Aesthetics." See also Rymer, "Wilderness Politics."

31. "DeHart, Independent Logger, Typical of Dwindling Breed," *Asheville Citizen*, February 10, 1974.

32. Hammond, "Clearcutting"; Lansky, "Myths"; Gilmour, interview; "Citizens Gather at Rally to Protest Clear-Cutting," *Times-News*, April 16, 1989.

33. McGee, "Clearcutting and Aesthetics," 541, 542, 544.

34. Cook, interview; Cut the Clearcutting! petition, Western North Carolina Alliance Archives.

35. Ibid.

36. Bolgiano, *Appalachian Forest*, 111–13; Robinson, *The Forest Service*, 77; Lewis, *Transforming*, 263–92.

37. Mastran and Lowerre, *Mountaineers and Rangers*, 144; Robinson, *The Forest Service*, 77.

38. Robinson, *The Forest Service*, 77; Bolgiano, *Appalachian Forest*, 113.

39. Robinson, *The Forest Service*, 77. Edward P. Cliff quoted in Hirt, *Conspiracy of Optimism*, 246.

40. Cliff, "Half a Century," 230–31. Cliff quoted in Hirt, *Conspiracy of Optimism*, 246. See also Robinson, *The Forest Service*, 77.

41. Robinson, *The Forest Service*, 77–78.

42. Mastran and Lowerre, *Mountaineers and Rangers*, 144; Robinson, *The Forest Service*, 78–79; Hirt, *Conspiracy of Optimism*, 251–56.

43. Bolgiano, *Appalachian Forest*, 113. Gifford Pinchot's son Gifford Bryce Pinchot was a founding member of the Natural Resources Defense Council board of directors. The younger Pinchot supported the organization's role in the Monongahela lawsuit. Some Forest Service personnel denounced the son as betraying his father's legacy, but Gifford Bryce believed he was upholding that legacy, since before his death the elder Pinchot had decried World War II era clearcuts as "tree butchery." See Miller, *Gifford Pinchot*, 357–61.

44. Hirt, *Conspiracy of Optimism*, 182–92, 229–33, 254–56, 260; Andrews, *Managing the Environment*, 308–11; Bolgiano, *Appalachian Forest*, 113; Robinson, *The Forest Service*, 79; Grumbine, "Policy," 255. Quote from Hirt, *Conspiracy of Optimism*, 254.

45. Hirt, *Conspiracy of Optimism*, 260–61; Andrews, *Managing the Environment*, 311; Bolgiano, *Appalachian Forest*, 113–14; Robinson, *The Forest Service*, 79.

46. Hirt, *Conspiracy of Optimism*, 261; Robinson, *The Forest Service*, 79–80; Mastran and Lowerre, *Mountaineers and Rangers*, 145. Quote from Robinson, *The Forest Service*, 79.

47. Bolgiano, *Appalachian Forest*, 114; Grumbine, "Policy," 255; Padgett, "Clearcutting the National Forests," 8.

48. Hirt, *Conspiracy of Optimism*, 261.

49. Ibid., 261–62; Bolgiano, *Appalachian Forest*, 114.

50. "Forest Chiefs Assail Ban on Clearcutting," *Asheville Citizen*, February 6, 1976.

51. Hays, *Wars in the Woods*, 16–19; Hirt, *Conspiracy of Optimism*, 261–62.

52. Quotes from Smith, "Green Paper Number 1," January 16, 1987; Padgett, "Clearcutting the National Forests," 9. See also National Forest Management Act of 1976; Smith, "Green Paper Number 2," February 12, 1987; Hirt, *Conspiracy of Optimism*, 260–65; Andrews, *Managing the Environment*, 311–12.

53. Quote from Padgett, "Clearcutting the National Forests," 10; Hirt, *Conspiracy of Optimism*, 260–65; Andrews, *Managing the Environment*, 311–12.

54. Hays, *Wars in the Woods*, 16–19. The conflict between "commodity forestry" and "ecological forestry" and the growing influence of ecological forestry over time are the subjects of Hays's illuminating book *Wars in the Woods*.

55. For a complete discussion of the timber emphasis within the USFS, see Clary, *Timber*. For analysis of "zoning" strategy, see Hirt, *Conspiracy of Optimism*, 162–66, 229–33. Also see Frome, *The Forest Service*, 187–88; Mastran and Lowerre, *Mountaineers and Rangers*, 167.

56. Multiple-Use Sustained-Yield Act, June 12, 1960; Hays, *American People*, 54, 56, 90–97; Frome, *The Forest Service*, 28.

57. Clary, *Timber*; Hirt, *Conspiracy of Optimism*, 1–39; Robinson, *The Forest Service*, 9–10, 14–16; Frome, *The Forest Service*, 71–79, 174–82, 190; Klyza, *Who Controls*, 67–108; Steen, "Origins and Significance."

58. Wilderness Act, September 3, 1964.

59. Turner, "Wilderness East"; Smith, "Eastern Wilderness"; Frome, *The Forest Service*, 187.

60. Roth, *Wilderness Movement, 1964–1980*.

61. Ibid., 19–22.

62. Ibid., 36–37.

63. Ibid., 37.

64. Ibid., 4–6, 39.

65. Ibid., 38–39.

66. Turner, "Wilderness East," quotes on 23.

67. This was the short title given in the Senate version of the document. The House version did not have a short title, and a short title was left off the final bill. See Scott, "Eastern Wilderness Areas Act."

68. Eastern Wilderness Areas Act, January 3, 1975.

SIX. Wilderness as Commons Enclosure

1. "Large Crowd Protests 'Wilderness," *Franklin Press*, July 13, 1978; "Park Plan Is Target of Protest," *Asheville Citizen*, July 12, 1978; Rymer, "Wilderness Politics"; Frome, *The Forest Service*, 194–95.

2. "Large Crowd Protests 'Wilderness' "; "Park Plan Is Target."

3. Mastran and Lowerre, *Mountaineers and Rangers*, 167–73; Rymer, "Wilderness Politics"; "Timber Industry Loss Questioned," *Asheville Citizen*, August 18, 1978; Ted Vaden, "Big Conservation Storm Hovering over Mountains," *Raleigh News and Observer*, July 30, 1978; Bolgiano, *Appalachian Forest*, 175; Cook, interview.

4. Mastran and Lowerre, *Mountaineers and Rangers*, 171; Cook, interview.

5. Historian Samuel Hays traces the decades-long national contest over forest management in his fine book *Wars in the Woods*. Hays frames the long series of disputes as a struggle between commodity forestry, on the one hand, and ecological forestry, on the other. This model has a great deal of explanatory power in the history of forest politics in western North Carolina. Commons users sometimes sided with "commodity forestry," as happened, for the most part, in the RARE II controversy. They sometimes sided with "ecological forestry," as happened in the case of the Southern Nantahala and in later battles over petroleum development and clearcutting.

6. Hirt, *Conspiracy of Optimism*, xli–xlv, 50–51, 131, 220; Mastran and Lowerre, *Mountaineers and Rangers*, 144; Vaden, "Big Conservation Storm."

7. Rymer, "Wilderness Politics"; "Gudger Questionnaire Shows Limited 'Wilderness' Support," *Asheville Citizen-Times*, April 30, 1978.

8. I include the newly designated Middle Prong Wilderness in this category, as it directly abutted existing Shining Rock Wilderness.

9. North Carolina Wilderness Act, 1984; "Taylor Crockett Remembers," *Wildlife in North Carolina*, February 1985, 18; "Forests and Trees," *Washington Post*, January 8, 1979; "Forest Service Seeking 36 Million More Aces for Timber and Mines," *New York Times*, January 5, 1979; "The Forest Service Opens 36 Million Acres and a Can of Worms," *New York Times*, January 7, 1979; Brian Sullam, "USDA Wilderness Proposal," *Journal of Commerce*, January 5, 1979.

10. Roth, *Wilderness Movement 1964–80*; Frome, *The Forest Service*, 188.

11. Frome, *The Forest Service*, 187–88; Cook, interview; Mastran and Lowerre, *Mountaineers and Rangers*, 167–72.

12. Turner, *Sierra Club*, 197.

13. For the pivotal role of the NFMA, see Hays, *Wars in the Woods*, 16–19.

14. Clyde Osborne, "New Wilderness Area Sites under Study," *Asheville Citizen-Times*, November 27, 1977; Frome, *The Forest Service*, 194.

15. Osborne, "New Wilderness Area Sites"; "Is Forest Service Neutral on Wilderness Issue?," *Asheville Citizen-Times*, December 18, 1977; "Forest Service Completes Wilderness Area Study," *Asheville Citizen-Times*, June 8, 1978.

16. "Is Forest Service Neutral."

17. Ibid.; Frome, *The Forest Service*, 189; Hirt, *Conspiracy of Optimism*, 229–30; "USDA Proposes Options for Usage of Wilderness," *Washington Post*, June 16, 1978.

18. "Is Forest Service Neutral"; "Forest Service Completes."

19. Klyza, *Who Controls*, 67–93; Frome, *The Forest Service*, 189–96; Cook, interview; Hays, *American People*, 15–19, 33–38, 41–45, 66–92.

20. Hirt, *Conspiracy of Optimism*, 162–66, 229–33; Klyza, *Who Controls*, 76–93; Andrews, *Managing the Environment*, 309; Cook, interview.

21. For a thorough discussion of the Forest Service's long-standing emphasis on

timber, see Clary, *Timber*, and for RARE II, see 176–77: "When wilderness threatened one of the material uses of a given area, the Forest Service was philosophically inclined to come down in favor of multiple use—though it was politically wise enough not to say so explicitly" (177). Also see Roth, *Wilderness Movement, 1964–80*, 54–61; for quote, see Cook, interview.

22. "Gudger Questionnaire"; "Survey Shows 'Limited Wilderness' Use Preferred," *Franklin Press*, May 11, 1978; "Forest Service Completes."

23. "Gudger Questionnaire"; "Survey Shows."

24. "Gudger Questionnaire"; "Survey Shows"; "Almost Three Million People Find Recreation in Pisgah during Year," *Asheville Citizen*, May 11, 1952; Mastran and Lowerre, *Mountaineers and Rangers*, 164; Ballew, interview; Taylor, "The Wilderness Question."

25. Quote in Frome, *The Forest Service*, 195.

26. "Not for Just a Few," *Franklin Press*, July 6, 1978. For a classic analysis of enclosure, see Thompson, *Whigs and Hunters*. For parallels between British and Appalachian enclosure history, see the introduction to Whisnant, *Modernizing*. For U.S. commons roots in English history, see Linebaugh, *Magna Carta Manifesto*; Crowe, "Tragedy of the Commons." For a discussion of commons thought in early New England conservation efforts, see Judd, *Common Lands*. For a discussion of contemporary Appalachian commons, see Hufford, "American Ginseng." For Appalachian national forests as commons, see Bolgiano, "National Forests." For U.S. enclosure case studies, see Schneider, "Enclosing the Floodplain"; Jacoby, "Class and Environmental History." For a treatment of southern uplands grazing commons enclosure, see Hahn, *Roots*; Durrill, "Producing Poverty"; Walpole, "Closing." For U.S. wilderness as enclosure, see Catton, *Inhabited Wilderness*; Johnson, "Conservation, Subsistence."

27. Osborne, "New Wilderness Area Sites"; Rymer, "Wilderness Politics"; Vaden, "Big Conservation Storm."

28. "Get the Facts and Write," *Franklin Press*, July 20, 1978.

29. "Not for Just a Few"; Vaden, "Big Conservation Storm."

30. In fact, between 1965 and 1971 wilderness proponents fought the National Park Service for proposing management plans for the Great Smoky Mountains National Park that threatened wilderness values through extensive road building. See Frome, *Battle for the Wilderness*, xlii, 176–86.

31. For an illuminating brief discussion of British enclosure as centuries-long process, see Snyder, "Understanding the Commons." For a treatment of cross-cultural commons enclosure processes, see McKay and Acheson, *Question of the Commons*. For commons management questions as struggles over resource allocation, see Baden and Noonan, *Managing the Commons*; and McKay and Acheson, *Question of the Commons*, especially McKay and Acheson, "Human Ecology."

32. For a classic treatment of class issues in commons struggles, see Thompson, *Whigs and Hunters*. See also Scott, *Domination*, 189–95. For class analysis of open-range issues in the New South, see Hahn, *Roots*, especially "Common Right and Commonwealth," 239–68, and "The Contours of Populism," 269–89. For a similar analysis of range issues in the North Carolina mountains, see Walpole, "Closing." For class and national forests, see Johnson, "Conservation, Subsistence." Also see

Jacoby, "Class and Environmental History," for class analysis and a discussion of absentee ownership in the Adirondacks forests.

33. "Not for Just a Few."

34. Osborne, "New Wilderness Area Sites."

35. Mastran and Lowerre, *Mountaineers and Rangers*, 170; Walter T. Buchanan, "Cites Timber as a Renewable Resource," *Franklin Press*, October 5, 1978.

36. Osborne, "New Wilderness Area Sites."

37. Frome, *Battle for the Wilderness*, 194–95; Mastran and Lowerre, *Mountaineers and Rangers*, 170; Osborne, "New Wilderness Area Sites"; "Not for Just a Few"; Vaden, "Big Conservation Storm"; Rymer, "Wilderness Politics."

38. "RARE Protest Sent to the President," *Franklin Press*, July 27, 1978; "Mineral Surveys Demanded on Proposed Wilderness Land," *Asheville Citizen*, September 1, 1978; Vaden, "Big Conservation Storm."

39. It is important to note that the Great Smoky Mountains National Park was not part of the National Wilderness Preservation System as established under the 1964 Wilderness Act. The legal differences between ordinary lands administered by the National Park Service and federally protected wilderness areas were substantial, but wilderness opponents routinely conflated the two. For more, see Frome, *Battle for the Wilderness*, xlii–xlvi, 176–86.

40. "RARE Protest Sent."

41. Ibid.

42. Ibid.

43. Ibid.

44. Ibid.

45. "Get the Facts and Write"; "Large Crowd Protests 'Wilderness'"; "Our Forests Are Proof," *Franklin Press*, September 28, 1978.

46. On timber versus other forest products, see Mastran and Lowerre, *Mountaineers and Rangers*, 164; "RARE Protest Sent"; "Gudger Opposes 'Any More Wilderness in WNC,'" *Franklin Press*, August 17, 1978; Vaden, "Big Conservation Storm."

47. Vaden, "Big Conservation Storm."

48. This set of ideas makes an interesting contrast with the idea of wilderness as sacred. See Cronon, "Trouble with Wilderness," and Nash, *Wilderness and the American Mind*, 156–60, for analyses of the divine wilderness idea.

49. Vaden, "Big Conservation Storm."

50. Bolgiano, *Appalachian Forest*, 175.

51. Mary Kelly, interview; Esther Cunningham, interview, September 9, 1999; Rymer, "Wilderness Politics"; Howe Crockett, "The Other Majorities Opinion," *Franklin Press*, August 3, 1978; Lester C. Waldroop Sr., "Wants Wilderness," *Franklin Press*, September 28, 1978.

52. "RARE Protest Sent."

53. Ibid.

54. Ibid.

55. Ibid. For an exploration of the pivotal relationship between automobiles and the wilderness movement in the first half of the twentieth century, see Sutter, *Driven Wild*. Debates in the second half of the century underscore the ongoing im-

portance of automobiles and other motorized vehicles in shaping wilderness politics. Like the wilderness advocates Sutter discusses, Southern Nantahala champions saw themselves as democratic wilderness promoters, though RARE II opponents cast wilderness as undemocratic.

56. "State Wildlife Officials Meet with Macon Sportsmen," *Franklin Press*, January 18, 1984; Vaden, "Big Conservation Storm."

57. Mastran and Lowerre, *Mountaineers and Rangers*, 169; "Ah, Wilderness . . . When Is Enough Enough?," *Watauga Democrat*, August 14, 1978.

58. Mastran and Lowerre, *Mountaineers and Rangers*, 171; "RARE II Meet in Town County," *Franklin Press*, July 20, 1978; "Company Would Mine in Wilderness Study Area," *Franklin Press*, July 27, 1978; Vaden, "Big Conservation Storm"; Rymer, "Wilderness Politics."

59. Buchanan, "Cites Timber."

60. Rymer, "Wilderness Politics"; Vaden, "Big Conservation Storm"; Cook, interview. USFS historians Mastran and Lowerre chronicle similar protests in other parts of the southern Appalachian region (*Mountaineers and Rangers*, 167–73).

61. Jay Hensley, "Timber Industry Loss Questioned," *Asheville Citizen*, August 18, 1978; Vaden, "Big Conservation Storm."

62. Mastran and Lowerre, *Mountaineers and Rangers*, 172; Vaden, "Big Conservation Storm"; "RARE Protest Sent"; "Why Do Citizens Burn Precious Dixie Forests?," *Asheville Citizen-Times*, April 16, 1978. For arson as a tool of commons defense, see Thompson, *Whigs and Hunters*, 147, 225–27; Jacoby, "Class and Environmental History"; and Walpole, "Closing."

63. Rogers quoted in Rymer, "Wilderness Politics."

64. Ibid.; "Congressman Hendon Inspects Olivine Deposits in Buck Creek," *Franklin Press*, June 15, 1981; "Hendon, Watt to Visit in District," *Franklin Press*, July 20, 1981; "Battle Waged on Wilderness Limits," *News and Observer*, June 14, 1981. For a useful in-depth discussion of Reagan's public lands policies, see Short, *Ronald Reagan*. Also see "The Reagan Antienvironmental Revolution," in Hays, *Beauty, Health, and Permanence*, 491–526; and "Our Land," in Lash, Gillman, and Sheridan, *A Season of Spoils*, 215–78. Brief discussions may be found in Hirt, *Conspiracy of Optimism*, 271–72; Andrews, *Managing the Environment*, 311–12; Klyza, *Who Controls*, 94–107; Frome, *The Forest Service*, 7–11.

65. "Wilderness Gets More Opposition," *Asheville Citizen*, September 20, 1978.

66. Kevin Marsh explores a series of specific instances of this kind of on-the-ground decision making in his fine study of national forest politics in the Pacific Northwest (*Drawing Lines*).

67. RARE II Final Environmental Statement; RARE II Southern Appalachian and Atlantic Coast States; Mastran and Lowerre, *Mountaineers and Rangers*, 167–72; "Is Forest Service Neutral"; "Forest Service Completes"; "Wilderness Plan Studied," *Asheville Citizen*, June 20, 1978; "Local Public Hearing on Wilderness July 11," *Franklin Press*, July 6, 1978; "Large Crowd Protests 'Wilderness.'"

68. Mastran and Lowerre, *Mountaineers and Rangers*, 169; Rymer, "Wilderness Politics."

69. Buchanan, "Cites Timber."

SEVEN. Wilderness as Commons Defense

1. The Middle Prong Wilderness Area was also new after RARE II, but as it was contiguous to Shining Rock, it was essentially a large extension of existing wilderness.

2. Rymer, "Wilderness Politics"; Lyman H. Ledbetter, "Sawmills Rest," *Franklin Press*, August 10, 1978; Howe Crockett, "The Other Majorities Opinion," *Franklin Press*, August 3, 1978.

3. J. S. Waldroop, "Favors Wilderness," *Franklin Press*, August 17, 1978; Ledbetter, "Sawmills Rest"; "Loggers Display Muscle," *Asheville Citizen-Times*, July 22, 1989.

4. For a complete discussion of the NFMA and the sea change it represented, see Hays, *Wars in the Woods*, 16–19.

5. Ted Vaden, "Big Conservation Storm Hovering over Mountains," *Raleigh News and Observer*, July 30, 1978. For the split between national groups and grassroots efforts, see Gottlieb, *Forcing the Spring*, 117–204; and Gottlieb, "Reconstructing Environmentalism."

6. Language emphasizing the large eastern population appeared frequently in the RARE II coverage. For examples, see "Carter Wilderness Initiative," *New York Times*, February 25, 1978; "Battle Waged on Wilderness Limits," *News and Observer*, January 14, 1981; "Forests and Trees," *Washington Post*, January 8, 1979.

7. Vaden, "Big Conservation Storm"; Jay Hensley, "Timber Industry Loss Questioned," *Asheville Citizen*, August 18, 1978.

8. Vaden, "Big Conservation Storm."

9. Rymer, "Wilderness Politics"; Martha Fort Prince, "Supports RARE II," *Franklin Press*, September 14, 1978; Crockett, "Taylor Crockett Remembers"; "Eighty Years in the Appalachian Woods," *Clay County Progress*, January 12, 1989; RARE II Southern Appalachian and Atlantic Coast States, 28.

10. Waldroop, "Favors Wilderness"; Crockett, "The Other Majorities Opinion"; Ledbetter, "Sawmills Rest"; Lester C. Waldroop Sr., "Wants Wilderness," *Franklin Press*, September 28, 1978; Clyde Osborne, "New Wilderness Area Sites under Study," *Asheville Citizen-Times*, November 27, 1977.

11. Rymer, "Wilderness Politics"; Crockett, "Taylor Crockett Remembers"; Taylor Crockett quoted in Fears, "Bear Hunting," 456–58.

12. Rymer, "Wilderness Politics."

13. Ibid.; Crockett, "Taylor Crockett Remembers."

14. "Eighty Years."

15. Crockett, "Taylor Crockett Remembers"; "Eighty Years."

16. Rymer, "Wilderness Politics"; Crockett, "Taylor Crockett Remembers." Other eastern wilderness advocates made the point that eastern lands could recover wilderness qualities. Benton MacKaye made this argument as early as 1929. See Sutter, *Driven Wild*, 175.

17. Waldroop, "Favors Wilderness"; Ledbetter, "Sawmills Rest."

18. Ledbetter, "Sawmills Rest."

19. Ibid.; Waldroop, "Favors Wilderness."

20. Crockett, "The Other Majorities Opinion"; Waldroop Sr., "Wants Wilderness."

21. Waldroop Sr., "Wants Wilderness"; Crockett, "The Other Majorities Opinion."

22. Crockett, "The Other Majorities Opinion"; Waldroop, "Favors Wilderness."

23. Waldroop Sr., "Wants Wilderness."

24. For payments in lieu of taxes, see Mastran and Lowerre, *Mountaineers and Rangers*, 145–46; H. Taylor Crockett, "Supports Wilderness Program," *Franklin Press*, September 21, 1978.

25. Crockett, "Supports Wilderness Program"; Crockett, "The Other Majorities Opinion"; Ledbetter, "Sawmills Rest."

26. Ledbetter, "Sawmills Rest"; Waldroop, "Favors Wilderness"; Crockett, "The Other Majorities Opinion."

27. Crockett, "Supports Wilderness Program." Crockett himself seemed less than enthusiastic about the prospect of hordes of tourists overrunning his beloved Nantahala, but he was willing to run this risk in order to protect the forest.

28. Ibid. For industry manipulation of numbers, see Hirt, *Conspiracy of Optimism*, 219–20, 255–56, 274–76; Mary Kelly, interview.

29. Crockett, "The Other Majorities Opinion"; Prince, "Supports RARE II"; Carl A. Reiche, "On RARE II," *Franklin Press*, October 5, 1978; Ledbetter, "Sawmills Rest."

30. Ledbetter, "Sawmills Rest"; Crockett, "The Other Majorities Opinion."

31. Waldroop, "Favors Wilderness"; Waldroop Sr., "Wants Wilderness"; Crockett, "The Other Majorities Opinion."

32. Waldroop, "Favors Wilderness"; Ledbetter, "Sawmills Rest."

33. Waldroop Sr., "Wants Wilderness"; Prince, "Supports RARE II." Alternative J was the last of the Forest Service's ten proposed alternatives. If enacted, it would make all RARE II study areas designated wilderness. All parties recognized that this alternative was not politically feasible (just as Alternative A, which took no action, was not politically feasible). Wilderness advocates charged that none of the other Forest Service alternatives offered acceptable levels of wilderness protection. National wilderness organizations advanced their own plan, Alternative W, which aimed to protect more—and different—wilderness than Forest Service Alternatives B through I without requiring the politically impossible total protection of Alternative J. See Hensley, "Timber Industry Loss Questioned"; RARE II Final Environmental Statement, v, 25–31; RARE II Southern Appalachian and Atlantic Coast States, 22–23, 28–29.

34. Waldroop, "Favors Wilderness."

35. "Wilderness Areas Favored in WNC," *Asheville Citizen*, November 24, 1978. For a full report of the responses, see RARE II Final Environmental Statement, U-40, U-41.

36. "Still Like to Drop It," *Franklin Press*, January 11, 1979.

37. "15-Million-Acre Addition to Wilderness Is Seen," *Washington Post*, January 4, 1979; "Wilderness Plan Revealed," *Asheville Citizen*, January 5, 1979; "Wilderness Designation Attacked as Too Large, Too Small," *Washington Post*, January 5, 1979; "Forest Service Seeking 36 Million More Acres for Timber and Mines," *New York Times*, January 5, 1979; "The Forest Service Opens 36 Million Acres and a Can of Worms," *New York Times*, January 7, 1979.

38. Roth, *Wilderness Movement, 1964–1980.*

39. Ibid.; Marsh, *Drawing Lines*, 126–27.

40. "Forest Service Seeking"; "The Forest Service Opens."

41. "Forests and Trees"; "Forest Service Seeking"; "The Forest Service Opens"; Brian Sullam, "USDA Wilderness Proposal," *Journal of Commerce*, January 5, 1979.

42. "Wilderness Plan Revealed"; "Sierra Club Scores Wilderness Proposal," *Asheville Citizen*, January 11, 1979.

43. Ibid.

44. Rymer, "Wilderness Politics"; "Wilderness Plan Revealed"; "Sierra Club Scores."

45. RARE II Final Environmental Statement, Q-5; "Wilderness Plan Revealed"; "Sierra Club Scores"; "Mineral Surveys Demanded on Proposed Wilderness Land," *Asheville Citizen*, September 1, 1978; "Study Says Mineral Potential High in Areas Proposed for Wilderness," *Asheville Citizen-Times*, September 17, 1978.

46. "Sierra Club Scores." For the role of timber organizing nationally, see Gottlieb, *Forcing the Spring*, 196; Hays, *Beauty, Health, and Permanence*, 300.

47. "Sierra Club Scores."

48. The eventual total in new wilderness was roughly 33,960 acres: 10,900 became Southern Nantahala, 7,900 became Middle Prong (these were the only two new wilderness areas, and Middle Prong abutted Shining Rock), 5,100 acres were added to Shining Rock, 3,680 to Ellicott Rock, 3,400 to Linville Gorge, and 2,980 to Joyce Kilmer–Slickrock. See North Carolina Wilderness Act of 1984, Public Law 98-324, June 19, 1984.

49. Charles Woodard, letter to the editor, *Franklin Press*, January 25, 1979.

50. "Still Like to Drop It."

51. "Forest Service Seeking"; "The Forest Service Opens"; "Forests and Trees."

52. North Carolina Wilderness Act of 1984; Rymer, "Wilderness Politics."

53. Crockett, "Taylor Crockett Remembers."

54. "What's Best? Think about It," *Franklin Press*, February 22, 1979.

55. "Still Like to Drop It."

EIGHT. Mobilizing Commons Defense

1. In *Who Controls the Public Lands?* Christopher M. Klyza identifies three historic strains of thought about public lands management in the United States. The first, economic liberalism, embraced the idea that public lands could best serve the national interest if they were fully opened to industrial development. The second, preservationism, argued that public lands could best serve the national interest by serving as reservoirs of undeveloped wilderness. The third, technocratic utilitarianism, espoused the view that a trained corps of expert technicians could best decide how to use public lands to serve the national interest. I argue that most longtime mountain residents rejected all three of these views and subscribed instead to a fourth way, a commons-inspired utilitarian model with a "use but don't abuse" approach to public lands management that valued multiple use and on-the-ground familiarity with the forest. The other theorist I have drawn heavily on is William Cronon, who described in his essay "The Trouble with Wilderness" the outlines and

limitations of the "wilderness model" of environmentalist thought that has historically dominated U.S. environmentalism. I have posited "commons environmentalism" as an alternative to the "wilderness model" Cronon describes.

2. For a useful in-depth discussion of Reagan's public lands policies, see Short, *Ronald Reagan*. Also see Hirt, *Conspiracy of Optimism*, 271–72; Andrews, *Managing the Environment*, 311–12; Klyza, *Who Controls*, 94–107; Frome, *The Forest Service*, 7–11.

3. Jack Brettler, "Environmentalists, Federal Lands Freeze Delaying 'Oil Boom' in Macon County?," *Franklin Press*, April 30, 1981; "Oil, Gas Leases OK'd for Two N.C. Forests," *News and Observer*, April 27, 1982.

4. John C. McCaslin, "Eastern Overthrust Belt Grabs Major's Interest," *Oil and Gas Journal*, October 20, 1980, 199.

5. Richard D. Lyons, "An Overthrust Belt Explored in the East," *New York Times*, March 24, 1980, D1.

6. John C. McCaslin, "Two Wildcats to Probe Montana's Disturbed Belt," *Oil and Gas Journal*, May 22, 1978, 167; Randy Sumpter, "Added Setasides Threaten Operations on Public Land," *Oil and Gas Journal*, March 13, 1978, 21; Bob Tippee, "Amoco Nudges Shell Out as Top 1977 Wildcatter," *Oil and Gas Journal*, March 20, 1978, 191; "Overthrust Belt Play Expanding in 1978," *Oil and Gas Journal*, April 10, 1978, 97.

7. "Overthrust Belt in Southeast Kentucky Yields Prolific Discovery," *Oil and Gas Journal*, May 1, 1978, 92; "Columbia Calls Appalachian Gas Strike 'Major,'" *Oil and Gas Journal*, July 30, 1979, 128; John C. McCaslin, "Another Gas Discovery Raises Virginia's Hopes," *Oil and Gas Journal*, October 8, 1979, 171; "Getting In on the Action," *Washington Post Magazine*, August 5, 1979, 10.

8. McCaslin, "Eastern Overthrust Belt Grabs."

9. Lyons, "An Overthrust Belt Explored."

10. "Broader Expanse Seen for Eastern Overthrust," *Oil and Gas Journal*, October 15, 1979, 92.

11. Ibid.; "Mountains of North Carolina May Have Significant Gas Reserves," *Franklin Press*, July 2, 1981, A6; John C. McCaslin, "New Drilling in Virginias Due Close Watch," *Oil and Gas Journal*, June 23, 1980, 171.

12. "Broader Expanse Seen"; Lyons, "An Overthrust Belt Explored"; McCaslin, "New Drilling in Virginias."

13. McCaslin, "New Drilling in Virginias"; John M. Berry, "Profit/Pain: Drilling Comes to Appalachia," *Washington Post*, May 24, 1981, F1; "Mountains of North Carolina."

14. For a discussion of energy issues in the national forests, see Frome, *The Forest Service*, 198–212.

15. Berry, "Profit/Pain."

16. Ibid.

17. Frome, *The Forest Service*, 201–2; Cook, interview.

18. Clyde Osborne, "Forest Oil Leases Backed," *Asheville Citizen*, July 1, 1980; Clyde Osborne, "Forest Supervisor Backs WNC Oil Exploration Plan," *Asheville Citizen*, September 17, 1980.

19. Frome, *The Forest Service*, 203; Liden, interview; Osborne, "Forest Oil Leases Backed."

20. Osborne, "Forest Oil Leases Backed."

21. Ibid.

22. "Oil, Gas Leases ok'd."

23. Sandy Ellis, "Board Approves Oil Exploration," *Franklin Press*, August 7, 1980; Brettler, "Environmentalists."

24. "It Could Be a Whiff That Went Away!," *Franklin Press*, August 7, 1980; "Don't Wait Too Late to Lock the Door!," *Franklin Press*, August 11, 1980.

25. "It Could Be a Whiff."

26. "Don't Wait Too Late," emphasis in original.

27. Osborne, "Forest Supervisor Backs"; "Forest Service Okays Oil Search," *Franklin Press*, September 18, 1980.

28. Clyde Osborne, "Oil Boom—What Would It Mean?," *Asheville Citizen*, November 3, 1980.

29. "Firm Seeks Oil and Gas Leases on Private Land," *Cherokee Scout*, reprinted in *Franklin Press*, February 26, 1981; Berry, "Profit/Pain."

30. "Firm Seeks Oil and Gas Leases."

31. "Mountains of North Carolina."

32. Clyde Osborne, "Oil Company Seeks Permits," *Asheville Citizen*, March 24, 1981; Clyde Osborne, "Company Asks for Oil Lease," *Asheville Citizen*, April 8, 1981; "Firm Seeks Oil and Gas Leases"; "Oil, Gas Leases Sought," *Franklin Press*, July 9, 1981.

33. Osborne, "Oil Boom."

34. Ibid.

35. Ibid.

36. Brettler, "Environmentalists."

37. Ibid.

38. "Our Land's Great; Let's Keep It That Way," *Franklin Press*, July 9, 1981.

39. Ibid.

40. "Atlantic Richfield Looking Forward to Working with People Here," *Franklin Press*, December 7, 1981.

41. Appalachian Land Ownership Task Force, *Who Owns Appalachia?*

42. "Land Study Shows Large Absentee Ownership Means Poorer Quality Of Life," upi report, April 2, 1981 (quote); "Appalachian Regional Study Finds Absentee Ownership of 43% of Land," *New York Times*, April 5, 1981; "Multinational Oil and Energy Conglomerates Gobbling Up Appalachia," upi report, April 16, 1981; Appalachian Land Ownership Task Force, *Who Owns Appalachia?*, 41–63, 138–40.

43. "Appalachian Regional Study"; "Multinational Oil and Energy Conglomerates"; Appalachian Land Ownership Task Force, *Who Owns Appalachia?*, 114–35, quote on 114.

44. Appalachian Land Ownership Task Force, *Who Owns Appalachia?*, 113–35, for strip mining, see 119–25, quotes, 119.

45. Ibid., 116–19; "It's Not Too Late to Plan Our Fate," *Franklin Press*, November 19, 1981.

46. "It's Not Too Late."

47. Esther Cunningham to Kathryn Newfont, September 21, 1997; Liden, interview; Florence Sherrill, interview; Mary Kelly, interview; Gilmour, interview.

48. Florence Sherrill, interview; Esther Cunningham, interviews.

49. Esther Cunningham, interviews.

50. Ibid.

51. Cunningham to Newfont; Florence Sherrill, interview; Esther Cunningham, interviews.

52. Esther Cunningham, interview, October 10, 1997; Florence Sherrill, interview; Esther Cunningham to Newfont; "4-H in Macon County" and "Macon Program for Progress," in Sutton, *Heritage*, 608, 606.

53. Esther Cunningham, interviews; Cunningham to Newfont.

54. Esther Cunningham, interviews; "4-H in Macon County."

55. Esther Cunningham, interview, October 10, 1997; "Cunningham Files for Commissioner," *Franklin Press*, January 10, 1980.

56. "Community Development Group Starts Its 32nd Year in Western North Carolina," *Franklin Press*, March 19, 1981; "Community Development Week Is April 11–18," *Franklin Press*, April 16, 1981; "Roy Taylor Elected President of Development Group," *Franklin Press*, January 19, 1983.

57. "Cunningham Files for Commissioner"; Esther Cunningham, interview, October 10, 1997; "Carson Community," in Sutton, *Heritage*, 609.

58. Esther Cunningham, interviews.

59. Esther Cunningham, interview, October 10, 1997; "Carson Community"; "Cunningham Files for Commissioner."

60. Esther Cunningham, interview, October 10, 1997.

61. Ibid.; Florence Sherrill, interview; George Sherrill, interview; Liden, interview. For examples of local coverage, see "Forest Oil Leases Backed," *Asheville Citizen*, July 2, 1980; "Oil Leases Recommended," *Asheville Times*, July 2, 1980; "Board Approves Oil Exploration," *Franklin Press*, August 7, 1980; "It Could Be a Whiff"; "Don't Wait Too Late"; "Oil, Gas Search Subject of Forum," *Asheville Citizen*, August 12, 1980; Osborne, "Forest Supervisor Backs"; "Forest Service Okays Oil Search"; Osborne, "Oil Boom"; "Oil Company Seeks Permits"; Osborne, "Company Asks for Oil Lease."

62. Esther Cunningham, interview, October 10, 1997.

63. Cunningham to Newfont; Esther Cunningham, interviews, October 10, 1997, August 17, 1998.

64. Appalachian Land Ownership Task Force, *Who Owns Appalachia?*

65. Ibid.; Esther Cunningham, interview, October 10, 1997; Esther Cunningham, Carson column, *Franklin Press*, July 23, 1981, A14.

66. Esther Cunningham, interview, October 10, 1997.

67. Ibid.; Gaventa, *Power and Powerlessness*.

68. Esther Cunningham, interview, October 10, 1997.

69. Cunningham to Newfont; Esther Cunningham, interview, October 10, 1997; Liden, interview; Florence Sherrill, interview; Mary Kelly, interview; Gilmour, interview. For more on the early history of WNC, see Newfont, "Grassroots Environmentalism."

70. For a discussion of kinship and community in western North Carolina, see Community Research Center, "A Socioeconomic Overview."

71. Liden, interview. For an examination of surface mining in the Appalachians,

see Montrie, *To Save the Land.* The Appalachian land-use study documented damage caused by surface coal mining. Appalachian Land Ownership Task Force, *Who Owns Appalachia?*

72. Esther Cunningham, interview, October 10, 1997; Liden, interview.

73. Esther Cunningham, interview, October 10, 1997; Cunningham to Newfont.

74. Esther Cunningham, interview, October 10, 1997; Liden, interview.

75. For examples, see Esther Cunningham, Carson columns, *Franklin Press*, January 14, 1982, and February 18, 1982.

76. Esther Cunningham, Carson columns, *Franklin Press*, January 14, 1982, and February 18, 1982; "Future of Forests Is Topic," *Asheville Citizen*, February 21, 1982.

77. "Forest Service Faces Facts for the {ap}80s," *Franklin Press*, March 1, 1982.

78. Esther Cunningham, interviews, October 10, 1997, November 16, 1998; Florence Sherrill, interview; George Sherrill, interview; "Macon County Home Demonstration Clubs and Extension Homemakers Association, 1935–1987," in Sutton, *Heritage*, 614.

79. "Forest Service Faces Facts."

80. Esther Cunningham, Carson column, *Franklin Press*, March 4, 1982; "Forest Service Faces Facts."

81. Esther Cunningham, Carson columns, *Franklin Press*, March 4, 1982, and April 1, 1982; "Watt a Threat to Western N.C.," *News and Observer*, April 11, 1982; "Pall of Menaces Growing over Mountains in N.C.," *News and Observer*, April 18, 1982; "Prospect of Mining Stirs Worry in N.C.," *News and Observer*, April 19, 1982; "Man versus Mountains," *News and Observer*, April 23, 1982; "Drilling Opposed, Severance Tax Proposed," *News and Observer*, April 28, 1982.

82. "More Loose Ends," *Franklin Press*, April 15, 1982; "WNC Oil Drilling Explained," *Asheville Citizen*, April 20, 1982; "WNC Oil, Gas Lease Requests Now Total Nearly Million Acres," *Franklin Press*, April 22, 1982; "Oil, Gas Leases OK'd."

83. Esther Cunningham, Carson column, *Franklin Press*, May 13, 1982.

84. Esther Cunningham, Carson column, *Franklin Press*, August 20, 1982.

85. "Oil Leases on Government Land Discussed," *Franklin Press*, September 1, 1982; Jim Baker, " 'Coon Power," *Asheville Citizen-Times*, October 14, 1979; "Local Coon Hunters Club Is Largest in the State," *Franklin Press*, August 11, 1982.

86. "Oil Leases on Government Land Discussed."

87. Ibid.

88. Esther Cunningham, Carson column, *Franklin Press*, November 5, 1982; "Conference on WNC Oil, Gas Development Set," *Franklin Press*, November 5, 1982; "Program Set on Oil, Gas Development in WNC," *Asheville Citizen*, November 4, 1982; "Western North Carolina Alliance Forum," *Accent*, no. 1 (Fall 1984): 2.

89. "Group Seeks to Preserve Environment in Region," *Asheville Citizen-Times*, April 5, 1984; "Group Seeks to Preserve Environment in Region," *Accent*, no. 1 (Fall 1984): 1; "Western North Carolina Alliance Forum," 2; "Experts Portray Gloomy Picture of Oil Drilling," *Asheville Citizen*, November 10, 1982; "Experts Paint Gloomy Oil Picture," *Franklin Press*, November 12, 1982.

90. "Experts Portray Gloomy Picture"; "Experts Paint."

91. Ibid.

92. "Experts Portray Gloomy Picture"; "Oil, Gas Drilling: A Judgment Call," *Asheville Citizen*, November 13, 1982.

93. "Kentucky Oil Fields Described to Local Group," *Franklin Press*, November 17, 1982.

94. Ibid.

95. Ibid.

96. Esther Cunningham, interview; Liden, interview; Cook, interview.

97. "Local Coon Hunters Club"; "Prospect of Mining."

98. "Local Coon Hunters Club"; Jim Cunningham, interview; "Cunningham Files for Commissioner"; for the importance of local networks to rural organizing, see Mary Kelly, interview.

99. Esther Cunningham, interview; Liden, interview; George Sherrill, interview; Gilmour, interview.

100. Mary Kelly, interview.

101. Liden, interview.

102. Esther Cunningham, interview, October 10, 1997; Liden, interview.

103. Mary Kelly, interview.

NINE. Clearcutting Returns

1. Padgett, "Clearcutting the National Forests," 2–3. For another example of clearcutting demonstrations' provoking shocked initial reactions from USFS personnel in the Southeast, see Cook, interview. For a piece addressing the issue of shocked response in the southern mountains, see McGee, "Clearcutting and Aesthetics."

2. Padgett, "Clearcutting the National Forests," 2–3; *Message from the President*.

3. U.S. Department of Agriculture, *National Forests in the Southern Appalachians*, 8.

4. Padgett, "Clearcutting the National Forests," 2.

5. Ibid., 7; Hirt, *Conspiracy of Optimism*, 131–44, 149–50. For a brief summary of paper industry history, including raw material supply issues, see Bartlett, *Troubled Waters*, 20–25. For U.S. papermaking history, see Smith, *History of Papermaking*.

6. For agency cooperation with industry, see Hays, *American People*. Eminent national forest historian Hays differentiates the period 1891–1920, dominated by a "silvicultural imperative," from the period 1920–75, the "evolution of an agency clientele." This clientele included the timber industry, which put increasing harvest pressures on the national forests throughout the period during and after World War II. Hays sees industry-agency rapprochement as solidifying during the 1950s on groundwork laid earlier, including by the Cooperative Sustained-Yield Program Congress authorized during World War II. He argues that the "sustained yield" idea slipped into a "sustained communities" concept, with the Forest Service accepting increased responsibility for supporting stable community economies. And Hays also traces the market shift from lumber to pulp as a key development of the postwar period (see 56–63). The 1965 trip Bob Padgett remembered is best understood against the backdrop of the patterns Hays traces, as is much else in western North

Carolina national forest history. Mead Corporation has published a self-history; see Mead Corporation, *In Quiet Ways*.

7. Clarke Morrison, "Clear-Cutting Foes: 'People Have Spoken,'" *Asheville Citizen-Times*, April 16, 1989; Mardell Griffin, "Clearcutting Petition Paraded throughout Asheville," *Mountain Times*, April 20, 1989. The four-hundred-year-old Bob Padgett Tulip Poplar in the Nantahala National Forest was named as a memorial to the lifelong forest advocate.

8. For a useful in-depth discussion of Reagan's public lands policies, see Short, *Ronald Reagan*. Also see Hirt, *Conspiracy of Optimism*, 271–72; Andrews, *Managing the Environment*, 311–12; Klyza, *Who Controls*, 94–107; Frome, *The Forest Service*, 7–11.

9. Short, *Ronald Reagan*, 53–54; Hirt, *Conspiracy of Optimism*, 270–71; Andrews, *Managing the Environment*, 311–12.

10. Mary Kelly, interview; Lansky, "Myths."

11. Short, *Ronald Reagan*, 103–5; Andrews, *Managing the Environment*, 260; Shabecoff, *Fierce Green Fire*, 209–10.

12. For Watt's role, see Short, *Ronald Reagan*, 55–80; Andrews, *Managing the Environment*, 314–15; Shabecoff, *Fierce Green Fire*, 152–53; Klyza, *Who Controls*, 59–61.

13. Hirt, *Conspiracy of Optimism*, xxi–xxv, xliv, 87–93, 113–17, 235–42, 266–67.

14. Frome, *The Forest Service*, 36–46; Robinson, *The Forest Service*, 26–32; Cook, interview; Padgett, "Clearcutting the National Forests," 2–4.

15. Padgett, "Clearcutting the National Forests," 7; Hirt, *Conspiracy of Optimism*, 271–73; Robinson, *The Forest Service*, 26–32; Frome, *The Forest Service*, 47.

16. Padgett, "Clearcutting the National Forests," 4; Hirt, *Conspiracy of Optimism*, 271–73.

17. Johnson, *Ready for Harvest*; Hirt, *Conspiracy of Optimism*, xli–xlv, 50–51, 131, 220; Mastran and Lowerre, *Mountaineers and Rangers*, 144; Shands, "The Lands Nobody Wanted."

18. Padgett, "Clearcutting the National Forests," 2–4; Hirt, *Conspiracy of Optimism*, 137.

19. Mastran and Lowerre, *Mountaineers and Rangers*, 144; Hirt, *Conspiracy of Optimism*, 245–46; Bolgiano, *Appalachian Forest*, 72; Padgett, "Clearcutting the National Forests," 4.

20. Hirt, *Conspiracy of Optimism*, 137; Mastran and Lowerre, *Mountaineers and Rangers*, 144; Walton R. Smith, "Green Paper Number 18," August 21, 1989, 2.

21. Johnson, *Ready for Harvest*; Walton R. Smith, "Green Paper Number 1," January 16, 1987; "Green Paper Number 5," August 3, 1987; "Green Paper Number 6," October 1, 1987; "Green Paper Number 7," December 1, 1987; "Green Paper Number 11," July 12, 1988; "Green Paper Number 15," March 1, 1989.

22. Shands, "The Lands Nobody Wanted"; Mastran and Lowerre, *Mountaineers and Rangers*, 7–10; Bolgiano, *Appalachian Forest*, 96–99.

23. Johnson, *Ready for Harvest*; Padgett, "Clearcutting the National Forests," 1; Mastran and Lowerre, *Mountaineers and Rangers*, 11, 38–39; Bolgiano, *Appalachian Forest*, 100–103, 113.

24. Bolgiano, *Appalachian Forest*, 94–99; Mastran and Lowerre, *Mountaineers and Rangers*, 32–37; Shands, "The Lands Nobody Wanted," 35–36.

25. Bolgiano, *Appalachian Forest*, 100–104; Shands, "The Lands Nobody Wanted," 36; Mastran and Lowerre, *Mountaineers and Rangers*, 77–80; Cook, interview; Hirt, *Conspiracy of Optimism*, xx, 44, 245.

26. Johnson, *Ready for Harvest*; Mastran and Lowerre, *Mountaineers and Rangers*, 39. According to Smith, the Forest Service never planned to cut the rare ancient stand that is now Joyce Kilmer but nonetheless had to justify the purchase price in timber terms. He said that he and his colleagues used German barrel stave prices to obtain timber values high enough to meet the seller's price.

27. Johnson, *Ready for Harvest*; Hirt, *Conspiracy of Optimism*, xx–xxi, 53–60, 80–81, 119–21, 131–34, 141–49; Mastran and Lowerre, *Mountaineers and Rangers*, 38.

28. Padgett, "Clearcutting the National Forests," 11; Walton R. Smith, "Green Paper Number 18," August 21, 1989; Hirt, *Conspiracy of Optimism*, 131–32.

29. Cook, interview; Frome, *The Forest Service*, 44–45; Robinson, *The Forest Service*, 32–36, 60–75, 265–66; Mastran and Lowerre, *Mountaineers and Rangers*, 168.

30. Quote from Robinson, *The Forest Service*, 43. See also Frome, *The Forest Service*, 52–53; Hirt, *Conspiracy of Optimism*, 274–75.

31. Padgett, "Clearcutting the National Forests"; Walton R. Smith, "Green Paper Number 15," March 1, 1989; "Green Paper Number 16," May 10, 1989; Frome, *The Forest Service*, 54–56.

32. Padgett, "Clearcutting the National Forests." 11–12; See also Frome, *The Forest Service*, 52–53, 55.

33. Robinson, *The Forest Service*, 43; Hirt, *Conspiracy*, 275.

34. Padgett, "Clearcutting the National Forests," 6; Mastran and Lowerre, *Mountaineers and Rangers*, 144; Rymer, "Wilderness Politics."

35. Johnson, *Ready for Harvest*. See also Mary Kelly, interview.

36. Mary Kelly, interview; "Large Crowd Protests 'Wilderness," *Franklin Press*, July 13, 1978; "RARE II Open House," *Franklin Press*, July 20, 1978; "Get the Facts and Write," *Franklin Press*, July 20, 1978.

37. For examples, see "Clearcut Is Held Up," *Accent*, no. 3 (Summer 1985); Walton R. Smith, "Green Paper Number 1," January 16, 1987; "Madison Residents Question Wisdom of Clearcutting," *Marshall News-Record*, November 24, 1988; "Craggy Clear-Cut Unpopular," *Asheville Citizen*, January 11, 1989; "Jackson Chapter of WNC Alliance Challenges Roaring Hole Clearcuts," *Sylva Herald and Ruralite*, January 12, 1989; "Clay County Clear-Cutting Opponents up in Arms," *Asheville Citizen*, February 3, 1989; "Sierra Club, WNC Alliance Challenge Timber Sale," *Asheville Times*, June 26, 1990; Mary Kelly, interview. See also Hirt, *Conspiracy of Optimism*, 162–66, 229–33. For more on the history of wilderness politics with particular attention to national forests, see Sutter, *Driven Wild*; Frome, *Battle for the Wilderness*; Roth, *Wilderness Movement, 1964–1980*; Marsh, *Drawing Lines*.

38. Hirt, *Conspiracy of Optimism*, 162–66, 229–33; Mary Kelly, interview.

39. For more on the early WNCA, see Newfont, "Grassroots Environmentalism."

40. Mary Kelly, interview; Gilmour, interview; Esther Cunningham, interviews, November 16, 1998, September 9, 1999; Walton Smith, "Green Paper Number 3," April 1, 1987; Johnson, *Ready for Harvest*.

41. Esther Cunningham, interview, October 10, 1997; *Accent*, no. 1 (Fall 1984): 3.

42. "Barbeque and Rally a Big Success" and "Clearcut Is Held Up," *Accent*, no. 3 (Summer 1985); Walton R. Smith, "Green Paper Number 1," January 16, 1987.

43. Walton R. Smith, "Green Paper Number 2," February 12, 1987, 4; "Green Paper Number 18," August 21, 1989, 3.

44. "Forestry Group Holds State Meeting at Coweeta," *Franklin Press*, August 3, 1978.

45. Walton R. Smith, "Green Paper Number 1," January 16, 1987.

46. Ibid.; "Barbeque and Rally a Big Success"; "Clearcut Is Held Up."

47. "Barbeque and Rally a Big Success"; "Clearcut Is Held Up."

48. Ibid.; Walton R. Smith, "Green Paper Number 7," December 1, 1987.

49. Walton R. Smith, "Green Paper Number 6," October 1, 1987; "Green Paper Number 8," February 2, 1988; "Barbeque and Rally a Big Success"; "Clearcut Is Held Up."

50. Walton R. Smith, "Green Paper Number 6," October 1, 1987; "Green Paper Number 8," February 2, 1988; "Barbeque and Rally a Big Success"; "Clearcut Is Held Up."

51. Mary Kelly, interview; Walton R. Smith, "Green Paper Number 6," October 1, 1987; "Green Paper Number 8," February 2, 1988; "Barbeque and Rally a Big Success"; "Clearcut Is Held Up."

52. Walton Smith photos in wnca archival slide collection; Mary Kelly, interview; Gilmour, interview; Walton R. Smith, "Green Paper Number 15," March 1, 1989; "Green Paper Number 16," May 10, 1989; "Clarence Hall and Walton Smith Present Data on Roaring Hole Timber Sale," "Mary Kelly Records Data while Clarence Hall 'Calls the Trees,'" "Dick Heywood and Rob Kelly Measure a Tree," *Accent*, no. 11 (Spring 1989): 9, 11, 15. For the role of "citizen scientists" and citizen-scientist alliances, see Hays, *Wars in the Woods* and *American People*.

53. "Forest Service Revises Plan," *Asheville Citizen*, February 8, 1985; "Forest Management," *Asheville Citizen-Times*, October 21, 1984.

54. "Forest Service Revises Plan"; "Forest Management"; Rymer, "Wilderness Politics"; Jim Baker, "Strange Bedfellows: Sportsmen, Conservationists, Lumbermen Align against Forest Service," *Asheville Citizen-Times*, January 13, 1980.

55. "State Wildlife Officials Meet with Macon Sportsmen," *Franklin Press*, January 18, 1984; "Decision on Boar Overruled," *Asheville Citizen*, July 18, 1985; "Corbin Named to Chair District Republican Party," *Franklin Press*, January 31, 1980.

56. "State Wildlife Officials Meet"; "Decision on Boar Overruled"; Taylor, "The Wilderness Question."

57. Taylor, "The Wilderness Question"; "Decision on Boar Overruled."

58. Ibid.

59. "State Wildlife Officials Meet."

60. Ibid.; Taylor, "The Wilderness Question."

61. "State Wildlife Officials Meet"; Taylor, "The Wilderness Question."

62. "Decision on Boar Overruled"; "Corbin Named to Chair"; "State Wildlife Officials Meet"; Eddie Sutton, "N.C. Wildlife Commission Got Some Good Suggestions," *Franklin Press*, January 24, 1984; Rymer, "Wilderness Politics."

63. "State Wildlife Officials Meet"; "Decision on Boar Overruled." Robinson eventually served as a Democratic state legislator.

64. "Decision on Boar Overruled."

65. "State Wildlife Officials Meet"; "Decision on Boar Overruled."

66. "Barbeque and Rally a Big Success."

67. Liden, interview; Mary Kelly, interview.

68. Mary Kelly, interview.

TEN. Commons Environmentalism Mobilized

1. Clarke Morrison, "Clear-Cutting Foes: 'People Have Spoken," *Asheville Citizen-Times*, April 16, 1989; Mardell Griffin, "Clearcutting Petition Paraded throughout Asheville," *Mountain Times*, April 20, 1989; "Citizens Gather at Rally to Protest Clear-Cutting," *Times-News*, April 16, 1989; Rusty Sivils, "Clearcut Rally Delivers 1000 Foot Long Petition," *Green Line* 3, no. 7 (1989); "Cut the Clearcutting Campaign," *Accent*, no. 12 (Summer 1989); Johnson, *Ready for Harvest*.

2. Griffin, "Clearcutting Petition"; Johnson, *Ready for Harvest*; Mary Kelly, "Alliance Mounts a 'Cut the Clearcutting' Campaign," *Accent*, no. 11 (Spring 1989).

3. Griffin, "Clearcutting Petition"; Walton R. Smith, "Green Paper Number 16," May 10, 1989; "Cut the Clearcutting Campaign," *Accent*, no. 12 (Summer 1989), including photo montage; unnumbered photos in WNCA archival collections. For an excellent exploration of commons culture in the southern Appalachian region, see Hufford, "American Ginseng."

4. Quote is from Mary Kelly, interview. For a rich exploration of contemporary commons culture in West Virginia, see American Folklife Center, "Tending the Commons" website.

5. Mary Kelly, interview; Griffin, "Clearcutting Petition."

6. Quote from Mary Kelly, interview. For the importance of NFMA, see Hays, *Wars in the Woods*, 16–19.

7. "Forest Management," *Asheville Citizen-Times*, October 21, 1984; "Public Reaction to 50 Year Plan" and "Alliance Opposes Clearcutting," *Accent*, no. 2 (Spring 1985); Johnson, *Ready for Harvest*; National Forest Management Act of 1976; "WNC Alliance Circulating Anti-Clearcutting Petition," *Mountain Times*, March 16, 1989; Mary Kelly, interview.

8. Walton R. Smith, "Green Paper Number 18," August 21, 1989, 2; Walton R. Smith, "Green Paper Number 1," January 16, 1987; Mary Kelly, interview; Esther Cunningham, interview, October 10, 1997; "Public Reaction to 50 Year Plan"; "Alliance Opposes Clearcutting"; "Forest Management."

9. Mary Kelly, interview; Esther Cunningham, interview, October 10, 1997; "Public Reaction to 50 Year Plan"; "Alliance Opposes Clearcutting"; "Forest Management"; Walton R. Smith, "Green Paper Number 1," January 16, 1987.

10. Liden, interview; George Sherrill, interview; "Public Reaction to 50 Year Plan"; "Alliance Opposes Clearcutting."

11. Liden, interview; Mary Kelly, interview; "Public Reaction to 50 Year Plan"; "Alliance Opposes Clearcutting."

12. "The Woodcutters . . . 4,150 Permits Issued in Pisgah Area," *Asheville Citizen-Times*, March 5, 1978; "Firewood Rules Announced," *Asheville Citizen*, August 24, 1979; *Accent* articles on meetings; "Public Reaction to 50 Year Plan"; "Alliance Op-

poses Clearcutting." For centrality of petty production, see Judd, *Common Lands*, 264.

13. For discussion of scenic commons, see O'Toole, "Tragedy of the Scenic Commons."

14. "Public Reaction to 50 Year Plan"; "Alliance Opposes Clearcutting"; "Forest Service Revises Plan," *Asheville Citizen*, February 8, 1985.

15. "War of the Woods," *Charlotte Observer*, February 18, 1989; "Opposition to Clear-Cutting Emotional, Ill-Informed," *Asheville Citizen-Times*, April 20, 1989; Johnson, *Ready for Harvest*.

16. "Forest Management"; "Forest Service Revises Plan."

17. "Public Reaction to 50 Year Plan."

18. Johnson, *Ready for Harvest*; Mary Kelly, interview; Taylor Crockett, "Eighty Years in the Appalachian Woodlands," *Clay County Progress*, January 12, 1989; Smith, "Green Paper Number 15," March 1, 1989; Bolgiano, *Appalachian Forest*, 230–31.

19. Liden, interview; "Alliance Opposes Clearcutting."

20. Hufford, "American Ginseng"; Johnson, *Ready for Harvest*.

21. George Sherrill, interview; "Alliance Opposes Clearcutting."

22. Liden, interview; George Sherrill, interview.

23. "Public Reaction to 50 Year Plan"; "Alliance Opposes Clearcutting"; "Forest Management"; "Forest Service Revises Plan."

24. Johnson, *Ready for Harvest*; "Grouse Hunting Is Best in Areas That Are Logged," *Franklin Press*, November 24, 1981. See also Mary Kelly, interview.

25. Johnson, *Ready for Harvest*; "Public Reaction to 50 Year Plan"; "Alliance Opposes Clearcutting"; "Forest Management"; "Forest Service Revises Plan."

26. "Forest Service Revises Plan"; "Public Reaction to 50 Year Plan"; "Alliance Opposes Clearcutting"; "Forest Management."

27. Esther Cunningham, interviews, October 10, 1997, November 16, 1998; Liden, interview.

28. "Forest Service Revises Plan"; "Forest Management"; Cook, interview; Mary Kelly, interview.

29. "Cut the Clearcutting Day! The People Have Spoken!" program in Monroe Gilmour, "Cut the Clearcutting" scrapbook, vol. 1, and in "Cut the Clearcutting" campaign file, Western North Carolina Alliance 1989 platform in Cut the Clearcutting! campaign file and Cut the Clearcutting! petition, all in Western North Carolina Alliance Archives.

30. Cronon, "Trouble with Wilderness"; White, "Are You an Environmentalist"; Hirt, *Conspiracy of Optimism*, 151–70. For the cultural importance of the commons, see Hufford, "American Ginseng," and Kirby, "Commoners and the Commons," chap. 3 in *Mockingbird Song*.

31. Mary Kelly, interview. For timber and the local economy, see Mastran and Lowerre, *Mountaineers and Rangers*. In Graham County 75 percent of the labor force was employed in timber-related jobs in the late 1970s, for example (169). See also "Forestry Is Important to Economy," *Asheville Citizen*, January 27, 1963; "$19 Million Forest Crop Means Big WNC Payoff," *Asheville Citizen*, June 18, 1972.

32. Smith, "Green Paper Number 18," August 21, 1989.

33. Smith, "Green Paper Number 4," June 1, 1987.

34. Smith, "Green Paper Number 5," August 3, 1987; "In Memoriam: Bob Padgett," *Accent*, no. 26 (Winter 1994).

35. Smith, "Green Paper Number 6," October 1, 1987, "Green Paper Number 8," February 24, 1988; Mary Kelly, interview; "Catherine A. Cotter Letter to Forest Service Chief Dale Robertson, 14 July 1987" and "Supplemental Request for Stay, 28 July 1987," in Western North Carolina Alliance Archives.

36. Smith, "Green Paper Number 8," February 24, 1988; "Green Paper Number 9," April 25, 1988.

37. Smith, "Green Paper Number 13," November 1, 1988; "Jackson Chapter of WNC Alliance Challenges Roaring Hole Clearcuts," *Sylva Herald and Ruralite*, January 12, 1989; "Clay County Clear-Cutting Opponents Up in Arms," *Asheville Citizen*, February 3, 1989; "Clarence Hall and Walton Smith Present Data on Roaring Hole Timber Sale," "Mary Kelly Records Data while Clarence Hall 'Calls the Trees,'" "Dick Heywood and Rob Kelly Measure a Tree," *Accent*, no. 11 (Spring 1989): 9, 11, 15.

38. Mary Kelly, interview; Smith, "Green Paper Number 12," September 28, 1988; "Clarence Hall and Walton Smith"; "Mary Kelly Records Data"; "Dick Heywood and Rob Kelly Measure."

39. Darry Wood, "Timber Targets," *Clay County Progress*, January 12, 1989, January 19, 1989, February 9, 1989; "Eyebrows Raising in Clear Cutting Issue," *Clay County Progress*, January 19, 1989; "Clay County Clear-Cutting Opponents"; "Rangers and Residents Square Off over Clear Cutting Issue," *Clay County Progress*, February 9, 1989.

40. Gilmour, interview; Ballew, interview; Brown, interview; Smith, "Green Paper Number 10," June 20, 1988; "Clearcutting May Be on Hold," *Black Mountain News*, September 21, 1989.

41. Mary Kelly, interview; Elizabeth Hunter, "USFS Prefers Clearcutting Method," *Yancey Journal*, March 8, 1989; Kelly, "Alliance Mounts"; "Resolution to Commit WNC Alliance to a 'Cut the Clearcutting' Campaign," January 15, 1989, and "Minutes of the WNCA Steering Committee Meeting, Hot Springs, N.C.," January 15, 1989, in Cut the Clearcutting! campaign file, Western North Carolina Alliance Archives.

42. Mary Kelly, interview; "Monroe Gilmour Memo to Mary Kelly: Discussion Draft on Stop Clearcutting Publicity Campaign," December 5, 1988, and "Cut the Clearcutting 'Game Plan' Outlined by Forest Management Task Force," December 10, 1988, in Cut the Clearcutting! campaign file, Western North Carolina Alliance Archives; Kelly, "Alliance Mounts."

43. Gilmour, interview; Mary Kelly, interview; Johnson, *Ready for Harvest* video.

44. Kelly, "Alliance Mounts," 8; Smith, "Green Paper Number 16," May 10, 1989; Mary Kelly, interview.

45. "Clearcutting Foes Gather Steam for Continued Push," *Black Mountain News*, February 2, 1989; "'Cut the Clearcutting' Campaign Involves Jackson County Citizens," *Sylva Herald and Ruralite*, February 16, 1989; "WNC Alliance Announces 'Cut the Clearcutting,'" *Asheville Advocate*, January 27, 1989; "Clear-Cutting Foes Express Regret at Champion News," *Asheville Citizen*, January 26, 1989.

46. "Clearcutting Protested by Local Western N.C. Alliance," *Tri-County News-*

Journal, February 2, 1989; "'Cut the Clearcutting' Campaign Getting Results," *Mountain Times*, February 9, 1989.

47. "'Cut the Clearcutting' Campaign Getting Results"; "Clearcutting Foes Gather Steam"; "Clear-Cutting Foes Express Regret."

48. "Clearcutting Foes Gather Steam"; "Clear-Cutting Foes Express Regret"; "'Cut the Clearcutting' Campaign Getting Results"; "Dick Heywood and Rob Kelly Measure," 15; Smith, "Green Paper Number 7," December 1, 1987, "Green Paper Number 8," February 24, 1988, "Green Paper Number 9," April 25, 1988.

49. "Anti-Clear-Cut Drive Picks Up Some Steam," *Asheville Citizen*, March 9, 1989. For examples of broad regional coverage, see Griffin, "Clearcutting Petition"; "Clearcut Rally Delivers"; "Clearcutting Foes Gather Steam"; Hunter, "USFS Prefers Clearcutting Method"; "Clearcutting Protested"; "Forest Service Clear-Cutting Is Focus of Debate," *Hendersonville Times-News*, February 19, 1989; "Jackson Chapter of WNC Alliance"; "WNC Alliance Announces 'Cut the Clearcutting'"; "Eyebrows Raising"; "Madison Residents Question Wisdom of Clearcutting," *Marshall News-Record*, November 24, 1988; "USFS Blasted for WNC Timber Sales," *Franklin Press*, January 4, 1989; "Clearcutting? WNC Alliance Hopes to Make It Dirty Word," *Mountaineer*, January 27, 1989; "Opposition Mounts against Clear-Cutting," *Highlander*, March 7, 1989; "Shelton Laurel Residents Oppose Clearcutting Plan," *Greeneville Sun*, January 27, 1989; "War of the Woods," *Charlotte Observer*, February 18, 1989; "Lighthawk Flyover Gives Bird's-Eye View of Forest Service Clearcutting in North Carolina," *Appalachian Reader*, Spring 1989. For photo contest, see flyer, "WNC Alliance and the 'Cut the Clearcutting Campaign' Announce: The Ugliest Clearcut Photo Contest," in Gilmour, "Cut the Clearcutting" scrapbook, vol. 1; "Contest Held to Find Photo of Ugliest Clear-Cut," *Asheville Citizen*, February 16, 1989; "WNC Alliance Photo Contest Centers on Clearcutting," *Asheville Times*, February 16, 1989; "'Ugliest Clearcut' Photo Contest Set," *Tri-County News-Journal*, February 23, 1989; "Ugly Clearcut Photo Contest," *Black Mountain News*, February 23, 1989; "Ugliest Clear-Cut Photo Contest Now Being Held," *Highlander*, March 7, 1989; "Award-Winning Clear-Cut Photo," *Asheville Citizen*, April 17, 1989.

50. "Clear-Cutting Seen from Above," *Hendersonville Times-News*, March 18, 1989; "Environment Guarded above by Lighthawk," *Asheville Citizen*, March 18, 1989; "Lighthawk Flyover Gives Bird's-Eye View."

51. "Anti-Clear-Cut Drive Picks Up Some Steam"; Mary Kelly, interview; "WNC Alliance Volunteers Circulated Petitions at Rose's," *Black Mountain News*, March 16, 1989; "WNC Alliance Circulating Anti-Clearcutting Petition," *Mountain Times*, March 16, 1989; "War of the Woods," *Charlotte Observer*, February 18, 1989.

52. "WNC Alliance Circulating Anti-Clearcutting Petition"; "Anti-Clear-Cut Drive Picks Up Some Steam"; Mary Kelly, interview; Clarke Morrison, "Clear-Cutting Foes: 'People Have Spoken," *Asheville Citizen-Times*, April 16, 1989; Griffin, "Clearcutting Petition."

53. Cook, interview; Hunter, "USFS Prefers Clearcutting Method."

54. Clarke Morrison, "Forest Management Plan Found Lacking," *Asheville Citizen*, September 30, 1989; "Public Wins a Victory on Clearcutting on NC Forests," *Accent*, no. 13 (Summer 1990).

55. Hirt, *Conspiracy of Optimism*, 272, 281; Andrews, *Managing the Environment*, 256–57, 333; Morrison, "Forest Management Plan Found Lacking." For an excellent analysis of nationwide forest politics in the last third of the twentieth century, see Hays, *Wars in the Woods*.

56. Morrison, "Forest Management Plan Found Lacking"; "Public Wins a Victory."

57. Mary Kelly, interview; "Public Wins a Victory"; Morrison, "Forest Management Plan Found Lacking."

58. "Public Opinion Makes a Difference! Revised Forest Plan 'Cuts the Clearcutting!" and "Here Lies Clearcutting," *Accent*, no. 27 (Spring 1994).

59. Ibid.; Hirt, *Conspiracy of Optimism*, 288–92; Andrews, *Managing the Environment*, 312–13, 334–35, 362–66.

60. Mary Kelly, interview; "wnc Alliance Members Tell Forest Service Chief How to Reinvent the Agency" and "Public Opinion Makes a Difference!," *Accent*, no. 27 (Spring 1994).

61. U.S. Department of Agriculture, *Land and Resource Management Plan: Amendment 5* and "Final Supplement to the Final Environmental Impact Statement"; "Public Opinion Makes a Difference!" and "wnc Alliance Members Tell Forest Service Chief."

62. On Cut the Clearcutting! Day there were around 15,500 signatures, but as stragglers came in, the number grew to over 20,000. Clearcutting petition, Western North Carolina Alliance Archives; Gilmour, personal correspondence in author's possession.

AFTERWORD

1. I draw parallels with the civil rights movement, which was not a single movement so much as an extensive series of local movements sharing the ultimate goal of full equality for African American citizens. Lunch-counter sit-ins in Nashville were not equivalent to voter registration drives in Atlanta, though both shared broad aims. Activists' campaigns, strategies, and immediate goals grew out of their particular contexts.

2. And yet, particularly in recent years, this invisibility begins to diminish. Pioneering scholars have begun to trace the outlines of a U.S. commons history, though not all whose work is relevant to the topic use that language. Among those whose studies contribute to this history are Richard Judd, Karl Jacoby, Brian Donahue, Theodore Catton, Martha Geores, Maria Montoya, Mark David Spence, Louis Warren, Ted Steinberg, Christine Keiner, Jake Kosek, Daniel W. Schneider, Benjamin Heber Johnson, Harry Watson, Stephen Hahn, and Wayne Durrill. These explorations especially treat forests and fisheries, with some attention also to grasslands. It is clear there is a great deal more to be done in all three of these arenas. Today's commons scholars are also fortunate to have fine theoretical scaffolding. Elinor Ostrom, Ramachandra Guha, Bonnie McKay, James Acheson, Fikret Berkes, Peter Linebaugh, Herbert Reid and Betsy Taylor, and other commons scholars have given us a range of tools with which to recognize, understand, and evaluate com-

mons systems. Folklorist Mary Hufford has also richly documented the continuing power of commons practice in one part of the nation. For all these reasons, this is a fine time to study commons.

3. In this list I have in mind natural-resource commons. Of course, there are also other forms of commons—bandwidth commons, scenic commons, and the like.

4. Among the exceptions, the pioneers in U.S. commons history are Richard Judd, Daniel W. Schneider, Benjamin Heber Johnson, Stephen Hahn, and Wayne Durrill.

5. See Ostrom, *Governing the Commons*; Linebaugh, *Magna Carta Manifesto*; Reid and Taylor, *Recovering the Commons*.

6. For Hardin's original piece, see Hardin, "Tragedy of the Commons"; for his later acknowledgment that it oversimplified, see McKay and Acheson, "Human Ecology"; for Ostrom's work delineating the contours of successful and unsuccessful commons systems, see Ostrom, *Governing the Commons*.

7. For transportation sector comparison, see Stern, *Economics of Climate Change*. For a sobering exploration of global deforestation, see Jensen and Draffan, *Strangely like War*.

BIBLIOGRAPHY

INTERVIEWS BY AUTHOR

Ballew, Betty, September 19, 1998
Brown, Roger, September 21, 1998
Cook, Pat, July 1, 1999
Cunningham, Esther, October 10, 1997, August 17, 1998, November 16, 1998,
    September 9, 1999
Cunningham, Jim, September 9, 1999
Gilmour, Monroe, August 21, 1998
Ivey, Norma, November 17, 1998
Jones, Peg, October 7, 1998
Kelly, Mary, November 13, 1998
Kelly, Rob, November 13, 1998
Lambe, Ron, October 19, 1998
Liden, David, October 17, 1998
Newman, Brownie, May 15, 1998
Sager, Mikki, August 28, 1997
Sherrill, Florence, November 16, 1998
Sherrill, George, November 16, 1998
Zellar, Janet Hoyle, January 15, 1998

LAWS AND STATUTES

Clarke-McNary Act, June 7, 1924
Eastern Wilderness Areas Act, January 3, 1975 (also known as the Omnibus
    Wilderness Areas Act)
Multiple-Use Sustained-Yield Act, June 12, 1960
National Forest Management Act, October 22, 1976
North Carolina Wilderness Act of 1984, Public Law 98-324, June 19, 1984
Weeks Act, March 1, 1911
Wilderness Act, September 3, 1964

MANUSCRIPT COLLECTIONS

Asheville Citizen-Times Archives, 14 O-Henry Ave., Asheville, N.C.
    Nantahala file
    National forests file
    Pisgah file

National Archives, College Park, Md. (NA)
    General Correspondence, 1901–40, Division of Land Acquisition, Record
        Group 95 (DLA)
    General Correspondence, 1914–50, Division of Wildlife Management, Record
        Group 95
    National Forest Reservation Commission Minutes, Office of the Chief,
        Record Group 95

North Carolina Collection, Wilson Library, University of North Carolina,
Chapel Hill
    Clippings collection
    Photographic archives
    Postcard collection

Pack Memorial Library Special Collections, Pack Memorial Library,
Asheville, N.C.
    Forest reserves file
    Nantahala file
    National forests file
    Pisgah file

Western North Carolina Alliance Archives, Asheville, N.C.
    1984–85 clippings files
    1988–89 clippings files
    Cut the Clearcutting! campaign file
    Cut the Clearcutting! petition
    Oil and gas file
    Oil and gas leasing map with pins
    Padgett, Bob. "Clearcutting the National Forests: Good or Bad?," January 1987
    Smith, Walton R. "Green Papers," forest management newsletters
    WNCA photo collection
    WNCA slide collection

NEWSPAPERS AND PERIODICALS

    Accent, WNCA newsletter
    Appalachian Voice
    Asheville Advocate
    Asheville Citizen
    Asheville Times
    Atlanta Journal
    Black Mountain News
    Carson Courier, Carson Community Development Association newsletter
    Charlotte Observer
    Cherokee Scout
    Clay County Progress
    Franklin Press

Greeneville Sun
Greenline (Asheville, N.C.)
Hendersonville Times-News
Highlander (Highlands, N.C.)
Journal of Commerce
Marshall News-Record
Mountain Times (Boone, N.C.)
New York Times
Oil and Gas Journal
Raleigh News and Observer
Sylva Herald and Ruralite
Tri-County News-Journal (Spruce Pine, N.C.)
Washington Post
Watauga Democrat (Boone, N.C.)
Wildlife in North Carolina
Yancey Journal

PERSONAL COLLECTIONS

Monroe Gilmour
Files
    Citizens against Clearcutting in the Asheville Watershed file box
Scrapbooks
    Citizens against Clearcutting in the Asheville Watershed
    Cut the Clearcutting, vol. 1
    Cut the Clearcutting, vol. 2
Videotapes
    Roger Brown, Citizens against Clearcutting in the Asheville Watershed
    Lighthawk coverage, May 1991
    Nancy Susan Reynolds awards, 1992
    Watershed coverage, 1991

Mary and Rob Kelly
    Waldee stick

Kathryn Newfont
    Esther Clouse Cunningham correspondence
    Richard Dillingham correspondence
    Elizabeth Giard correspondence
    Monroe Gilmour correspondence

PRIMARY AND SECONDARY SOURCES

Agee, James, and Walker Evans. *Let Us Now Praise Famous Men: Three Tenant Families.* Boston: Houghton Mifflin, 1969.
Alexander, Warren. "In Huckleberry Time Courtin's a Pleasure." In Parris, *Mountain Bred*, 291–93. Interview by John Parris.

Allen, Barbara, and Thomas J. Schlereth, eds. *Sense of Place: American Regional Cultures*. Lexington: University Press of Kentucky, 1990.

Allen, Bill. "Save Our Cumberland Mountains: Growth and Change within a Grassroots Organization." In Fisher, *Fighting Back in Appalachia*, 85–99.

Altherr, Thomas L., and John F. Reiger. "Academic Historians and Hunting: A Call for More and Better Scholarship." *Environmental History Review* 19, no. 3 (1995): 39–56.

American Chestnut Foundation. http://www.acf.org/history.php. Accessed June 10, 2010.

American Folklife Center, Library of Congress. "Tending the Commons: Folklife and Landscape in Southern West Virginia." http://memory.loc.gov/ammem/collections/tending/index.html. Accessed June 20, 2009.

Anderson, David G., and Eeva Berglund, eds. *Ethnographies of Conservation: Environmentalism and the Distribution of Privilege*. New York: Berghahn Books, 2003.

Andrews, Richard N. L., ed. *Land in America: Commodity or Natural Resource?* Lexington, Mass.: D. C. Heath, 1978.

———. *Managing the Environment, Managing Ourselves: A History of American Environmental Policy*. New Haven, Conn.: Yale University Press, 1999.

Appalachian Land Ownership Task Force. *Who Owns Appalachia? Land Ownership and Its Impact*. Lexington: University Press of Kentucky, 1983.

Appalachian Voices. http://www.appvoices.org/index.php?/site/mtr_overview/. Accessed June 15, 2010.

Archives of Appalachia, Eastern Tennessee State University. "Harvesting the Hardwoods: Logging, Lumbering, and Forestry in Southern Appalachia." http://www.etsu.edu/cass/Archives/Subjects/Hardwoods/intro.htm. Accessed June 10, 2010.

Armstrong, Susan J., and Richard G. Botzler, eds. *Environmental Ethics: Divergence and Convergence*. New York: McGraw-Hill, 1993.

Arthur, John Preston. *A History of Watauga County, North Carolina, with Sketches of Prominent Families*. Richmond, Va.: Everett Waddey Company, 1915; repr., Charleston, S.C.: Nabu Press, 2010.

———. *Western North Carolina: A History*. 1914; Spartanburg, S.C.: Reprint Company, 1973.

"Aunt Arie." In Wigginton, *The Foxfire Book*, 15–30. Interview by Mike Cook and Paul Gillespie.

Ayers, Edward L. *The Promise of the New South: Life after Reconstruction*. New York: Oxford University Press, 1992.

Ayers, Edward L., Patricia Nelson Limerick, Stephen Nissenbaum, and Peter S. Onuf. *All over the Map: Rethinking American Regions*. Baltimore, Md.: Johns Hopkins University Press, 1996.

Baden, John A., and Douglas S. Noonan, eds. *Managing the Commons*. Bloomington: Indiana University Press, 1998.

Barth, Gunther. *Fleeting Moments: Nature and Culture in American History*. New York: Oxford University Press, 1990.

Bartlett, Richard A. *Troubled Waters: Champion International and the Pigeon River Controversy*. Knoxville: University of Tennessee Press, 1995.

Bauer, Rainer Lutz. "Economic Differentiation and the Divided Responses of Spanish Galician Farmers to Reforestation of the Commons under Franco." *Social Science History* 29, no. 2 (2005): 175–205.

Bean, Michael J. *The Evolution of National Wildlife Law*. New York: Praeger, 1983.

Beaver, Patricia D. *Rural Community in the Appalachian South*. Lexington: University Press of Kentucky, 1986.

Beaver, Patricia D., and Burton L. Purrington, eds. *Cultural Adaptation to Mountain Environments*. Athens: University of Georgia Press, 1984.

Billings, Dwight B., Gurney Norman, and Katherine Ledford, eds. *Backtalk from Appalachia: Confronting Stereotypes*. Lexington: University Press of Kentucky, 1999.

Bilsky, Lester J. *Historical Ecology: Essays on Environment and Social Change*. Port Washington, N.Y.: Kennikat Press, 1980.

Bird, Elizabeth Ann R. "The Social Construction of Nature: Theoretical Approaches to the History of Environmental Problems." *Environmental Review* 11, no. 4 (1987): 255–64.

Black, Brian. "Oil Creek as Industrial Apparatus: Re-creating the Industrial Process through the Landscape of Pennsylvania's Oil Boom." *Environmental History* 3, no. 2 (1998): 210–29.

Blue Ridge National Heritage Area. http://www.blueridgeheritage.com/about. Accessed April 14, 2010.

Bolgiano, Chris. *The Appalachian Forest: A Search for Roots and Renewal*. Mechanicsburg, Pa.: Stackpole Books, 1998.

———. *Living in the Appalachian Forest: True Tales of Sustainable Forestry*. Mechanicsburg, Pa.: Stackpole Books, 2002.

———, ed. *Mighty Giants: An American Chestnut Anthology*. Bennington, Vt.: American Chestnut Foundation, 2007.

———. "National Forests as the New Appalachian Commons." Paper presented at the Appalachian Studies Association meeting, Abingdon, Va., 1999.

Bowes, Michael D., and John V. Krutilla. *Multiple-Use Management: The Economics of Public Forestlands*. Washington, D.C.: Resources for the Future, 1989.

Bradley, Wallace. "Hot Biscuits and Sourwood Honey." In Parris, *Roaming the Mountains*, 27–29. Interview by John Parris.

Bramlett, Jim, and Robin Briggs. *The Road to Nowhere*. Research Triangle Park: University of North Carolina Center for Public Television, 1997.

Brinkley, Douglas. *The Wilderness Warrior: Theodore Roosevelt and the Crusade for America*. New York: HarperCollins, 2009.

Bromley, Daniel M. "Land and Water Problems in an Institutional Perspective." *American Journal of Agricultural Economics* 64 (2002): 834–44.

———, ed. *Making the Commons Work*. San Francisco: Institute for Contemporary Studies, 1992.

———. "Property Rights as Authority Systems: The Role of Rules in Resource Management." In *Emerging Issues in Forest Policy*, edited by Peter M. Nemetz, 453–70. Vancouver: University of British Columbia Press, 1992.

Brooks, Paul. *The House of Life: Rachel Carson at Work*. Boston: Houghton Mifflin, 1972.

———. *Speaking for Nature: How Literary Naturalists from Henry David Thoreau to Rachel Carson Have Shaped America*. Boston: Houghton Mifflin, 1980.

Brown, Catherine, and Celie Newton Maddox. "Women and the Land: A Suitable Profession." *Landscape Architecture*, May 1982, 65–69.

Brown, Margaret Lynn. *The Wild East: A Biography of the Great Smoky Mountains*. Gainesville: University Press of Florida, 2000.

Brownhill, Leigh. "Gendered Struggles for the Commons: Food Sovereignty, Tree-Planting, and Climate Change." *Women and Environments* 74/75 (2007): 34–37.

Brubaker, Sterling, ed. *Rethinking the Federal Lands*. Washington, D.C.: Resources for the Future, 1984.

Brundage, W. Fitzhugh, ed. *Where These Memories Grow: History, Memory, and Southern Identity*. Chapel Hill: University of North Carolina Press, 2000.

Brunk, Robert S., ed. *May We All Remember Well: A Journal of the History & Cultures of Western North Carolina*. Vol. 1. Asheville, N.C.: Robert S. Brunk Auction Services, 1997.

Buck, Susan J. "Cultural Theory and Management of Common Property Resources." *Human Ecology* 17 (1989): 101–16.

———. "No Tragedy on the Commons." *Environmental Ethics* 7 (1985): 49–61.

Bullard, Robert D. *Confronting Environmental Racism: Voices from the Grassroots*. Boston: South End Press, 1993.

———. *Dumping in Dixie: Race, Class, and Environmental Quality*. Boulder, Colo.: Westview Press, 1990.

———, ed. *Unequal Protection: Environmental Justice and Communities of Color*. San Francisco: Sierra Club Books, 1993.

Bumgarner, Ed. "Bear-Huntin' Men Know the Feeling." In Parris, *Roaming the Mountains*, 175–77. Interview by John Parris.

Burg, David F. *Chicago's White City of 1893*. Lexington: University Press of Kentucky, 1976.

Burnett, Edmund Cody. "Hog Raising and Hog Driving in the Region of the French Broad River." *Agricultural History* 20, no. 2 (1946): 86–103.

Burress, Bob. See Jeff Fears, "Bear Hunting." In Wigginton, *Foxfire 5*, 437–94. Interview by Jeff Fears, with Randall Hardy, Danny Brown, Eddie Brown, and Mark Burdette.

Buxton, Barry M., ed. *The Great Forest: An Appalachian Story*. Boone, N.C.: Appalachian Consortium Press, 1985.

Caldecott, Leonie, and Stephanie Leland, eds. *Reclaim the Earth: Women Speak Out for Life on Earth*. London: Women's Press, 1983.

Calhoun, Granville. "Talk about Catching Fish." In Parris, *Mountain Bred*, 202–4. Interview by John Parris.

———. "When Every Day Was Thanksgiving." In Parris, *These Storied Mountains*, 199–201. Interview by John Parris.

Carpenter, Bob. "Hunting Tales." In Wigginton, *The Foxfire Book*, 274–75.

Carpenter, Harley. "Hunting Tales." In Wigginton, *The Foxfire Book*, 279–82.

Carson, Rachel. *The Sense of Wonder*. New York: Harper and Row, 1956.

———. *Silent Spring*. 1962; New York: Fawcett, 1964.

Cartmill, Matt. *A View to a Death in the Morning: Hunting and Nature through History*. Cambridge, Mass.: Harvard University Press, 1993.

Castro, Alfonso Peter. "Njukiine Forest: Transformation of a Common-Property Resource." *Forest & Conservation History* 35, no. 4 (1991): 160–68.

Catton, Theodore. "From Game Refuges to Ecosystem Assessments: Wildlife Management on the Western National Forests." *Journal of the West* 38, no. 4 (1999): 36–44.

———. *Inhabited Wilderness: Indians, Eskimos, and National Parks in Alaska*. Albuquerque: University of New Mexico Press, 1997.

Chastain, Nate. "Hunting Tales." In Wigginton, *The Foxfire Book*, 274–75.

Cheek, Angie, Lacy Hunter Nix, and Foxfire students, eds. *The Foxfire 40th Anniversary Book: Faith, Family, and the Land*. New York: Anchor Books, 2006.

Cheney, Jim. "Eco-feminism and Deep Ecology." *Environmental Ethics* 9 (Summer 1987): 115–45.

Clark, Sandra H. B. *Geology of the Southern Appalachian Mountains*. U.S. Department of the Interior, U.S. Geological Survey Scientific Investigations Map 2830, 2008.

Clark, Thomas D. *The Greening of the South: The Recovery of Land and Forest*. Lexington: University Press of Kentucky, 1984.

Clary, David A. *Timber and the Forest Service*. Lawrence: University Press of Kansas, 1986.

Clawson, Marion. *Forest for Whom and for What?* Baltimore, Md.: Johns Hopkins University Press for Resources for the Future, 1975.

Cliff, Edward P. "Half a Century in Forest Conservation." USDA, Forest Service, Washington Office, History Unit, 1981. Interview.

Coalition for Appalachian Ministry. *Erets: Land: The Church and Appalachian Land Issues*. Amesville, Ohio: Coalition for Appalachian Ministry, 1984.

Cogdill, Jerald. See Jeff Fears, "Bear Hunting." In Wigginton, *Foxfire 5*, 437–94. Interview by Jeff Fears, with Randall Hardy, Danny Brown, Eddie Brown, and Mark Burdette.

Colonial and State Records of North Carolina, Acts of the North Carolina General Assembly, 1745, vol. 23, 218–19.

Community Research Center. "A Socioeconomic Overview of Western North Carolina for the Nantahala-Pisgah Forests." Southern Appalachian Center, Mars Hill College, 1979.

Conner, Minyard. "Hunting Tales." In Wigginton, *The Foxfire Book*, 287–88.

Conrad, David E. *The Land We Cared For . . . A History of the Forest Service's Eastern Region*. USDA, Forest Service, Region 9, 1997.

Corkran, David H. *The Carolina Indian Frontier*. Columbia: University of South Carolina Press, 1970.

Cosgrove, Denis E. "Landscape and Social Formation: Theoretical Considerations." In *Social Formation and Symbolic Landscape*, 13–38. Totowa, N.J.: Barnes and Noble, 1984.

Cowdrey, Albert E. *This Land, This South: An Environmental History*. Lexington: University Press of Kentucky, 1983.

Cox, Thomas R., Robert S. Maxwell, Phillip Drennon Thomas, and Joseph J. Malone. *This Well-Wooded Land: Americans and Their Forests from Colonial Times to the Present*. Lincoln: University of Nebraska Press, 1985.

Cradle of Forestry. http://www.cradleofforestry.com/. Accessed June 15, 2010.

Crane, Verner W. *The Southern Frontier, 1670–1732*. Ann Arbor: University of Michigan Press, 1929.

Crockett, Taylor. "Eighty Years in the Appalachian Woodlands." *Clay County Progress*, January 12, 1989. Interview by David Wheeler.

———. "Hunting Tales." In Wigginton, *The Foxfire Book*, 283–84, 285–87.

———. "Taylor Crockett Remembers." *Wildlife in North Carolina*, February 1985, 18–22. Interview by Lawrence S. Early and Curtis Wooten.

Cronon, William. *Changes in the Land: Indians, Colonists, and the Ecology of New England*. New York: Hill and Wang, 1983.

———. *Nature's Metropolis: Chicago and the Great West*. New York: W. W. Norton, 1991.

———. "The Trouble with Wilderness; or, Getting Back to the Wrong Nature." In Cronon, *Uncommon Ground*, 69–90.

———, ed. *Uncommon Ground: Toward Reinventing Nature*. New York: W. W. Norton, 1995.

———. "The Uses of Environmental History." *Environmental History Review* 17, no. 3 (1993): 1–22.

Crosby, Alfred W. *The Columbian Exchange: Biological and Cultural Consequences of 1492*. Westport, Conn.: Greenwood Press, 1986.

Crowe, Beryl. "The Tragedy of the Commons Revisited." In Hardin and Baden, *Managing the Commons*, 54–55.

Daniel, Pete. *Standing at the Crossroads: Southern Life since 1900*. New York: Hill and Wang, 1986.

Davidson, Debra J., and Scott Frickel. "Understanding Environmental Governance: A Critical Review." *Organization and Environment* 17, no. 4 (2004): 471–92.

Davis, Donald Edward. *Homeplace Geography: Essays for Appalachia*. Macon, Ga.: Mercer University Press, 2006.

———. *Where There Are Mountains: An Environmental History of the Southern Appalachians*. Athens: University of Georgia Press, 2000.

Decker, D. J., and G. R. Goff, eds. *Valuing Wildlife: Economic and Social Perspectives*. Boulder, Colo.: Westview Press, 1987.

Delcourt, Hazel R., and Paul A. Delcourt. "Pre-Columbian Native American Use of Fire on Southern Appalachian Landscapes." *Conservation Biology* 11, no. 4 (1997): 1010–11.

Delcourt, Paul A., and Hazel R. Delcourt. "The Influence of Prehistoric Human-Set Fires on Oak-Chestnut Forests in the Southern Appalachians." *Castanea* 63, no. 3 (1998): 37–45.

De Moor, Martina, Leigh Shaw-Taylor, and Paul Warde, eds. *The Management of*

Common Land in North West Europe, c. 1500–1850. Turnhout: Brepols Publishers, 2002.

Dendy, Mae. "Wild Buckberries Mean a Cold Bread Pie Feast." *Asheville Citizen*, September 16, 1979. Interview by John Parris.

Denevan, William. "The Pristine Myth: The Landscape of the Americas in 1492." *Annals of the Association of American Geographers* 82 (1992): 369–85.

Devall, Bill, ed. *Clearcut: The Tragedy of Industrial Forestry*. San Francisco: Sierra Club Books and Earth Island Press, 1993.

Diamond, Irene, and Gloria Feman Orenstein, eds. *Reweaving the World: The Emergence of Ecofeminism*. San Francisco: Sierra Club Books, 1990.

Dick, Everett. *The Lure of the Land: A Social History of the Public Lands from the Articles of Confederation to the New Deal*. Lincoln: University of Nebraska Press, 1970.

Diegues, Antonio Carlos. "Social Movements and the Remaking of the Commons in the Brazilian Amazon." In Goldman, *Privatizing Nature*, 54–75.

Dillingham, Hoyte. See Bolgiano, *The Appalachian Forest*, 229–32. Interview by Chris Bolgiano.

Discover Life in America, Great Smoky Mountains National Park All Taxa Biodiversity Inventory. "Smokies Species Tally, December 10, 2009." http://www.dlia.org/abti/new_science/discoveries.shtml. Accessed April 14, 2010.

Dixon, Melvin. *Ride Out the Wilderness: Geography and Identity in Afro-American Literature*. Urbana: University of Illinois Press, 1987.

Dobson, Andrew, and Derek Bell, eds. *Environmental Citizenship*. Cambridge, Mass.: MIT Press, 2006.

Donahue, Brian. *Reclaiming the Commons: Community Farms and Forests in a New England Town*. New Haven, Conn.: Yale University Press, 2001.

Dorman, Robert L. *A Word for Nature: Four Pioneering Environmental Advocates, 1845–1913*. Chapel Hill: University of North Carolina Press, 1998.

Doughty, Robin W. *Feather Fashions and Bird Preservation: A Study in Nature Protection*. Berkeley: University of California Press, 1975.

Dowie, Mark. *Losing Ground: American Environmentalism at the Close of the Twentieth Century*. Cambridge, Mass.: MIT Press, 1995.

Drake, Richard B. "Southern Appalachia and the South: A Region within a Section." In Inscoe, *Southern Appalachia and the South*, 18–27.

Dunaway, Wilma A. *The First American Frontier: Transition to Capitalism in Southern Appalachia, 1700–1860*. Chapel Hill: University of North Carolina Press, 1996.

Duncan, Barbara R. "American Ginseng in Western North Carolina: A Cross-Cultural Examination." In Brunk, *May We All Remember Well*, 1:201–13.

———. *Living Stories of the Cherokee*. Chapel Hill: University of North Carolina Press, 1998.

Dunlap, Riley E., and Angela G. Mertig, eds. *American Environmentalism: The U.S. Environmental Movement, 1970–1990*. Philadelphia: Taylor and Francis, 1992.

Dunlap, Thomas R. *Saving America's Wildlife*. Princeton, N.J.: Princeton University Press, 1981.

———. "Sport Hunting and Conservation, 1880–1920." *Environmental Review* 12, no. 1 (1988): 51–80.

Dunn, Durwood. *Cades Cove: The Life and Death of a Southern Appalachian Community, 1818–1937.* Knoxville: University of Tennessee Press, 1988.

Durrill, Wayne. "Producing Poverty: Local Government and Economic Development in a New South County, 1874–1884." *Journal of American History* 71, no. 4 (1985): 764–81.

Eller, Ronald D. "Land as Commodity: Industrialization of the Appalachian Forests, 1880–1940." In Buxton, *The Great Forest,* 27–42.

———. *Miners, Millhands, and Mountaineers: Industrialization of the Appalachian South, 1880–1930.* Knoxville: University of Tennessee Press, 1982.

———. *Uneven Ground: Appalachia since 1945.* Lexington: University Press of Kentucky, 2008.

Evans, Sara M., and Hary C. Boyte. *Free Spaces: The Sources of Democratic Change in America.* New York: Harper and Row, 1986.

Fears, Jeff. "Bear Hunting." In Wigginton, *Foxfire 5,* 437–94.

Feeney, David, Fikret Berkes, Bonnie J. McCay, and James M. Acheson. "The Tragedy of the Commons: Twenty-Two Years Later." *Human Ecology* 18 (1990): 1–19.

Finger, John R. *Cherokee Americans: The Eastern Band of Cherokees in the Twentieth Century.* Lincoln: University of Nebraska Press, 1991.

Fink, Leon. *The Maya of Morganton: Work and Community in the Nuevo New South.* Chapel Hill: University of North Carolina Press, 2007.

Fischer, Frank. *Citizens, Experts, and the Environment: The Politics of Local Knowledge.* Durham, N.C.: Duke University Press, 2000.

Fisher, Stephen L., ed. *Fighting Back in Appalachia: Traditions of Resistance and Change.* Philadelphia: Temple University Press, 1993.

Flippen, John Brooks. "The Nixon Administration, Timber, and the Call of the Wild." *Environmental History Review* 19, no. 2 (1995): 37–54.

Flores, Dan. "Place: An Argument for Bioregional History." *Environmental History Review* 18, no. 4 (1994): 1–18.

Fortmann, Louise, and John W. Bruce. *Whose Trees: Proprietary Dimensions of Forestry.* Boulder, Colo.: Westview Press, 1988.

Foster, David R. "Conservation Lessons & Challenges from Ecological History." *Forest History Today,* Fall 2000, 2–11.

Fox, Stephen. *The American Conservation Movement: John Muir and His Legacy.* Madison: University of Wisconsin Press, 1981.

Francis, Mark, Lisa Cashdan, and Lynn Paxson. *Community Open Spaces: Greening Neighborhoods through Community Action and Land Conservation.* Washington, D.C.: Island Press, 1984.

Franklin, Wayne, and Michael Steiner, eds. *Mapping American Culture.* Iowa City: University of Iowa Press, 1992.

Fraser, Walter J., Jr., R. Frank Saunders Jr., and Jon L. Wakelyn, eds. *The Web of Southern Social Relations: Women, Family, and Education.* Athens: University of Georgia Press, 1985.

Freedman, Estelle. "Separatism as Strategy: Female Institution Building and American Feminism, 1870–1930." *Feminist Studies* 5, no. 3 (1979): 512–29.

Freinkel, Susan. *American Chestnut: The Life, Death, and Rebirth of a Perfect Tree.* Berkeley: University of California Press, 2007.

Frisch, Michael. *A Shared Authority: Essays on the Craft and Meaning of Oral and Public History.* Albany: State University of New York Press, 1990.

Fritzboger, Martina Bo. *A Windfall for the Magnates: The Development of Woodland Ownership in Denmark c. 1150–1830.* Odense: University Press of Southern Denmark, 2004.

Frome, Michael. *Battle for the Wilderness.* 3rd ed. Salt Lake City: University of Utah Press, 1997.

———. *The Forest Service.* Boulder, Colo.: Westview Press, 1984.

———. *Whose Woods These Are: The Story of the National Forests.* New York: Doubleday & Company, 1962.

Gale, Bob. "The Scent of Hickory and the Agony of Da Feet." Paper presented at the Appalachian Studies Association meeting, Snowshoe, W. Va., 2000.

Gates, Barbara T., and Ann B. Shteir, eds. *Natural Eloquence: Women Reinscribe Science.* Madison: University of Wisconsin Press, 1997.

Gaventa, John. *Power and Powerlessness: Quiescence and Rebellion in an Appalachian Valley.* Urbana: University of Illinois Press, 1980.

Gennett, Andrew. *Sound Wormy: Memoir of Andrew Gennett, Lumberman.* Edited by Nicole Hayler. Athens: University of Georgia Press, 2002.

Geores, Martha E. *Common Ground: The Struggle for Ownership of the Black Hills National Forest.* Lanham, Md.: Rowman and Littlefield, 1996.

Gillette, Elizabeth R., ed. *Action for Wilderness.* San Francisco: Sierra Club, 1972.

Gohdes, Clarence, ed. *Hunting in the Old South: Original Narratives of the Hunters.* Baton Rouge: Louisiana State University Press, 1967.

Goldman, Michael, ed. *Privatizing Nature: Political Struggles for the Global Commons.* New Brunswick, N.J.: Rutgers University Press, 1998.

Gonzales, George A. *Corporate Power and the Environment: The Political Economy of U.S. Environmental Policy.* Lanham, Md.: Rowman and Littlefield, 2001.

Gottlieb, Robert. "Beyond NEPA and Earth Day: Reconstructing the Past and Envisioning a Future for Environmentalism." *Environmental History Review* 19, no. 4 (1995): 1–14.

———. *Forcing the Spring: The Transformation of the American Environmental Movement.* Washington, D.C.: Island Press, 1993.

———. "Reconstructing Environmentalism: Complex Movements, Diverse Roots." *Environmental History Review* 17, no. 4 (1993): 1–19.

Gould, Lewis L. "First Lady as Catalyst: Lady Bird Johnson and Highway Beautification in the 1960s." *Environmental Review* 10, no. 2 (1986): 76–92.

———. *Lady Bird Johnson and the Environment.* Lawrence: University Press of Kansas, 1988.

Grantham, Dewey. *The Life and Death of the Solid South: A Political History.* Lexington: University Press of Kentucky, 1988.

———. *Southern Progressivism: The Reconciliation of Progress and Tradition.* Knoxville: University of Tennessee Press, 1983.

Griffin, Glenn. See Jeff Fears, "Bear Hunting." In Wigginton, *Foxfire 5*, 437–94. Interview by Jeff Fears, with Randall Hardy, Danny Brown, Eddie Brown, and Mark Burdette.

Groth, Paul. "Lot, Yard, and Garden: American Distinctions." *Landscape* 30, no. 3 (1990): 29–35.

Grumbine, R. Edward. "Policy in the Woods." In Devall, *Clearcut*, 253–61.

Gugliotta, Angela. "Class, Gender, and Coal Smoke: Gender Ideology and Environmental Injustice in Pittsburgh, 1868–1914." *Environmental History* 5, no. 2 (2000): 165–93.

Guha, Ramachandra. "Radical American Environmentalism and Wilderness Preservation: A Third World Critique." *Environmental Ethics* 11, no. 1 (1989): 71–83.

———. *The Unquiet Woods: Ecological Change and Peasant Resistance in the Himalaya*. Berkeley: University of California Press, 1990.

Guha, Ramachandra, and J. Martinez-Alier. *Varieties of Environmentalism: Essays North and South*. London: Oxford University Press, 1998.

Hahn, Steven. "Hunting, Fishing, and Foraging: Common Rights and Class Relations in the Postbellum South." *Radical History Review* 26, no. 10 (1982): 38–43.

———. *Roots of Southern Populism: Yeoman Farmers and the Transformation of the Georgia Upcountry, 1850–1890*. New York: Oxford University Press, 1983.

Hahn, Steven, and Jonathan Prude, eds. *The Countryside in the Age of Capitalist Transformation: Essays in the Social History of Rural America*. Chapel Hill: University of North Carolina Press, 1985.

Haile, Margaret Wallis. *Dillinghams of Big Ivy, Buncombe County, N.C. and Related Families*. Baltimore, Md.: Gateway Press, 1979.

Hall, Jacquelyn Dowd. "Disorderly Women: Gender and Labor Militancy in the Appalachian South." *Journal of American History* 73 (September 1986): 354–82.

———. "Partial Truths." *Signs* 14 (Winter 1989): 902–11.

———. "Private Eyes, Public Women: Images of Class and Sex in the Urban South, Atlanta, Georgia, 1913–1915." In *Work Engendered: Toward a New History of Labor*, edited by Ava Baron, 243–72. Ithaca, N.Y.: Cornell University Press, 1991.

Hall, Jacquelyn Dowd, James Leloudis, Robert Korstad, Mary Murphy, Lu Ann Jones, and Christopher B. Daly. *Like a Family: The Making of a Southern Cotton Mill World*. Chapel Hill: University of North Carolina Press, 1987.

Hall, Jacquelyn Dowd, and Anne Firor Scott. "Women in the South." In *Interpreting Southern History: Historiographical Essays in Honor of Sanford W. Higginbotham*, edited by John B. Boles and Evelyn Thomas Nolen, 454–509. Baton Rouge: Louisiana State University Press, 1987.

Hall, Robert L., and Carol B. Stack, eds. *Holding On to the Land and the Lord: Kinship, Ritual, Land Tenure, and Social Policy in the Rural South*. Athens: University of Georgia Press, 1982.

Hall, William L. "Influences of the National Forests in the Southern Appalachians." *Journal of Forestry* 17 (1919): 402–7.

———. "To Remake the Appalachians: A New Order in the Mountains That Is Founded on Forestry." *World's Work* 28 (July 1914): 321–38.

Hammond, Herb. "Clearcutting: Ecological and Economic Flaws." In Devall, *Clearcut*, 25–32.

Haraway, Donna. *Primate Visions: Gender, Race, and Nature in the World of Modern Science*. New York: Routledge, 1989.

Hardin, Garrett. "The Tragedy of the Commons." *Science* 162 (1968): 1243–48.

Hardin, Garrett, and John Baden, eds. *Managing the Commons*. San Francisco: W. H. Freeman, 1977.

Hatley, Tom. *The Dividing Paths: Cherokees and South Carolinians through the Era of Revolution*. New York: Oxford University Press, 1993.

Hawks, Joanne V., and Sheila L. Skemp, eds. *Sex, Race, and the Role of Women in the South*. Jackson: University Press of Mississippi, 1983.

Hays, Samuel P. *The American People and the National Forests: The First Century of the U.S. Forest Service*. Pittsburgh: University of Pittsburgh Press, 2009.

———. *Beauty, Health, and Permanence: Environmental Politics in the United States, 1955–1985*. Cambridge: Cambridge University Press, 1987.

———. *Conservation and the Gospel of Efficiency: The Progressive Conservation Movement, 1890–1920*. New York: Atheneum Books, 1980.

———. *Wars in the Woods: The Rise of Ecological Forestry in America*. Pittsburgh: University of Pittsburgh Press, 2007.

Heidbrink, Ingo Klaus. "The Oceans as the Common Property of Mankind from Early Modern Period to Today." *History Compass* 6, no. 2 (2008): 659–72.

Hewitt, Nancy A. "Beyond the Search for Sisterhood." In *Unequal Sisters: A Multicultural Reader in U.S. Women's History*, edited by Vicki L. Ruiz and Ellen Carol DuBois, 1–19. New York: Routledge, 1994.

Hewitt, Nancy A., and Suzanne Lebsock. *Visible Women: New Essays on American Activism*. Urbana: University of Illinois Press, 1993.

Hibbard, Benjamin Horace. *A History of Public Land Policies*. 1924; Madison: University of Wisconsin Press, 1965.

Hicks, George L. *Appalachian Valley*. New York: Holt, Rinehart and Winston, 1976.

Hill, Sarah H. *Weaving New Worlds: Cherokee Women and Their Basketry*. Chapel Hill: University of North Carolina Press, 1997.

Hinsdale, Mary Ann, Helen M. Lewis, and S. Maxine Waller. *It Comes from the People: Community Development and Local Theology*. Philadelphia: Temple University Press, 1995.

Hirt, Paul W. *A Conspiracy of Optimism: Management of the National Forests since World War Two*. Lincoln: University of Nebraska Press, 1994.

———. "Institutional Failure in the U.S. Forest Service: A Historical Perspective." *Research in Social Problems and Public Policy* 7 (1999): 217–39.

Houston, Rachel. "The Coon-Huntin' Woman of the Hills." In Parris, *These Storied Mountains*, 140–43. Interview by John Parris.

Howell, Benita J., ed. *Culture, Environment, and Conservation in the Appalachian South*. Urbana: University of Illinois Press, 2002.

———. "Mountain Foragers in Southeast Asia and Appalachia: Cross-Cultural

Perspectives on the 'Mountain Man' Stereotype." In Obermiller and Philliber, *Appalachia in an International Context*, 131–40.

Howkins, A. "Economic Crime and Class Law: Poaching and the Game Laws, 1840–1880." In *The Imposition of Law*, edited by Sandra B. Burman and Barbara E. Harrell-Bond, 273–87. New York: Academic Press, 1979.

Hoy, Suellen. "'Municipal Housekeeping': The Role of Women in Improving Urban Sanitation Practices, 1880–1917." In *Pollution and Reform in American Cities, 1870–1930*, edited by Martin V. Melosi, 173–98. Austin: University of Texas Press, 1980.

Hsiung, David C. "Geographic Determinism and Possibilism: Interpretations of the Appalachian Environment and Culture in the Last Century." *Journal of the Appalachian Studies Association* 4 (1992): 14–23.

Hudson, Charles. *Knights of Spain, Warriors of the Sun: Hernando de Soto and the South's Ancient Chiefdoms*. Athens: University of Georgia Press, 1998.

———. *The Southeastern Indians*. Knoxville: University of Tennessee Press, 1976.

Hufford, Mary. "American Ginseng and the Idea of the Commons." *Folklife Center News* 19, nos. 1 and 2 (1997): 3–18.

———. "Building the Commons: Folklore, Citizen Science, and the Ecological Imagination." *Indian Folklife* 1, no. 3 (2000): 15–16.

———. *Chaseworld: Foxhunting and Storytelling in New Jersey's Pine Barrens*. Philadelphia: University of Pennsylvania Press, 1992.

Hughes, D. M. "When Parks Encroach upon People: Expanding National Parks in the Rusitu Valley, Zimbabwe." *Cultural Survival Quarterly* 20, no. 1 (1996): 36–40.

Hunt, James L. *Marion Butler and American Populism*. Chapel Hill: University of North Carolina Press, 2007.

Hurley, Andrew. *Environmental Inequalities: Class, Race, and Industrial Pollution in Gary, Indiana, 1945–1980*. Chapel Hill: University of North Carolina Press, 1995.

Huth, Hans. *Nature and the American Mind: Three Centuries of Changing Attitudes*. Berkeley: University of California Press, 1957.

Hynes, H. Patricia. "Ellen Swallow, Lois Gibbs, and Rachel Carson: Catalysts of the American Environmental Movement." *Woman of Power* 9 (Spring 1988): 37–41, 78–80.

———. *The Recurring Silent Spring*. New York: Pergamon Press, 1989.

Igler, David. "When Is a River Not a River? Reclaiming Nature's Disorder in *Lux v. Haggin*." *Environmental History* 1, no. 2 (1996): 52–69.

Inscoe, John. *Mountain Masters: Slavery and the Sectional Crisis in Western North Carolina*. Knoxville: University of Tennessee Press, 1989.

———, ed. *Southern Appalachia and the South: A Region within a Region*. Proceedings of the Appalachian Studies Conference. Boone: Appalachian Consortium Press, 1991.

Jackson, J. B. *Discovering the Vernacular Landscape*. New Haven, Conn.: Yale University Press, 1984.

———. *The Necessity for Ruins and Other Topics*. Amherst: University of Massachusetts Press, 1985.

Jackson, Kenneth T. *Crabgrass Frontier: The Suburbanization of the United States.* New York: Oxford University Press, 1985.

Jacobs, Harvey M., ed. *Who Owns America? Social Conflict over Property Rights.* Madison: University of Wisconsin Press, 1998.

Jacoby, Karl. "Class and Environmental History: Lessons from 'The War in the Adirondacks." *Environmental History* 2, no. 3 (1997): 324–42.

———. *Crimes against Nature: Squatters, Poachers, Thieves, and the Hidden History of American Conservation.* Berkeley: University of California Press, 2003.

Jeffrey, Julie Roy. "'There Is Some Splendid Scenery': Women's Responses to the Great Plains Landscape." *Great Plains Quarterly* 8, no. 2 (1988): 69–78.

Jensen, Derrick, and George Draffan. *Strangely like War: The Global Assault on Forests.* White River Junction, Vt.: Chelsea Green Publishing, 2003.

John, DeWitt. *Civic Environmentalism: Alternatives to Regulation in States and Communities.* Washington, D.C.: Congressional Quarterly Press, 1994.

Johnson, Anne Lewis. *Ready for Harvest: Clearcutting in the Southern Appalachians.* Whitesburg, Ky.: Appalshop Film and Video, 1993.

Johnson, Benjamin Heber. "Conservation, Subsistence, and Class at the Birth of Superior National Forest." *Environmental History* 4, no. 1 (1999): 80–99.

Jones, Eric T., Rebecca J. McLain, and James Weigand, eds. *Nontimber Forest Products in the United States.* Lawrence: University Press of Kansas, 2002.

Judd, Richard. *Common Lands, Common People: The Origins of Conservation in Northern New England.* Cambridge, Mass.: Harvard University Press, 1997.

———. *Natural States: The Environmental Imagination in Maine, Oregon, and the Nation.* Washington, D.C.: Resources for the Future Press, 2004.

Justen, Norton. *So Sweet to Labor: Rural Women in America, 1865–1895.* New York: Viking Press, 1979.

Kahn, Si. *The Forest Service and Appalachia.* John Hay Whitney Foundation, 1974.

Kaminer, Wendy. *Women Volunteering: The Pleasure, Pain, and Politics of Unpaid Work from 1830 to the Present.* Garden City, N.Y.: Doubleday, 1984.

Kaplan, Temma. *Crazy for Democracy: Women in Grassroots Movements.* New York: Routledge, 1997.

Kaufman, Polly Welts. *National Parks and the Woman's Voice: A History.* Albuquerque: University of New Mexico Press, 1996.

Kayden, Jerold S. "Private Property Rights, Government Regulation, and the Constitution: Searching for a Balance." In *Land Use in America,* edited by H. Diamond and P. Noonan, 257–77. Washington, D.C.: Island Press, 1996.

Keeper of the Mountains Foundation. http://mountainkeeper.blogspot.com/. Accessed June 15, 2010.

Keiner, Christine. *The Oyster Question: Scientists, Watermen, and the Maryland Chesapeake Bay since 1880.* Athens: University of Georgia Press, 2010.

Kellert, Stephen R. *From Kinship to Mastery: Biophilia in Human Evolution and Development.* Washington, D.C.: Island Press/Shearwater Books, 1997.

Kellert, Stephen R., and Joyce K. Berry. *Knowledge, Affection, and Basic Attitudes toward Animals in American Society.* American Attitudes, Knowledge, and Behaviors toward Wildlife and Natural Habitats, Phase III. Washington, D.C.: U.S. Fish and Wildlife Service, 1980.

Kelley, Mary, ed. *Woman's Being Woman's Place: Female Identity and Vocation in American History*. Boston: Hall, 1979.

Kemmis, Daniel. *Community and the Politics of Place*. Norman: University of Oklahoma Press, 1990.

Kempton, Willett, James Boster, and Jennifer Hartley. *Environmental Values in American Culture*. Cambridge, Mass.: MIT Press, 1995.

Kephart, Horace. *Our Southern Highlanders: A Narrative of Adventure in the Southern Appalachians and a Study of Life among the Mountaineers*. 1913; Knoxville: University of Tennessee Press, 1984.

Kerber, Linda. "Separate Spheres, Female Worlds, Woman's Place: The Rhetoric of Women's History." *Journal of American History* 75, no. 1 (1988): 9–39.

Kheel, Marti. "The Liberation of Nature: A Circular Affair." *Environmental Ethics* 7 (Summer 1985): 135–49.

King, Ynestra. "What Is Ecofeminism?" *Nation*, December 12, 1987, 702, 730–32.

Kirby, Jack Temple. *Mockingbird Song: Ecological Landscapes of the South*. Chapel Hill: University of North Carolina Press, 2006.

———. *Poquosin: A Study of Rural Landscape and Society*. Chapel Hill: University of North Carolina Press, 1995.

———. *Rural Worlds Lost: The American South, 1920–1960*. Baton Rouge: Louisiana State University Press, 1986.

Kline, Benjamin. *First along the River: A Brief History of the U.S. Environmental Movement*. San Francisco: Acada Books, 1997.

Klyza, Christopher. *Who Controls the Public Lands? Mining, Forestry, and Grazing Policies, 1870–1990*. Chapel Hill: University of North Carolina Press, 1996.

Knott, Catherine Henshaw. *Living with the Adirondack Forest: Local Perspectives on Land Use Conflicts*. Ithaca, N.Y.: Cornell University Press, 1998.

Koeniger, A. Cash. "Climate and Southern Distinctiveness." *Journal of Southern History* 54 (February 1988): 21–44.

Kolodny, Annette. *The Land before Her: Fantasy and Experience of the American Frontiers, 1630–1860*. Chapel Hill: University of North Carolina Press, 1984.

———. *The Lay of the Land: Metaphor as Experience and History in American Life and Letters*. Chapel Hill: University of North Carolina Press, 1984.

Koppes, Clayton R. "Efficiency/Equity/Esthetics: Towards a Reinterpretation of American Conservation." *Environmental Review* 11, no. 2 (1987): 127–46.

Kosek, Jake. *Understories: The Political Life of Forests in New Mexico*. Durham, N.C.: Duke University Press, 2006.

Kury, Channing, ed. *Enclosing the Environment: NEPA's Transformation of Conservation into Environmentalism*. Albuquerque: University of New Mexico Press, 1985.

Langston, Nancy. *Forest Dreams, Forest Nightmares: The Paradox of Old Growth in the Inland West*. Seattle: University of Washington Press, 1996.

Lanier, Parks, Jr., ed. *The Poetics of Appalachian Space*. Knoxville: University of Tennessee Press, 1991.

Lansky, Mitch. "Myths of the Benign Industrial Clearcut." In Devall, *Clearcut*, 47–49.

Lash, Jonathan, Katherine Gillman, and David Sheridan. *A Season of Spoils: The*

Story of the Reagan Administration's Attack on the Environment. New York: Pantheon Books, 1984.

Leach, Melissa, and Cathy Green. "Gender and Environmental History: From Representation of Women and Nature to Gender Analysis of Ecology and Politics." *Environment and History* 3 (1997): 343–70.

Lear, Linda J. "Rachel Carson's Silent Spring." *Environmental History Review* 17, no. 3 (1993): 23–48.

Leavitt, Emily Stewart. *Animals and Their Legal Rights: A Survey of American Laws from 1641–1978.* Washington, D.C.: Animal Welfare Institute, 1978.

Lewis, James G. *The Forest Service and the Greatest Good: A Centennial History.* Durham, N.C.: Forest History Society, 2005.

Lewis, Michael, ed. *American Wilderness: A New History.* New York: Oxford University Press, 2007.

Lewis, Ronald L. *Transforming the Appalachian Countryside: Railroads, Deforestation, and Social Change in West Virginia, 1880–1920.* Chapel Hill: University of North Carolina Press, 1998.

Limerick, Patricia Nelson. "Forestry and Modern Environmentalism: Ending the Cold War." *Journal of Forestry* 100 (December 2002): 46–50.

Linebaugh, Peter. *The Magna Carta Manifesto: Liberties and Commons for All.* Berkeley: University of California Press, 2008.

Link, William. *The Paradox of Southern Progressivism, 1880–1930.* Chapel Hill: University of North Carolina Press, 1992.

Little, Charles E. *The Dying of the Trees: The Pandemic in America's Forests.* New York: Penguin Books, 1995.

Little, Priscilla Cortelyou, and Robert C. Vaughan, eds. *A New Perspective: Southern Women's Cultural History from the Civil War to Civil Rights.* Charlottesville: Virginia Foundation for the Humanities, 1989.

Logan, John Henry. *A History of the Upper Country of South Carolina; from the Earliest Periods to the Close of the War of Independence.* Charleston, S.C.: S. G. Courtenay, 1859; repr., General Books LLC, 2010.

Lu, Flora. "'The Commons' in an Amazonian Context." In Nonini, *The Global Idea,* 41–52.

Luke, Timothy. *Capitalism, Democracy, and Ecology: Departing from Marx.* Urbana: University of Illinois Press, 1999.

Lund, Thomas A. *American Wildlife Law.* Berkeley: University of California Press, 1980.

Lutts, Ralph H. "Like Manna from God: The American Chestnut Trade in Southwestern Virginia." *Environmental History* 9, no. 3 (2004): 497–525.

Lynch, Barbara Deutsch. "The Garden and the Sea: U.S. Latino Environmental Discourse and Mainstream Environmentalism." *Social Problems* 40 (February 1993): 108–18.

MacCormack, Carol P., and Marilyn Strathern, eds. *Nature, Culture, and Gender.* Cambridge: Cambridge University Press, 1980.

Maher, Neil. *Nature's New Deal: The Civilian Conservation Corps and the Roots of the American Environmental Movement.* New York: Oxford University Press, 2007.

Marburg, Sandra Lin. "Women and Environment: Subsistence Paradigms, 1850–1950." *Environmental Review* 8, no. 1 (1984): 7–22.

Marden, P. G., and A. M. Schwartz. "Comparative Regional Issues: Land Use and Environmental Planning in the Adirondacks and Appalachians." In *Appalachia/America*, edited by W. Somerville, 89–98. Proceedings of the 1980 Appalachian Studies Conference, East Tennessee State University. Boone: Appalachian Consortium Press, 1980.

Marks, Stewart A. *Southern Hunting in Black and White: Nature, History, and Ritual in a Carolina Community.* Princeton, N.J.: Princeton University Press, 1991.

Marsh, Kevin R. *Drawing Lines in the Forest: Creating Wilderness Areas in the Pacific Northwest.* Seattle: University of Washington Press, 2007.

Martin, William H., et al., eds. *Biodiversity of the Southeastern United States.* New York: John Wiley, 1993.

Marx, Leo. *The Machine in the Garden: Technology and the Pastoral Ideal in America.* New York: Oxford University Press, 1964.

Mastran, Shelley Smith, and Nan Lowerre. *Mountaineers and Rangers: A History of Federal Forest Management in the Southern Appalachians, 1900–81.* Washington, D.C.: USDA, 1983.

Maurer, Bill. "Colonial Policy and the Construction of the Commons: An Introduction." *Plantation Society in the Americas* 4, nos. 2–3 (1997): 113–33.

McConnell, Grant. "The Multiple-Use Concept in Forest Service Policy." *Sierra Club Bulletin* 44, no. 7 (1959): 14–28.

McCormick, John. *Reclaiming Paradise: The Global Environmental Movement.* Bloomington: Indiana University Press, 1980.

McCullough, Robert. *The Landscape of Community: A History of Communal Forests in New England.* Hanover, N.H.: University Press of New England, 1995.

McDonald, Michael J., and John Muldowny. *TVA and the Dispossessed: The Resettlement of Population in the Norris Dam Area.* Knoxville: University of Tennessee Press, 1982.

McGarity, Eileen M. "From NIMBY to Civil Rights: The Origins of the Environmental Justice Movement." *Environmental History* 2, no. 3 (1997): 301–23.

McGee, Charles E. "Clearcutting and Aesthetics in the Southern Appalachians." *Journal of Forestry* 68, no. 9 (1970): 540–44.

McKay, Bonnie J. "The Culture of the Commoners: Historical Observations on Old and New World Fisheries." In McKay and Acheson, *The Question of the Commons,* 195–216.

———. *Oyster Wars and the Public Trust: Property, Law, and Ecology in New Jersey History.* Tucson: University of Arizona Press, 1998.

McKay, Bonnie J., and James M. Acheson. "Human Ecology." In McKay and Acheson, *The Question of the Commons,* 1–34.

———, eds. *The Question of the Commons: The Culture and Ecology of Communal Resources.* Tucson: University of Arizona Press, 1987.

McKean, Margaret, and Elinor Ostrom. "Common Property Regimes in the Forest: Just a Relic from the Past?" *Unasylva 180* 46 (1995).

McKinney, Gordon. *Southern Mountain Republicans, 1865–1900: Politics and the Appalachian Community*. Chapel Hill: University of North Carolina Press, 1978.

McLeod, Dawn. *Down to Earth Women: Those Who Care for the Soil*. Edinburgh: Blackwood, 1982.

Mead Corporation. *In Quiet Ways: George H. Mead, the Man and the Company*. Dayton, Ohio: Privately printed by Mead Corporation, 1970.

Medford, W. Clark. *The Early History of Haywood County*. Waynesville, N.C.: Miller Printing Company, 1961.

Melosi, Martin V. "Energy and Environment in the United States: The Era of Fossil Fuels." *Environmental Review* 11, no. 3 (1987): 167–88.

———. "Equity, Eco-racism and Environmental History." *Environmental History Review* 19, no. 3 (1995): 1–16.

———. *Garbage in the Cities: Refuse, Reform, and the Environment, 1880–1980*. Chicago: Dorsey Press, 1981.

Merchant, Carolyn. *The Death of Nature: Women, Ecology, and the Scientific Revolution*. San Francisco: Harper and Row, 1980.

———. *Earthcare: Women and the Environment*. New York: Routledge, 1996.

———. *Ecological Revolutions: Nature, Gender, and Science in New England*. Chapel Hill: University of North Carolina Press, 1989.

———. "Women of the Progressive Conservation Movement, 1900–1916." *Environmental Review* 8 (Spring 1984): 57–86.

Merrill, Karen. *Public Lands and Political Meaning: Ranchers, the Government, and the Property between Them*. Berkeley: University of California Press, 2002.

Message from the President of the United States, Transmitting a Report of the Secretary of Agriculture in Relation to the Forests, Rivers, and Mountains of the Southern Appalachian Region. Washington, D.C.: U.S. Government Printing Office, 1902.

Mighetto, Lisa. *Wild Animals and American Environmental Ethics*. Tucson: University of Arizona Press, 1991.

———. "Wildlife Protection and the New Humanitarianism." *Environmental Review* 12 (Spring 1988): 37–49.

Miller, Char, ed. *American Forests, Nature, Culture, and Politics: Development of Western Resources*. Lawrence: University Press of Kansas, 1997.

———. *Gifford Pinchot and the Making of Modern Environmentalism*. Washington, D.C.: Shearwater Press, 2001.

Miller, Char, and Hal Rothman, eds. *Out of the Woods: Essays in Environmental History*. Pittsburgh: University of Pittsburgh Press, 1997.

Mitchell, John Hanson. *Trespassing: An Inquiry into the Private Ownership of Land*. Reading, Mass.: Addison-Wesley, 1998.

Mitchell, Robert D., ed. *Appalachian Frontiers: Settlement, Society, & Development in the Preindustrial Era*. Lexington: University Press of Kentucky, 1991.

Monk, Janice. "Approaches to the Study of Women and Landscape." *Environmental Review* 8, no. 1 (1984): 23–33.

Montoya, Maria. *Translating Property: The Maxwell Land Grant and the Conflict over Land in the American West, 1840–1900*. Berkeley: University of California Press, 2002.

Montrie, Chad. "Expedient Environmentalism: Opposition to Coal Surface Mining in Appalachia and the United Mine Workers of America, 1945–1975." *Environmental History* 5, no. 1 (2000): 75–98.

———. *Making a Living: Work and the Environment in the United States*. Chapel Hill: University of North Carolina Press, 2008.

———. *To Save the Land and the People: A History of Opposition to Surface Coal Mining in Appalachia*. Chapel Hill: University of North Carolina Press, 2003.

Mooney, James. *James Mooney's History, Myths, and Sacred Formulas of the Cherokees*. 1891, 1900; repr., Asheville, N.C.: Bright Mountain Books, 1992.

Morley, Margaret Warner. *The Carolina Mountains*. New York: Houghton Mifflin, 1913.

Morrone, Michele, and Geoffrey L. Buckley, eds., *Mountains of Injustice: Social and Environmental Justice in Appalachia*. Athens: Ohio University Press, 2011.

Mull, J. Alex. *Tales of Old Burke*. Morganton, N.C.: News Herald Press, 1975.

Nash, Roderick. *The Rights of Nature: A History of Environmental Ethics*. Madison: University of Wisconsin Press, 1989.

———. *Wilderness and the American Mind*. 3rd ed. New Haven, Conn.: Yale University Press, 1982.

National Park Service. "Great Smoky Mountains National Park: Nature & Science." http://www.nps.gov/grsm/naturescience/index.htm. Accessed April 14, 2010.

———. "U.S. World Heritage Sites: Great Smoky Mountains National Park." http://www.nps.gov/history/worldheritage/grsm.htm. Accessed April 14, 2010.

Nevins, Deborah. "The Triumph of Flora: Women and the American Landscape, 1890–1935." *Antiques* 127 (April 1985): 904–22.

Newfont, Kathryn. "Commons Environmentalism Mobilized: The Western North Carolina Alliance and the Cut the Clearcutting! Campaign." In *Mountains of Injustice: Social and Environmental Justice in Appalachia*, edited by Michele Morrone and Geoffrey L. Buckley. Athens: Ohio University Press, 2011.

———. "Grassroots Environmentalism: The Origins of the Western North Carolina Alliance." *Appalachian Journal* 27, no. 1 (Fall 1999): 46–61.

———. "Moving Mountains: Forest Politics and Commons Culture in Western North Carolina, 1964–1994." PhD diss., University of North Carolina, Chapel Hill, 2001.

Nguiffo, Samual-Alain. "In Defense of the Commons: Forest Battles in Southern Cameroon." In Goldman, *Privatizing Nature*, 102–19.

Nicholson, Max. *The New Environmental Age*. New York: Cambridge University Press, 1987.

Nickens, T. Edward. "A Brief Glance Backwards." *Wildlife in North Carolina* 64, no. 1 (2000): 14.

Nobel Prize. Press release, "The Sveriges Riksbank Prize in Economic Sciences in Memory of Alfred Nobel 2009." http://nobelprize.org/nobel_prizes/economics/laureates/2009/press.html. Accessed July 8, 2010.

Nonini, Donald M., ed. *The Global Idea of "The Commons."* 2007; New York: Berghahn Books, 2008.

Norman, Gurney. "Notes on the Kentucky Cycle." In Billings, Norman, and Ledford, *Backtalk from Appalachia*, 327–32.

North Carolina Wildlife Resources Commission. http://www.ncwildlife.org/.
Accessed June 15, 2010.

Norwood, Vera. "Heroines of Nature: Four Women Respond to the American
Landscape." *Environmental Review* 8 (Spring 1984): 34–57.

———. *Made from This Earth: American Women and Nature.* Chapel Hill:
University of North Carolina Press, 1993.

———. "The Nature of Knowing: Rachel Carson and the American
Environment." *Signs: Journal of Women in Culture and Society* 12 (Summer 1987):
740–60.

Norwood, Vera, and Janice Monk, eds. *The Desert Is No Lady: Southwestern
Landscapes in Women's Writing and Art.* New Haven, Conn.: Yale University
Press, 1987.

Obermiller, Philip J., and William W. Philliber. *Appalachia in an International
Context: Cross-National Comparisons of Developing Regions.* Westport, Conn.:
Praeger, 1994.

Oelschlaeger, Max. *The Idea of Wilderness from Prehistory to the Age of Ecology.* New
Haven, Conn.: Yale University Press, 1991.

Olmsted, Frederick Law. *A Journey in the Back Country.* New York: Mason
Brothers, 1860; repr., n.p.: Corner House Publishers, 1972.

Ostrom, Elinor. *Governing the Commons: The Evolution of Institutions for Collective
Action.* New York: Cambridge University Press, 1991.

O'Toole, Randal Lee. *An Economic View of RARE II.* Eugene, Ore.: Cascade
Holistic Economic Consultants, 1978.

———. *Reforming the Forest Service.* Washington, D.C.: Island Press, 1988.

———. "The Tragedy of the Scenic Commons." In Baden and Noonan, *Managing
the Commons,* 181–87.

Otto, John Solomon. "The Decline of Forest Farming in Southern Appalachia."
Journal of Forest History, January 1983, 18–27.

Paehlke, Robert C. *Environmentalism and the Future of Progressive Politics.* New
Haven, Conn.: Yale University Press, 1989.

Pancake, Ann. "Similar Outcroppings from the Same Strata: The Synonymous
'Development' Imagery of Appalachian Natives and Natural Resources."
Journal of Appalachian Studies 6, nos. 1 and 2 (2000): 100–108.

Parris, John. *Mountain Bred.* Asheville, N.C.: Citizen Times Publishing Company,
1967.

———. *My Mountains, My People.* Asheville, N.C.: Citizen Times Publishing
Company, 1957.

———. *Roaming the Mountains with John Parris.* Asheville, N.C.: Citizen Times
Publishing Company, 1955.

———. *These Storied Mountains.* Asheville, N.C.: Citizen Times Publishing
Company, 1972.

Pepper, David. *The Roots of Modern Environmentalism.* Dover, N.H.: Croom
Helm, 1984.

Perdue, Charles L., Jr., and Nancy J. Martin-Perdue. "Appalachian Fables and
Facts: A Case Study of the Shenandoah National Park Removals." *Appalachian
Journal* 7, nos. 1–2 (1979–80): 84–104.

————. "'To Build a Wall around These Mountains': The Displaced People of Shenandoah." *Magazine of Albemarle County History* 49 (1991): 48–71.

Petulla, Joseph M. *American Environmental History.* Columbus, Ohio: Merrill Publishing Company, 1988.

Phillips, Sarah T. *This Land, This Nation: Conservation, Rural America, and the New Deal.* New York: Cambridge University Press, 2007.

Pierce, Daniel S. *The Great Smokies: From Natural Habitat to National Park.* Knoxville: University of Tennessee Press, 2000.

Pinchot, Gifford. *Biltmore Forest.* Chicago: Lakeside Press, 1893; repr., New York: Arno Press, 1970.

————. *Breaking New Ground.* New York: Harcourt Brace, 1947.

Pisani, Donald J. "Forests and Conservation, 1865–1890." *Journal of American History* 72 (September 1985): 340–59.

Plant, Judith, ed. *Healing the Wounds: The Promise of Ecofeminism.* Philadelphia: New Society Publishers, 1989.

Pless, Lenoir. "Bear Hunter." See Jeff Fears, "Bear Hunting." In Wigginton, *Foxfire 5,* 437–94. Interview by Jeff Fears, with Randall Hardy, Danny Brown, Eddie Brown, and Mark Burdette.

Plumwood, Val. "Ecofeminism: An Overview and Discussion of Positions and Arguments." *Australasian Journal of Philosophy* supp. 64 (June 1986): 120–38.

Polanyi, Karl. *The Great Transformation.* New York: Farrar and Rinehart, 1944.

Pollan, Michael. "Afterword: The Garden's Prospects in America." In *Keeping Eden: A History of Gardening in America,* edited by Walter T. Punch, 261–65. Boston: Little, Brown, 1992.

Pomeroy, Kenneth B., and James G. Yoho. *North Carolina Lands: Ownership, Use, and Management of Forest and Related Lands.* Washington, D.C.: American Forestry Association, 1964.

Powell, William S., ed. *Dictionary of North Carolina Biography.* Chapel Hill: University of North Carolina Press, 1996.

Prebble, John. *The Highland Clearances.* London: Secker and Warburg, 1963.

Press, Daniel. *Democratic Dilemmas in the Age of Ecology: Trees and Toxics in the American West.* Durham, N.C.: Duke University Press, 1994.

Pudup, Mary Beth, Dwight B. Billings, and Altina L. Waller, eds. *Appalachia in the Making: The Mountain South in the Nineteenth Century.* Chapel Hill: University of North Carolina Press, 1995.

Pulido, Laura. *Environmentalism and Economic Justice: Two Chicano Struggles in the Southwest.* Tucson: University of Arizona Press, 1996.

Pyne, Stephen J. *Fire in America: A Cultural History of Wildland and Rural Fire.* Princeton, N.J.: Princeton University Press, 1982.

Quam-Wickham, Nancy. "'Cities Sacrificed on the Altar of Oil': Popular Opposition to Oil Development in 1920s Los Angeles." *Environmental History* 1, no. 2 (1998): 187–209.

Raine, James Watt. *The Land of the Saddle-Bags: A Study of the Mountain People of Appalachia.* 1924; Detroit: Singing Tree Press, 1969.

Redclift, Michael. "In Our Own Image: The Environment and Society as Global Discourse." *Environment and History* 1 (1995): 111–23.

Rees, Judith. *Natural Resources: Allocation, Economics, and Policy*. New York: Routledge, 1990.

Reid, Herbert, and Betsy Taylor. *Recovering the Commons: Democracy, Place, and Global Justice*. Urbana: University of Illinois Press, 2010.

Reiger, John. *American Sportsmen and the Origins of Conservation*. 1975; Corvallis: Oregon State University Press, 2001.

Rensberger, Boyce. *The Cult of the Wild*. Garden City, N.Y.: Anchor Press/Doubleday, 1977.

Rhoades, Verne. *Federal Forest Purchases and Forest Recreation*. Circular no. 9, North Carolina Geological and Economic Survey. Chapel Hill: North Carolina State Government, 1924.

Robbins, Roy M. *Our Landed Heritage: The Public Domain, 1776–1970*. Lincoln: University of Nebraska Press, 1976.

Robinson, Glen O. *The Forest Service: A Study in Public Land Management*. Baltimore, Md.: Johns Hopkins Press, 1975.

Roland, Charles P. *The Improbable Era: The South since World War II*. Lexington: University Press of Kentucky, 1975.

Rome, Adam W. "Coming to Terms with Pollution: The Language of Environmental Reform, 1865–1916." *Environmental History* 1, no. 3 (1996): 6–28.

Rosenthal, Dorothy B. *Environmental Case Studies: Southeastern Region*. New York: John Wiley and Sons, 1996.

Roth, Darlene Rebecca. *Matronage: Patterns in Women's Organizations, Atlanta, Georgia, 1890–1940*. Brooklyn: Carlson, 1994.

Roth, Dennis M. *The Wilderness Movement and the National Forests, 1964–1980*. Washington, D.C.: USDA, Forest Service, 1984.

———. *The Wilderness Movement and the National Forests: 1980–84*. Washington, D.C.: USDA, Forest Service, 1988.

Rothman, Hal K. *The Greening of a Nation?: Environmentalism in the U.S. since 1945*. Wadsworth Publishing, 1997.

———. *Saving the Planet: The American Response to the Environment in the Twentieth Century*. Chicago: Ivan R. Dee, 2000.

Rothrock, Mary. "Carolina Traders among the Overhill Cherokee, 1690–1760." *East Tennessee Historical Society Publications* 1 (1929): 3–18.

Rubin, Charles T. *The Green Crusade: Rethinking the Roots of Environmentalism*. New York: Free Press, 1994.

Russell, Edmund P., III. "Lost among the Parts per Billion: Ecological Protection and the United States Environmental Protection Agency, 1970–1993." *Environmental History* 2, no. 1 (1997): 29–51.

Rymer, Russ. "Wilderness Politics." *Atlanta Journal Weekly Magazine*, October 24, 1982.

Sale, Kirkpatrick. *The Green Revolution: The American Environmental Movement, 1962–1992*. New York: Hill and Wang, 1993.

Salstrom, Paul. *Appalachia's Path to Dependency: Rethinking a Region's Economic History, 1730–1940*. Lexington: University Press of Kentucky, 1994.

Sarvis, Will. "An Appalachian Forest: Creation of the Jefferson National Forest and Its Effects on the Local Community." *Forest & Conservation History* 37, no. 4 (1993): 169–78.

———. "Fisheries and Wildlife Management: Part of the History of the Jefferson National Forest." *Virginia Forests*, Summer 1992, 6–8.

———. "The Mount Rogers National Recreation Area and the Rise of Public Involvement in Forest Service Planning." *Environmental History Review* 18, no. 2 (1994): 41–65.

Schenck, Carl Alwin. *The Birth of Forestry in America: Biltmore Forest School 1898–1913.* Minnesota Historical Society, 1955; repr., Forest History Society and the Appalachian Consortium, 1974.

Schmitt, Peter J. *Back to Nature: The Arcadian Myth in Urban America.* 1969; Baltimore, Md.: Johns Hopkins University Press, 1990.

Schneider, Daniel W. "Enclosing the Floodplain: Resource Conflict on the Illinois River, 1880–1920." *Environmental History* 1, no. 2 (1996): 70–96.

Schrepfer, Susan R. *Nature's Altars: Mountains, Gender, and American Environmentalism.* Lawrence: University Press of Kansas, 2005.

Scott, Anne Firor. *Making the Invisible Woman Visible.* Urbana: University of Illinois Press, 1984.

———. *Natural Allies: Women's Associations in American History.* Urbana: University of Illinois Press, 1991.

Scott, Douglas W. "Eastern Wilderness Areas Act: What's in a Name?" *Wild Earth* 11, no. 1 (2001): 24.

Scott, James C. *Domination and the Arts of Resistance: Hidden Transcripts.* New Haven, Conn.: Yale University Press, 1990.

———. *Seeing like a State: How Certain Schemes to Improve the Human Condition Have Failed.* New Haven, Conn.: Yale University Press, 1999.

Sears, John F. *Sacred Places: American Tourist Attractions in the Nineteenth Century.* New York: Oxford University Press, 1989.

Sedjo, Roger A. "Ecosystem Management: An Uncharted Course for Public Forests." *Resources* 121 (Fall 1995): 10, 18–20.

———, ed. *Governmental Interventions, Social Needs, and the Management of U.S. Forests.* Washington, D.C.: Resources for the Future, 1983.

Seitz, Virginia R. *Women, Development, and Communities for Empowerment in Appalachia.* Albany: State University of New York Press, 1995.

Shabecoff, Philip. *A Fierce Green Fire: The American Environmental Movement.* New York: Hill and Wang, 1993.

Shands, William E. "The Lands Nobody Wanted: The Legacy of the Eastern National Forests." In Steen, *Origins of the National Forests*, 19–44.

Shands, William E., Perry R. Hagenstein, and Marissa T. Roche. *National Forest Policy: From Conflict toward Consensus.* Washington, D.C.: Conservation Foundation, 1979.

Shands, William E., and Robert G. Healy. *The Lands Nobody Wanted.* Washington, D.C.: Conservation Foundation, 1977.

Shapiro, Henry D. *Appalachia on Our Mind: The Southern Mountains and Mountaineers in the American Consciousness, 1870–1920.* Chapel Hill: University of North Carolina Press, 1978.

Sheppard, Muriel Earley. *Cabins in the Laurel.* 1935; Chapel Hill: University of North Carolina Press, 1991.

Short, C. Brant. *Ronald Reagan and the Public Lands: America's Conservation Debate, 1979–1984.* College Station: Texas A&M University Press, 1989.

Siehl, George H. "Forest Service's Roadless Area Review and Evaluation (RARE II)." Washington, D.C.: Library of Congress, Congressional Research Service, 1980.

Silver, Timothy. *Mount Mitchell and the Black Mountains: An Environmental History of the Highest Peaks in Eastern North America.* Chapel Hill: University of North Carolina Press, 2003.

———. *A New Face on the Countryside: Indians, Colonists, and Slaves in South Atlantic Forests, 1500–1800.* Cambridge: Cambridge University Press, 1990.

Smathers, George Henry. *The History of Land Titles in Western North Carolina.* Asheville, N.C.: Miller Printing Company, 1938.

Smith, Allen E. "Eastern Wilderness: A Small Price to Pay for a Large Heritage." *Sierra Club Bulletin*, October 1976, 18–22.

Smith, Charles Dennis. "The Appalachian National Park Movement, 1885–1901." *North Carolina Historical Review* 37 (January 1960): 38–65.

Smith, David C. *History of Papermaking in the United States (1691–1969).* New York: Lockwood Publishing Company, 1970.

Snedeker, Rodney J., and Michael A. Harmon. "Identification and Preservation of Nineteenth and Twentieth Century Homesites in the Pisgah and Nantahala National Forests." Appalachian Cultural Resources Workshop Papers, National Park Service. http://www.nps.gov/history/history/online_books/sero/appalachian/sec4.htm.

Snyder, Gary. "Understanding the Commons." In Armstrong and Botzler, *Environmental Ethics*, 227–31.

Snyder, Lynn Page. "'The Death-Dealing Smog over Donora, Pennsylvania': Industrial Air Pollution, Public Health Policy, and the Politics of Expertise, 1948–1949." *Environmental History Review* 18, no. 1 (1994): 117–39.

Sondley, F. A. *A History of Buncombe County North Carolina.* 1930; Spartanburg, S.C.: Reprint Company, 1977.

Soroos, Marvin S. "The International Commons: A Historical Perspective." *Environmental Review* 12, no. 1 (1988): 1–22.

Southern Appalachian Man and the Biosphere. "The SAMAB Reserve." http://www.samab.org/About/reserve.html. Accessed April 14, 2010.

Spagna, Ana Maria. *Now Go Home: Wilderness, Belonging, and the Crosscut Saw.* Corvallis: Oregon State University Press, 2004.

Spence, Mark David. *Dispossessing the Wilderness: Indian Removal and the Making of the National Parks.* New York: Oxford University Press, 2000.

Starnes, Richard. *Creating the Land of the Sky: Tourism and Society in Western North Carolina.* Tuscaloosa: University of Alabama Press, 2005.

Steen, Harold K. "The Origins and Significance of the National Forest System." In Steen, *Origins of the National Forests*, 3–9.

———, ed. *Origins of the National Forests: A Centennial Symposium.* Durham, N.C.: Forest History Society, 1992.

———. *The U.S. Forest Service: A History*. Seattle: University of Washington Press, 1976.

Steinberg, Ted. "Down to Earth: Nature, Agency, and Power in History." *American Historical Review* 107, no. 3 (2002): 798–820.

Stern, Nicholas. *The Economics of Climate Change: The Stern Review*. London: Cambridge University Press, 2007.

Stewart, Bruce E. *Moonshiners and Prohibitionists: The Battle Over Alcohol in Southern Appalachia*. Lexington: University Press of Kentucky, 2011.

Stewart, Carrie. "Carrie Stewart." In Wigginton, *Foxfire 5*, 495–511. Interview by Lynn Butler.

Stewart, Mart A. *"What Nature Suffers to Groe": Life, Labor, and Landscape on the Georgia Coast, 1680–1920*. Athens: University of Georgia Press, 1996.

Stilgoe, John R. *Borderland: Origins of the American Suburb, 1820–1939*. New Haven, Conn.: Yale University Press, 1989.

———. *Common Landscape of America, 1580 to 1845*. New Haven, Conn.: Yale University Press, 1982.

Stine, Jeffrey K. "Environmental Politics in the American South: The Fight over the Tennessee-Tombigbee Waterway." *Environmental History Review* 15, no. 1 (1991): 1–24.

———. *Mixing the Waters: Environment, Politics, and the Building of the Tennessee-Tombigbee Waterway*. Akron, Ohio: University of Akron Press, 1993.

Straw, Richard A., and H. Tyler Blethen. *High Mountains Rising: Appalachia in Time and Place*. Urbana: University of Illinois Press, 2004.

Sutter, Paul S. *Driven Wild: How the Fight against Automobiles Launched the Modern Wilderness Movement*. Seattle: University of Washington Press, 2002.

Sutter, Paul S., and Christopher J. Manganiello, eds. *Environmental History and the American South: A Reader*. Athens: University of Georgia Press, 2009.

Sutton, Jessie, ed. *The Heritage of Macon County, North Carolina*. Winston-Salem, N.C.: Hunter Publishing, 1987.

Swain, Martha H. "The Public Role of Southern Women." In Hawks and Skemp, *Sex, Race, and the Role of Women*, 37–58.

Szakos, Joe. "Practical Lessons in Community Organizing in Appalachia: What We've Learned at Kentuckians for the Commonwealth." In Fisher, *Fighting Back in Appalachia*, 101–21.

Tabachnick, David Edgemon. "Fence of Ownership: Common Property versus Individual Property Regimes in England, France, Africa, and the United States." PhD diss., University of Wisconsin, 2002.

Taylor, Alan. "Unnatural Inequalities: Social and Environmental Histories." *Environmental History* 1, no. 4 (1996): 6–19.

Taylor, Betsy. " 'Place' as Pre-political Grounds of Democracy: An Appalachian Case Study in Class Conflict, Forest Politics, and Civic Networks." *American Behavioral Scientist* 52, no. 6 (2009): 826–45.

Taylor, David A. *Ginseng: The Divine Root*. Chapel Hill, N.C.: Algonquin Books, 2006.

Taylor, Mark. "The Wilderness Question." *Wildlife in North Carolina*, March 1978, 9–17.

Terrie, Philip G. *Contested Terrain: A New History of Nature and People in the Adirondacks.* Syracuse, N.Y.: Syracuse University Press, 1997.

Thelen, David. *Paths of Resistance: Tradition and Dignity in Industrializing Missouri.* New York: Oxford University Press, 1986.

Thomas, Keith. *Man and the Natural World: A History of Modern Sensibility.* New York: Pantheon, 1983.

Thompson, E. P. *Whigs and Hunters: The Origins of the Black Act.* New York: Pantheon, 1975.

Tilly, Louise, and Patricia Gurin, eds. *Women, Politics, and Change.* New York: Russell Sage Foundation, 1990.

Tindall, George. *The Emergence of the New South, 1913–1945.* Baton Rouge: Louisiana State University Press, 1967.

Tober, James A. *Who Owns the Wildlife? The Political Economy of Conservation in Nineteenth-Century America.* Westport, Conn.: Greenwood Press, 1981.

Turner, James Morton. "Wilderness East: Reclaiming History." *Wild Earth* 11, no. 1 (2001): 19–27.

Turner, Tom. *Sierra Club: 100 Years of Protecting Nature.* New York: Harry N. Abrams, 1991.

United Nations Educational, Scientific, and Cultural Organization. "Biosphere Reserve Information, United States of America: Southern Appalachian." http://www.unesco.org/mabdb/br/brdir/directory/biores .asp?mode=gen&code=USA+44. Accessed April 14, 2010.

———. "World Heritage: Great Smoky Mountains National Park." http://whc .unesco.org/en/list/259. Accessed April 14, 2010.

U.S. Central Intelligence Agency. *World Factbook.* http://www.cia.gov/library/ publications/the-world-factbook/rankorder/2147rank.html. Accessed June 10, 2010.

U.S. Congress, Senate Committee on Energy and Natural Resources. *Roadless Area Review and Evaluation (RARE II).* Washington, D.C.: Government Printing Office, 1978.

U.S. Department of Agriculture (USDA). "Final Supplement to the Final Environmental Impact Statement." In *Land and Resource Management Plan.*

———. "FY 2009 National Forest Acreage." http://www.fs.fed.us/land/staff/lar/ 2009/LAR_Table_04.html. Accessed June 11, 2010.

———. *Land and Resource Management Plan: Nantahala and Pisgah National Forests. Amendment 5.* Atlanta: USDA, Forest Service, Southern Region, 1994.

———. *Nantahala National Forest, North Carolina.* Washington, D.C.: USDA, 1986. Map.

———. *National Forests in the Southern Appalachians.* Washington, D.C.: USDA, Forest Service, 1940.

———. *Pisgah National Forest, North Carolina.* Washington, D.C.: USDA, 1986. Map.

———. RARE II Final Environmental Statement, Roadless Area Review and Evaluation. Washington, D.C.: USDA, Forest Service, January 1979.

———. RARE II Southern Appalachian and Atlantic Coast States, Supplement to Draft Environmental Statement, Roadless Area Review and Evaluation. Washington, D.C.: USDA, Forest Service, June 1978.

———. *Report of the Secretary of Agriculture on the Southern Appalachian and White Mountain Watersheds*. Washington, D.C.: Government Printing Office, 1908.

———. *The Use of National Forest Reserves: Regulations and Instructions*. Washington, D.C.: USDA, Forest Service, 1905.

Usner, Daniel H., Jr. *Indians, Settlers, and Slaves in a Frontier Exchange Economy: The Lower Mississippi Valley before 1783*. Chapel Hill: University of North Carolina Press, 1992.

Van Sickle, Charles, and Robert S. Turner. "The Southern Appalachian Man and the Biosphere Program—a Model for Management Need-Based Research." Paper presented at the Southern Forest Science Conference, Atlanta, Ga., 2001. http://www.samab.org/pdfs/SamabModel.pdf.

Vig, Norman, and Michael Kraft. *Environmental Policy in the 1980s: Reagan's New Agenda*. Washington, D.C.: Congressional Quarterly, 1984.

———. *Environmental Policy in the 1990s*. 3rd ed. Washington, D.C.: Congressional Quarterly, 1996.

Vinson, Frank B. "Conservation and the South, 1890–1920." PhD diss., University of Georgia, 1971.

Waldroop, Grady. "Hunting Tales." In Wigginton, *The Foxfire Book*, 278.

Waldroop, Jake. "Hunting Tales." In Wigginton, *The Foxfire Book*, 278–79.

———. See Jeff Fears, "Bear Hunting." In Wigginton, *Foxfire 5*, 437–94. Interview by Jeff Fears, with Randall Hardy, Danny Brown, Eddie Brown, and Mark Burdette.

Wallach, Bret. "The Slighted Mountains of Upper East Tennessee." *Annals of the Association of American Geographers* 71, no. 3 (1981): 359–73.

Walpole, Matthew R. "The Closing of the Open Range in Watauga County, N.C." *Appalachian Journal* 16, no. 4 (1989): 320–35.

Warner, Sam Bass. *To Dwell Is to Garden: A History of Boston's Community Gardens*. Boston: Northeastern University Press, 1987.

Warren, Karen J. "Feminism and Ecology: Making Connections." *Environmental Ethics* 9 (Spring 1987): 3–20.

———. "The Power and Promise of Ecological Feminism." *Environmental Ethics* 12 (Summer 1990): 125–46.

Warren, Louis S. *The Hunter's Game: Poachers and Conservationists in Twentieth-Century America*. New Haven, Conn.: Yale University Press, 1997.

Watson, Harry. "'The Common Rights of Mankind': Subsistence, Shad, and Commerce in the Early Republican South." *Journal of American History* 83 (1996): 13–43.

Watts, Marvin. "Hunting Tales." In Wigginton, *The Foxfire Book*, 284–85.

Webb, Andy. "Hunting Tales." In Wigginton, *The Foxfire Book*, 276–78.

Wellock, Thomas R. "Stick It in L.A.! Community Control and Nuclear Power in California's Central Valley." *Journal of American History* 84, no. 3 (1997): 942–78.

Westmacott, Richard. *African-American Gardens and Yards in the Rural South*. Knoxville: University of Tennessee Press, 1992.

Wheeler, William Bruce, and Michael J. McDonald. *TVA and the Tellico Dam.* Knoxville: University of Tennessee Press, 1986.

Whisnant, Anne Mitchell. "Parkway Politics: Class, Culture, and Tourism in the Blue Ridge." PhD diss., University of North Carolina at Chapel Hill, 1997.

———. *Super-Scenic Motorway: A Blue Ridge Parkway History.* Chapel Hill: University of North Carolina Press, 2006.

Whisnant, David E. *All That Is Native and Fine: The Politics of Culture in an American Region.* Chapel Hill: University of North Carolina Press, 1983.

———. *Modernizing the Mountaineer: People, Power, and Planning in Appalachia.* Boone, N.C.: Appalachian Consortium Press, 1981.

White, Richard. "'Are You an Environmentalist or Do You Work for a Living?': Work and Nature." In Cronon, *Uncommon Ground,* 171–85.

———. *The Organic Machine.* New York: Hill and Wang, 1995.

Wigginton, Eliot, ed. *The Foxfire Book: Hog Dressing, Log Cabin Building, Mountain Crafts and Foods, Planting by the Signs, Snake Lore, Hunting Tales, Faith Healing, Moonshining, and Other Affairs of Plain Living.* New York: Doubleday, 1972.

———, ed. *Foxfire 5: Ironmaking, Blacksmithing, Flintlock Rifles, Bear Hunting, and Other Affairs of Plain Living.* Garden City, N.Y.: Anchor Press/Doubleday, 1979.

Williams, John Alexander. "A Regionalism within Regionalisms: Three Frameworks for Appalachian Studies." In Inscoe, *Southern Appalachia and the South,* 4–17.

Williams, Michael. *Americans and Their Forests: A Historical Geography.* New York: Cambridge University Press, 1989.

Williams, Michael Ann. "'When I Can Read My Title Clear': Anti-environmentalism and Sense of Place in the Great Smoky Mountains." In Howell, *Culture, Environment, and Conservation,* 87–99.

Williams, Samuel Cole, ed. *Early Travels in the Tennessee Country, 1540–1800.* Johnson City, Tenn.: Watauga Press, 1928.

Woodward, C. Vann. *The Burden of Southern History.* New York: Vintage Books, 1960.

———. *Origins of the New South, 1877–1913.* Baton Rouge: Louisiana State University Press, 1951.

———. *The Strange Career of Jim Crow.* New York: Oxford University Press, 1957.

Worster, Donald. *Dust Bowl: The Southern Plains in the 1930s.* New York: Oxford University Press, 1979.

———, ed. *The Ends of the Earth: Perspectives on Modern Environmental History.* New York: Cambridge University Press, 1988.

———. "Nature and the Disorder of History." *Environmental History Review* 18, no. 2 (1994): 1–15.

———. *Nature's Economy: A History of Ecological Ideas.* Cambridge: Cambridge University Press, 1977.

———. *Rivers of Empire: Water, Aridity, and the Growth of the American West.* New York: Oxford University Press, 1985.

———. "The Two Cultures Revisited: Environmental History and the Environmental Sciences." *Environment and History* 2 (1996): 3–14.

———. *Under Western Skies: Nature and History in the American West.* New York: Oxford University Press, 1992.

———. *The Wealth of Nature: Environmental History and the Ecological Imagination.* New York: Oxford University Press, 1993.

Wright, Gavin. *Old South, New South: Revolutions in the Southern Economy since the Civil War.* New York: Basic Books, 1986.

Yale Environment 360. "Leveling Appalachia: The Legacy of Mountaintop Removal Mining." http://e360.yale.edu/content/feature.msp?id=2198. Accessed June 15, 2010.

Yarnell, Susan L. *The Southern Appalachians: A History of the Landscape.* Washington, D.C.: USDA, 1998.

Yett, Jane. "Women and Their Environments: A Bibliography for Research and Teaching." *Environmental Review* 8, no. 1 (1984): 86–94.

Zoellner, Magaline. "I Used to Wear Blue Jeans All the Time . . ." In Wigginton, *Foxfire 5,* 67–76. Interview by Richard Henslee and Tinker McCoy.

based resistance to, 190–91, 271; and Biltmore Estate, 58–59; in British Isles, 22–23; and clearcutting, 265, 271–72; defined, 9–10; and national forests, 73, 123, 188, 272; as ongoing threat in southern Appalachians, 129, 161, 171; patterns in, 18; and petroleum development, 215, 223; resistance to, 18; and stock law, 36–37, and timber removal, 43; and wilderness advocacy, 168–69, 171, 176, 181–82; and wilderness opposition, 129, 146–48, 154–56, 158, 163–65, 167. *See also* commons

Enka, 47

environmental movement, U.S., 10–11

erosion: affecting waterways, 20; after timber removal, 42, 43, 64, 65; control efforts by USFS, 74, 94, 95, 234, 236; as issue in clearcutting controversy, 136; as issue in petroleum development, 221; in mountain formation, 4

even-aged timber management, 132, 133–34, 233–34, 236–37; and fifty-year draft management plan, 254, 255; and generational divide among foresters, 237–39; and Monongahela case, 134–38; and WNCA anticlearcutting, 260. *See also* all-aged timber management; clearcut timber harvesting

Evison, Boyd, 128, 130

Extension Homemakers, 208, 210

Exxon, 192, 195

fence-cutting, 58, 271; fence destruction by fire, 36–37

fence law. *See* stock law

fencing, 30; of animals, 34, 35; at Biltmore Estate, 50, 58; of crops, 28, 97; in Dillingham controversy, 112, 113, 114; fenceposts, 39, 82, 83, 99, 122; in Nantahala deer stations, 119. *See also* fence-cutting; stock law

Fernow, Bernard, 51, 55

fire: cataclysmic western fires of 1910, 68–69; intentional woods-burning, 24, 116–17; as tool of commons defense, 37, 165, 271; in wake of timber harvests, 42, 48, 64, 65. *See also* arson; fire suppression

fire suppression: local cooperation in firefighting, 165; local men as firefighters and fire guards, 97–98, 117–18; by USFS, 74, 95, 116–18, 236. *See also* arson; fire.

firewood, 82, 97, 127, 130, 161, 256, 272; as commons concern, 157, 161, 254–55; in Forest Charter, 22; USFS permits, 7, 99, 122, 126–27, 131, 272; in woodlot tracts, 30. *See also* gathering commons

Fish, Lloyd, 42

fishing commons, 7, 19–20; Chase Ambler fishing trip and Appalachian park idea, 61–62; fisherman confrontation with Carl Schenck, 59–60. *See also* wildlife commons

flooding: forests as preventing, 67–68; in 1901, 64; in 1907, 68

Fontana Dam, 128

Foreign Hardwood Log Company, 44

Foster, Fred, 146

Fouts, Canada, 86

Fraser fir, 7, 126, 131

free-use permits, 122–23

friendly condemnation, 80, 104–5

Friends of the Earth, 144–45

"Future of Appalachia" conference (1981), 212

galax, 2, 15–16, 122, 157; as nontimber forest product, 82; and USFS lands, 7, 15–16, 126, 131. *See also* gathering commons

Garden and Forest, 55, 61

Gash, Leander, 31

gathering commons, 7, 19, 21, 31–32, 121–22. *See also* berry buckets; blackberries; bloodroot; blueberries; buckberries; chestnut; firewood gathering; Fraser fir; galax; ginseng; huckleberry pickers; medicinal

258–59, 262, 266–67; incompatibility with clearcutting, 239, 241; and Monongahela case, 134–38; and petroleum issue, 201, 211, 217, 220, 224–25; and Pisgah deer herd, 120–21; and RARE II opposition, 156, 160–63; and USFS, 131; and wilderness advocacy, 169, 173–76, 176–79, 181–82. *See also* North Carolina Wildlife Resources Commission; wildlife commons

hunting commons, 7, 19, 20–21. *See also* wildlife commons

Huskins, J. C., 71

Ingall, O. D., 84–88, 97–98, 107–9, 111

inholdings, 56, 60, 96

international biosphere reserve system. *See* Southern Appalachian Biosphere Reserve; United Nations international biosphere reserve system

Izaak Walton League, 136–38, 140, 230

Jefferson National Forest, 78, 117–18

Jenkins, McKinley, 256–58

John Hay Whitney Foundation, 103

Jones, Nell, 209

Joseph LeConte Sierra Club group, 185–86

Journal of Forestry, 102, 109, 133

Joyce Kilmer Memorial Forest, 93, 143, 145, 150, 217, 236. *See also* Joyce Kilmer–Slickrock Creek Primitive Area; Joyce Kilmer–Slickrock Creek Wilderness Area

Joyce Kilmer–Slickrock Creek Primitive Area, 143

Joyce Kilmer–Slickrock Creek Wilderness Area, 145, 150, 217

Kearney, Lewis, 219–20, 222

Kelly, Mary, 130, 225–26, 262–64; and clearcutting issue, 245, 251, 253, 261, 262–64, 266–68; and RARE II, 161

Kelly, Rob, 262, 268

Kentuckians for the Commonwealth, 225

Kircher, Joseph C., 93

Kuwait Petroleum Corporation, 219–20

land acquisition by USFS, 87–94; smallholder frustration, 90, 108–11

land condemnation issue, 79–80, 95, 104, 106

Landers, Haze, 239, 259

land titles, 89

leather-tanning industry, 13, 39, 41–42, 45, 122. *See also* Champion Fibre Company; tanbark

Ledbetter, Lyman, 177, 179, 180–82

Liden, David, 190–91, 211, 213–15; and Appalachian Land Ownership Task Force, 205, 207; and clearcutting issue, 249, 250, 254, 259, 263, 268; and petroleum leasing issue, 220–21, 223–26; and Western North Carolina Alliance, 240–41. *See also* Appalachian Land Ownership Task Force; Western North Carolina Alliance

Lieberman, Garland, 186

Lincoln Memorial University, 212

Linville Gorge, 142, 186

Little Laurel timber sale, 240, 242–44

Little River Lumber Company, 76–77, 115

livestock commons, 21–22, 31, 119. *See also* grazing commons

livestock trade, 13, 32–35

Loveday, Lisa, 266–67

Lovill, Edward, 35

Macon County, 42, 102, 126, 146; forest management, 241, 243, 246; hunting, 124, 248; mineral development, 188, 206; oil and gas exploration, 190, 197, 202–4, 207; oil leasing, 215–20, 222, 224; PTA, 209; and RARE II, 154–56, 158, 159, 162, 168, 173, 177, 179, 182; tourism, 129, 180

Smith, Walton R., 234–38; clearcutting critique, 140, 234, 253–54; as volunteer forester trainer, 243–45; as WNCA anticlearcutting leader, 240–45, 249, 250, 253–54, 261–65, 268, 269

Smoky Mountains purchase unit, 75, 76–77, 98, 115 (dissolved 1923)

snakeroot. *See* seneca

Society of American Foresters, 102

Southern Appalachian Biosphere Reserve, 5

Southern Appalachian Hardwood Producers Association, 149–50, 167, 180, 186; name change, 167. *See also* Southern Appalachian Multiple-Use Council

Southern Appalachian Multiple-Use Council, 167, 186. *See also* Southern Appalachian Hardwood Producers Association

Southern Blue Ridge geological province, 5, 6, 10

Southern Nantahala Wilderness Area, 148, 168–69, 172, 173–87 passim, 272

special-use permits, 98–99, 121

species loss, 10, 270, 274

squirrel, 28; and chestnut, 38, 40; and clearcuts, 258; hunters in Monongahela lawsuit, 135

Standard Oil Company, 191

Standing Indian Campground, 169, 173, 176, 178

stereotyping: of Appalachian people, 11–12, 14, 109, 171, 200; of Arab people, 219; of Native American people, 23–24; of wilderness advocates, 176

Stewart, Carrie, 38

Stimson, Henry L., 74

stock law, 22, 34, 35–38. *See also* cattle; chestnut; grazing commons; hogs; range masters; sheep; turkey

Stone, J. Herbert, 117

Swafford, Verlon, 158–59, 160, 161–63, 164

Szakos, Joe, 225

Taft, Howard, presidential administration, 53, 69, 74

Tameler, Karl L., 197, 216–17

tanbark, 32, 41–42, 99, 122. *See also* gathering commons; leather-tanning industry

tax revenue issue: for high corporate ownership counties, 205–6; for USFS host counties, 101–4. *See also* Payments in Lieu of Taxes Act (1976)

Taylor, Mark, 129–31

Taylor, Roy, 139, 166

Tayrien, Dave, 200–201

technocratic expertise emphasis in USFS, 53–54, 151–52, 310–11n1

telephones, as USFS benefit, 98

tenantry: in Appalachians, 34, 98, 105–6; on USFS lands, 93–94, 97–99, 105–6

Tennessee Valley Authority (TVA), 69, 73, 91, 103, 105, 127; and condemnation/displacement issue, 95, 104, 105, 128, 272

Thompson, Peter G., 45

Thrash, Tom, 154

timber harvests, 30; in Appalachian boom period, 42–48; at Appalachian peak, 45, 91; and clearcutting, 260–61; in Depression-era Appalachians, 91; in postwar Appalachians, 152, 159–60, 180; small operators in, 63, 122, 131, 254–55; social effects of, 47; as threat to commons, 168–69, 176, 181, 182, 188; in United States, 43, 232–33. *See also* clearcut timber harvesting; selective harvesting; timber industry; timber management; timber program in USFS; timber resources

timber industry, 4; in Appalachians, 4, 43–46, 48, 62, 65, 261; Appalachian landholding of, 204–5; and clearcutting, 259; land acquisition, legal issues in, 71–72, 89–90, 100, 112–15; land-acquisition tactics of, 72, 89–90, 108, 111; land sales to USFS of, 77, 78, 88, 92, 100, 109; local

ENVIRONMENTAL HISTORY AND THE AMERICAN SOUTH

Pharsalia: An Environmental Biography of a Southern Plantation, 1780–1880
Lynn A. Nelson

An Everglades Providence: Marjory Stoneman Douglas and the American Environmental Century
Jack E. Davis

Spirits of the Air: Birds and American Indians in the South
Shepard Krech III

Environmental History and the American South: A Reader
Paul S. Sutter and Christopher J. Manganiello, eds.

Making Catfish Bait out of Government Boys: The Fight against Cattle Ticks and the Transformation of the Yeoman South
Claire Strom

The Oyster Question: Scientists, Watermen, and the Maryland Chesapeake Bay since 1880
Christine Keiner

My Work Is That of Conservation: An Environmental Biography of George Washington Carver
Mark D. Hersey

Conserving Southern Longleaf: Herbert Stoddard and the Rise of Ecological Land Management
Albert G. Way

Blue Ridge Commons: Environmental Activism and Forest History in Western North Carolina
Kathryn Newfont

War upon the Land: Military Strategy and the Transformation of Southern Landscapes during the American Civil War
Lisa M. Brady

CPSIA information can be obtained at www.ICGtesting.com
Printed in the USA
BVOW07s1157100714

358731BV00002B/47/P